Assessing Learners with Special Needs

An Applied Approach

Assessing Learners with Special Needs

An Applied Approach

EIGHTH EDITION

Terry Overton
Stephen F. Austin State University

PEARSON

Boston Columbus Indianapolis New York San Francisco Upper Saddle River
Amsterdam Cape Town Dubai London Madrid Milan Munich Paris Montréal Toronto
Delhi Mexico City São Paulo Sydney Hong Kong Seoul Singapore Taipei Tokyo

Vice President and Editorial Director: Jeffery W. Johnston
Executive Editor: Ann Castel Davis
Editorial Assistant: Janelle Criner
Development Editor: Bryce Bell
Executive Field Marketing Manager: Krista Clark
Senior Product Marketing Manager: Christopher Barry
Project Manager: Kerry Rubadue
Program Manager: Joe Sweeney
Operations Specialist: Deidra Skahill
Text Designer: S4Carlisle Publishing Services

Design Director: Diane Lorenzo
Cover Art: Getty Images
Media Producer: Autumn Benson
Media Project Manager: Tammy Walters
Full-Service Project Management: S4Carlisle Publishing Services
Composition: S4Carlisle Publishing Services
Printer/Binder: LSC Communications
Cover Printer: LSC Communications
Text Font: Sabon

For my family

And especially my husband.

NEW TO THE EIGHTH EDITION

The process of monitoring and assessing students in the general education environment who have academic and behavioral challenges continues to evolve as a result of changes in federal regulations and research focusing on best practices in assessment and instruction. The eighth edition of *Assessing Learners with Special Needs: An Applied Approach* was written to reflect these changes in the assessment process and to provide the learner with information about the newly revised instruments used in assessing learners with educational challenges. This new edition, converted primarily to an e-text, provides a new presentation format and a new format for assessing student mastery of material through interactive learning activities.

Like earlier editions, the primary focus of this text is to provide students with a practical approach to learning about the complex procedures that are part of the assessment process. This new edition includes:

- *Embedded Videos:* Embedded videos provide helpful examples of chapter content.
- **Check Your Understanding** *Interactive Exercises:* These interactive exercises provide an opportunity for readers to apply their learning and monitor their progress in the learning and assessment process. These activities are included in electronic format with feedback provided to the students following each response.
- *Interactive* **Chapter Quizzes:** At the end of each chapter, a pop-up multiple-choice quiz assesses students' understanding of chapter content.
- *Interactive Pretest:* This pretest in Chapter 1, which includes feedback, helps assess understanding of course material at the outset.
- *Interactive* **Course Progress Monitoring Activities:** At the end of each part, this pop-up assessment allows students to monitor their progress as they master the material presented.
- *Chapter 4:* This chapter includes a discussion of reliability and validity issues of text accommodations and alternative assessments.

ORGANIZATION OF THE TEXT

This text presents complex concepts in a step-by-step discussion and provides students with practice exercises for each step. Students are introduced to portions of assessment instruments, protocols, and scoring tables as part of their practice exercises. Students participate in the educational decision-making process using data from classroom observations, curriculum-based assessment, functional behavioral assessment, and norm-referenced assessment.

This text is divided into four parts. Part 1, Introduction to Assessment, introduces students to the basic concepts in assessment and types of assessment. This part also presents the legal issues of assessment in the Individuals with Disabilities Education Act (IDEA) of 2004 and discusses ethical concerns related to assessment.

Part 2, Technical Prerequisites of Understanding Assessment, addresses the topics of descriptive statistics, reliability, and validity.

Part 3, Assessing Students, presents the mechanics of both informal and formal assessment. Students practice curriculum-based assessment, behavioral assessment, and norm-referenced assessment.

Part 4, Interpretation of Assessment Results, discusses interpretation of data for classroom interventions, eligibility decisions, and educational planning. Numerous case studies are included in this section.

SPECIAL FEATURES OF THE EIGHTH EDITION

Each chapter of this edition contains the following special features to help facilitate a better understanding of content.

- *Chapter Outcomes:* Each chapter begins with Chapter Outcomes to serve as an advance organizer to help prepare readers for the expectations for learning in the chapter.
- *Check Your Understanding:* These interactive exercises provide an opportunity for readers to monitor their progress in the learning and assessment process. These activities are included in electronic format with the feedback provided to the students following each response.
- *Embedded Videos:* These point-of-use videos illustrate various assessment techniques and strategies in context.
- *Test Review Tables:* These tables in Part 3 summarize the assessment instruments covered in their respective chapters.
- *Chapter Summary:* The summary provides an overview of the learning outcomes covered in the chapter.
- *Chapter Quiz:* This end-of-chapter interactive quiz enables readers to gauge their understanding of the chapter as a whole.
- *Course Progress Monitoring Activity:* Students complete a pre-test at the beginning of Chapter 1 and at the end of each part of the text to gauge their progress toward achieving learning targets. By completing this activity, students experience progress monitoring of their content knowledge.

SUPPLEMENTS

The eighth edition has an enhanced supplement support package, including an *Instructor's Manual* with test items, PowerPoint slides, and computerized test bank and assessment software. All of these items were developed exclusively for this text, and are available to instructors for download at www.pearsonhighered.com.

Online *Instructor's Manual* with Test Bank

The *Instructor's Manual* (ISBN: 978-0-13-394889-9) is organized by chapter and contains numerous resources and test items.

TestGen

TestGen (ISBN: 978-0-13-401912-3) is a powerful test generator that you install on your computer and use in conjunction with the TestGen testbank file for your text. Assessments may be created for both print or testing online.

Online PowerPoint Slides

PowerPoint slides (978-0-13-401945-1) highlight key concepts and summarize content.

ACKNOWLEDGMENTS

I would like to express my sincere gratitude to my former colleagues and the many students at the University of Texas–Brownsville and my current colleagues and students at Stephen F. Austin State University.

Thanks to the following reviewers: Laura Baylot Casey, University of Memphis; Sara Hines, Hunter College–CUNY; Jennifer Madigan, San Jose State University; Gilbert Stiefel, Eastern Michigan University.

Brief Contents

Contents

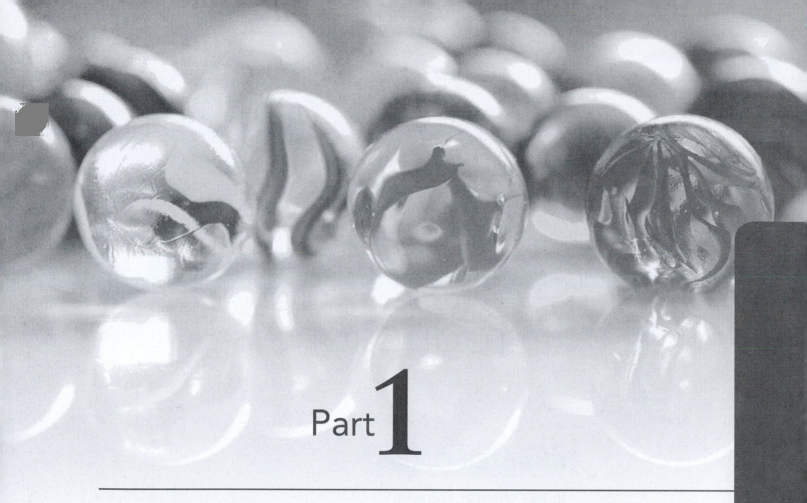

Part 1

Introduction to Assessment

1 Introduction

CHAPTER FOCUS

In this chapter you will:

- Learn about the history of assessment
- Learn about the traditional and contemporary models of assessment
- Apply the contemporary assessment model to a scenario
- Analyze scenarios and determine the type of assessment needed
- Synthesize the strategies used in the referral process
- Evaluate a referral case scenario

This introductory chapter presents an overview of the assessment process in general education in today's educational environment, reflecting current emphasis on inclusion and accountability in education for all children. The evaluation of student progress in general education occurs regularly. Teachers employ a problem-solving process incorporating intervention strategies in the classroom setting as well as screening and assessment of students who, even with appropriate interventions, require additional support. Various types of assessment are presented along with considerations of assessment of the child as a whole.

Before you begin this course, take this short pretest of some of the concepts covered in the text. As you finish each of the four major parts of the textbook, you will find additional Progress Monitoring Tests to assess your knowledge as you move through the course. By the end of the course, you should have mastered the content, and this will be reflected in the results of your tests. Click here, respond, and read your feedback for each item.

● ASSESSMENT: A NECESSARY PART OF TEACHING

Testing is one method of evaluating progress and determining student outcomes and individual student needs. Testing, however, is only one form of assessment. Assessment includes many formal and informal methods of evaluating student progress and behavior.

Assessment happens every day in every classroom for the purpose of informing the teacher about needed instructional interventions. A teacher observes the behaviors of a student solving math problems. The teacher then checks the student's answers and determines the student's ability to solve that particular type of math problem. If the student made mistakes, the teacher determines the types of errors and decides what steps must be taken to correct the miscalculations. This is one type of assessment. The teacher observes behavior, gathers information about the student, and makes instructional changes according to the information obtained.

In the routine assessment of students, behavior is observed, progress is monitored and evaluated, and interventions are planned when students do not make needed progress. With effective interventions that are based on scientific research, few students will require additional assessment or special support services. Students who do not respond to intensive interventions and continue to have academic difficulties may require additional assessment and evaluation for possible special education support. This process, known as response to intervention or (RTI), should result in only 3–5% of students requiring a full evaluation for exceptional learning needs or special education. The very best assessment practices, however, must adhere to legal mandates, ethical standards, and basic principles of measurement. Teachers and other educational personnel have a professional responsibility to be accountable for each decision about assessment. Therefore, knowledge of the fundamentals of assessment and the various types of assessment is necessary.

The process of assessment plays an important role in the determination of student outcomes. The Individuals with Disabilities Education Act of 1997 amendments, the Elementary and Secondary Education Act (ESEA) of 2001, and the Individuals with Disabilities Education Improvement Act of 2004 place more emphasis on the assessment of all students for measuring attainment of educational standards within the general curriculum (*Federal Register*, 1999, 2006; Individuals with Disabilities Education Improvement Act of 2004 Conference Committee Report, 2004, as cited in IDEA 2004; PL 107–110, 2002; Ysseldyke, Nelson, & House, 2000). Although the percentage of students receiving special education support continues to increase, so has the percentage of students in those programs graduating with regular high school diplomas. The rate has increased from 63.8% of all students with disabilities graduating from high school with a regular diploma in 2011 (Office of Special Education Programs, Data Accountability Center, 2013). It is of concern that despite the increasing numbers of students with special needs graduating with diplomas, nearly 40% of the students receiving special

FIGURE 1.1 Graduation Data for 47 States of 2008–2012 Cohort

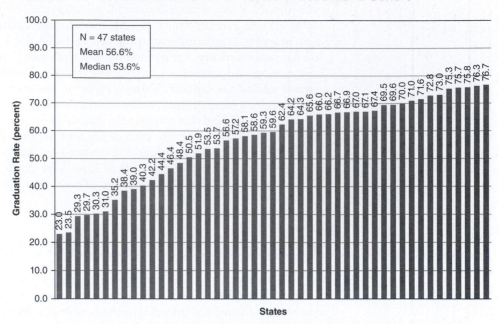

education support services do not. This underscores the need for more emphasis on the accountability of professionals serving special education students in ensuring these students progress successfully in the general education curriculum. You might want to know about your own state's graduation rate of students with exceptionalities. Figure 1.1 presents data reported by 47 states on students within disability categories who graduated with a general education diploma for the 2010–2011 academic year (National Dropout Prevention Center, 2013). These data are based on a cohort of students with disabilities who entered the ninth grade during the fall of 2007 and graduated by the spring of 2011. Table 1.1 presents data on students who graduated with a regular diploma by disability category.

Educational accountability efforts include improving education and achievement for all students, and especially improving the educational outcomes for culturally, linguistically, and ethnically diverse students, who continue to be represented in disproportionate numbers in several categories of special education (*Federal Register*, 2006; U.S. Department of Education, 1999, 2000). Federal regulations specifically target additional procedures and funding to address the disproportionate numbers of students of various ethnic groups who are found eligible for special education when this may be the result of other cultural factors. The regulations also address students who may be denied services as a result of cultural or linguistic differences. The under- or overrepresentation of students from various ethnic or linguistically different groups among those receiving special education services is called disproportionality. When too many students are found to be eligible from a specific ethnic group, it is known as overrepresentation of that group. For example, American Indian/Alaska Native students were 2.89 times more likely to receive special education and related services for developmental delay than any other group (U.S. Department of Education, 2009). Further explanation of disproportionality is provided in Chapter 2.

On January 8, 2002, the Elementary and Secondary Education Act of 2001 was enacted (PL 107–110, 2002). This legislation further emphasized educators' accountability for the academic performance of all children. *Accountability* in this sense means statewide assessment of all students to measure their performance against standards of achievement. Assessment of students with disabilities is based on the same principles as assessment of students in general education. Students with exceptional learning needs are required to take statewide exams or alternative exams to measure their progress within the general education curriculum. Teachers and other educational personnel

TABLE 1.1

Percentage of Students Ages 14 through 21 Exiting IDEA, Part B, and School, who *Graduated with a Regular High School Diploma*, by Year and Disability Category: 2001–02 through 2010–11

Disability	2001–02	2002–03	2003–04	2004–05	2005–06	2006–07	2007–08	2008–09	2009–10	2010–11
All disabilities	51.4	52.5	54.5	54.4	56.7	56.0	59.0	60.6	62.6	63.6
Austism	54.0	54.0	58.2	55.6	57.7	58.8	63.2	64.4	66.2	64.8
Deaf-blindness[a]	49.7	57.7	51.6	53.7	64.5	74.3	56.8	63.6	60.0	51.6
Emotional disturbance	32.2	35.6	38.4	40.1	43.4	42.7	45.6	47.4	49.9	52.3
Hearing impairments	67.1	67.1	67.6	69.6	68.9	67.0	69.7	71.7	71.8	73.1
Intellectual disabilities	38.5	37.8	38.9	35.1	37.2	37.6	37.6	38.7	40.7	39.9
Multiple disabilities	45.7	46.6	47.8	43.1	44.6	45.5	45.7	48.1	47.6	47.2
Orthopedic impairments	57.4	57.7	62.7	62.0	62.0	59.9	62.0	61.2	62.8	62.3
Other health impairments	59.3	60.0	60.5	61.9	63.6	62.4	66.5	67.3	69.2	70.0
Specific learning disabilities	57.0	57.7	59.6	59.6	61.7	60.7	64.2	65.5	67.4	68.4
Speech or language impairments	56.0	59.6	61.2	64.9	67.4	66.5	66.6	68.3	70.3	72.6
Traumatic brain injury	65.0	64.2	61.8	62.8	65.0	62.6	64.9	67.9	68.0	67.7
Visual impairments	71.5	69.5	73.4	72.4	72.1	69.7	77.1	75.0	77.9	78.6

Source: U.S. Department of Education, Office of Special Education Programs, Data Analysis System (DANS), OMB #1820-0521: "Report of Children with Disabilities Exiting Special Education," 2001–02 through 2010–11. These data are for the 50 states, DC, BIE schools, PR, and the four outlying areas with the following exceptions. For 2004–05, data for Washington and DC were not available. For 2005–06, data for DC were not available. For 2006–07, data for Vermont and Washington were not available. For 2007–08, data for Texas, Vermont, and DC were not available. For 2008–09, data for Vermont were not available. For 2010–11, data for BIE schools were not available. Data for 2001–02 through 2009–10 were accessed spring 2012. Data for 2010–11 were accessed fall 2012. For actual data used, go to http://www.ed.gov/about/reports/annual/osep.

[a]Percentages are based on fewer than 200 students exiting special education and school.

Note: Graduated with a regular high school diploma refers to students ages 14 through 21 served under *IDEA*, Part B, who exited an educational program through receipt of a high school diploma identical to that for which students without disabilities were eligible. These were students with disabilities who met the same standards for graduation as those for students without disabilities. As defined in 34 CFR section 300.102(a)(3)(iv), "the term *regular high school diploma* does not include an alternative degree that is not fully aligned with the State's academic standards, such as a certificate or a general educational development credential (GED)." The U.S Department of Education collects data on seven categories of exiters from special education (i.e., the Part B program in which the student was enrolled at the start of the reporting period). The categories include five categories of exiters from both special education and school (i.e., *graduate with a regular school diploma, received a certificate, dropped out, reached maximum age for services,* and *died*) and two categories of exiters from special education, but not school (i.e., *transferred to regular education and moved, known to be continuing* in education). The seven categories are mutually exclusive. This exhibit provides percentages for only one category of exiters from both special education and school (i.e., *graduated with a regular high school diploma*). For data on all seven categories of exiters, see exhibit 35. Percentage was calculated by dividing the number of students ages 14 through 21 served under *IDEA*, Part B, reported under the disability category who *graduated with a regular high school diploma* for the year by the total number of the students ages 14 through 21 served under *IDEA*, Part B, reported under the disability category in the five exit-from-both-special education-and-school categories for that year, then multiplying the result by 100. The percentages of students who exited special education and school by graduating as required under *IDEA* and included in this report are not comparable to the graduation rates required under the *Elementary and Secondary Education Act* of 1965, as amended (*ESEA*). The data used to calculate percentages of students who exited special education and school by graduating are different from those used to calculate graduation rates. In particular, states often use data such as the number of students who graduated in four years with a regular high school diploma and the number of students who entered high school four years earlier to determine their graduation rates under *ESEA*. For 2001–02 through 2004–05, data are from a cumulative 12-month reporting period, which may have varied from state to state. For 2005–06 through 2010–11, data are from the reporting period between July 1 and June 30 of the referenced year.

TABLE 1.2

Time in General Education Setting by Disability Category

Type of Disability	All Environments	Regular School, Time Inside General Class			Separate School for Students with Disabilities	Separate Residential Facility	Parentally Placed in Regular Private Schools[1]	Home-Bound/ Hospital Placement	Correctional Facility
		Less Than 40 Percent	40–79 Percent	80 Percent or More					
1	2	3	4	5	6	7	8	9	10
Visual impairments	100.0	11.8	13.3	63.8	5.5	3.7	1.3	0.6	#
2011									
All students with disabilities	**100.0**	**14.0**	**19.8**	**61.1**	**3.0**	**0.3**	**1.1**	**0.4**	**0.3**
Autism	100.0	33.7	18.2	39.0	7.7	0.5	0.6	0.3	#
Deaf-blindness	100.0	32.5	10.5	27.0	18.1	8.4	0.7	2.8	#
Developmental delay	100.0	16.3	19.6	62.5	0.8	0.1	0.6	0.2	#
Emotional disturbance	100.0	20.6	18.0	43.2	13.2	1.9	0.2	1.1	1.8
Hearing impairments	100.0	13.0	16.8	56.7	8.6	3.4	1.3	0.2	0.1
Intellectual disability	100.0	48.8	26.6	17.0	6.2	0.4	0.3	0.5	0.2
Multiple disabilities	100.0	46.2	16.4	13.0	19.2	1.7	0.3	3.0	0.1
Orthopedic impairments	100.0	22.2	16.3	54.0	4.7	0.2	0.8	1.7	0.1
Other health impairments[2]	100.0	10.0	22.7	63.5	1.6	0.2	1.0	0.9	0.3
Specific learning disabilities	100.0	6.8	25.1	66.2	0.5	0.1	0.8	0.1	0.3
Speech or language impairments	100.0	4.5	5.5	86.9	0.3	#	2.6	0.1	#
Traumatic brain injury	100.0	20.5	22.8	48.5	5.2	0.5	0.8	1.7	0.1
Visual impairments	100.0	11.3	13.1	64.3	5.9	3.8	1.1	0.6	#

—Not available.

Rounds to zero.

[1]Students who are enrolled by their parents or guardians in regular private schools and have their basic education paid through private resources, but receive special education services at public expense. These students are not included under "Regular school, time inside general class" (columns 3 through 5).

[2]Other health impairments include having limited strength, vitality, or alertness due to chronic or acute health problems such as a heart condition, tuberculosis, rheumatic fever, nephritis, asthma, sickle cell anemia, hemophilia, epilepsy, lead poisoning, leukemia, or diabetes.

Note: Data are for the 50 states, the District of Columbia, and the Bureau of Indian Education schools. Detail may not sum to totals because of rounding. Some data have been revised from previously published figures.

Source: U.S. Department of Education, Office of Special Education Programs, Individuals with Disabilities Education Act (IDEA) database, retrieved May 22, 2013, from http://tadnet.public .tadr.t..org/pages/712. (This table was prepared May 2013.)

must make decisions about the types of evaluations and tests and any accommodations that might be needed for statewide assessments in order to include students receiving special education support in accountability measures (*Federal Register*, 2006).

Inclusion of students with disabilities within the context of the general education classroom setting for more than 40% of the school day has increased to nearly 81% and will continue to increase due to the IDEA 2004 emphasis on general curriculum (*Federal Register*, 2006; U.S. Department of Education, 2013) and the accountability standards of the ESEA (PL 107–110, 2002). This increase of students with disabilities in the general education environment results in common expectations for educational standards and common assessment (*Federal Register*, 2006; PL 107–110, 2002; U.S. Department of Education, 1999). Table 1.2 displays the percent of time in various educational settings by disability category.

In November of 2004, the Individuals with Disabilities Education Improvement Act was completed by the congressional conference committee and signed into law on December 3, 2004. This law reauthorized the original IDEA and aligned it with the ESEA of 2002. In the 2004 Individuals with Disabilities Improvement Act, known as IDEA 2004, additional emphasis was placed on setting high standards of achievement for students with disabilities. These high standards should reflect the general education curriculum and must be assessed by statewide assessment of all students. Like the ESEA, IDEA 2004 requires that school systems and state education agencies collect data to document student achievement. This most recent reauthorization of the original IDEA places higher standards of accountability on teachers and schools to ensure student achievement. The rules and regulations that govern state educational systems and local school systems were completed and reported in the *Federal Register* in 2006. Additional aspects of the law and the assessment requirements are presented in Chapter 2.

● HISTORICAL AND CONTEMPORARY MODELS OF ASSESSMENT

Since the original public law was implemented in 1975, the typical process of assessment has included identification of specific deficits within a student that appeared to be the cause of the student's difficulty in the general education curriculum. The historical assessment model meant that when a general education teacher noticed that a student was having difficulty in the classroom, a referral was made to a multidisciplinary team. The multidisciplinary team, composed of assessment personnel such as a school psychologist, speech clinician, and educational testing specialist, then evaluated the student. The traditional model of assessment is presented in Figure 1.2.

FIGURE 1.2 The Traditional Model of Assessment

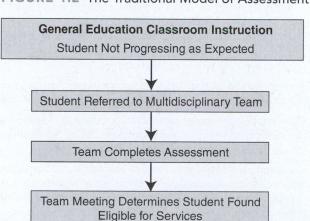

The team members and the child's parents then determined if the student met criteria for one of the categories of special education (McNamara & Hollinger, 2003). These categories are presented in Figure 1.3.

Research studies found varying referral practices, and professionals in the field subsequently have recommended reform in the referral process. For a discussion of historical research issues that influenced current practice and legislation, refer to the Research and Issues section at the end of this chapter.

Alternative practices such as prereferral interventions strategies emerged (Graden, Casey, & Bonstrom, 1985; Graden, Casey, & Christenson, 1985). These interventions were intended to address bias in the referral process and prevent unnecessary additional assessment and are now part of the RTI model. The use of RTI resulted in decreasing the rate of referrals (Marston, 2005) and improving the process of determining which students require additional special education support

FIGURE 1.3 Disabilities Defined in IDEA for Which Students Are Eligible for Special Education Services

Autism	A developmental disability significantly affecting verbal and nonverbal communication and social interaction, generally evident before age 3, that adversely affects a child's educational performance. Other characteristics often associated with autism are engagement in repetitive activities and stereotyped movements, resistance to change in daily routines, and unusual responses to sensory experiences. Autism does not apply if a child's educational performance is adversely affected primarily because the child has an emotional disturbance. A child who manifests the characteristics of autism after age 3 could be identified as having autism if other criteria are met.
Deaf-blindness	Concomitant hearing and visual impairments, the combination of which causes such severe communication and other developmental and educational needs that the child cannot be accommodated in special education programs solely for children with deafness or children with blindness.
Deafness	A hearing impairment that is so severe that the child is impaired in processing linguistic information through hearing, with or without amplification, and that adversely affects a child's educational performance.
Emotional disturbance	A condition exhibiting one or more of the following characteristics over a long period of time and to a marked degree that adversely affects a child's educational performance: (A) An inability to learn that cannot be explained by intellectual, sensory, or health factors (B) An inability to build or maintain satisfactory interpersonal relationships with peers and teachers (C) Inappropriate types of behaviors or feelings under normal circumstances (D) A general pervasive mood of unhappiness or depression (E) A tendency to develop physical symptoms of fears associated with personal or school problems (F) Emotional disturbance includes schizophrenia. The term does not apply to children who are socially maladjusted, unless it can be determined that they met other criteria for emotional disturbance.
Hearing impairment	An impairment in hearing, whether permanent or fluctuating, that adversely affects a child's educational performance but that is not included under the definition of deafness.
Intellectual disability	Significantly subaverage general intellectual functioning existing concurrently with deficits in adaptive behavior and manifested during the developmental period that adversely affects educational performance.
Multiple disabilities	Concomitant impairments (such as mental retardation–blindness or mental retardation–orthopedic impairment), the combination of which causes such severe educational needs that the child cannot be accommodated in special education programs solely for one of the impairments. Multiple disabilities does not include deaf-blindness.

FIGURE 1.3 Continued

Orthopedic impairment	Severe orhopedic impairment that adversely affects a child's educational performance. The term includes impairments caused by congenital anomaly, impairments caused by disease (e.g., poliomyelitis, bone tuberculosis), and impairments from other causes (e.g., cerebral palsy, amputations, and fractures or burns that cause contractures).
Other health impairment	Having limited strength, vitality, or alertness, including a heightened alertness to environmental stimuli, that results in limited alertness with respect to the educational environment that is due to chronic or acute health problems such as asthma, attention deficit disorder or attention deficit hyperactivity disorder, diabetes, epilepsy, a heart condition, hempophilia, lead poisoning, leukemia, nephritis, rheumatic fever, sickle cell anemia, and Tourette's syndrome, and adversely affects a child's educational performance.
Specific learning disability	A disorder in one or more of the basic psychological processes involved in understanding or using language, spoken or written, that may manifest itself in the imperfect ability to listen, speak, read, write, spell, or do mathematical calculations, including conditions such as perceptual disabilities, brain injury, minimal brain dysfunction, dyslexia, and developmental aphasia.
Speech or language impairment	A communication disorder, such as stuttering, impaired articulation, a language impairment, or a voice impairment, that adversely affects a child's educational performance.
Traumatic brain injury	An acquired injury to the brain caused by an external force, resulting in total or partial functional disability or psychosocial impairment, or both, that adversely affects a child's educational performance. Traumatic brain injury applies to open or closed head injuries resulting in impairments in one or more areas such as cognition, language, memory, attention, reasoning, abstract thinking, judgment, problem-solving, and sensory, perceptual, and motor abilities; psychosocial behavior; physical functions; information processing; and speech. Traumatic brain injury does not apply to brain injuries that are congenital or degenerative, or to brain injuries induced by brain trauma.
Visual impairment including blindness	An impairment in vision that, even with correction, adversely affects a child's educational performance. The term includes both partial sight and blindness.

services (Barnett, Daly, Jones, & Lentz, 2004). When interventions are used to improve learning and prevent additional learning problems, they are known as early intervening services.

Early Intervening Services

The inconsistent practices of the historic referral and assessment model resulted in the increasing rates of children referred for assessment and subsequently served in special education. The 2004 Individuals with Disabilities Education Improvement Act to IDEA began with congressional findings, which listed areas that the act sought to improve, including the use of prereferral interventions or early intervening services. The goal of increasing the use of early intervening services is, as often as possible, to address each student's needs within the general education classroom and to prevent additional assessment. Congress stated:

> Over 30 years of research and experience has demonstrated that the education of children with disabilities can be made more effective by providing incentives for whole school approaches and pre-referral intervention to reduce the need to label children as disabled in order to address their learning needs. (Individuals with Disabilities Education Improvement Act, 2004)

New regulations that outline the practices expected in IDEA 2004 require school systems to provide appropriate interventions for children who are at risk of having academic or behavioral difficulty. These interventions are referred to in the regulations as *early intervening services*. Particular emphasis is given to students in kindergarten through third grade and students who may be represented disproportionally; however, all students K–12 may receive these services. Early intervening services include those available to all children in the general education curriculum, such as general teaching methods, remedial instruction, and tutoring. In addition, schools are expected to use research-based methods for intervention and to document these efforts. These efforts may be included as part of the school's response to intervention methods, or RTI methods, for the prevention of learning problems and, if not successful, the data collected through RTI may be used to document possible learning and behavioral problems. Response to intervention is covered in depth in Chapter 7.

● THREE-TIER MODEL OF INTERVENTION

A three-tier model has been effectively employed for both academic and behavioral interventions. This model illustrates that all children's progress in core academic subjects should be monitored routinely. Monitoring can occur using standardized instruments such as state-mandated assessment tools, teacher-made tests, and measures of general academic performance in the classroom. Students whose performance on these measures is markedly discrepant from that of their peers are considered to be at risk of academic or behavioral problems; these students receive tier-two interventions, such as remedial assistance or tutoring. Using research-based instructional strategies, the teacher applies recommended interventions over a period of time, documenting results. Watch this video to review the three-tier model, learn some of the reasons behind the new methods, and see examples of implementation.

If interventions do not result in improved student performance, the teacher may request assistance through the teacher assistance team, which can recommend that a student receive intensive interventions that are designed to address a specific area of weakness or difficulty. If the child continues to struggle, he or she may be referred for evaluation for possible special education eligibility. The three-tier model is presented in Figure 1.4.

FIGURE 1.4 A Three-Tier Model

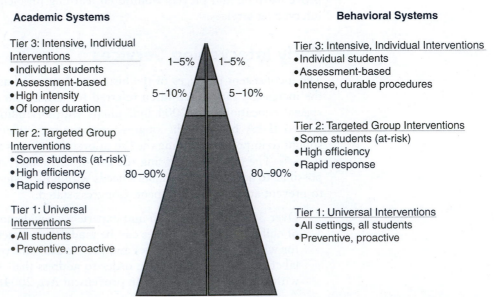

Three-Tier Model of School Supports

Academic Systems

Tier 3: Intensive, Individual Interventions
- Individual students
- Assessment-based
- High intensity
- Of longer duration

Tier 2: Targeted Group Interventions
- Some students (at-risk)
- High efficiency
- Rapid response

Tier 1: Universal Interventions
- All students
- Preventive, proactive

1–5%   1–5%

5–10%   5–10%

80–90%   80–90%

Behavioral Systems

Tier 3: Intensive, Individual Interventions
- Individual students
- Assessment-based
- Intense, durable procedures

Tier 2: Targeted Group Interventions
- Some students (at-risk)
- High efficiency
- Rapid response

Tier 1: Universal Interventions
- All settings, all students
- Preventive, proactive

Source: Adapted from: Batsche, G., et al. (2005). *Response to intervention: Policy considerations and implementation.* Alexandria, VA: National Association of State Directors of Special Education. Used with permission.

The more frequent use of better interventions is a step forward in the prevention of unnecessary evaluation and the possibility of misdiagnosis and overidentification of special education students. The use of specific academic interventions based on the type of academic performance problems may prevent inappropriate special education referrals. Teachers can determine the possible reason for the academic difficulty, provide an intervention, and determine if the intervention improves performance. Halgren and Clarizio (1993) found that 38% of students in special education were either reclassified or terminated from special education. This indicates a need for more specific identification of the learning or behavioral problems through referral and initial assessment.

Gopaul-McNicol and Thomas-Presswood (1998) caution that teachers of students whose primary language is not English often consider bilingual education or English as a Second Language (ESL) classes as prereferral interventions. In other research on referral and assessment practices involving Asian American students, Poon-McBrayer and Garcia (2000) found that prereferral interventions were limited and did not reflect the approaches needed to assist with language development; in this study, students were referred for evaluation when language interventions might have resolved their difficulties. Teachers of students with cultural and linguistic differences should employ prereferral intervention strategies that promote language acquisition in addition to an ESL or bilingual curriculum. In one study, the RTI model was applied to English Language Learners (ELLs) who were at risk of reading disabilities (Linan-Thompson, Vaughn, Prater, & Cirino, 2006). In this study, students whose primary language was Spanish received intensive interventions using evidence-based practices and made significant gains, thereby circumventing the need for special education referral. Finch (2012) called for additional research to determine the effectiveness of RTI with individuals from diverse linguistic, ethnic, and cultural backgrounds.

In this video, you will learn important components of the special education referral process.

● CONTEMPORARY MODEL OF ASSESSMENT

Difficulties with the traditional approach to referral and assessment led educators to look for more effective methods. The goal of the contemporary model of assessment is to resolve the academic or behavioral challenges experienced by the student so that he or she can experience success in the general education setting. This problem-solving model emphasizes finding a solution rather than determining eligibility or finding a special education placement. The contemporary model is presented in Figure 1.5. As noted in the model, several methods of assessment and intervention are employed before referral and comprehensive evaluation are considered. These methods include informal assessment techniques used in the general education environment. The team and the child's parents discuss the results.

Interventions are implemented and additional data are gathered to determine if the intervention was successful. When the interventions result in less improvement than had been expected, the team meets to discuss additional strategies or interventions. When a student is referred, it is only to assist in finding a solution or appropriate intervention. The intervention may or may not include special education support.

Read the following Case Study and respond to the questions asked in the Check Your Understanding activity that follows.

Case Study

Jaime entered kindergarten 3 months after his family moved into the school district. He had not attended preschool, and his mother had little time to devote to school-readiness skills. Jaime lives with his mother, father, and three older siblings.

FIGURE 1.5 The Contemporary Assessment Model

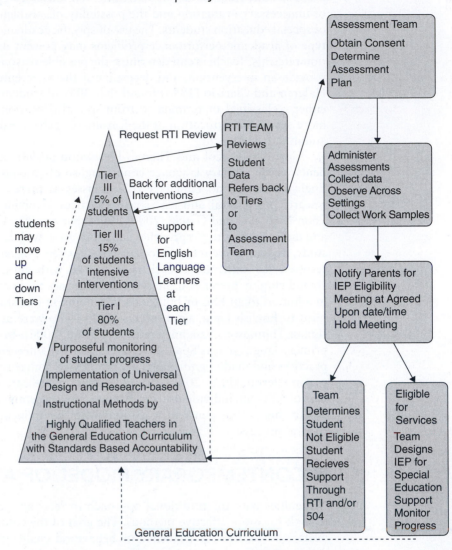

Jaime had experiences around other children in his extended family; however, Jaime had no experience in a structured learning environment. Within the first few weeks of school, Jaime's kindergarten teacher, Mrs. Johnson, began activities to teach phonemic awareness and used teaching methods that have been found to be effective in published reading studies. His teacher observed Jaime within the general classroom instructional activities and checked his understanding of the tasks he was asked to complete. His teacher routinely observed all students to make certain that they were following along and participating as expected. Mrs. Johnson frequently measured her students' progress using curriculum-based measurement tools. During this assessment, Mrs. Johnson noted that Jaime was not progressing as expected.

● EVALUATING STUDENT PROGRESS IN THE CLASSROOM

Teachers use several methods to assess student progress in the classroom. Teacher-made tests, quizzes, and other types of classroom-based informal assessment are often the initial means by which a student's progress is measured. Teachers may develop assessments directly from curriculum materials. This type of assessment is curriculum-based assessment. Curriculum-based assessment is commonly used to measure a student's performance within a specific classroom curriculum, such as reading, writing, or mathematics.

Teachers may first notice that a student is having difficulty progressing as expected by taking frequent measurements of the student's classroom performance. These frequent measurements using the curriculum that is being taught are called curriculum-based measurements. Research supports curriculum-based measurement as an effective method of monitoring the progress of both general and special education students (Deno, 2003; Fuchs, Deno, & Mirkin, 1984; Fuchs, Fuchs, Hamlett, Phillips, & Bentz, 1994). This method is presented in detail in Chapter 6.

When students are tested for mastery of a skill or an objective, the assessment is called criterion-related assessment, and tests of this type may be labeled criterion-referenced tests. Criterion-referenced tests compare the performance of a student to a given criterion.

Another type of assessment used in the classroom requires students to create a product that demonstrates their skills or competency; the assessment of their creation is called performance assessment. The assessment of a collection of various types of products or assessments collected over time that demonstrate student progress is known as portfolio assessment. Take a look at this video, and see the various types of products that might be included in portfolio assessments. Assessment that includes interaction or teaching and prompting to determine a student's potential to learn a skill is known as dynamic assessment. In dynamic assessment, the teacher assesses the student's ability or capacity to learn a new skill rather than testing for mastery of the skill.

Learning *how* the student performs tasks may also provide insight into the nature of the academic or behavioral difficulty. Observing the steps a student takes to solve a problem or complete a task can benefit the teacher as well as the student. The teacher might ask the student to verbalize the steps taken while reading a paragraph for content or while solving a math equation and then note the types or patterns of errors the student made during the process. This type of analysis is known as error analysis (e.g., $7 \times 3 = 10$; the student added rather than multiplied the numbers). Teachers also develop checklists to identify students who have mastered skills, tasks, or developmental expectations appropriate to their grade level. Checklists can be found in some commercial materials or school curriculum guides. Placement in the specific curriculum within the general education classroom may be based on a student's performance on skills listed on these commercial checklists or on other curriculum-based assessment results.

Current reform movements in special education and general education emphasize the changing role of assessment in special education (U.S. Department of Education, 2004). The result of this trend was the encouragement of nontraditional methods of assessment and the inclusion of students with disabilities in statewide accountability and competency testing (IDEA amendments, 1997). Including students with disabilities in district and statewide assessment, or high-stakes testing, is necessary to determine the effectiveness of educational programs (Ysseldyke, Thurlow, Kozleski, & Reschly, 1998). These statewide assessments are used to monitor progress of individual schools and school systems. The ESEA requires schools to show adequate yearly progress, or AYP, in order to demonstrate that students are mastering the curriculum in the general classroom (PL 107–110, 2002). AYP is measured using the results of statewide assessments. Students with disabilities who are determined to be unable to participate in these statewide assessments are to be tested using alternative assessments to measure attainment of standards. Teachers will be required to use a variety of assessment techniques to assess student competency and mastery of educational goals and objectives.

In the past, a student was referred for testing, evaluated by team members, and, if determined eligible for special education services, given an individualized education program (IEP) and placed in a special education setting. Although these steps were reported nationally as those most commonly followed in the evaluation process (Ysseldyke & Thurlow, 1983), they do not include the step of prereferral intervention.

Prior to assessing a student to determine if the student has exceptional learning needs, the teacher assistance team should evaluate the environment to determine if it supports the learning process. This type of assessment, called ecological assessment or environmental assessment, reflects a major trend toward considering the environment and assessing students in their natural environment (Overton, 2003; Reschly, 1986). One example of environmental assessment is presented in Figure 1.6.

FIGURE 1.6 Assessing the Academic Environment

Assessment of Academic Environment

Name of Student _____

Class: _____

Duration of observation:_____ minutes.

Check all that are observed during this observational period.

Physical Environmental Factors

_____ Seating: Individual student desks

_____ Seating: Group tables

_____ Seating: Student desks grouped in pairs or groups of four

_____ Material organized for quick student access and use

_____ Target student's materials organized

Classroom Behavioral Structure

_____ Classroom expectations (rules) posted

_____ Verbal praise for effort of students

_____ Verbal praise for target student

_____ Quiet redirection for target student when needed

_____ Inconsequential minor behaviors are ignored

_____ Transitions were smooth

_____ Time lapse to begin task less than 3 minutes (for class)

_____ Time lapse to begin task less than 3 minutes (for target student)

_____ Time lapse to begin task 5 minutes or more (for class)

_____ Time lapse to begin task 5 minutes or more (for target student)

_____ Noise level consistent with task demands

_____ Classwide behavior plan used

Classroom Teacher's Instructional Behaviors

_____ Task expectations explained verbally

_____ Task expectations explained visually (on board, etc.)

_____ Task modeled by teacher

_____ Cognitive strategies modeled by teacher first (thinking aloud)

Teacher–Student Interactions

_____ Academic behavior/responses shaped by teacher for all students

_____ Teacher used proximity as a monitoring technique for all students

_____ Teacher used proximity for reinforcement technique for all students

_____ Teacher used one-on-one instruction to clarify task for all students

Teacher–Target Student Interactions

_____ Academic behavior/responses shaped by teacher for target student

_____ Teacher used proximity as a monitoring technique for target student

_____ Teacher used proximity for reinforcement technique for target student

_____ Teacher used one-on-one instruction to clarify for target student

FIGURE 1.6 Continued

Classroom Academic Structure

_____ Anticipatory set for lesson/activity

_____ Task completed by group first before individuals are expected to complete task

_____ Academic behavior/responses modeled/assisted by peers

_____ Expected response or task made by pairs, groups, or teams

_____ Expected response made by individual students

_____ Tasks, instructions were structured and clear to students

_____ Tasks, instructions were unclear to target student

_____ A variety of teaching methods (direct instruction, media, manipulatives) used

Extended Learning Experiences

_____ Advanced organizers used; cues and prompts presented to class

_____ Homework assignment appropriate (at independent level, not emerging skill level)

_____ Homework instructions are clear

_____ Homework assignment is displayed in consistent place in room (board, etc.)

_____ Students use daily planner or other technique for homework/classwork

_____ Homework assignment is planned for reinforcement of skill rather than extension of work not completed during class

Other concerns of academic environment:

Source: From "Promoting Academic Success through Environmental Assessment," by Terry Overton, 2004, *Intervention in School and Clinic, 39*(3), pp. 149–150. Copyright 2004 by PRO–ED, Inc. Adapted with permission.

CHECK YOUR UNDERSTANDING

Check your understanding of the different types of assessment presented in the previous section by completing Activity 1.2.

Messick (1984) proposed a two-phase assessment strategy that emphasizes pre-referral assessment of the student's learning environment. The information needed during Messick's first phase includes

1. evidence that the school is using programs and curricula shown to be effective not just for students in general but for the various ethnic, linguistic, and socio-economic groups actually served by the school in question;

2. evidence that the students in question have been adequately exposed to the curriculum by virtue of not having missed too many lessons because of absence or disciplinary exclusion from class and that the teacher has implemented the curriculum effectively;

3. objective evidence that the child has not learned what was taught;

4. evidence that systematic efforts were or are being made to identify the learning difficulty and to take corrective instructional action, such as introducing reme-dial approaches, changing the curriculum materials, or trying a new teacher.

It is no longer considered acceptable to refer students who have difficulty in the general classroom without interventions unless they appear to be experiencing severe learning or behavioral problems or are in danger of harming themselves or others. Early intervention strategies have had positive effects. The problem-solving method requires the team to determine an effecive solution for the student's academic or behav-ioral difficulties. As part of this problem-solving strategy, a prereferral checklist may be used by the intervention team to clarify the target areas of difficulty and generate

---

* From "Assessment in Context: Appraising Student Performance in Relation to Instructional Quality," by S. Messick, 1984, *Educational Researcher, 13*, p. 5. Copyright 1984 by American Educational Research Association. Reprinted by permission of SAGE Publications.

hypotheses for interventions. An example of a prereferral checklist is presented in Figure 1.7. For a review of the referral process, watch this **video** and find out more about the connection of referral to the assessment of students with exceptionalities.

FIGURE 1.7 A Prereferral Checklist to Determine Whether All Necessary Interventions Have Been Attempted

Prereferral Checklist

Name of Student _____

Concerned Teacher _____

Briefly describe area of difficulty:

1. Curriculum evaluation:

   _____ Material is appropriate for age and/or grade level.
   _____ Instructions are presented clearly.
   _____ Expected method of response is within the student's capability.
   _____ Readability of material is appropriate.
   _____ Prerequisite skills have been mastered.
   _____ Format of materials is easily understood by students of same age and/or grade level.
   _____ Frequent and various methods of evaluation are employed.
   _____ Tasks are appropriate in length.
   _____ Pace of material is appropriate for age and/or grade level.

2. Learning environment:

   _____ Methods of presentation are appropriate for age and/or grade level.
   _____ Tasks are presented in appropriate sequence.
   _____ Expected level of response is appropriate for age and/or grade level.
   _____ Physical facilities are conducive to learning.

3. Social environment:

   _____ Student does not experience noticeable conflicts with peers.
   _____ Student appears to have adequate relationships with peers.
   _____ Parent conference reveals no current conflicts or concerns within the home.
   _____ Social development appears average for age expectancy.

4. Student's physical condition:

   _____ Student's height and weight appear to be within average range of expectancy for age and/or grade level.
   _____ Student has no signs of visual or hearing difficulties (asks teacher to repeat instructions, squints, holds papers close to face to read).
   _____ Student has had vision and hearing checked by school nurse or other health official.
   _____ Student has not experienced long-term illness or serious injury.
   _____ School attendance is average or better.
   _____ Student appears attentive and alert during instruction.
   _____ Student appears to have adequate motor skills.
   _____ Student appears to have adequate communication skills.

5. Intervention procedures (changes in teaching strategies that have been attempted):

   _____ Consultant has observed student:

Setting	Date	Comments
1.		
2.		
3.		

FIGURE 1.7 **Continued**

```
_____ Educational and curriculum changes were made:

    Change                          Date            Comments
1.

2.

3.

_____ Behavioral and social changes were made:

    Change                          Date            Comments
1.

2.

3.

_____ Parent conferences were held:

    Date                            Comments
1.

2.

3.

_____ Additional documentation is attached.
```

● DESIGNING AN ASSESSMENT PLAN

When team members decide that a comprehensive assessment will be needed in order to determine effective interventions, they must construct an assessment plan. Federal law mandates that evaluation measures used during the assessment process are those measures specifically designed to assess areas of concern (IDEA amendments of 2004). (Specific laws pertaining to the education of individuals with disabilities are discussed in Chapter 2.) Using appropriate early intervention strategies, a teacher observes the specific skills of learning difficulty and documents the lack of progress or the lack of response to the specific interventions. The team must determine which instruments will be administered, which additional methods of data collection will be used, and which special education professionals are needed to complete the assessment. Federal law also requires that the instruments selected are valid for their intended purpose. For example, if the student has been referred for problems with reading comprehension, the appropriate assessment instrument would be one of good technical quality that has been designed to measure reading problems—specifically, reading comprehension skills. In addition to requiring selection of the appropriate tests, the law mandates that persons administering specific tests be adequately trained to do so and that more than a single instrument be used to determine eligibility for special services. To meet these mandates, the educator must design an individual assessment plan for each student. Maxam, Boyer-Stephens, and Alff (1986) recommended that each evaluation team follow these specific steps in preparing an assessment plan:

1. Review all of the screening information in each of the seven areas (health, vision, hearing, speech and language skills, intellectual, academic, prevocational/vocational).

2. Determine what area or areas need further evaluation.

3. Determine the specific data-collection procedures to use (interviews, observation of behavior, informal or formal techniques, standardized tests).

4. Determine persons responsible for administering the selected procedures. These persons must be trained or certified if the assessment instrument calls for specific qualifications.

In addition to federal mandates and recommendations from professionals in the field of special education, the professional organizations of the American Psychological Association, the American Educational Research Association, and the National Council on Measurement in Education have produced the **Standards for Educational and Psychological Testing** (1999), which clearly defines acceptable professional and ethical standards for individuals who test children in schools. (Several of these standards are included in later chapters of this text.) The APA *Standards* (1999) emphasize the importance of using tests for the purpose intended by the test producer and place ethical responsibility for correct use and interpretation on the person administering and scoring tests in the educational setting. Other professional organizations, such as the Council for Exceptional Children and the National Association of School Psychologists, have ethics and standards that apply to assessment. These are presented in Chapter 2.

A student who has been referred for an initial evaluation may be found eligible for services according to the definitions of the various disabling conditions defined in federal law. (Refer to Figure 1.2)

The Comprehensive Evaluation

When a student has not had success in a learning environment after several prereferral strategies have been applied, the prereferral intervention team meets to determine the next step that will be taken in meeting the needs of that student. The team might recommend a comprehensive evaluation or perhaps a new educational intervention or alternative, such as a change in teaching methods, schedule, accommodations, or classroom teachers. If the team members recommend a comprehensive evaluation, they design an assessment plan.

The types of assessment that may be used in a comprehensive evaluation are varied and depend on the student's needs. Some instruments used are norm-referenced tests or assessment devices. These instruments determine how well a student performs on tasks when compared with students of the same age or grade level. These tests are also standardized tests. This means that the tests feature very structured and specific directions for administration, formats, scoring, and interpretation procedures. These specifics, written in the test manual, must be followed to ensure that the tests are used in the manner set forth by the test developers. Refer to Table 1.3 to compare the various types of tests used in assessing learners.

In addition to standardized norm-referenced tests, team members use informal methods such as classroom observations, interviews with teachers and parents, and criterion-referenced instruments. A team of designated professionals and the parents of the student comprise the individualized education program (IEP) team. The team reviews the results from the assessments in the eligibility meeting. This meeting will determine what educational changes may be necessary to provide the best instruction for the student.

---

* From *Assessment: A Key to Appropriate Program Placement* (Report No. CE 045 407, pp. 11–13), by S. Maxam, A. Boyer-Stephens, and M. Alff, 1986, Columbia, MO: University of Missouri, Columbia, Department of Special Education and Department of Practical Arts and Vocational-Technical Education. (ERIC Document Reproduction Service No. ED 275 835.) Copyright © 1986 by the authors. Reprinted by permission.

TABLE 1.3			

Types of Assessment

Type of Assessment	Purpose of Assessment	Who Administers Assessment	When Assessment Is Used
Ecological Assessment	To determine classroom environmental influences or contributions to learning	Teacher or intervention team member, such as special education teacher	Any time students appear to have learning or behavioral difficulties
Norm-Referenced Tests	To compare a specific student's ability with that of same-age students in national sample	Teacher (group tests); teachers, school psychologists, educational diagnosticians, other members of IEP team (individual tests)	When achievement or ability needs to be assessed for annual, triennial, or initial evaluations
Standardized Tests	Tests given with specific instructions and procedures—often are also norm-referenced	Teacher and/or members of intervention/IEP teams, such as school psychologists or educational diagnosticians	When achievement or ability need to be assessed for annual, triennial, or initial evaluations
Error Analysis	To determine a pattern of errors or specific type of errors	Teacher and other personnel working with student	Can be used daily or on any type of assessment at any time
Curriculum-Based Assessment	To determine how student is performing using actual content of curriculum	Teacher	To measure mastery of curriculum (chapter tests, etc.)
Curriculum-Based Measurement	To measure progress of a specific skill against an aim line	Teacher	Daily or several times each week
Dynamic Assessment	To determine if student has potential to learn a new skill	Teacher and/or other members of intervention or IEP team	Can be used daily, weekly, or as part of a formal evaluation
Portfolio Assessment	To evaluate progress over time in specific area	Teacher and/or members of intervention or IEP team	Over a specific period of time or specific academic unit or chapters
Criterion-Referenced Tests	To assess a student's progress in skill mastery against specific standards	Teacher and/or members of intervention or IEP team	To determine if student has mastered skill at end of unit or end of time period
Criterion-Related Tests	To assess student's progress on items that are similar to objectives or standards	Teacher and/or members of intervention or IEP team	Same as criterion-referenced tests
Checklists, Rating Scales, Observations	To determine student's skill level or behavioral functioning	Teacher and/or members of intervention or IEP team	Curriculum placement determination or behavioral screening

During the eligibility meeting, the IEP team may determine that the student is eligible for special education services based on information collected through the evaluation process. If the student is eligible, an IEP, or individualized education program, must be written for the student. If, however, the student is not eligible for special education services, the team considers an **alternative plan**, including educational intervention suggestions for the student. Alternative planning may include a plan for accommodations in the general classroom setting under Section 504. This law (presented in Chapter 2) requires that students who have disabilities or needs but who are not eligible to receive services under IDEA must have accommodations for their needs or disabilities in the regular classroom setting. A 504 accommodation plan is designed to implement those accommodations. Figure 1.8 presents a sample 504 accommodation plan.

FIGURE 1.8 Sample 504 Plan

504 Accommodation Plan

Name of Student _____ Date _____

1. Describe the concern for this student's achievement in the classroom setting: _____

2. Describe or attach the existing documentation for the disability or concern (if documentation exists). _____

3. Describe how this affects the student's major life activities. _____

4. The Child Study Team/504 Team has reviewed the case and recommends the following checked accommodations:

Physical Characteristics of Classroom or Other Environment

_____ Seat student near teacher.

_____ Teacher to stand near student when instructions are provided.

_____ Separate student from distractors (other students, air-conditioning or heating units, doorway).

Presentation of Instruction

_____ Student to work with a peer during seatwork time.

_____ Monitor instructions for understanding.

_____ Student to repeat all instructions back to teacher.

_____ Provide a peer tutor.

_____ Provide a homework helper.

_____ All written instructions require accompanying oral instructions.

_____ Teacher to check student's written work during working time to monitor for understanding.

_____ Student may use tape recorder during lessons.

Assignments

_____ Student requires reduced workload.

_____ Student requires extended time for assignments.

_____ Student requires reduced stimuli on page.

_____ Student requires that work be completed in steps.

_____ Student requires frequent breaks during work.

_____ Student requires use of tape recorder for oral responses.

_____ Student requires lower-level reading/math problems.

_____ No penalty for handwriting errors.

_____ No penalty for spelling errors.

_____ No penalty for grammatical errors.

FIGURE 1.8 Continued

Additional Accommodations for Medical Concerns (List)

_____

_____

Additional Accommodations for Behavioral Concerns (List)

_____

_____

Additional Resources for Parents (List)

_____

_____

Participating Committee Members

_____

_____

_____

CHECK YOUR UNDERSTANDING

Check your understanding of the referral process presented in the previous section by completing Activity 1.3.

When the referred child is 3 years of age or younger and eligibility for services has been determined, the law requires that team members and the child's parents collaborate in designing an individual family service plan (IFSP). The IFSP differs from the IEP in that the family's needs as well as the child's needs are addressed.

● ASSESSING THE WHOLE CHILD: CULTURAL CONSIDERATIONS

The 1997 IDEA amendments (presented in Chapter 2) required that state educational systems report the frequency of occurrence of disabilities and the race/ethnicity of students with disabilities. As reported in the literature for several years, particular groups of students from cultural and linguistically diverse backgrounds were found to be overrepresented in some categories of disabilities. The number of children ages 3 to 21 receiving special education support from various ethnic and racial groups is presented in Table 1.4.

It has been observed that the disproportionate rate of occurrence of students from various ethnic and cultural backgrounds happens in the disability categories that rely heavily on "clinical judgment"—learning disabilities, mild mental retardation, and emotional disturbances (Harry & Anderson, 1995). Fujiura and Yamaki (2000) reported troubling patterns indicating that students from homes that fall in the range of poverty and that structurally include a single parent are at increased risk for disabilities. Although there may be increased risk involved in environments that lack resources and support for single parents, the educational assessment of students from various cultural and linguistic backgrounds must be completed cautiously, fairly, and from the perspective of the child as a whole. Educators must keep the individual child's cultural, ethnic, and linguistic background in the forefront during the evaluation process.

Concern over the disproportionate rate of children from various ethnic and cultural groups being represented in special education categories resulted in directives to state educational agencies in IDEA 2004. The new version of IDEA includes specific mandates to states to make certain that policies and procedures are in place to prevent the disproportionate representation of ethnic groups in special education. Chapter 2 discusses these new requirements.

TABLE 1.4

Children 3 to 21 Years Old Served Under Individuals with Disabilities Education Act (IDEA), Part B, by Race/Ethnicity and Type of Disability: 2010–11 and 2011–12

Type of Disability	2010–11								2011–12							
	Total	White	Black	Hispanic	Asian	Pacific Islander	American Indian/ Alaska Native	Two or More Races	Total	White	Black	Hispanic	Asian	Pacific Islander	American Indian/ Alaska Native	Two or More Races
1	2	3	4	5	6	7	8	9	10	11	12	13	14	15	16	17
	Number of children served															
All disabilities	6,437,297	3,518,029	1,214,830	1,311,765	145,912	19,581	91,823	135,357	6,404,630	3,436,115	1,196,695	1,355,780	147,704	19,203	88,675	160,458
Autism	417,576	256,646	56,150	67,967	22,473	1,194	3,162	9,984	455,349	274,355	61,628	77,714	24,592	1,151	3,418	12,491
Deaf-blindness	1,512	867	155	355	69	10	24	32	1,583	890	158	397	65	16	26	31
Developmental delay	381,575	216,587	70,905	63,804	10,489	1,866	8,068	9,856	393,138	215,164	73,250	68,045	10,578	1,806	7,830	16,465
Emotional disturbance	389,299	210,011	106,474	52,310	3,430	1,083	5,860	10,131	373,154	199,929	100,412	51,698	3,224	980	5,381	11,530
Hearing impairments	78,134	39,360	11,517	20,505	3,962	397	937	1,456	78,448	38,409	11,412	21,617	4,156	402	841	1,611
Intellectual disability	448,120	212,415	127,322	83,070	9,904	1,203	6,199	8,007	434,586	203,247	120,492	85,206	10,018	1,239	5,679	8,705
Multiple disabilities	130,158	76,727	25,553	20,251	3,549	420	1,577	2,081	132,986	76,726	24,901	22,483	3,681	471	1,952	2,772
Orthopedic impairments	63,266	35,123	7,776	16,112	2,248	182	563	1,262	61,716	33,919	7,430	15,875	2,289	180	534	1,489
Other health impairments[1]	716,116	457,138	128,143	94,004	9,563	2,285	8,743	16,240	742,866	465,223	134,232	102,785	10,083	2,032	8,771	19,740
Specific learning disabilities	2,361,044	1,172,937	478,072	584,252	34,786	8,072	38,736	44,189	2,302,961	1,118,435	464,337	591,664	34,192	8,064	36,988	49,281
Speech or language impairments	1,396,282	808,295	194,225	299,096	43,731	2,703	17,225	31,007	1,372,870	778,171	189,926	307,379	43,075	2,692	16,570	35,057
Traumatic brain injury	25,727	16,039	4,031	4,086	595	75	345	556	25,969	16,006	4,041	4,254	609	77	329	653
Visual impairments	28,488	15,884	4,507	5,953	1,113	91	384	556	29,004	15,641	4,476	6,663	1,142	93	356	633
	Percentage distribution of children served															
All disabilities	100.0	100.0	100.0	100.0	100.0	100.0	100.0	100.0	100.0	100.0	100.0	100.0	100.0	100.0	100.0	100.0
Autism	6.5	7.3	4.6	5.2	15.4	6.1	3.4	7.4	7.1	8.0	5.1	5.7	16.6	6.0	3.9	7.8
Deaf-blindness	#	#	#	#	#	0.1	#	#	#	#	#	#	#	0.1	#	#
Developmental delay	5.9	6.2	5.8	4.9	7.2	9.5	8.8	7.3	6.1	6.3	6.1	5.0	7.2	9.4	8.8	10.3
Emotional disturbance	6.0	6.0	8.8	4.0	2.4	5.5	6.4	7.5	5.8	5.8	8.4	3.8	2.2	5.1	6.1	7.2
Hearing impairments	1.2	1.1	0.9	1.6	2.7	2.0	1.0	1.1	1.0	1.1	1.0	1.6	2.8	2.1	0.9	1.0
Intellectual disability	7.0	6.0	10.5	6.3	6.8	6.1	6.8	5.9	6.8	5.9	10.1	6.3	6.8	6.5	6.4	5.4

Number served as a percent of total enrollment[2]

Disability type													
Multiple disabilities	2.0	2.2	1.5	2.4	2.1	1.7	2.1	2.2	2.1	1.7	2.5	2.2	2.2	1.7
Orthopedic impairments[1]	1.0	1.0	1.2	1.5	0.6	0.6	0.9	1.0	0.6	1.2	1.5	0.9	0.6	0.9
Other health impairments[1]	11.1	13.0	7.2	6.6	10.5	9.5	11.7	13.5	11.2	7.6	6.8	10.6	9.9	12.3
Specific learning disabilities	36.7	33.3	44.5	23.8	39.4	42.2	41.2	32.5	38.8	43.6	23.1	42.0	41.7	30.7
Speech or language impairments	21.7	23.0	22.8	30.0	16.0	18.8	13.8	22.6	15.9	22.7	29.2	14.0	18.7	21.8
Traumatic brain injury	0.4	0.5	0.3	0.4	0.3	0.4	0.4	0.5	0.3	0.3	0.4	0.4	0.4	0.4
Visual impairments	0.4	0.5	0.5	0.8	0.4	0.4	0.5	0.5	0.4	0.5	0.8	0.5	0.4	0.4

Disability type													
All disabilities	**13.0**	**13.6**	**15.4**	**11.5**	**6.4**	**16.3**	**12.9**	**13.4**	**11.5**	**11.5**	**6.3**	**10.7**	**16.2**	**12.6**
Autism	0.8	1.0	0.7	0.6	1.0	0.6	0.9	1.1	0.8	0.7	1.1	0.6	0.6	1.0
Deaf-blindness	#	#	#	#	#	#	#	#	#	#	#	#	#	#
Developmental delay	0.8	0.8	0.9	0.6	0.5	1.4	0.8	0.8	0.9	0.6	0.5	1.0	1.4	1.3
Emotional disturbance	0.8	0.8	1.3	0.5	0.1	1.0	0.8	0.8	1.3	0.4	0.1	0.5	1.0	0.9
Hearing impairments	0.2	0.2	0.1	0.2	0.2	0.2	0.2	0.2	0.1	0.2	0.2	0.2	0.2	0.1
Intellectual disability	0.9	0.8	1.6	0.7	0.4	1.1	0.9	0.8	1.5	0.7	0.4	0.4	1.0	0.7
Multiple disabilities	0.3	0.3	0.3	0.2	0.2	0.3	0.3	0.3	0.3	0.2	0.2	0.3	0.4	0.2
Orthopedic impairments[1]	0.1	0.1	0.1	0.1	0.1	0.1	0.1	0.1	0.1	0.1	0.1	0.1	0.1	0.1
Other health impairments[1]	1.4	1.8	1.6	0.8	0.4	1.5	1.5	1.8	1.7	0.9	0.4	1.1	1.6	1.6
Specific learning disabilities	4.8	4.5	6.0	5.1	1.5	6.9	4.7	4.4	5.9	5.0	1.5	4.5	6.8	3.9
Speech or language impairments	2.8	3.1	2.5	2.6	1.9	3.0	2.8	3.0	2.4	2.6	1.8	1.5	3.0	2.8
Traumatic brain injury	0.1	0.1	0.1	0.0	#	0.1	0.1	0.1	0.1	#	#	#	0.1	0.1
Visual impairments	0.1	0.1	0.1	0.1	#	0.1	0.1	0.1	0.1	0.1	#	0.1	0.1	#

Rounds to zero.

[1]Other health impairments include having limited strength, vitality, or alertness due to chronic or acute health problems such as a heart condition, tuberculosis, rheumatic fever, nephritis, asthma, sickle cell anemia, hemophilia, epilepsy, lead poisoning, leukemia, or diabetes.

[2]Based on the total enrollment in public schools, prekindergarten through 12th grade, by race/ethnicity.

Note: Data include only those children served for whom race/ethnicity and type of disability were reported. Although data are for the 50 states and the District of Columbia, data limitations result in inclusion of a small (but unknown) number of students from Bureau of Indian Education and Puerto Rican schools. For these reasons, totals may differ from those shown in other tables. Race categories exclude persons of Hispanic ethnicity. Detail may not sum to totals because of rounding.

Source: U.S. Department of Education, Office of Special Education Programs, Individuals with Disabilities Education Act (IDEA) database, retrieved June 10, 2013, from http://tadnet.public.tadnet.org/pages/712; and National Center for Education Statistics, Common Core of Data (CCD), "State Nonfiscal Survey of Public Elementary/Secondary Education," 2010–11 and 2011–12. (This table was prepared June 2013.)

Portes (1996) posed the question, "What is it about culture and ethnicity that accounts for significant differences in response to the schooling process and its outcomes?" (p. 351). Portes further reasoned that differences in response to schooling are not fixed characteristics of students, but are more likely the learned behaviors and identities associated with school. Many variables seem to be associated with a greater likelihood of being found eligible for special education, including being male, having socioeconomic needs, being from a minority culture, and being suspended (Sullivan & Bal, 2013). Behavioral challenges and suspensions are examples of how students' experiences with school may contribute to the referral and identification process. Educators must continue to strive for methods of assessment that are fair to all students. Burnette's earlier recommendations (1998) of strategies for improving accuracy in the assessment process in order to reduce disproportionate representation of minorities in special education remain important today:

- Ensure that staff know requirements and criteria for referral and are kept abreast of current research affecting the process.
- Check that the student's general education program uses instructional strategies appropriate for the individual, has been adjusted to address the student's area of difficulty, includes ongoing communication with the student's family, and reflects a culturally responsive learning environment.
- Involve families in the decision to refer to special education in ways that are sensitive to the family's cultural background.
- Use only tests and procedures that are technically acceptable and culturally and linguistically appropriate.
- Ensure that testing personnel have been trained in conducting these particular assessments and interpreting the results in a culturally responsive manner.
- Include personnel who understand how racial, ethnic, and other factors influence student performance in the eligibility decision.
- When eligibility is first established, record a set of firm standards for the student's progress and readiness to exit special education.

The early writings of Lev Vygotsky concerning special education students' development and assessment cautioned professionals to be certain that the disability was not in "the imagination of the investigators" (Vygotsky, 1993, p. 38). Vygotsky also emphasized that the qualitative aspect of assessment in determining strengths and weaknesses is just as important as the concern for quantifiable deficits in children. Vygotsky reminded educators that children with disabilities should be viewed in light of their developmental processes in their various environments (Gindis, 1999; Vygotsky, 1993).

The way a student adapts to his or her environment, including culture and school, has a profound impact on that student's ability to have a successful school experience. Today the IDEA amendments call for educational equity and reform as well as emphasize the use of a variety of early intervening services and assessment techniques that will be useful in educational planning rather than assessment only for determining eligibility. The remaining chapters of this text present educators with both formal and informal assessment and evaluation procedures to be used in educational planning and intervention.

The following section is a brief review of the historic research and issues that influence current practice and changes in legislation. Additional information about legislation is presented in Chapter 2.

● RESEARCH AND ISSUES

1. Special education programs in previous years proved to have mixed results, and this contributed to the inclusion of students with exceptional learning needs in the general education curriculum and setting (Detterman & Thompson, 1997, 1998; Keogh, Forness, & MacMillan, 1998; Symons & Warren, 1998).

2. Research suggests referral practices in the past were inconsistent and may have been contributing to bias in the referral, assessment, and eligibility process. For example, studies found (1) that males were referred more frequently than females and that students with a previous history of difficulties tended to be referred more often (Del'Homme, Kasari, Forness, & Bagley, 1996); (2) that female teachers referred students with behavioral problems more frequently than their male colleagues (McIntyre, 1988); (3) that teachers referred students with learning and behavioral problems more often than those with behavioral problems alone (Soodak & Podell, 1993); and (4) that teacher referrals were global in nature and contained subjective rather than objective information in more than half the cases (Reschly, 1986; Ysseldyke, Christenson, Pianta, & Algozzine, 1983).

3. According to research, a teacher's decision to refer may be influenced by the student's having a sibling who has had school problems as well as by the referring teacher's tolerance for certain student behaviors; the teacher with a low tolerance for particular behaviors may more readily refer students exhibiting those behaviors (Thurlow, Christenson, & Ysseldyke, 1983).

4. Early research indicated that, nationwide, more than 90% of the students referred for evaluation were tested. Of those tested, 73% were subsequently found eligible for services in special education (Algozzine, Christenson, & Ysseldyke, 1982). More recently, Del'Homme et al. (1996) found that 63% of the students in their study who were referred subsequently received special education services. Students who are referred are highly likely to complete the evaluation process and receive special education services. In another study, 54% of the students referred for assessment were determined to be eligible (Fugate, Clarizio, & Phillips, 1993).

5. In a study by Hosp, Hosp, and Dole (2011), bias in predictive validity of universal reading screening measures was found, and this points to the importance of using multiple screening measures before making a decision, for example, that a specific student may need additional interventions.

6. When IDEA was reauthorized in 2004, it included language for districts in which disproportionality had been found to address this through the use of IDEA funds, up to 15%, to provide early intervening services. The goal was to reduce disproportionality of individuals from various ethnic or racial groups by assisting students to achieve in the general education setting. It has since been determined (Government Accountability Office [GAO], 2013) that state definitions of disproportionality in fact influenced the outcomes. In other words, in some states the definitions may be written in such a way that the districts were not found to have disproportionality but when another state's definition was applied, disproportionality would be found.

CHAPTER SUMMARY

In this chapter you:

- Learned about the history of assessment
- Learned about the traditional and contemporary models of assessment
- Applied the contemporary assessment model to a scenario
- Analyzed scenarios and determined the type of assessment needed
- Synthesized the strategies used in the referral process
- Evaluated a referral case scenario

THINK AHEAD

The steps of the evaluation process are structured by both federal and state laws. The federal mandates are presented in Chapter 2. Why is it necessary to have laws that regulate the assessment process in education?

CHAPTER QUIZ

Complete the Chapter Quiz to measure your understanding of the content in this chapter.

2 Laws, Ethics, and Issues

CHAPTER FOCUS

In this chapter you will:

- Learn the federal regulations covering the assessment process
- Apply regulations to case scenarios
- Analyze cases to determine compliance with regulations
- Synthesize the meaning of regulations
- Evaluate case scenarios for compliance and ethical issues

● THE LAW: PUBLIC LAW 94–142 AND IDEA

During the 1970s, substantial legal changes for persons with disabilities occurred. Much of the pressure for these changes came from parents and professionals. Another influential source affecting the language of the law was litigation in the civil court system. In 1975, the Education for All Handicapped Children Act, referred to as **Public Law 94–142**, was passed, and 2 years later the regulations were completed (Education of the Handicapped Act [EHA], 1975; *Federal Register*, 1977). Several reauthorizations of the original legislation have occurred. With each reauthorization, amendments have been added. Many provisions of IDEA concern the process of assessment. The law mandates that state education agencies (SEAs) ensure that proper assessment procedures are followed (*Federal Register*, 1992).

Although the original law has been in effect for three decades, professional educators must continue to monitor compliance with the mandates within each local education agency (LEA). Informed teachers and parents are the best safeguards for compliance in every school.

In 1986, the Education for the Handicapped Act Amendments, PL 99–457, were passed. The final regulations, written in 1993 (*Federal Register*, 1993), were developed to promote early intervention for preschool children and infants with special needs or developmental delays. Additional changes were added in the 1997 amendments of IDEA. Specific issues concerning preschool education for children with exceptional needs are now incorporated into IDEA. The assessment of infants, toddlers, and preschool children is discussed in Chapter 11.

In 2004, the Individuals with Disabilities Education Improvement Act was signed into law. This law was designed to address the portions of IDEA that needed improvement and to align this legislation with the Elementary and Secondary Education Act of 2002. The changes included in this improvement act focused on

- increasing accountability for achievement by students with disabilities;
- reducing the amount of paperwork that educators and other professionals needed to complete;
- reducing noninstructional time spent by teachers (time spent completing paperwork and attending meetings);
- providing additional avenues to resolve disagreements between schools and parents;
- increasing early intervention activities and aligning this effort with ESEA;
- improving teacher quality;
- mandating efforts by state education agencies to decrease disproportionality of ethnic and culture representations in special education; and
- improving discipline policies of earlier legislation.

As a review of the main principles of IDEA, watch this video and see how these principles relate to the assessment process.

Once a bill such as the Individuals with Disabilities Education Improvement Act has been signed by the president and becomes law, regulations are put into place to delineate the legal guidelines for implementing the law. It may take quite some time to write regulations, especially if the law is a lengthy one. Once the law is passed, each state must use the law and regulations to ensure that all of the public schools in the state implement the law according to the federal regulations. In addition, states may interpret some components in a different way and pass state laws and write regulations that the schools within that state must implement. The state cannot elect to ignore, or not implement, federal mandates; however, the specific manner in which states implement the law can be determined by each state. There may be additions to the federal law but not deletions of mandatory laws. For example, a state may decide to provide a variety of intensive services to all infants and toddlers with suspected developmental delays, but a state cannot refuse to provide services to children ages 3–5 with developmental delays or other known impairments.

Once the state regulations are written, individual districts may further determine district policies for each district within the state. For example, although it may not be part of federal or state law, an individual district might develop a policy of offering complete comprehensive evaluations for each student in special education who is exiting the school system due to graduation or reaching the age at which public school services will no longer be provided (age 22). The federal law requires a summary evaluation for exiting students; however, a comprehensive evaluation is not required. In this particular case, the district policy is offering more services than are mandated by law.

This chapter contains sections of the law that directly affect the assessment of children and youth of school age. Additional legal issues regarding high-stakes assessment are presented in Chapter 5. IDEA and IDEA 2004 topics presented in this chapter are listed in Table 2.1.

TABLE 2.1

IDEA Topics Presented in Chapter 2

- Early intervening services
- Initial evaluations
- Parental consent
- Procedural safeguards
- Nondiscriminatory assessment
- Disproportionality of ethnic and cultural groups
- Determining needed evaluation data
- Evaluating children with specific learning disabilities
- Meeting the needs of persons with ADHD
- Multidisciplinary team evaluations
- The IEP team
- IDEA regular education teacher requirements
- Determining eligibility
- Parent participation
- Developing the IEP
- Considerations of special factors
- Transition services
- Due process
- Impartial due process hearings

● IDEA AND ASSESSMENT

IDEA is a federal law containing mandates to promote fair, objective assessment practices and due process procedures, the foundations for legal recourse when parents or schools disagree with evaluation or placement recommendations. Teachers should be aware of the law and strive to maintain compliance with it in testing students, recommending placement, and developing IEPs. Teachers can help their local education agencies comply by following guidelines, meeting timelines, and correctly performing educational functions specified in the law.

As presented in Chapter 1, early intervening services should be implemented prior to a referral for the initial evaluation, or the first evaluation of a student to determine if special education services are needed. Following the early intervening activities and documentation collected, students who continue to struggle may then be referred for an initial evaluation.

Initial Evaluations

The provisions of IDEA as amended by the recent improvement act are presented throughout this chapter. The regulations have timeline requirements for completing the comprehensive evaluation and also provide guidance for situations in which the timeline may be extended or changed.

A parent, teacher, or others who know and work with a student in school, can initiate the referral process. Before a student can receive special education support services in a general education classroom or in a special education setting, members of the multidisciplinary team must complete a comprehensive individual evaluation of the student's needs. This evaluation should reflect consideration of the specific academic, behavioral, communicative, cognitive, motor, and sensory areas of concern. This comprehensive educational evaluation must be completed before eligibility can be determined. The IDEA 2004 requires that this comprehensive evaluation be completed within a specific timeframe of 60 days from the date that the parent signs a consent form for the evaluation. A state may select a different deadline, such as 45 days, or accept the federal timeframe. Additional specifications are presented in the law that address how the timeframe may be adjusted when a child transfers to a different school after the parent has signed the consent form. In addition, the law allows for flexibility of the timeframe if the parents do not produce the child for the evaluation or if the parents refuse to consent to the evaluation.

Parental Consent

The initial preplacement comprehensive evaluation cannot take place without parental notice about the assessment procedures and informed consent. The school should make reasonable efforts to obtain the consent for the initial evaluation. Informed consent means that the parent understands what school personnel want to do, such as the procedures that will be completed as part of the assessment. The consent provided by the parent for the initial evaluation does not mean the parent has also consented to special education support services.

When parents refuse to give consent for the initial evaluation, the school is not obligated to provide special education support services. School personnel can, however, seek due process or mediation procedures in order to seek a ruling requiring the assessment. The school is not required to conduct due process proceedings and is not required to provide special education support services.

For children who are a ward of the state and are not living with their parents, or children whose parents no longer legally have educational authority for their children as determined through the court system, the consent form is not required if the parents cannot be located. According to federal regulations, *parental consent* means that the parent, guardian, or surrogate parent has been fully informed of all educational activities to which she or he is being asked to consent. When a parent gives consent for an initial evaluation the parent is indicating that she or he has been fully informed of the evaluation procedures, has been told why school personnel believe these measures are necessary, and has agreed to the evaluation.

The federal regulations regarding informed consent require that the parent has been provided with all information in her or his native language or mode of communication. If the parent does not speak English, the information must be conveyed verbally or in writing in the parent's native language. In areas where languages other than English are prevalent, education agencies often employ bilingual personnel to translate assessment and placement information as necessary. Additionally, many state education agencies provide consent forms and parents' rights booklets in languages other than English. IDEA's statement regarding mode of communication sends a clear message that parents with visual or hearing impairments must be accommodated. The education agency must make every effort to provide sign interpreters for parents with hearing impairments who sign to communicate and large-type or Braille materials for parents with visual impairments who read in this fashion.

IDEA 2004 includes provisions for allowing school systems to pursue the evaluation of a student without parental consent if the school system follows the due process procedures within the law under certain conditions. Should parents refuse services that have been found to be necessary following the evaluation, the school system is not held responsible for the provision of such services. In addition, this law states that parental consent for evaluation is not to be considered as consent for receiving special education services.

The 2004 law addresses obtaining consent from parents when their child is a ward of the state in which they live. Local school systems must attempt to locate these parents and obtain consent for evaluation and receipt of services. However, if the parents cannot be found, the school can complete an initial evaluation without parental consent.

Parents must be notified of any action proposed by the local school regarding initial evaluations and options considered by IEP teams. These are among the many procedural safeguards provided to parents under federal law. The law includes requirements about when parents should receive notice of their rights.

Within the procedural safeguards information, the law requires that parents (1) be informed of the procedures and safeguards for obtaining an initial evaluation, (2) receive prior notice before any actions related to their child are taken, (3) be informed of their rights with regard to informed consent, (4) are made aware of how to obtain their student's records and who has access to those records, and (5) are informed of the process to follow when they have complaints as well as the procedures used in resolving those complaints.

Parental consent must be obtained before the school releases any student records to a third party. If, for example, school personnel want a student's records to be mailed to a psychologist in private practice, the student's parents must give written consent for them to release the records. Further, parents have the right to know exactly which records are to be mailed and to whom.

Federal law requires that school personnel inform parents before any special placement is effected. Parental consent is considered mandatory in order for the services to be implemented and it may be revoked at any time. For example, if parents agree to special education resource services for their child for 1 hour per day, and it is later recommended that the child receive services for 3 hours per day, they may revoke their approval of special education services if they believe it to be in the best interest of their child to do so. Should parents revoke their consent to provision of special education services, they are guaranteed the rights of due process. The special education services must be terminated and the school must provide written notice of when the termination will occur. School personnel are granted the same rights of due process and may decide to file a complaint against parents. (Due process is discussed in greater depth later in this chapter.)

The Check Your Understanding exercises included with this text provide opportunity for you to monitor your own progress in learning the assessment process. Complete this activity for Chapter 2.

CHECK YOUR UNDERSTANDING

Check your understanding of procedures for initial evaluations by completing Activity 2.1.

Nondiscriminatory Assessment

Many of the requirements that guide professionals in the assessment process are concerned with fair testing practice. IDEA 2004 regulations relating to nondiscriminatory assessment are consistent with the original regulations. The regulations of 1999 included a statement regarding the assessment of students with limited English proficiency. These requirements have been expanded so that educational professionals must regard language differences as they select and administer instruments and as they present results to parents who may not speak English.

This section of the law requires that multiple measures be used to obtain an accurate view of a child to determine if that child has a disability. It further states that the results of these evaluations are to be used to determine the content of the child's individualized education program (IEP). This underscores that the purpose of evaluation is to provide meaningful information that will assist in the design of a program of intervention rather than the simple evaluation of a child to determine if that child is eligible for special services. In addition, the law requires that the instruments used for assessment must be technically sound or, in other words, valid for such purposes.

Nondiscriminatory assessment is mandated by federal law to ensure fairness and objectivity in testing. This section of the law requires that the instruments or techniques used in the assessment process are not racially, ethnically, or culturally biased. This section of the law sets forth the minimum criteria for nondiscriminatory assessment practice in special education. It requires that the mode of communication typically used by the student be used in the assessment process and that the form of communication used will be the one in which the child can best demonstrate his or her ability. Like the communication standards written for parental consent, this section mandates that school personnel find and use such appropriate methods as sign language or Braille if necessary to assess the student's ability in the fairest and most objective manner.

The assessment of students with limited proficiency or emerging proficiency in English is especially difficult. Assessment personnel must make certain that the instruments they use to assess students who have not mastered English assess skills and abilities other than English language skills. Additional considerations for the assessment of students who are not proficient in English are provided in determining specific learning disabilities, which is presented later in this chapter.

The act of 2004 clearly indicates that measures of a student's school performance other than tests should be used in the evaluation process. The multidisciplinary team must weigh this input in arriving at decisions regarding any instructional interventions or referral for special services. Moreover, information gathered should be for the purpose of enabling the student to participate as often as possible in the general education curriculum. All assessment must be conducted with the goal of providing functional information that will be of benefit to the student.

Proper assessment of referred children means that schools must ensure that tests are administered by trained personnel in the manner specified by the test producer. The examiner's manuals that are included with testing materials contain information regarding the qualifications test administrators should possess, and it is essential that administrators understand the information provided in these manuals before working with students. Examples of testing errors made by professionals who do not comply with this section of IDEA include administering tests or sections of a test to a group of students when the test was designed for individual administration, giving directions to students in writing when the manual specifies that they should be issued orally, and allowing additional time to complete an item on timed items. When an examiner fails to follow directions specified by the developer of a standardized test, the results may lead to inaccurate interpretations and poor recommendations. In this regard, the testing has been unfair to the student.

The best and most consistent practice for using standardized instruments is to follow the directions provided for administration. There are times, however, when the best practice for determining an *estimate* of the student's ability may require adaptation of the standardized directive. For example, when assessing a very young child who has a high level of anxiety or a child with limited cognitive ability, it may be necessary for an examiner to request that the parent or primary caretaker remain in the room, perhaps with the child sitting on the parent's lap. The parent in such situations may assist with some of the assessment items (such as providing translations if the young child has difficulty with articulation). In such cases, the 1999 regulations require that any modifications to testing procedures be explained in the written evaluation report. In such situations, an estimate of the child's ability has been obtained. This would require that additional measures, both standardized and nonstandardized, be incorporated into the assessment before making a decision about the student's eligibility.

The assessment of a student must include the use of multiple measures designed for evaluating specific educational needs. The law indicates that no single instrument should be used to determine eligibility. Before the passage of the original law (PL 94–142), numerous students were discriminated against because of conclusions based on a single IQ score. Often this resulted in placement in restrictive settings, such as institutions or self-contained classrooms, rather than in the implementation of more appropriate educational interventions. In addition to federal mandates, court cases, such as *Larry P. v. Riles* (1984), have had a significant impact on discriminatory testing practices. This case and others are presented in Chapter 10.

Assessment can be discriminatory in other ways. The law mandates that the instruments used to assess one skill or area do not discriminate or unduly penalize a student because of an existing impairment. For example, a student with speech articulation problems who is referred for reading difficulties should not be penalized on a test that requires him to pronounce nonsense syllables. Such a student may incorrectly articulate sounds because of the speech condition, and his articulation errors might be counted as reading errors, resulting in scores that are not truly indicative of his actual decoding skills. IDEA also requires that students be assessed in all areas of suspected disability and that sensory, motor, and emotional areas should be included when appropriate. Assessment personnel must consider all possible areas of need, even those that are not typically associated or linked with the area of weakness that might have been the initial focus of concern. For example, it is not uncommon for students with specific learning disabilities to have difficulty in more than one academic area (e.g., spelling, writing, reading). Likewise, a student who is referred because of immature social skills and inappropriate behavior might also demonstrate developmental and learning problems. Often, when referral information is initially submitted, background information is too limited to determine whether the student is having emotional problems, specific learning problems, or might be below average in general intellectual ability. In one case, a young student referred because of behavioral problems was found after assessment to have a mild hearing impairment. Appropriate audiological and educational interventions prevented further behavioral problems from developing and helped to remediate this student's academic skills.

The law also requires that the tests or instruments employed for assessment be psychometrically adequate. Test consumers are required to have an understanding of general testing principles and the accuracy with which inferences about students' cognitive, academic, and behavioral functioning can be made using such instruments. Examiners should possess an understanding of the reliability and validity of specific standardized instruments in order to have confidence in the instrument's accuracy in measuring a student's performance or skills. Reliability and validity concepts are reviewed in Chapter 4.

The law encourages the use of a variety of assessment devices and requires the participation of several professionals in the decision-making process. Using varied assessment materials helps professionals arrive at a more holistic view of the student. The professional expertise provided by a multidisciplinary team aids in promoting fair and objective assessment and ultimately results in optimal intervention and placement decisions.

CHECK YOUR UNDERSTANDING

Check your understanding of fair assessment practices by completing Activity 2.2.

Discriminatory test practices concerned with test bias—examiner bias, for example—are presented in the section "Research and Issues Concerning IDEA" later in this chapter. The IDEA Improvement Act of 2004 includes additional statements regarding the initial assessment and reevaluation of students that require the consideration of data derived from various sources during previous assessments.

In addition to the specifications about nondiscriminatory assessment, the regulations include requirements about students who transfer from one school to another in the same school year and encourage schools to complete pending or incomplete evaluations. The evaluation must include assessment of all areas of suspected special needs and related services that the child may require to determine his or her educational needs.

Determining Needed Evaluation Data

Since the regulations require that all possible areas of disability need to be evaluated, they also provide guidance on how to determine which data are needed in order to determine the child's educational needs. The data should be collected from classroom formal and informal assessments, observations, school records, current levels of performance, and any high-stakes assessment data. These specifications are outlined for evaluations and reevaluations. Some of these types of data are collected on all students, such as high-stakes testing data or classroom performance data. Other data would be collected during the initial evaluation or reevaluation process. Data may include input and information from the parents of the referred student.

IDEA calls on professionals and parents alike to determine what data may be needed to obtain the most accurate picture of the child's current ability and educational needs. The law requires that any services provided are designed to assist the student in meeting the measurable goals of the IEP. The law further requires that the student participate in the general education curriculum unless there are data to indicate that this would not be appropriate. Students with disabilities may require alternate or modified versions of state-mandated achievement tests, which should be noted in the IEP, and these data may be included in the review. It might also be the decision of the multidisciplinary team that such students be educated in settings different from those of their age and grade peers. Federal law requires that the IEP team review data from a variety of sources and, in the case of reevaluation of a student receiving special services, determine whether enough data exist to support that student's continued eligibility. In such cases, the student is not subjected to comprehensive formal testing to complete the review for continued placement unless her or his parents request it. Although these comprehensive assessments are not mandatory in reevaluations in federal law, specific states or district policies may require more extensive testing for the reevaluation. The student's academic, behavioral, and social progress data are reviewed by the multidisciplinary team, but any testing that occurs generally consists of only those measures of current educational or behavioral functioning unless parents request additional measures. For example, a student who excels in math but has a specific reading disability likely will not undergo reevaluation of her or his math skills unless the parents specifically request that math skills are reevaluated as well as reading skills.

Additional regulations specify that the IEP team may conduct its review of the existing data without a meeting at which all involved parties are present. If the team determines that additional data are needed, the appropriate testing is conducted to obtain the needed data. If additional data are not needed, the parents are notified of this and informed that they have the right to request additional assessment. If the parents request additional assessment, the team is required to complete testing before determining that the child should continue receiving special education support.

● EVALUATING CHILDREN WITH SPECIFIC LEARNING DISABILITIES

Federal law includes not only the definition of the term *learning disabilities* (see Chapter 1) but also guidelines to assist in determining whether a learning disability exists. Until the reauthorization of IDEA 2004, the law stated that a learning disability was indicated when a student exhibited a significant discrepancy between cognitive ability and academic achievement. Using the "significant discrepancy" model meant that a student with a learning disability would likely struggle in acquiring basic skills in reading, writing, and mathematics during the elementary years— at least until a significant discrepancy between ability and achievement could be determined. Research has indicated that students can benefit from instructional interventions during the early elementary years, and the revised law reflects this research. In order to find that a student has a specific learning disability, the determination must include the use of additional measures and cannot be based only on a learning discrepancy model.

This section of the law indicates that the eligibility determination must include measures such as response to intervention (RTI) methods that have been found to be effective using scientific research methods. The team may use other methods (e.g., those that indicate difficulties in processing information) that have been found through research to be effective in the diagnostic process. The state criteria cannot require the use of the former discrepancy model. Additional information about response to intervention is provided in Chapter 7.

According to this operational definition and elaboration on determining eligibility, a student can be found to have a specific learning disability in academic areas, such as reading, math, or written language. These weaknesses can be found in reading fluency, reading comprehension, basic reading skills, math problem solving, calculation, oral and written expression, and listening comprehension. When the referred student has been receiving appropriate instruction prior to the referral, these weaknesses in the specific learning areas mentioned are found when the student is compared with grade-level peers on measures including but not limited to statewide assessments. The regulations promote instructional interventions early in the student's schooling that may result in the student's needs being met in the general education classroom. Should those interventions not result in the progress expected, they become data that are used in determining eligibility for special services. The team may determine that other data are needed as well.

The regulations include exclusionary statements that require the team to consider and make certain that the identified learning disability is not the result of cognitive disability; emotional disorders; cultural, linguistic, economic, or environmental disadvantage; or limited proficiency in English. Moreover, the student cannot be found to have a learning disability if this is the result of disabilities in hearing, vision, or physical or motor disabilities. The regulations require that the team consider multiple sources of data in an effort to make the determination that the learning disability is not the result of these other factors.

● MEETING THE NEEDS OF PERSONS WITH ATTENTION DISORDERS

When PL 94–142 was revised, attention disorders were studied by the U.S. Department of Education (U.S. Department of Education, 1991) for possible addition as a new disability category under IDEA. The decision was made that attention disorders (e.g., attention deficit disorder, or ADD) did not need a separate category because students with these disorders who had educational needs were already served, for the most part, as students with learning or behavioral disabilities. If the criteria for either specific learning disabilities or emotional disturbance were not met, the student could be served in an appropriate setting under the category of Other Health Impairment, "in instances where the ADD is a chronic or acute health problem that results in limited alertness, which adversely affects educational performance" (U.S. Department of Education, 1991, p. 3). The terms *attention deficit disorder* and *attention deficit hyperactivity disorder* (ADHD) are included among the disorders listed in the category Other Health Impairment (§ 300.8[c][9][i], IDEA, 1997).

If the attention disorder does not significantly impair the student's ability to function in the regular classroom, the student may be served in the regular classroom under the provisions of Section 504 of the Rehabilitation Act of 1973 (discussed later in this chapter). This law requires that students be given reasonable accommodations for their disability in the general education environment. Students with attention disorders must undergo a comprehensive evaluation by a multidisciplinary team to determine whether they are eligible for services and, if so, whether they would be better served by the provisions of IDEA or of Section 504.

● IEP TEAM EVALUATION

To decrease the possibility of subjective and discriminatory assessment, IDEA regulations mandate that the comprehensive evaluation be conducted by members of a multidisciplinary IEP team. If the team has determined during screening and has specified in the assessment plan that the student needs further evaluation in speech, language, reading, and social/behavioral skills, then a speech-language clinician, a special education teacher or educational diagnostician, and a school psychologist will be members of the assessment team. The team may obtain additional information from the parents, the classroom teacher, the school nurse, the school counselor, the building principal, and other school personnel. Figure 2.1 describes the responsibilities of the various members who might be on the IEP team.

In compliance with the nondiscriminatory section of the law, team members employ several types of assessment and collect different types of data. Because the law requires that a variety of methods be used in assessment, the team should make use of classroom observations, informal assessment measures, and parent interviews. Additional data provided by outside sources or from previous assessment should also be considered.

IDEA amendments specify that the IEP team be composed of professionals representing a variety of disciplines and the student's parent(s), all of whom collaborate in reaching a decision regarding possible interventions and the student's eligibility for services. Each member of the IEP team contributes carefully documented information to the decision-making process.

The amendments require that, at minimum, the IEP team include the child's parents, a general education teacher (if the child is or may be participating in the general education environment), a special education teacher, a supervisor of special education services who is knowledgeable about general curriculum and local resources, and someone who is able to interpret the instructional implications of evaluation results. In many cases, one person may fulfill more than one role on the IEP team. The school or parent may invite others as long as they have knowledge of the child or the services that will be provided. Together, the IEP team and other professionals, as appropriate, determine eligibility based on federal and state criteria.

IEP Team Member Attendance. At one time, federal law and subsequent regulations written for IDEA required that all team members attend all IEP team meetings in their entirety, even though they may not have had new information to contribute. In an effort to clarify team members' responsibilities and to decrease

FIGURE 2.1 The IEP Team: Who's Who?

Team members include, in addition to the child's parents, the following:

Team Member	Responsibilities
School nurse	Initial vision and hearing screens, checks medical records, refers health problems to other medical professionals.
Special education teacher	Consultant to regular classroom teacher during prereferral process; administers educational tests, observes in other classrooms, helps with screening and recommends IEP goals, writes objectives, and suggests educational interventions.
Special education supervisor	May advise all activities of special education teacher, may provide direct services, guides placement decisions, recommends services.
Educational diagnostician	Administers norm-referenced and criterion-referenced tests, observes student in educational setting, makes suggestions for IEP goals and objectives.
School psychologist	Administers individual intelligence tests, observes student in classroom, administers projective instruments and personality inventories; may be under supervision of a doctoral-level psychologist.
Occupational therapist	Evaluates fine motor and self-help skills, recommends therapies, may provide direct services or consultant services, may help obtain equipment for student needs.
Physical therapist	Evaluates gross motor functioning and self-help skills, living skills, and job-related skills necessary for optimum achievement of student; may provide direct services or consultant services.
Behavioral consultant	Specialist in behavior management and crisis intervention; may provide direct services or consultant services.
School counselor	May serve as objective observer in prereferral stage, may provide direct group or individual counseling, may schedule students and help with planning of student school schedules.
Speech-language clinician	Evaluates speech-language development, may refer for hearing problems, may provide direct therapy or consultant services for classroom teachers.
Audiologist	Evaluates hearing for possible impairments, may refer students for medical problems, may help obtain hearing aids.
Physician's assistant	Evaluates physical condition of student and may provide physical exams for students of a local education agency, refers medical problems to physicians or appropriate therapists, school social worker, or visiting teacher.
Home-school coordinator; school social worker or visiting teacher	Works directly with family; may hold conferences, conduct interviews, and administer adaptive behavior scales based on parent interviews; may serve as case manager.
Regular education teacher	Works with the special education team, student, and parents to develop an environment that is appropriate and as much like that of general education students as possible; implements prereferral intervention strategies.

the amount of time teachers spent away from their classrooms, new statements were included in IDEA 2004 regarding attendance. The law includes the following statements:

A member of the IEP Team described in paragraphs (a)(2) through (a)(5) of this section is not required to attend an IEP Team meeting, in whole or in part, if the parent of a child with a disability and the public agency agree, in writing, that the attendance of the member is not necessary because the member's area of the curriculum or related services is not being modified or discussed in the meeting.

These statements indicate that a team member is not required to attend an IEP meeting if he or she is not presenting new information in written form or during discussion. If the member wishes to contribute to the meeting but cannot attend, with the parent's and school's consent, the member may submit her or his contribution in written form. Parental consent to either excusal or nonattendance must be given in writing.

As you watch this video on the multidiciplinary team, identify how each professional contributes to the IEP meeting.

● DETERMINING ELIGIBILITY

IDEA 2004 amendments include definitions and some fairly global criteria for determining eligibility for services for students with the following disabilities: autism, deaf-blindness, deafness, hearing impairment, intellectual disabilities or cognitive impairments, multiple disabilities, orthopedic impairment, emotional disturbance, specific learning disability, speech or language impairment, traumatic brain injury, and visual impairment, including blindness. Most states have more specific criteria for determining eligibility for services, and many use different terms for the conditions stated in the law. For example, some states use the term *perceptual disability* rather than *learning disability*.

The decision that the student is eligible for special education services or that she or he should continue in the general education classroom without special interventions should be based on data presented during the eligibility meeting by the team members. Parents are to be active participants in this meeting. School personnel should strive to make parents feel comfortable in the meeting and should welcome and carefully consider all of their comments and any additional data they submit. If the student is found eligible for services, the team discusses educational interventions and specific special education services and related services. Federal requirements mandate that students who receive special services are educated with their nondisabled peers unless there is evidence that this is inappropriate. Related services are those determined by the IEP team to be necessary for the student to benefit from the instructional goals of the IEP. Examples of related services include psychological services, early identification of children with disabilities, and therapeutic recreation. The 2004 regulations specifically added the related services of interpreting for students who are deaf or hard of hearing and services of the school nurse.

The Improvement Act of 2004 includes statements regarding when a student should *not* be found eligible for services. The rules for determining eligibility are aimed at preventing students from being determined eligible for special education solely on the basis of no instruction or limited instruction in reading or math. The special rule regarding appropriate instruction references the Elementary and Secondary Education Act, linking ESEA with IDEA specifically with regard to "essential reading components." Under ESEA, the essential components of reading are phonemic awareness, an understanding of phonics, vocabulary development, reading fluency (including oral reading skills), and reading comprehension (PL 107–110, § 103[3]).

Students may not be found eligible for special education services solely on the basis of having limited English proficiency. In other words, students with limited skills in speaking, reading, and understanding the English language must have other causative factors that result in the need for special education or related services. This section of the law also provides that even if a student may be ineligible for special services because of little or inappropriate instruction in one academic area, she or he may be found eligible for services because of a disability in another academic area that has been documented through evaluation.

CHECK YOUR UNDERSTANDING

Check your understanding of the roles of multidisciplinary team members by completing Activity 2.3.

● PARENT PARTICIPATION

Every effort should be made to accommodate parents so that they may attend all multidisciplinary team conferences pertaining to their child's education. Federal requirements emphasize the importance of parental attendance.

The importance of parent involvement was underscored in the original provisions of PL 99–457. The amendments required that the intervention plan, called the Individual Family Service Plan (IFSP), be designed to include the family members. As mentioned in Chapter 1, the IFSP identifies family needs relating to the child's development that, when met, will increase the likelihood of successful intervention. Legislation governing the provision of special education services emphasizes the role of the family in the life of the child with a disability (Turnbull, 1990).

IDEA amendments of 1997 and those of 2004 further stressed the importance of parent participation by including the parents on the IEP team and by encouraging parents to submit additional information to be used during the eligibility and planning process. These regulations also require that the parent be given a copy of the evaluation report as well as documentation of eligibility upon the completion of testing and other evaluation materials.

IDEA 2004 added provisions for parents to be involved in the educational planning process of their child without having to convene the whole IEP team for changes in the educational program. This law allows modifications to a student's educational program if her or his parents and school personnel, such as the child's general education or special education teacher, agree. For example, the parents and teachers may agree to a change in the amount of time spent in various instructional arrangements, without convening the entire IEP committee.

As you watch this video, observe how the special education administrator presents the parent's rights about agreeing with and signing the IEP.

● DEVELOPING THE INDIVIDUALIZED EDUCATION PROGRAM

Every student receiving special education services must have an individualized education program or plan (IEP) that is written in compliance with the requirements of IDEA. Current levels of educational performance may include scores such as grade-level scores, age-equivalent scores, and/or standard scores. In addition, present level-of-performance information should include classroom performance measures and classroom behavior. Measurable long-term goals, or annual goals, must be included in the IEP. Every area in which special education services are provided must have an annual goal. The IEP is driven by the data and results of the evaluation.

IDEA amendments of 2004 specified all the information that needs to be included on the IEP. These requirements are presented in the following section.

The first requirement is that the IEP include a statement of the student's current level of functioning and, most important, how the student's disability affects her or his involvement in the general education program. The IEP team also must consider the extent to which the student can participate in state-mandated assessments. Information regarding state-mandated assessments, or high-stakes testing, is provided in Chapter 5. IEP requirements tied to statewide assessment reflect this awareness of accountability in the education of students with disabilities.

Federal regulations also state that a student should be educated in the **least restrictive environment** (LRE). Yell (1995) provided guidance to assist with the determination of LRE. These guidelines include considerations for the integration of students with disabilities with nondisabled students to the extent possible. This might mean that a student with disabilities requires some educational or behavioral

CHECK YOUR UNDERSTANDING

Review the data and the IEP statements in Activity 2.4. Are these statements accurate for the data included? Are changes needed?

CHECK YOUR UNDERSTANDING

Check your understanding of the term *least restrictive environment* and other requirements of IDEA by completing Activity 2.5.

support in settings that are away from the general classroom; however, if this is needed, educational personnel must provide reasoning and justification that this setting is necessary. In other words, the student was not able to learn in the general setting or perhaps the student had significant behavior challenges that resulted in adversely affecting the learning of other students. As you watch this video, identify the continuum of services and which of the options represents the LRE.

Each of these requirements mandates that the IEP team consider the *specific* needs of individual students with disabilities, including those with limited English proficiency. These specific needs, which have been determined through effective assessment, must be addressed in the IEP, and the student's progress toward articulated goals must be monitored and reviewed at least annually by the IEP team.

TRANSITION SERVICES

The section of federal regulations dealing with the content of the IEP also addresses the transitioning needs of students who are nearing their graduation from high school.

IDEA stresses the importance of transition services to prepare students 16 years old or older for a work or postsecondary environment. When appropriate, younger students may also be eligible for such services. The law underscores the importance of early planning and decisions by all members affected, including the student. Planning for the needed transition procedures and services typically begins in the student's sophomore or junior year of high school. IDEA amendments emphasize transition services to a greater extent than they do other regulations.

The regulations extend rights to the student at the age of majority in accordance with individual state laws. The age of majority is the age at which a child is no longer considered to be a minor; in many states, this age is 18. School personnel are responsible for communicating to the student—and to her or his parents—that the student's rights under the law are now in the hands of the student rather than her or his parents. Moreover, the law requires that the student be informed of the transfer of rights a year before she or he attains the age of majority.

The 2004 amendments add specificity regarding transitional assessment and appropriate annual goals. The law emphasizes that postsecondary goals be measurable and that they should be based on the results of assessment in areas of education, employment, and daily living skills as appropriate.

CHECK YOUR UNDERSTANDING

Check your understanding of the legal requirements of the Individuals with Disabilities Education Improvement Act of 2004 by completing Activity 2.6.

LEARNERS WITH SPECIAL NEEDS AND DISCIPLINE

Federal regulations include specific mandates about students with special needs who have committed disciplinary infractions. The school district must ensure that the student has the correct IEP in place, that the IEP makes specific reference to the student's behavioral issues, and that the IEP lists strategies to address the student's behavioral needs. (These strategies include a functional behavioral assessment, or FBA, which is covered in detail in Chapter 9.) If the parent and school personnel determine that the student's inappropriate behavior is the result of the IEP not being implemented correctly, it is the school's legal responsibility to correct implementation procedures. The removal of a student from the typical school environment to an alternative setting for disciplinary reasons when the behavior may be in part due to the child's disability can constitute removal from the appropriate educational services specified in the IEP. Therefore, protections are included in the law. The 2004 regulations indicate that if parents and IEP members can provide proof that the student's behavior is the result of a disability or that the disability has a substantial relationship to the behavior, the student may not be removed from the school setting. Certain behaviors, however, do result in automatic removal from the school setting for a period of 45 days. These behaviors involve use of illegal drugs, possession of weapons on school grounds, and engagement in activity that results in extreme bodily injury to another.

● DUE PROCESS

IDEA was influenced to a large degree by parent organizations and court cases involving individuals with disabilities and their right to a free, appropriate education. When schools implement the provisions of the law, occasionally differences arise between the schools providing the service and the parents of the student with the disability. Therefore, IDEA contains provisions for parents and schools to resolve their differences. These provisions are called *due process provisions*.

Procedural safeguards occur throughout the portions of the law concerned with assessment. For example, parental informed consent is considered a procedural safeguard designed to prevent assessment and placement of students without parents' knowledge. Parents may withdraw their consent to assessment or placement at any time. Other provisions promote fairness in the decision-making process. Included in these provisions are the rights of parents to examine all educational records of their child, to seek an independent educational evaluation of their child, and to a request a hearing to resolve differences between themselves and the local education agency (LEA) or service providers.

IDEA amendments of 1997 include a significant addition in the area of due process. The amendments promote mediation as a method of resolving disagreements between parents and their local school agency. The amendments mandate local education agencies to provide mediation at no cost to parents. The mediation process is voluntary on the part of both the school and parents. This process cannot be used by a local education agency to delay parental rights to a hearing or to deny any other rights provided in the regulations. The mediation process must be conducted by qualified and impartial trained mediators who are included on a list maintained by each state.

IDEA 2004 adds a requirement for a resolution session to be held with the parents and school personnel within 15 days of the filing of a complaint. This session is an attempt to resolve the complaint in a timely and mutually agreeable manner so that a formal hearing can be avoided. During this session, the school may not have an attorney present unless the parents are accompanied by their attorney. This resolution session may be waived if the parents and school personnel all agree in writing to do so. Parents may choose to waive the resolution meeting and instead schedule a mediation meeting.

The parents of a student who has been evaluated by the multidisciplinary team may disagree with the results yielded by the assessment process. Should this occur, they have the right to obtain an independent evaluation by an outside examiner. The independent educational evaluation is provided by a qualified professional not employed by the local education agency. Should independent evaluation results differ from those obtained by school personnel, the school must pay for the evaluation. An exception to this requirement occurs if the school initiates an impartial due process hearing to resolve the different results and the hearing officer finds in favor of the school. In this case, the parents would be responsible for paying for the independent evaluation. If, however, the hearing finds in favor of the parents, the school is responsible for payment.

● IMPARTIAL DUE PROCESS HEARING

The parents and school are provided with procedures for filing complaints and requesting an impartial due process hearing. In a third-party hearing, the parents and the school may individually explain their side of the disagreement before an impartial hearing officer, a person qualified to hear the case. In some states, third-party hearing officers are lawyers; in other states, the hearing officers are special education professionals, such as college faculty who teach special education courses to prepare teachers.

Parents should be advised before the hearing that although counsel (an attorney) is not required for the hearing, they do have the right to secure counsel as well as experts to give testimony. After hearing each side of the complaint, the hearing officer reaches a decision. A finding in favor of the parents requires the LEA to comply with the ruling or appeal to a state-level hearing. If favor is found with the school, the parents must comply. If the parents do not wish to comply, they have the right to request a state-level hearing or file an appeal with a civil court.

While the school and parents are involved with due process and hearing procedures, the student remains in the classroom setting in which she or he was placed before the complaint was filed. This requirement has been called the *stay-put provision*.

● SECTION 504

Section 504 of the Rehabilitation Act of 1973 includes many of the same concepts, such as procedural safeguards and evaluation, as those in IDEA. The law extends beyond the categories listed in IDEA and beyond the public school environment. This law is a civil rights law, and its purpose is to prevent discrimination against individuals with disabilities in programs receiving federal financial assistance. Students with disabilities are protected from discrimination in schools receiving federal financial assistance under Section 504, whether or not they are protected by IDEA. The law extends its educational regulations to include postsecondary environments, such as colleges and universities. It is used to protect the educational rights of persons with chronic health conditions in the public education setting who may not be specifically protected under IDEA, such as students with ADHD who do not need full special education support because they have no other significant learning disability.

Notable differences between IDEA and Section 504 were summarized by Yell (1997). These differences are presented in Table 2.2.

TABLE 2.2

Differences between IDEA and 504

Component	IDEA	Section 504
Purpose of Law	• Provides federal funding to states to assist in education of students with disabilities • Substantive requirements attached to funding	• Civil rights law • Protects persons with disabilities from discrimination in programs or services that receive federal financial assistance • Requires reasonable accommodations to ensure nondiscrimination
Who Is Protected?	• Categorical approach • Thirteen disability categories • Disability must adversely impact educational performance	• Functional approach • Students (a) having a mental or physical impairment that affects a major life activity, (b) with a record of such an impairment, or (c) who are regarded as having such an impairment • Protects students in general and special education

(Continued)

TABLE 2.2

Differences between IDEA and 504 (*Continued*)

Component	IDEA	Section 504
FAPE	• Special education and related services are provided at public expense, meet state requirements, and are provided in conformity with the IEP • Substantive standard is educational benefit	• General or special education and related aids and services • Requires a written education plan • Substantive standard is equivalency
LRE	• Student must be educated with peers without disabilities to the maximum extent appropriate • Removal from integrated settings is allowed only when supplementary aids and services are not successful • Districts must have a continuum of placement available	• School must ensure that students are educated with their peers without disabilities
Evaluation and Placement	• Protection in evaluation procedures • Requires consent prior to initial evaluation and placement • Evaluation and placement decisions have to be made by a multidisciplinary team • Requires evaluation of progress toward IEP goals annually and reevaluation at least every 3 years	• Does not require consent; requires notice only • Requires periodic reevaluation • Reevaluation is required before a significant change in placement
Procedural Safeguards	• Comprehensive and detailed notice requirements • Provides for independent evaluations • No grievance procedure • Impartial due process hearing	• General notice requirements • Grievance procedure • Impartial due process hearing
Funding	• Provides for federal funding to assist in the education of students with disabilities	• No federal funding
Enforcement	• U.S. Office of Special Education Programs (OSEP) (can cut off IDEA funds) • Complaints can be filed with state's department of education	• Compliance monitoring by state educational agency (SEA) • Complaint can be filed with Office of Civil Rights (OCR) (can cut off all federal funding)

Source: Yell, *The Law and Special Education*, Table 6.2, "Differences between IDEA and 504," © 1998. Reproduced by permission of Pearson Education, Inc.

CHECK YOUR UNDERSTANDING

Check your understanding of IDEA and Section 504 by completing Activity 2.7.

For the purposes of assessment and educational planning, Section 504 seeks to meet the needs of students according to how their conditions affect their daily functioning. This places the emphasis of assessment and program planning on a student's current functioning within that activity and calls for reasonable accommodations. For a college student with a specific learning disability, for example, reasonable accommodations may include taking exams in a quiet room with extended time because of attention deficit disorder or waiving a foreign language requirement because of a specific learning disability in written language.

As you watch this video, identify the differences in the definition of disability in Section 504 and how this benefits some students in an educational setting.

● RESEARCH AND ISSUES CONCERNING IDEA

IDEA states that each school agency shall actively take steps to ensure that parents participate in the IEP process in several ways. First, parents must agree by informed consent to an initial evaluation of their child and before placement in a special education program occurs. The 1997 amendments added the provision that parents must consent prior to the reevaluation. Parents also participate in the decision-making process regarding eligibility. Following the eligibility determination, parents participate in the development of the IEP and in the review of their child's progress toward the goals specified in the IEP. Parental participation in IEP processes is a legal mandate—not a simple courtesy extended by the multidisciplinary team or LEA.

Informed consent is one of the first ways to ensure parental involvement and procedural safeguards. However, informed consent is confounded by issues such as parental literacy, parental comprehension of the meaning of legal terminology, and the amount and quality of time professionals spend with parents explaining testing and special education. Parents' rights materials may be difficult to understand because of their use of highly specialized vocabulary. According to an early study involving observation and analysis of interactions in IEP conferences, parents' rights were merely "glossed over in the majority of conferences" (Goldstein, Strickland, Turnbull, & Curry, 1980, p. 283). This suggests that sufficient time may not be allotted to discussing issues of central concern to parents. Changes in the 1997 amendments are designed to promote genuine parental involvement in educational assessment and planning.

In an early review of decisions and reports from the Office of Civil Rights (OCR) concerned with the question of procedural safeguards and parental involvement, Katsiyannis (1994) found that the typical sequence of the referral/screening process denied procedural safeguards at the prereferral stage. Parents should be informed of procedural safeguards at the time their child is screened to determine whether additional assessment will be conducted. Educators should keep in mind that the new regulations stress parental involvement during all stages of the assessment and planning process. These regulations provide the minimum guidelines for professionals; best practice dictates that parents should be involved throughout their child's education (Sheridan, Cowan, & Eagle, 2000).

Parents actively participate in the IEP conference by contributing to the formulation of long-term goals and short-term objectives for their children. In the past, in traditional IEP conferences, parents were found to be passive and to attend merely to receive information (Barnett, Zins, & Wise, 1984; Brantlinger, 1987; Goldstein et al., 1980; Goldstein, & Turnbull, 1982; Vaughn, Bos, Harrell, & Lasky, 1988; Weber & Stoneman, 1986). Parents are now considered to be equal team members in the IEP process.

An area of additional concern involves working with parents of culturally, linguistically, or environmentally diverse backgrounds. Professionals should make certain that materials and concepts presented are at the appropriate level. Special education or legal concepts are complex for many persons who are not familiar with the vocabulary and process. For persons who do not speak English as a primary language, legal terms and specialized concepts may be difficult even though materials are presented in the individual's native language. These concepts may be different from educational concepts of their birth or native culture. Salend and Taylor (1993) suggested that the parents' level of acculturation be considered, noting that children may become acculturated much more quickly than their parents. In addition, Salend and Taylor reminded educators to consider the family's history of discrimination and the family structure, as these factors might have an impact on the family's interactions with school personnel. Educational professionals should make every effort to be certain that all parents are familiar with the special education process, services available, and their expected role during the assessment and IEP processes.

● ISSUES OF NONDISCRIMINATORY ASSESSMENT

Perhaps no other area in the field of psychoeducational assessment has received more attention than that of nondiscriminatory assessment. Much of this attention centers around the overrepresentation of minority students in special education classes. Minority overrepresentation is found to occur when the percentage of minority students enrolled in particular special education classes is larger than the percentage of minority students enrolled in the local education agency. For example, if classes for students with intellectual disabilities were made up of 28% minority students, but only 12% of the local education agency was made up of minorities, the local education agency's special education classes would have an overrepresentation of minority students.

In 2009, the U.S. Department of Education reported that students from minority ethnic groups continue to be at greater risk for receiving special education and related services overrepresentation. This overrepresentation is illustrated by findings of the Office of Civil Rights, which reported that although African Americans account for 16% of the total population in schools, 32% of students in settings for persons with mild intellectual disabilities and 29% of students diagnosed as having moderate mental retardation are African American. In addition, African Americans account for 24% of students identified as "emotionally disturbed," and 18% of students identified as having specific learning disabilities. An analysis of 5-year trends during the period of 2004–2008 indicated that slight decreases were noted in the percentage of African American students who were within the learning disabilities and intellectual disabilities categories; however, this varied by state and interacted to some degree with socioeconomic status of the states, with poorer states having lower percentages of some minorities in some categories (Zhang, Katsiyannis, Ju, & Roberts, 2014). Zhang et al. found that Hispanic students tended to be underrepresented in some states and generally African Americans were represented with the greatest percentage of all groups, with American Indians and Alaskan Natives coming in second in representation. In a meta-analysis of English learners, Gage and colleagues noted that Hispanics were underrepresented in the category of emotional disturbance and that this varied by district (Gage, Gersten, Sugai, & Newman-Gonchar, 2013).

Much of the blame for the overrepresentation of minorities in special education has been attributed to referral and evaluation practices. In a review by Skiba et al., the authors concluded that the initial referral may be influenced by the referring teacher's own self-efficacy or confidence and perceived ability in working with students from cultures other than the teacher's own culture (2008). In addition, among the reasons for bias reviewed by Skiba at el. were referral, testing bias, assessment, and evaluation. The amount of attention given to the assessment process may be due in part to IDEA's emphasis on nondiscriminatory assessment. The law clearly states that educational agencies should use evaluation procedures that are not racially or culturally discriminatory. This can have many implications in the assessment of students who have linguistic differences and those who come from culturally different backgrounds or deprived environments. The following list of problems of bias in assessment is adapted from Reynolds and Lowe (2009, pp. 332–557).*

1. *Inappropriate content.* Students from minority populations may lack exposure to certain items on the assessment instrument.

2. *Inappropriate standardization samples.* Ethnic minorities were not represented in the normative sample at the time of development of the instrument.

---

*Reynolds, C. R., & Lowe, P. A. (2009). "The Problem of Bias in Psychological Assessment." In T. Gutkin & C. R. Reynolds (Eds.), *The Handbook of School Psychology* (4th ed., pp. 339–340). Hoboken, NJ: Wiley.

3. *Examiner and language.* White, English-speaking examiners may intimidate students of color and students from different linguistic backgrounds.

4. *Inequitable social consequences.* Because of discriminatory assessment practices, minority students may be relegated to lower educational placements, which may ultimately result in lower-paying jobs.

5. *Measurement of different constructs.* White test developers designed instruments assumed to measure academic or cognitive ability for all students. When used with minority students, however, the instruments may measure only the degree to which these students have been able to absorb white, middle-class culture.

6. *Different predictive validity.* Instruments designed to predict the educational or academic outcome or potential for white students might not do so for minority students.

7. *Qualitatively distinct minority and majority aptitude and achievement.* This suggests that persons from various ethnic groups are qualitatively different, and therefore tests designed to measure aptitude in one group cannot adequately measure the aptitude of another group.

Additional problems in biased assessment include overinterpretation of test results. This means that an examiner may report to have assessed a trait, attribute, or characteristic that the instrument is not designed to measure (Flaugher, 1978). For example, an examiner might report a cognitive ability level or a behavioral trait based on the results of a student's academic achievement test. The assessment is inaccurate because the test was designed to measure academic achievement only.

Another problem that may arise in assessment is testing students whose dominant language is not English. Although some instruments are published in languages other than English, such as Spanish, the translations may result in different conceptual meanings and influence test performance and test results (Fradd & Hallman, 1983). Lopez (1995) recommended that norm-referenced instruments not be used with bilingual students for several reasons:

1. Norms are usually limited to small samples of minority children.

2. Norming procedures routinely exclude students with limited English proficiency.

3. Test items tap information that minority children may not be familiar with because of their linguistically and culturally different backgrounds.

4. Testing formats do not allow examiners the opportunity to provide feedback or to probe into the children's quality of responses.

5. The tests' scoring systems arbitrarily decide what the correct responses are based on majority culture paradigms.

6. Standardized testing procedures assume that children have appropriate test-taking skills.

IDEA mandates that the evaluation of students for possible special education services must involve the use of tests that have been validated for the purpose for which they are used. IDEA regulations contain language requiring that, at minimum, professionals be trained in assessment and, more specifically, that training or expertise is available to enable the examiner to evaluate students with disabilities.

Of all of the controversial issues in nondiscriminatory assessment, the most controversial is that of IQ testing for the purpose of determining eligibility for services under the diagnostic category of Intellectual Disability. One professional in the field (Jackson, 1975) called for banning the use of IQ tests. Some state and local education agencies, either by litigation or voluntarily, have discontinued the use of IQ tests with minority students. Evidence indicates, however, that IQ scores continue to be the most influential test score variable in the decision-making process

(Sapp, Chissom, & Horton, 1984), and are valid predictors of academic achievement over time (Freberg, Vandiver, Watkins, & Canivez, 2008). MacMillan and Forness (1998) argued that IQ testing might only be a peripheral factor in placement decisions rather than the determining factor. They concluded that the use of IQ scores might in fact disallow eligibility to students who are truly in need of support services. The trend in assessment to use more functional measures instead of relying heavily on traditional cognitive assessment may be the result of disproportionality in special education and the questioning of bias in the assessment process.

IDEA requires that other data, such as comments from parents and teachers and adaptive behavior measures, be considered in the decision-making process and that parents are active throughout the process. Professionals must take extra care when informing parents of the assessment process, including the reasons for the assessment and possible benefits the results may yield in guiding educational decisions. In a review of hearing cases involving parents who refused to consent to assessment, it was found that parents often thought the assessment process would be harmful or would result in a predetermined placement (Etscheidt, Clopton, & Haselhuhn, 2012). This underscores the need for open communication with parents that includes checking for parents' understanding of the assessment and IEP process. Yell, Katsiyannis, Ennis, and Losinski (2013) indicate that not involving the parents in the IEP process is one of the major errors made by schools.

CHECK YOUR UNDERSTANDING

Check your understanding of IDEA 2004 provisions regarding disproportionality and other issues by completing Activity 2.8.

Disproportionality. Disproportionality refers to the overrepresentation or underrepresentation of specific minority groups within specific categories of special education eligibility. The research indicating that students from different ethnic, cultural, or linguistic backgrounds were at greater risk for receiving special education services strongly influenced IDEA revisions. To decrease disproportionality, the law emphasizes the importance of early intervention services that, when judiciously selected and implemented, can prevent inappropriate or unnecessary placement in special education.

The regulations of IDEA 2004 include specific methods that states must follow to be accountable for making efforts to reduce disproportionality. State education agencies are mandated to collect and report data on the following: (1) types of impairments of students identified as eligible to receive services, (2) placement or educational environments of students, (3) the incidence of disciplinary actions, and (4) the duration of disciplinary measures, including suspensions and expulsions of students who are served under special education. All of these data are to be reported, and when specific data indicate problematic disproportionality, the state educational agency is mandated to review the data and, if necessary, revise the methods and policies for identification and placement of students in special education.

● THE MULTIDISCIPLINARY TEAM AND THE DECISION-MAKING PROCESS

IDEA regulations call for a variety of professionals and the parents of the student to be involved in the assessment and IEP processes. When all members of the IEP multidisciplinary team are integrally involved in decision making, the appropriateness of decisions is enhanced.

Inconsistencies in decisions about eligibility made by teams have been found specifically in situations where mild disabilities, such as learning disabilities, are involved (Bocian, Beebe, MacMillan, & Gresham, 1999; MacMillan, Gresham, & Bocian, 1998). These researchers concluded that various forms of evidence, such as behaviors observed by teachers, may have weighed heavily in the decision-making process. MacMillan, Gresham, and Bocian (1998) postulated that eligibility decisions for students with mild disabilities may be based on educational need more than actual legal criteria.

● LEAST RESTRICTIVE ENVIRONMENT

IDEA is designed to provide special education support services in the least restrictive environment. In most cases, this means that a student who is identified as having special needs will be served in the general education classroom unless there are justifiable reasons for the student to be educated in a special education setting.

Research conducted by the U.S. Department of Education indicates that there has been an increasing trend to serve students with disabilities in the general education classroom environment for most of the school day (U.S. Department of Education, 2012). Table 2.3 illustrates this trend.

The implementation of least restrictive environment guidelines and, more specifically, of inclusion mandates has been interpreted through litigation in several state and federal courts (Kubicek, 1994; Lipsky & Gartner, 1997; Yell, 1997). In summary, the courts have interpreted that the least restrictive environment decision must first consider placement in a regular education environment with additional supplementary aids if needed. If the general education environment will be equal to or better than the special education setting for the student, she or he should be placed in the regular classroom with typically developing peers. The student's academic and nonacademic needs must be considered in any placement decision. This includes consideration of the benefits of social interaction in nonacademic activities and environments. The IEP team must also review the effect that the student with special needs will have on the teacher in terms of time and attention required and the effect that student may have on her or his peers in the general classroom. If the educational services required for the student with a disability can be better provided in the segregated setting, the student may be placed in a special education environment.

Research has produced interesting results regarding inclusion in general education settings. One study that surveyed secondary students found that many expressed a preference for a pull-out program for meeting their educational needs but enjoyed inclusion for the social benefits of interacting with their peers without disabilities (Klinger, Vaughn, Schumm, Cohen, & Forgan, 1998). Some of the students in this study stated that the general education environment was simply too noisy. Bennett, Lee, and Lueke (1998) stated that inclusion decisions should consider parents' expectations.

● IMPARTIAL HEARINGS

The procedural safeguards provided through due process seek to involve the parents in all stages of the IEP process rather than only during third-party hearings. Due process provisions specify at least 36 grounds for either schools or parents to seek a hearing (Turnbull, Turnbull, & Strickland, 1979). If abused, the process could result in chaos in the operation of school systems. The years since the law was enacted have witnessed a great deal of interpretation of uncertain issues through the judicial system (Turnbull, 1986).

Due process may be discriminatory because its cost may be prohibitive for some families in terms of both financial and human resources (Turnbull, 1986). Because the financial, time, and emotional investment required for carrying out due process procedures may be burdensome, educators are concerned that due process as stipulated in IDEA may, in some cases, be yet another vehicle that increases rather than decreases discriminatory practices.

The 1997 amendments that provide specific guidelines for mediation may result in more timely and economical resolutions. Engiles, Fromme, LeResche, and Moses (1999) suggested strategies that schools and personnel can implement to increase participation in mediation of parents of culturally and linguistically diverse backgrounds. These researchers remind educators that some persons from various

TABLE 2.3

Increasing Trend of Students with Disabilities Ages 6–21 Served in Each General Education Environment: 1989–2011

Type of disability	All environments	Regular school, time inside general class			Separate school for students with disabilities	Separate residential facility	Parentally placed in regular private schools[1]	Home-bound/ hospital placement	Correctional facility
		Less than 40 percent	40–79 percent	80 percent or more					
1	2	3	4	5	6	7	8	9	10
All students with disabilities									
1989	100.0	24.9	37.5	31.7	4.5	1.0	—	0.6	—
1990	100.0	25.0	36.4	33.1	4.2	0.9	—	0.5	—
1994	100.0	22.4	28.5	44.8	3.0	0.7	—	0.6	—
1995	100.0	21.5	28.5	45.7	3.1	0.7	—	0.5	—
1996	100.0	21.4	28.3	46.1	3.0	0.7	—	0.5	—
1997	100.0	20.4	28.8	46.8	2.9	0.7	—	0.5	—
1998	100.0	20.0	29.9	46.0	2.9	0.7	—	0.5	—
1999	100.0	20.3	29.8	45.9	2.9	0.7	—	0.5	—
2000	100.0	19.5	29.8	46.5	3.0	0.7	—	0.5	—
2001	100.0	19.2	28.5	48.2	2.9	0.7	—	0.4	—
2002	100.0	19.0	28.7	48.2	2.9	0.7	—	0.5	—
2003	100.0	18.5	27.7	49.9	2.8	0.7	—	0.5	—
2004	100.0	17.9	26.5	51.5	3.0	0.6	—	0.4	—
2005	100.0	16.7	25.1	54.2	2.9	0.6	—	0.4	—
2006	100.0	16.4	23.8	54.8	2.9	0.4	1.0	0.4	0.4
2007	100.0	15.4	22.4	56.8	3.0	0.4	1.1	0.4	0.4
2008	100.0	14.9	21.4	58.5	2.9	0.4	1.1	0.4	0.4

2009

All students with disabilities	100.0	14.6	20.7	59.4	3.0	0.4	1.2	0.4	0.4
Autism	100.0	34.8	18.3	37.4	8.0	0.6	0.7	0.3	#
Deaf-blindness	100.0	33.3	13.3	21.6	19.1	9.9	0.6	2.3	0.2
Developmental delay	100.0	16.2	20.5	61.6	0.9	0.1	0.6	0.2	#
Emotional disturbance	100.0	22.2	18.8	40.6	13.2	2.0	0.2	1.1	2.0
Hearing impairments	100.0	14.7	17.0	54.6	8.2	4.0	1.3	0.2	0.1
Intellectual disability	100.0	48.2	26.7	17.4	6.3	0.4	0.3	0.5	0.3
Multiple disabilities	100.0	45.5	16.2	13.2	19.6	1.9	0.4	2.9	0.2
Orthopedic impairments	100.0	23.6	16.3	52.2	5.1	0.2	0.9	1.7	0.1
Other health impairments[2]	100.0	10.8	23.8	61.4	1.6	0.2	1.1	0.9	0.3
Specific learning disabilities	100.0	8.0	26.6	63.3	0.6	0.1	0.9	0.2	0.4
Speech or language impairments	100.0	4.6	5.6	86.3	0.3	#	3.1	0.1	#
Traumatic brain injury	100.0	21.5	23.8	46.4	5.2	0.6	0.7	1.7	0.2
Visual impairments	100.0	12.0	13.5	62.6	6.2	3.6	1.4	0.7	#

2010

All students with disabilities	100.0	14.2	20.0	60.5	3.0	0.4	1.2	0.4	0.3
Autism	100.0	34.1	18.1	38.5	7.9	0.5	0.6	0.3	#
Deaf-blindness	100.0	33.4	11.9	22.9	18.2	9.6	0.7	3.3	#
Developmental delay	100.0	16.1	19.6	62.5	0.9	0.1	0.6	0.2	#
Emotional disturbance	100.0	21.3	18.3	42.2	13.1	2.0	0.2	1.1	1.9
Hearing impairments	100.0	14.1	16.7	56.2	8.2	3.4	1.2	0.2	0.1
Intellectual disability	100.0	47.7	26.8	17.9	6.2	0.4	0.2	0.5	0.3
Multiple disabilities	100.0	46.0	15.9	13.0	19.7	1.8	0.4	3.1	0.2
Orthopedic impairments	100.0	22.9	16.2	53.3	4.9	0.2	0.8	1.7	0.1
Other health impairments[2]	100.0	10.6	23.0	62.5	1.6	0.2	1.0	0.9	0.3
Specific learning disabilities	100.0	7.4	25.5	65.2	0.6	0.1	0.9	0.2	0.3
Speech or language impairments	100.0	4.7	5.5	86.5	0.3	#	2.9	0.1	#

(Continued)

TABLE 2.3

Increasing Trend of Students with Disabilities Ages 6–21 Served in Each General Education Environment: 1989–2011 (Continued)

Type of disability	All environments	Regular school, time inside general class			Separate school for students with disabilities	Separate residential facility	Parentally placed in regular private schools[1]	Home-bound/hospital placement	Correctional facility
		Less than 40 percent	40–79 percent	80 percent or more					
1	2	3	4	5	6	7	8	9	10
2011									
All students with disabilities	100.0	14.0	19.8	61.1	3.0	0.3	1.1	0.4	0.3
Autism	100.0	33.7	18.2	39.0	7.7	0.5	0.6	0.3	#
Deaf-blindness	100.0	32.5	10.5	27.0	18.1	8.4	0.7	2.8	#
Developmental delay	100.0	16.3	19.6	62.5	0.8	0.1	0.6	0.2	#
Emotional disturbance	100.0	20.6	18.0	43.2	13.2	1.9	0.2	1.1	1.8
Hearing impairments	100.0	13.0	16.8	56.7	8.6	3.4	1.3	0.2	0.1
Intellectual disability	100.0	48.8	26.6	17.0	6.2	0.4	0.3	0.5	0.2
Multiple disabilities	100.0	46.2	16.4	13.0	19.2	1.7	0.3	3.0	0.1
Orthopedic impairments	100.0	22.2	16.3	54.0	4.7	0.2	0.8	1.7	0.1
Other health impairments[2]	100.0	10.0	22.7	63.5	1.6	0.2	1.0	0.9	0.3
Specific learning disabilities	100.0	6.8	25.1	66.2	0.5	0.1	0.8	0.1	0.3
Speech or language impairments	100.0	4.5	5.5	86.9	0.3	#	2.6	0.1	#
Traumatic brain injury	100.0	20.5	22.8	48.5	5.2	0.5	0.8	1.7	0.1
Visual impairments	100.0	11.3	13.1	64.3	5.9	3.8	1.1	0.6	#

—Not available.

Rounds to zero.

[1]Students who are enrolled by their parents or guardians in regular private schools and have their basic education paid through private resources, but receive special education services at public expense. These students are not included under "Regular school, time inside general class" (columns 3 through 5).

[2]Other health impairments include having limited strength, vitality, or alertness due to chronic or acute health problems such as a heart condition, tuberculosis, rheumatic fever, nephritis, asthma, sickle cell anemia, hemophilia, epilepsy, lead poisoning, leukemia, or diabetes.

Note: Data are for the 50 states, the District of Columbia, and the Bureau of Indian Education schools. Detail may not sum to totals because of rounding. Some data have been revised from previously published figures.

Source: U.S. Department of Education, Office of Special Education Programs, Individuals with Disabilities Education Act (IDEA) database, retrieved October 13, 2014, from h :es.ed.gov/programs/digest/d13/tables/dt13_204.60.asp.

cultures do not believe that they should be involved in educational decisions, and others may not welcome the involvement of school personnel in family or personal matters. Increasing parental involvement and communication between parents and schools from the prereferral stage through the decision-making stage may decrease the need for both mediation and third-party hearings.

Difficulties with the hearing process were likely the impetus behind changing the 2004 amendments to include the option of resolution sessions. This allows parents and the school another opportunity to resolve issues about which they disagree in a more timely manner and without the costs typically associated with hearings. Should parents or schools exhaust the hearing process without satisfaction, the right remains for either party to take the case through the civil court system. IDEA continues to be interpreted through the judicial system.

● ETHICS AND STANDARDS

In addition to the legal requirements that govern the process of assessment and planning in special and general education, ethical standards for practice have been established by professional organizations. In special education, standards of practice and policies have been set forth by the Council for Exceptional Children. The National Association of School Psychologists has established standards and ethics for professionals in the school psychology field. And the American Educational Research Association, the American Psychological Association, and the National Council on Measurement in Education have established the *Standards for Educational and Psychological Testing* (1999). These professional groups have policies regarding the education and assessment of students from culturally and linguistically diverse backgrounds.

Although professionals in the field of education and educational psychology are required by law to follow federal regulations and mandates, the standards and ethics are established by professional groups to encourage professionalism and best practice. Information about the standards, codes, and policies that are relevant to assessment and special education are included in the following pages.

The Ethical Principles & Practice Standards set forth by the Council for Exceptional Children (CEC) are similar to the federal regulations governing assessment, use of goals and objectives for planning, record keeping and confidentiality, and decision-making practices.

The National Association of School Psychologists' *Principles for Professional Ethics* (2010) includes standards that cover all areas of practice for psychologists working in the school setting and includes specific standards for assessment. Specifically, Principle II concerns competence and professional responsibility in assessment and record-keeping practices, and these guidelines are consistent with the legal requirements for assessment and the evaluation process.

The *Standards for Educational and Psychological Testing* also contain standards for all areas of testing and are consistent with the federal regulations. For example, the standards include language regarding the use of multiple measures in reaching decisions about an individual's functioning, following standardized administration procedures, and confidentiality of test results and test instruments. The standards require examiners to consider various explanations of why a student might have performed as she or he did and use a variety of assessment methods rather than relying only on a single instrument or a single explanation. These standards require the examiner to be fully qualified to administer specific instruments and procedures to assess a student's ability and behavior. For additional information, refer to the *Standards for Educational and Psychological Testing* (American Research Association, American Psychological Association, & National Council on Measurement in Education, 1999).

CHECK YOUR UNDERSTANDING

Check your understanding of ethical decisions in the assessment process by completing Activity 2.9.

Digital Concerns and Ethical Practices

Changing technologies require that individuals who provide assessment in the schools think purposefully about how these technologies may impact professional practice and ethics (Armistead,& Provenzano, 2014). As you will see throughout the text in later chapters, many assessment instruments are now scored and interpreted using computer programs or online scoring housed on a publisher's website. New technology can ease test administration, scoring, and interpretation and can be more time efficient. However, these new practices raise several questions that each evaluator must consider. Of particular concern are the uses of technology in the assessment process and in the areas of keeping assessment records. For example:

1. How can the examiner make certain that all input into a scoring program is accurate, and how are errors detected?

2. How will the interpretation by a computer differ from the interpretation by the highly trained professional?

3. How can the examiner make certain that the interpretation and computer-generated report include the specific behavioral observations made during the assessment process?

4. How will information obtained from other individuals (parent interviews, teacher conferences, classroom observations) be considered and included in the report?

5. How secure will electronic data and reports be if generated and held by a third party?

6. How are confidentiality and parents' rights considered in this process of electronic storage of data?

In addition to the concerns regarding the assessment practice, the individual practitioner should be concerned with how each practitioner secures and protects electronic technology and the information held therein. For example, computer-generated assessment, scoring, and interpretation must be password protected and held on a secure computer. Any records that are actively being generated must be protected and storage must be secure. Imagine the ethical and legal concerns of the examiner who discovers that a laptop with data and records has been stolen or a flash drive has been misplaced. Emerging technologies will continue to change the practice of assessment and will continue to require professionals to be concerned with how legal and ethical standards can be upheld.

CHAPTER SUMMARY

In this chapter you:

- Learned the federal regulations covering the assessment process
- Applied regulations to case scenarios
- Analyzed cases to determine compliance with regulations
- Synthesized the meaning of regulations
- Evaluated case scenarios for compliance and ethical issues

THINK AHEAD

Procedures used to interpret the results of a student's performance on test instruments involve basic statistical methods, which are presented in Chapter 3. Do you think tests using the same numerical scales can easily be compared?

CHAPTER QUIZ

Now complete the Chapter Quiz for Chapter 2 and assess your understanding of the legal regulations for the practice of assessment of learners with special needs and learning challenges.

Once you have completed that exercise, assess your progress by completing the Course Progress Monitoring Activity. This activity will let you know if you are moving toward target for course objectives.

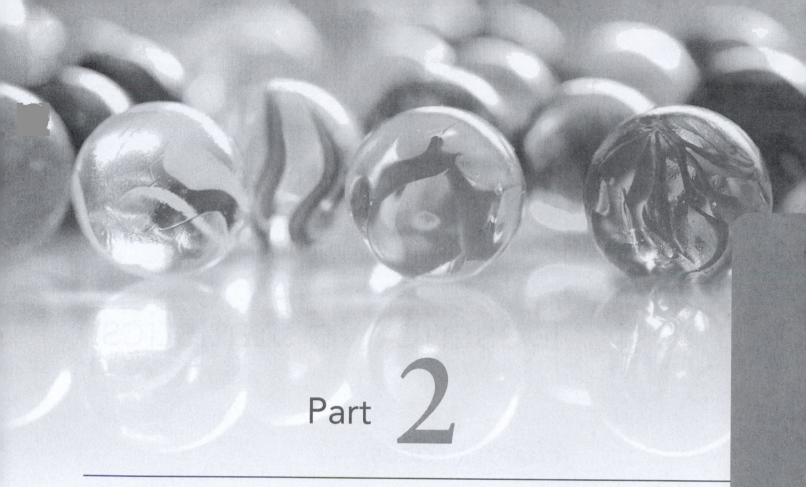

Part 2

Technical Prerequisites of Understanding Assessment

3 Descriptive Statistics

CHAPTER FOCUS

In this chapter you will:

- Learn measurement terms and operations
- Apply steps of measurement operations
- Analyze when and why the measurement operations are used
- Synthesize the results of measurement operations
- Evaluate results of measurement operations to determine significance for classroom practice

● WHY IS MEASUREMENT IMPORTANT?

Psychoeducational assessment using standardized instruments historically has been applied in the educational decision-making process. To properly use standardized instruments, one must understand test-selection criteria, basic principles of measurement, administration techniques, and scoring procedures. Careful interpretation of test results relies on these abilities. Thus, research that questions the assessment competence of special educators and other professionals is frightening because the educational future of so many individuals is at risk.

The careful study of measurement by professionals in the field of special education follows research about common mistakes made in the field. Several studies in the early 1980s made note of the typical types of mistakes made by teachers, administrators, psychologists, and other professionals in the field of special education. Algozzine and Ysseldyke (1981) found that professionals identified students as eligible for special education services when the students' test scores were within the average range and relied instead on referral information to make decisions. Ysseldyke, Algozzine, Richey, and Graden (1982) found that data presented during educational planning conferences played little, if any, part in the members' decisions. Still other researchers found that professionals continued to select poor-quality assessment instruments when better tests were available (Davis & Shepard, 1983; Ysseldyke, Algozzine, Regan, & Potter, 1980).

Research by Huebner (1988, 1989) indicated that professionals made errors in the diagnosis of learning disabilities more frequently when scores were reported in percentiles. This reflects inadequate understanding of data interpretation. Eaves (1985) noted there were often common errors made by professionals during the assessment process. Some of the most common mistakes that test examiners made were simple errors such as calculation and scoring errors.

Research that pointed out the occurrence of such errors heightened awareness of the importance of educators needing a basic understanding of the measurement principles used in assessment. The *Standards for Educational and Psychological Testing* (AERA, APA, & NCME, 1999) warned that when special educators have little or no training in the basic principles of measurement, assessment instruments could be misused.

Much of the foundation of good practice in psychoeducational assessment lies in a thorough understanding of test reliability and validity as well as basic measurement principles. Although revisions in policies governing the provision of special education services have occurred since the 1980s, thorough and effective assessment of students by members of the multidisciplinary team is still integral to the team's decision making. For this reason, this chapter is designed to promote the development of a basic understanding of general principles of measurement and the application of those principles.

● GETTING MEANING FROM NUMBERS

Any teacher who scores a test, either published or teacher-made, will subtract the number of items a student missed from the number of items presented to the student. This number, known as the raw score, is of little value to the teacher unless a frame of reference exists for that number. The frame of reference might be comparing the number of items the student answered correctly with the number the student answered correctly the previous day (e.g., Monday, 5 out of 10 responses correct; Tuesday, 6 out of 10 responses correct). The frame of reference might be a national sample of students of the same age who attempted the same items in the same manner on a norm-referenced standardized test. In all cases, teachers must clearly understand what can and cannot be inferred from numerical data gathered on small samples of behavior known as *tests*.

The techniques used to obtain raw scores are discussed in Chapter 5. Raw scores are used to obtain the other scores presented in this chapter.

● REVIEW OF NUMERICAL SCALES

Numbers can denote different meanings from different scales. The scale that has the least meaning for educational measurement purposes is the **nominal scale**. The nominal scale consists of numbers used only for identification purposes, such as student ID numbers or the numbers on race cars. These numbers cannot be used in mathematical operations. For example, if race cars were labeled with letters of the alphabet rather than with numerals, it would make no difference in the outcome of the race. Numbers on a nominal scale function like names.

When numbers are used to rank the order of objects or items, those numbers are said to be on the **ordinal scale**. An ordinal scale is used to rank the order of the winners in a science fair. The winner has the first rank, or number 1, the runner-up has the second rank, or number 2, and so on. In this scale, the numbers have the quality of identification and indicate greater or lesser quality. The ordinal scale, however, does not have the quality of using equidistant units. For example, suppose the winners of a bike race were ranked as they came in, with the winner ranked as first, the runner-up as second, and the third bike rider as third. The distance between the winner and the second-place bike rider might be 9 seconds, and the difference between the second- and third-place bike riders might be 30 seconds. Although the numbers do rank the bike riders, they do not represent equidistant units.

Numbers that are used for identification that rank greater or lesser quality or amount and that are equidistant are numbers used on an **interval scale**. An example is the scale used in measuring temperature. The degrees on the thermometer can be added or subtracted—a reading of 38°F is 10° less than a reading of 48°F. The interval scale does not have an absolute-zero quality. For example, zero degrees does not indicate that there is no temperature. Also, the numbers used on an interval scale cannot be used in other mathematical operations, such as multiplication. Is a reading of 100°F really four times as hot as 25°F? An interval scale used in assessment is the IQ scale. IQ numbers are equidistant, but they do not possess additional numerical properties. A person with an IQ of 66 cannot be called two-thirds as smart as a person with an IQ of 99.

When numbers on a scale are equidistant from each other and have a true meaning of absolute zero, they can be used in all mathematical operations. This **ratio scale** allows for direct comparisons and mathematical manipulations.

When scoring tests and interpreting data, it is important to understand which numerical scale the numbers represent and to realize the properties and limitations of that scale. Understanding what test scores represent may decrease errors such as attributing more meaning to a particular score than should be allowed by the nature of the numerical scale.

● DESCRIPTIVE STATISTICS

When assessing a student's behavior or performance for the purpose of educational intervention, it is often necessary to determine the amount of difference or deviance that the student exhibits in a particular area from the expected level for the student's age or grade. By looking at how much difference exists in samples of behavior, educational decision makers and parents can appropriately plan interventions. As previously mentioned, obtaining a raw score will not help with educational planning unless the evaluator has a frame of reference for that score. A raw score may have meaning when it is compared with previous student performance, or it may be used to gain information from another set of scores called derived scores. Derived scores may be scores such as percentile ranks, standard scores, grade equivalents, age equivalents, or language quotients. Many derived scores obtain meaning from large sets of data or large samples of scores. By observing how a large sample of students of the same age or in the same grade performed on the same tasks, it becomes possible to compare a particular student with the large group to see if that student performed as well as the group, better than the group, or not as well as the group.

Large sets of data are organized and understood through methods known as descriptive statistics. As the name implies, these are statistical operations that help educators understand and describe sets of data.

● MEASURES OF CENTRAL TENDENCY

One way to organize and describe data is to see how the data fall together, or cluster. This type of statistics is called measures of central tendency. Measures of central tendency are methods to determine how scores cluster—that is, how they are distributed around a numerical representation of the average score.

One common type of distribution used in assessment is called a normal distribution. A normal distribution has particular qualities that, when understood, help with the interpretation of assessment data. A normal distribution hypothetically represents the way test scores would fall if a particular test were given to every single student of the same age or in the same grade in the population for whom the test was designed. If educators could administer an instrument in this way and obtain a normal distribution, the scores would fall in the shape of a bell curve, as shown in Figure 3.1.

In a graph of a normal distribution of scores, a very large number of the students tested are represented by all of the scores in the middle, or the "hump" part, of the curve. Because fewer students obtain extremely high or low scores, their scores are plotted or represented on the extreme ends of the curve. It is assumed that the same number of students obtained the higher scores as obtained the lower scores. The distribution is symmetric, or equal, on either side of the vertical line. Normal distribution is discussed throughout the text. One method of interpreting norm-referenced tests is to assume the principles of normal distribution theory and employ the measures of central tendency.

FIGURE 3.1 Normal Distribution of Scores, Shown by the Bell Curve

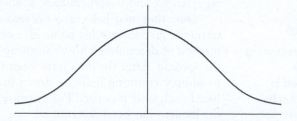

● AVERAGE PERFORMANCE

Although educators are familiar with the average grade of C on a letter-grade system (interval scale), the numerical ranking of the C grade might be 70 to 79 in one school and 76 to 84 in another. If the educator does not understand the numerical meaning of *average* for a student, the letter grade of C has little value. The educator must know how the other students performed and what score indicates average performance, what score denotes excellent performance, and what score signifies poor performance. To determine this, the teacher must determine what is considered *average* for that specific set of data.

One way to look at a set of data is to rank the scores from highest to lowest. This helps the teacher see how the group as a whole performed. After ranking the data in this fashion, it is helpful to complete a frequency distribution by counting how frequently each score occurred. Here is a data set of 39 test scores, which the teacher ranked and then counted to record frequency.

Data Set A

Score	Tally	Frequency
100	I	1
99	I	1
98	II	2
94	II	2
90	IIII	5
89	IIII II	7
88	IIII IIII	10
82	IIII I	6
75	II	2
74	I	1
68	I	1
60	I	1

By arranging the data in this order and tallying the frequency of each score, the teacher can determine a trend in the performance of the class.

Another way to look at the data is to determine the most frequently occurring score, or the mode. The mode can give the teacher an idea of how the group performed because it indicates the score or performance that occurred most often. The mode for Data Set A was 88 because it occurred 10 times. In Data Set B (Activity 3.2), the mode was 70.

Some sets of data have two modes or two most frequently occurring scores. This type of distribution of scores is known as a bimodal distribution. A distribution with three or more modes is called a multimodal distribution.

A clear representation of the distribution of a set of data can be illustrated graphically with a frequency polygon. A frequency polygon is a graph with test scores represented on the horizontal axis and the number of occurrences, or frequencies, represented on the vertical axis, as shown for Data Set A in Figure 3.2.

Data that have been rank ordered and for which a mode or modes have been determined give the teacher some idea of how students performed as a group. Another method of determining how the group performed is to find the middlemost score, or the median. After the data have been rank ordered, the teacher can find the median by simply counting halfway down the list of scores; however, each score must be listed each time it occurs. For example, here is a rank-ordered set of data for which the median has been determined.

CHECK YOUR UNDERSTANDING

Check your understanding of the descriptive statistics presented in the previous section by completing Activity 3.2.

FIGURE 3.2 Frequency Polygon for Data Set A

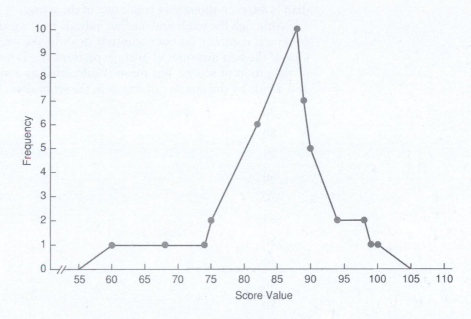

100	79
97	79
89	79
85	68
85	62
78	60

78 median score

CHECK YOUR UNDERSTANDING

Check your understanding of the descriptive statistics presented in the previous section by completing Activity 3.3.

Refer to page 85 in this text. Rank order the following set of data, complete a frequency count, and determine the mode.

The median score has 50% of the data listed above it and 50% of the data listed below it. In this example, six of the scores are listed above 78 and six are listed below the median. Notice that although 78 is the median, it is not the mode for this set of data. In a normal distribution, which is distributed symmetrically, the median and the mode are represented by the same number.

In a set of data with an even number of scores, the median is the middlemost score even though the score may not actually exist in that set of data. For example,

100

96

95

90

85

83

82

80

78

77

The scores 85 and 83 occur in the middle of this distribution; therefore, the median is 84, even though 84 is not one of the scores.

Although the mode and median indicate how a group performed, these measures of central tendency do not accurately describe the average, or typical, performance. One of the best measures of average performance is the arithmetic average, or **mean,** of the group of scores. The mean is calculated as a simple average: Add the scores and divide by the number of scores in the set of data. For example:

90

80

75

60

70

65

80

100

80

80

780 / 10 = 78

The sum of the scores is 780. There are 10 scores in the set of data. Therefore, the sum, 780, is divided by the number of scores, 10. The average, or typical, score for this set of data is 78, which represents the arithmetic average.

Often teachers choose to use the mean score to represent the average score on a particular test or assignment. If this score seems to represent the typical performance on the specific test, the teacher may assign a letter grade of C to the numerical representation of the mean score. However, as discussed next, extremely high or low scores can render the mean misrepresentative of the average performance of the class.

Using measures of central tendency is one way teachers can determine which score represents an average performance for a particular group on a particular measure. This aids the teacher in monitoring student progress and knowing when a student is performing well above or well below the norm, or average, of the group.

The mean can be affected by an extreme score, especially if the group is composed of only a few students. A very high score can raise the mean, whereas a very low score can lower the mean. For this reason, the teacher may wish to omit an extreme score before averaging the data. If scores seem to be widely dispersed, or scattered, using measures of central tendency may not be in students' best interests. Moreover, such scatter might suggest that the teacher needs to qualitatively evaluate the students' performance and other factors such as his or her teaching methods.

In research and test development, it is necessary to strive for and understand the normal distribution. Because of the symmetrical quality of the normal curve, the mean, median, and mode are all represented by the same number. For example, on tests measuring intelligence, the mean IQ is 100. One hundred is also the middlemost score (median) and the most frequently occurring score (mode). In fact, more than 68% of all of IQ scores will cluster within one standard deviation, or one determined typical unit, above and below the score of 100. The statistic known as *standard deviation* is very important in special education assessment when the use of tests that compare an individual student with a norm-referenced group is necessary. Finding the standard deviation is one method of calculating difference in scores, or variability of scores, known as *dispersion*.

CHECK YOUR UNDERSTANDING

Check your understanding of the descriptive statistics presented in the previous section by completing Activity 3.4.

CHECK YOUR UNDERSTANDING

Check your understanding of the measures of central tendency presented in the previous section by completing Activity 3.5.

● HOW CAN CLASSROOM TEACHERS USE MEASURES OF CENTRAL TENDENCY?

As noted in the activities from the previous sections of the chapter, teachers can use the raw score data they obtain on classroom tests to see how specific students are progressing. For example, close examination of all scores might reveal an extreme score that informs the teacher that a student is acquiring and retaining material at a much higher or lower level than other students in the classroom. In addition to learning about student progress, raw score data from classroom testing or assignment scores can inform the teacher about practices in the classroom. Read the following case study and respond to the questions in Activity 3.6.

Case Study 1

Mr. Lambert completed the science unit on astronomy and administered the end-of-unit exam to assess content knowledge of the material. A total of 50 items were on the exam and each item was worth 2 points for a total possible score of 100. Upon completion of the exam, Mr. Lambert began grading the tests. Of the 20 students in his class, he noted the following set of data and arranged the scores from the highest to the lowest:

72, 70, 62, 59, 51, 49, 42, 40, 38, 38, 38, 38, 38, 37, 37, 37, 37, 36, 36, 35

CHECK YOUR UNDERSTANDING

By examining the data, at first glance, what might be plausible reasons for the scores? Answer the questions in Activity 3.6 about Mr. Lambert's class.

● MEASURES OF DISPERSION

Because special educators must determine the degree or amount of difference exhibited by individuals in behaviors, skills, or traits, they must employ methods of calculating difference from the average or expected score. Just as measures of central tendency are used to see how sets of data cluster together around an average score, measures of dispersion are used to calculate how scores are spread from the mean.

The way that scores in a set of data are spread apart is known as the *variability of the scores*, or how much the scores vary from each other. When scores fall very close together and are not widely spread apart, the data are described as not having much variability, or variance.

Compare the following two sets of data.

Data Set I		Data Set J	
100	75	98	75
98	75	96	75
95	75	87	75
91	72	78	75
88	70	75	72
87	69	75	72
82	68	75	72
80	67	75	72
75	51	75	72
75	50	75	72

An easy way to get an idea about the spread is to find the range of scores. The range is calculated by subtracting the lowest score from the highest score.

Set I	Set J
$100 - 50 = 50$	$98 - 72 = 26$

The range for Set J is about half that of Set I. It appears that Set I has more variability than Set J. Look at the sets of data again. Both sets have the same median and the same mode, yet they are very different in terms of variability. When the means are calculated, it seems that the data are very similar. Set I has a mean of 77.15, and Set J has a mean of 77.05. By using only measures of central tendency, the teacher may think that the students in both of these classes performed in a very similar manner on this test. Yet one set of data has approximately twice the spread, or variability, of scores. In educational testing, it is necessary to determine the deviation from the mean in order to have a clearer picture of how students in groups such as these performed. By calculating the variance and the standard deviation, the teacher can find out the typical amount of difference from the mean. By knowing these typical or standard deviations from the mean, the teacher will be able to find out which scores are a significant distance from the average score.

To find the standard deviation of a set of scores, the variance must first be calculated. The variance can be described as the degree or amount of variability or dispersion in a set of scores. Looking at data sets I and J, one could probably assume that Set I would have a larger variance than Set J.

Step 1		Step 2		
Difference		**Multiply by Itself**		**Squared**
$100 - 77.15 =$	22.85	$22.85 \times$	$22.85 =$	522.1225
$98 - 77.15 =$	20.85	$20.85 \times$	$20.85 =$	434.7225
$95 - 77.15 =$	17.85	$17.85 \times$	$17.85 =$	318.6225
$91 - 77.15 =$	13.85	$13.85 \times$	$13.85 =$	191.8225
$88 - 77.15 =$	10.85	$10.85 \times$	$10.85 =$	117.7225
$87 - 77.15 =$	9.85	$9.85 \times$	$9.85 =$	97.0225
$82 - 77.15 =$	4.85	$4.85 \times$	$4.85 =$	23.5225
$80 - 77.15 =$	2.85	$2.85 \times$	$2.85 =$	8.1225
$75 - 77.15 =$	-2.15	$-2.15 \times$	$-2.15 =$	4.6225
$75 - 77.15 =$	-2.15	$-2.15 \times$	$-2.15 =$	4.6225
$75 - 77.15 =$	-2.15	$-2.15 \times$	$-2.15 =$	4.6225
$75 - 77.15 =$	-2.15	$-2.15 \times$	$-2.15 =$	4.6225
$75 - 77.15 =$	-2.15	$-2.15 \times$	$-2.15 =$	4.6225
$72 - 77.15 =$	-5.15	$-5.15 \times$	$-5.15 =$	26.5225
$70 - 77.15 =$	-7.15	$-7.15 \times$	$-7.15 =$	51.1225
$69 - 77.15 =$	-8.15	$-8.15 \times$	$-8.15 =$	66.4225
$68 - 77.15 =$	-9.15	$-9.15 \times$	$-9.15 =$	83.7225
$67 - 77.15 =$	-10.15	$-10.15 \times$	$-10.15 =$	103.0225
$51 - 77.15 =$	-26.15	$-26.15 \times$	$-26.15 =$	683.8225
$50 - 77.15 =$	-27.15	$-27.15 \times$	$-27.15 =$	737.1225

Four steps are involved in calculating the variance.

Step 1: To calculate the amount of distance of each score from the mean, subtract the mean for the set of data from each score.

Step 2: Find the square of each of the difference scores found in Step 1 (multiply each difference score by itself).

Step 3: Find the total of all of the squared score differences. This is called the *sum of squares.*

Step 4: Calculate the average of the sum of squares by dividing the total by the number of scores.

Step 5: Sum of squares: 3,488.55

Step 6: Divide the sum of squares by the number of scores.

$$3{,}488.55 / 20 = 174.4275$$

Therefore, the variance for Data Set I = 174.4275.

CHECK YOUR UNDERSTANDING

Check your understanding of the measures of dispersion presented in the previous section by completing Activity 3.7.

● STANDARD DEVIATION

Once the variance has been calculated, only one more step is needed to calculate the standard deviation. The standard deviation helps the teacher determine how much distance from the mean is typical and how much is considered significant.

The standard deviation of a set of data is the square root of the variance.

$$\text{Standard deviation} = \sqrt{\text{Variance}}$$

Because the variance for Data Sets I and J has already been calculated, merely enter each number on a calculator and hit the square root button. If a calculator is not available, use the square root tables located in most introductory statistics textbooks.

The square root of the variance for Data Set I is 13.21. Therefore, any test score that is more than one standard deviation above or below the mean score, either 13.21 above the mean or 13.21 below the mean, is considered significant. Look at Data Set I. The test scores that are more than one standard deviation above the mean (77.15) are 100, 98, 95, and 91. The scores that are more than one standard deviation below the mean are 51 and 50. These scores represent the extremes for this distribution and may well receive the extreme grades for the class: As and Fs. Figure 3.3 illustrates the distribution of scores in Data Set I.

Look at Data Set J. To locate significantly different scores, find those that are one or more standard deviations away from the mean of 77.05. Which scores are considered to be a significant distance from the mean?

FIGURE 3.3 Distribution for Data Set I

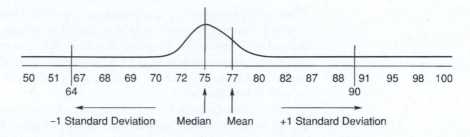

FIGURE 3.4 Percentages of Population That Fall within Standard Deviation Units in a Normal Distribution

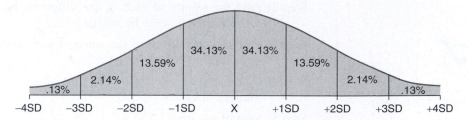

Standard Deviation and the Normal Distribution

In a normal distribution, the standard deviations represent the percentages of scores shown on the bell curve in Figure 3.4. More than 68% of the scores fall within one standard deviation above or below the mean. A normal distribution is symmetrical and has the same number representing the mean, median, and mode. Notice that approximately 95% of scores are found within two standard deviations above and below the mean (Figure 3.4). To clarify the significance of standard deviation, it is helpful to remember that one criterion for the diagnosis of intellectual disability is an IQ score of more than two standard deviations below the mean. The criterion of two standard deviations above the mean is often used to determine that a student's intellectual ability is within the gifted range. Using a standard deviation of 15 IQ points, an individual with an IQ of 70 or less and a subaverage adaptive behavior scale score might be classified as being within the range of mental intellectual disability, whereas an individual with an IQ of 130 or more may be classified as gifted. The American Association on Intellectual and Developmental Disability (AAIDD) classification system allows additional flexibility by adding five points to the minimum requirement: That is, the student within the 70–75 IQ range may also be found eligible for services under the category of intellectual disability if there are additional supporting data.

CHECK YOUR UNDERSTANDING

Check your understanding of the measures of dispersion presented in the previous section by completing Activity 3.8.

● MEAN DIFFERENCES

Test results such as those discussed in the preceding section should be interpreted with caution. Many tests that have been used historically to diagnose disabilities such as mental retardation have been shown to exhibit *mean differences*. A specific cultural or linguistic group may have a different mean or average score than that reported for most of the population; this is a mean difference. Accordingly, minority students should not be judged by an acceptable average for a different population. This issue is elaborated on in Chapter 9, "Measures of Intelligence and Adaptive Behavior."

● SKEWED DISTRIBUTIONS

When small samples of populations are tested or when a fairly restricted population is tested, the results may not be distributed in a normal curve. Distributions can be skewed in a positive or negative direction. When many of the scores are below the mean, the distribution is said to be positively skewed and will resemble the distribution in Figure 3.5. Notice that the most frequently occurring scores (mode) are located below the mean.

When a large number of the scores occurs above the mean, the distribution is said to be negatively skewed, as shown in Figure 3.6. Notice that the mode and median scores are located above the mean.

FIGURE 3.5 Positively Skewed Distribution

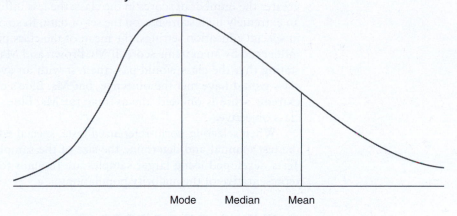

Mode   Median   Mean

FIGURE 3.6 Negatively Skewed Distribution

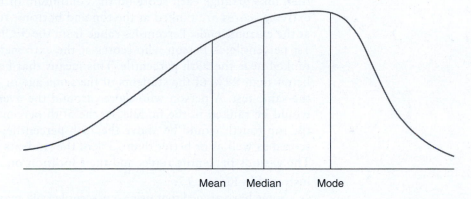

Mean   Median   Mode

Figures 3.5 and 3.6 illustrate different ways that groups of scores fall, cluster, and are dispersed. As already discussed, extreme scores can change the appearance of a set of scores. Often, when working with scores from teacher-made tests, one or two scores can be so extreme that they influence the way the data are described. That is, the scores may influence or pull the mean in one direction. Consider the following examples.

Mr. Brown	Ms. Blue
100	100
92	92
86	86
80	80
78	78
78	78
78	78
75	75
74	74
72	6
813 / 10 = 81.3	745 / 10 = 74.5

These sets of data are very similar except for the one extremely low score. The greater the number of scores in the class, the less influence an extremely low score or an extremely high score has on the set of data. In small classes like those often found in special education settings, the mean of the class performance is more likely to be influenced by an extreme score. If Mr. Brown and Ms. Blue each had a class objective stating that the class would pass the test with an average score of 80, Mr. Brown's class would have met the objective, but Ms. Blue's class would not have. When the extreme score is omitted, the average for Ms. Blue's class is 82.1, which meets the class objective.

When selecting norm-referenced tests, special educators must take care to read the test manual and determine the size of the sample used in the norming process. Tests developed using larger samples are thought to result in scores that are more representative of the majority population.

● TYPES OF SCORES

Percentile ranks and *z* scores provide additional ways of looking at data. Percentile ranks arrange each score on the continuum of the normal distribution. The extreme scores are ranked at the top and bottom; very few people obtain scores at the extreme ends. Percentiles range from the 99.9th percentile to less than the 1st percentile. A person who scores at the extremely high end of a test may be ranked near the 99th percentile. This means that he or she scored as well as or better than 99% of the students of the same age or in the same grade who took the same test. A person who scores around the average, say 100 on an IQ test, would be ranked in the middle, or the 50th percentile. A person who scores in the top fourth would be above the 75th percentile; in other words, the student scored as well as or better than 75% of the students in that particular age group. The various percentile ranks and their location on a normal distribution are illustrated in Figure 3.7.

Some have argued that using a percentile rank may not convey information that is as meaningful as other types of scores, such as *z* scores (May & Nicewander, 1994, 1997). DeGruijter (1997) argued that May and Nicewander were faulty in their reasoning regarding percentile ranks and stated that percentile ranks are not inferior indicators of ability.

Some tests use *T* scores to interpret test performance. *T* scores have an average or mean of 50 and standard deviation of 10. One standard deviation above the mean would be expressed as a *T* score of 60, and 40 would represent one standard deviation below the mean.

Another type of score used to describe the data in a normal distribution is called a *z* *score*. A *z* score indicates where a score is located in terms of standard

FIGURE 3.7 Relationship of Percentiles and Normal Distribution

Source: From *Assessing special students* (3rd ed., p. 63) by J. McLoughlin and R. Lewis, 1990, Upper Saddle River, NJ: Merrill/Prentice Hall. Copyright 1990 by Prentice Hall. Adapted with permission.

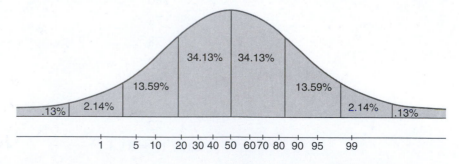

FIGURE 3.8 Relationship of z Scores and the Normal Distribution

Source: From *Assessing special students* (3rd ed., p. 63) by J. McLoughlin and R. Lewis, 1990, Upper Saddle River, NJ: Merrill/Prentice Hall. Copyright 1990 by Prentice Hall. Adapted with permission.

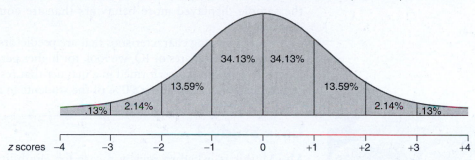

deviation units. The mean is expressed as 0, one standard deviation above the mean is expressed as +1, two standard deviations above as +2, and so on, as illustrated in Figure 3.8. Standard deviation units below the mean are expressed as negative numbers. For example, a score that is one standard deviation below the mean is expressed using z scores as −1, and a score that is two standard deviations below is expressed as −2.

Stanines are used to report many group-achievement test scores. Stanines divide the scores into nine groups and are reported as 1 through 9, with a mean of 5. The standard deviation unit of stanines is 2. This indicates that students who fall between the 3rd and 7th stanines are within the range expected for their age or grade group.

Deciles are scores that are reported in 10 groups ranging from a score of 10 for the lowest grouping to 100 for the highest group of scores. Each grouping represents 10% of the obtained scores.

Case Study 2

Mr. Garza received a report from the school counselor regarding a student whom he had referred for an assessment of self-esteem. The student, Jorge, completed a norm-referenced questionnaire that assessed his feelings of self-confidence about school, his peers, and his family. When the counselor met with Mr. Garza, she reported the following scores for Jorge.

Self-Confidence with Peer Relationships	5th percentile rank
Self-Confidence with Family Relationships	95th percentile rank
Self-Confidence in Ability at School	12th percentile rank

In this case, self-confidence is something that is valued or consistent with better behavior and higher achievement. In other words, the more confidence a student reports, the better he or she may be able to function in school with peers, and with family members at home. Jorge's responses resulted in his being ranked at the 5th percentile in self-confidence with peers. This means that about 95% of students his age who were in the norming group for this assessment instrument reported feeling more confident about their peer relationships. According to Jorge's responses, how confident is he about his ability to get along with his family? How confident is he in his ability to perform at school?

Because self-confidence is something that is valued, higher percentile ranks indicate that the student has confidence while lower percentile ranks indicate that he or she is not very confident about his or her ability.

When we assess behaviors that are impacting learning in a negative way, such as distractibility or signs of depression, we want percentile ranks to be lower. In other words, a percentile rank of 15 indicates that about 85% of students in the sample displayed more behaviors that are consistent with distractibility or depression.

When assessing characteristics that are predictors of higher school achievement, such as cognitive scores or IQ, we look for higher percentile ranks to indicate higher ability. A student who performed in a manner that resulted in a percentile rank of 90 performed better than about 90% of the students in the norm sample.

Case Study 3

Ms. Mathis is asked to review a case for eligibility determination. The student has been referred for an evaluation due to general low achievement and observed low ability across both academic and behavioral measures. As Ms. Mathis reviews the file, she must be aware of the requirements for the various types of special education categories. For example, to be considered for support services for intellectual disability (ID), a student should have cognitive functioning that is significantly subaverage as well as deficits in adaptive behavior. For example, subaverage functioning is considered to be at least two standard deviations below the average score (American Association on Intellectual and Developmental Disabilities, 2011). This means that for a measure with an average of 100 and a standard deviation of 15, a student's score on a cognitive measure should generally be below 70. The student's file includes cognitive assessment scores of 68, 62, and 65 and adaptive behavioral functioning that is significantly below the levels expected. Ms. Mathis knew that the scores were within the range of intellectual disability. Further consideration by Ms. Mathis revealed that there were several areas in which the student would need additional support for optimal functioning in school, home, and the community. For this reason, Ms. Mathis examined the adaptive behavior scales carefully before she attended the eligibility meeting. Since the purpose of assessment is to obtain data that will assist in educational planning, Ms. Mathis noted all areas in which the student was found to be below developmental expectations. At the conclusion of the meeting, Ms. Mathis was able to construct meaningful individualized education program (IEP) objectives to address school, home, and community functioning.

CHAPTER SUMMARY

In this chapter you:

- Learned measurement terms and operations
- Applied steps of measurement operations
- Analyzed when and why measurement operations are used
- Synthesized the results of measurement operations
- Evaluated results of measurement operations to determine significance for classroom practice

THINK AHEAD

Now that you know how to compare students' scores with each other, you will read about how to compare tests. You will learn how to determine whether tests are reliable and valid. Do you think a test must be both reliable and valid to obtain information about a student's abilities?

CHAPTER QUIZ

Now complete the Chapter Quiz, which includes Figure 3.9, to measure your understanding of the content in this chapter.

FIGURE 3.9 Relationships among Different Types of Scores in a Normal Distribution

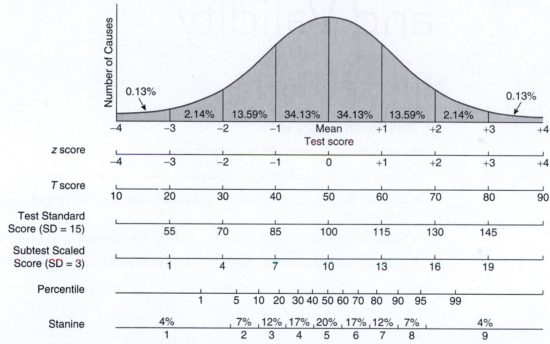

Source: McLoughlin & Lewis, "Relationships among different types of scores in a normal distribution," p. 61, *Assessing Special Students,* © 1994 by Pearson Education, Inc. Reproduced by permission of Pearson Education, Inc.

4 Reliability and Validity

CHAPTER FOCUS

In this chapter you will:

- Learn the types of reliability and validity

- Apply reliability and validity concepts to data

- Analyze the benefits of reliability and validity for specific types of assessment

- Synthesize the meaning of reliability and validity research in assessment

- Evaluate assessment instruments based on their reliability and validity data

● RELIABILITY AND VALIDITY IN ASSESSMENT

It is important that the assessment methods used in teaching provide accurate information. Usually, inferences are made from test data. In each school district, these inferences and subsequent interpretations of test results may change or set the educational future of hundreds of students each school year. An understanding of the concepts of reliability and validity aids the educator in determining test accuracy and dependability as well as how much faith can be placed in the use of instruments in the decision-making process.

Reliability in assessment refers to the confidence that can be placed in an instrument to yield the same score for the same student if the test were administered more than once and to the degree with which a skill or trait is measured consistently across items of a test. Teachers administering tests of any type, formal or informal, must be aware that error will be present to some degree during test administration. Statistical methods for estimating the probable amount of error and the degree of reliability allow professionals to select instruments with the lowest estimate of error and the greatest degree of reliability. Because educators use assessment as a basis for educational intervention and placement decisions, the most technically adequate instruments are preferred.

● CORRELATION

One concept important to the understanding of reliability in assessment is correlation. Correlation is a method of determining the degree of relationship between two variables. Reliability is determined by the degree of relationship between the administration of an instrument and some other variable (including a repeated administration of the same instrument). The greater the degree of the relationship, the more reliable the instrument.

Correlation is a statistical procedure calculated to measure the relationship between two variables. The two variables might be two administrations of the same test, administration of equivalent forms of the same test, administration of one test and school achievement, or variables such as amount of time spent studying and final exam grades. In short, correlation is a method of determining whether two variables are associated with each other and, if so, how much.

There are three types of correlations between variables: positive, negative, and no relationship. The degree of relationship between two variables is expressed by a correlation coefficient (r). The correlation coefficient will be a number between +1.00 and −1.00. A −1.00 or +1.00 indicates a perfect degree of correlation. In reality, perfect correlations are extremely rare. A correlation coefficient of 0 indicates no relationship.

The closer to +1.00 the coefficient, the stronger the degree of the relationship. Hence, an r of 0.78 represents a stronger relationship than 0.65. When relationships are expressed by coefficients, the positive or negative sign does not indicate the strength of a relationship, but indicates the direction of the relationship. Therefore, r values of −0.78 and +0.78 are of equal strength.

Positive Correlation

Variables that have a positive relationship are those that move in the same direction. This means that when test scores representing one variable in a set are high, scores representing the other variable also are high, and when the scores on one variable are low, scores on the other variable are low. Look at the following list of scores. Students who made high scores on a reading ability test (mean = 100) also had fairly high classroom reading grades at the end of the 6-week reporting period. Therefore, the data appear to show a positive relationship between the ability measured on the reading test (variable Y) and the students' performance in the reading curriculum in the classroom (variable X).

	Scores on the Reading Ability Test (Variable Y)	Reading Grade at End of 6 Weeks (Variable X)
John	109	B+
Gustavo	120	A+
Sue	88	C−
Mary	95	B+
George	116	A−
Fred	78	D−
Kristy	140	A+
Jake	135	A
Jason	138	A
Miko	95	B−
Jamie	85	C+

This positive relationship is effectively illustrated by plotting the scores on these two variables on a scattergram (Figure 4.1). Each student is represented by a single dot on the graph. The scattergram shows clearly that as the score on one variable increased, so did the score on the other variable.

The more closely the dots on a scattergram approximate a straight line, the nearer to perfect is the correlation. Hence, a strong relationship will appear more linear. Figure 4.2 illustrates a perfect positive correlation (straight line) for the small set of data shown here.

FIGURE 4.1 Scattergram Showing Relationship between Scores on Reading Ability Test and Reading Grade for 6 Weeks

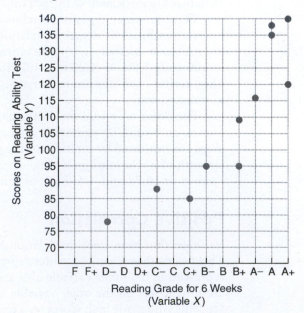

FIGURE 4.2 Scattergram Showing a Perfect Positive Correlation

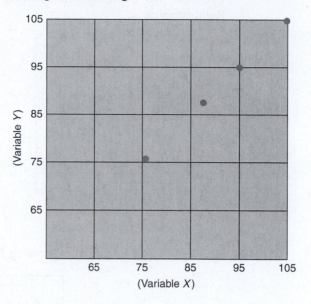

	Test 1 (**Variable** *Y*)	Test 2 (**Variable** *X*)
Jorge	100	100
Bill	95	95
Jennifer	87	87
Isaac	76	76

Check your understanding of positive correlation by completing Activity 4.1.

CHECK YOUR UNDERSTANDING

Examples of other variables that would be expected to have a positive relationship are number of days present in class and semester grade, number of chapters studied and final exam grade, and number of alcoholic drinks consumed and mistakes on a fine-motor test.

Negative Correlation

A negative correlation occurs when high scores on one variable are associated with low scores on the other variable. Examples of probable negative correlations are number of days absent and test grades, number of hours spent at parties and test grades, and number of hours missed from work and amount of hourly paycheck.

When the strength of a relationship is weak, the scattergram will not appear to have a distinct line. The less linear the scattergram, the weaker the correlation. Figure 4.3 illustrates scattergrams representing weak positive and weak negative relationships.

No Correlation

When data from two variables are not associated or have no relationship, the *r* = 0.00. No correlation will be represented on a scattergram by the absence of any linear direction, either positive or negative. Figure 4.4 illustrates a scattergram of variables with no relationship.

FIGURE 4.3 Scattergrams Showing (a) Weak Positive and (b) Weak Negative Relationships

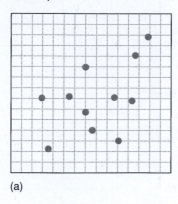

(a)

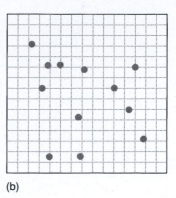

(b)

FIGURE 4.4 Scattergram Showing No Relationship

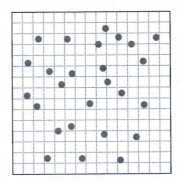

● METHODS OF MEASURING RELIABILITY

A teacher who administers a mathematics ability test to a student on a particular day and obtains a standard score of 110 (mean = 100) might feel quite confident that the student has ability in math above expectancy for that student's age level. Imagine that a teacher recommended a change in the student's educational placement based on the results of that particular math test and later discovered that the math test was not reliable. Educators must be able to have confidence that test instruments used will yield similar results when administered at different times. Professionals must know the degree to which they can rely on a specific instrument.

Different methods can be used to measure the reliability of test instruments. Reliability statistics are calculated using correlational methods. One correlational method used is the Pearson's Product Moment correlation, known as Pearson's *r*. Pearson's *r* is a commonly used formula for data on an interval or a ratio scale, although other methods are used as well. Correlational studies of the reliability of tests involve checking reliability over time or of items within the test, known as internal consistency. For such studies, the procedures of test–retest, equivalent forms, split-half, and statistical methods called Kuder–Richardson formulas may be used.

Test–Retest Reliability

One way to determine the reliability of a test is to measure the correlation of test scores obtained during one administration with the scores obtained on a repeated administration. The assumption of test–retest reliability is that the trait being measured is one that is stable over time. If the trait being measured remains constant, the readministration of the instrument will result in scores very similar to the first scores, and thus the correlation between the two administrations will be positive.

Many of the traits measured in psychoeducational assessment are variable and respond to influencing factors or changes over time, such as instruction or student maturity. The readministration of an instrument for reliability studies should therefore be completed within a fairly short time period in an effort to control the influencing variables that occur naturally in the educational environment of children and youth. Typically, the longer the interval between test administrations, the greater the chance of variation in the obtained scores. Conversely, the shorter the interval between the two test administrations, the less likelihood there is that students will be influenced by time-related factors (experience, education, etc.). The difficulty with readministering the same instrument within a short period of time is that the student may remember items on the test. This *practice effect* most likely would cause the scores obtained on the second administration to be higher than the original scores, which would influence the correlation. The shorter the interval between administrations, the greater the possibility of practice effect; the longer the interval, the greater the influence of time variables.

The disadvantages of test–retest methods for checking test reliability have led to the use of other methods.

Equivalent Forms Reliability

To control the influence of time-related and practice-effect variables of test–retest methods, test developers may choose to use equivalent forms reliability, also called alternate forms reliability. In this method, two forms of the same instrument are used. The items are matched for difficulty on each test. For example, if three items for phonetic attack of consonant blends are included on one version of a reading test, three items of the same nature must be included at the same level on the alternate form of the test. During the reliability study, each student is administered both forms, and the scores obtained on one form of the test are then paired with the scores obtained on the equivalent form. The following are scores obtained on equivalent forms of a hypothetical reading test.

The *Best-Ever Diagnostic Reading Test* (x = 100)*

	Form 1	Form 2
Miguel	82	85
Hannah	76	78
Bill	89	87
Randy	54	56
Ysobel	106	112
Sara	115	109

*x = mean of sample

This positive correlation indicates a fairly high reliability using equivalent forms reliability. In reality, an equivalent forms reliability study would involve a much larger sample of students. If this example had been an equivalent forms study using a large national sample, the educator could assume that both forms of the *Best-Ever Reading Diagnostic Test* are measuring the tested trait with some consistency.

If the test developer of the *Best-Ever Reading Diagnostic Test* also wanted the test to measure the stability of the trait over time, the manual would recommend that an interval of time pass between the administration of each form of the test. In using equivalent forms for measuring stability over time, the reliability coefficient usually will not be as high as in the case of administering the same form of a test a

CHECK YOUR UNDERSTANDING

Check your ability to distinguish between positive, negative, or no correlation by completing Activity 4.2.

second time. In the case of administering equivalent forms over a period of time, the influence of time-related variables will decrease the reliability coefficient as well as the practice effect that occurs in a test–retest reliability study of the same instrument.

Several published achievement and diagnostic tests that are used in special education consist of two equivalent forms. The advantage of this format is that it provides the educator with two tests of the same difficulty level that can be administered within a short time frame without the influence of practice effect. Often, local educational agencies practice a policy of administering one of the equivalent forms before the IEP team writes short-term objectives for the year and of administering the second form following educational interventions near the end of the school year. Educators administer the second form of the test to determine whether educational objectives were achieved.

Internal Consistency Measures

Several methods allow a test developer to determine the reliability of the items on a single test using one administration of the test. These methods include split-half reliability, Kuder–Richardson (K–R) 20, and coefficient alpha.

Split-Half Reliability. Test developers rely often on the split-half method of determining reliability because of its ease of use. This method uses the items available on the instrument, splits the test in half, and correlates the two halves of the test. Because most tests have the items arranged sequentially, from the easiest items at the beginning of the test to the most difficult items at the end, the tests are typically split by pulling every other item, which in essence results in two equivalent half-forms of the test. Because this type of reliability study can be performed in a single administration of the instrument, split-half reliability studies are often completed even though other types of reliability studies are used in the test development. Although this method establishes reliability of one half of the test with the other half, it does not establish the reliability of the entire test. Because reliability tends to increase with the number of items on the test, using split-half reliability may result in a lower reliability coefficient than that calculated by another method for the entire test (Mehrens & Lehmann, 1978). In this case, the reliability may be statistically adjusted to account for the variance in length (Mehrens & Lehmann, 1978).

Kuder–Richardson 20 and Coefficient Alpha. As the name implies, internal consistency reliability methods are used to determine how much alike items are to other items on a test. An advantage of this type of reliability study is that a single test administration is required. This reflects the unidimensionality in measuring a trait rather than the multidimensionality (Walsh & Betz, 1985).

Internal consistency is computed statistically by using either the Kuder–Richardson (K–R) 20 formula for items scored only right or wrong or the coefficient alpha formula for items when more than one point is earned for a correct response (Mehrens & Lehmann, 1978).

When a high correlation coefficient is expressed by an internal consistency formula such as K–R 20 or coefficient alpha, the educator can be confident that the items on the instrument measure the trait or skill with some consistency. These methods measure the consistency of the items but not the consistency or dependability of the instrument across time, as do the test–retest method and the use of equivalent forms in separate test administrations.

Interrater Reliability

Many of the educational and diagnostic tests used in assessing special learners are standardized with very specific administration, scoring, and interpretation instructions. Tests with a great deal of structure reduce the amount of influence that individual examiners may have on the results of the test. Some tests, specifically tests that allow the examiner to make judgments about student performance, have a greater possibility of influence by test examiners. In other words, there may be more of a chance that a score would vary from one examiner to another if the same student were tested by different examiners. On tests such as these, it is important to check the interrater reliability, or interscorer reliability. This can be accomplished by administering the test and then having an objective scorer also score the test results. The results of the tests scored by the examiner are then correlated with the results obtained by the objective scorer to determine how much variability exists between the test scores. This information is especially important when tests with a great deal of subjectivity are used in making educational decisions.

Case Study

Mrs. Umeki received a new student in her fifth-grade class. In the student's records were educational testing data. Because of difficulty in reading, the student had been assessed in her previous school using a brief screening reading test that assessed all reading levels by using a simple list of most common words. The student's scores did not indicate any reading difficulty, yet Mrs. Umeki noticed that the student was struggling with the fifth-grade reader.

One aspect of technically reliable academic instruments is the number of items and the representativeness of the domain being assessed. In this case, the student was assessed with a very short instrument that did not adequately assess the domain of skills that comprise fifth-grade-level reading, such as comprehension, decoding, recognition, oral fluency, and silent reading fluency. Mrs. Umeki decided to assess the student using a comprehensive reading test that measured all aspects of reading expected of a student in the fifth grade. This administration indicated that the student was actually able to complete most reading tasks successfully at the third-grade reading level. This comprehensive reading test was more predictive of the student's actual instructional level in reading.

● WHICH TYPE OF RELIABILITY IS THE BEST?

Different types of reliability studies are used to measure consistency over time, consistency of the items on a test, and consistency of the test scored by different examiners. An educator selects assessment instruments for specific purposes according to the child's educational needs. The reliability studies and information in the test manual concerning reliability of the instrument are important considerations for the educator when determining which test is best for a particular student. An educator should select the instrument that has a high degree of reliability related to the purpose of assessment. An adequate reliability coefficient would be 0.60 or greater, and a high degree of reliability would be above 0.80. For example, if the examiner is interested in measuring a trait over time, the examiner should select an instrument in which the reliability or consistency over time has been studied. If the examiner is more concerned with the instrument's ability to determine student behavior using an instrument that allows for a great degree of examiner judgment, the examiner should check the instrument's interrater reliability.

CHECK YOUR UNDERSTANDING

Check your understanding of the different methods of studying reliability by completing Activity 4.3.

Reliability for Different Groups

The calculation of the reliability coefficient is a group statistic and can be influenced by the make-up of the group. The best tests and the manuals accompanying those tests will include information regarding the reliability of a test with different age or grade levels and even the reliability of a test with populations that differ on demographic variables such as cultural or linguistic backgrounds. The information in Table 4.1 illustrates how reliability may vary across different age groups.

● STANDARD ERROR OF MEASUREMENT

In all psychoeducational assessment, there is a basic underlying assumption: Error exists. Errors in testing may result from situational factors such as a poor testing environment or the health or emotions of the student, or errors may occur because of inaccuracies in the test instrument. Error should be considered when tests are administered, scored, and interpreted. Because tests are small samples of behavior observed at a given time, many variables can affect the assessment process and cause variance in test scores. This variance is called *error* because it influences test results. Professionals need to know that all tests contain error and that a single test score may not accurately reflect the student's true score. Salvia and Ysseldyke (1988a) stated, "A true score is a hypothetical value that represents a person's score when the entire domain of items is assessed at all possible times, by all appropriate testers" (p. 369). The following basic formula should be remembered when interpreting scores:

$$\text{Obtained score} = \text{True score} + \text{Error}$$

Conversely,

$$\text{Obtained score} - \text{True score} = \text{Error}$$

True score is never actually known; therefore, a range of possible scores is calculated. The error is called the standard error of measurement, and an instrument with a large standard error of measurement would be less desirable than an instrument with a small standard error of measurement.

To estimate the amount of error present in an individual obtained score, the standard error of measurement must be obtained and applied to each score. The standard deviation and the reliability coefficient of the instrument are used to calculate the standard error of measurement. The following formula will enable the educator to determine the standard error of measurement when it has not been provided by the test developer in the test manual.

$$SEM = SD \sqrt{1-r}$$

where *SEM* = the standard error of measurement

SD = the standard deviation of the norm group of scores obtained during development of the instrument

r = the reliability coefficient

Figure 4.5 uses this formula to calculate the standard error of measurement for an instrument with a given standard deviation of 3 and a reliability coefficient of 0.78. The manual for this test would probably report the *SEM* as 1.4. Knowing the *SEM* allows the teacher to calculate a range of scores for a particular student, thus providing a better estimate of the student's true ability. Using the *SEM* of 1.4, the teacher adds and subtracts 1.4 to/from the obtained score. If the obtained score is 9 (mean = 10), the teacher adds and subtracts the *SEM* to the obtained score of 9:

$$9+1.4 = 10.4$$

$$9-1.4 = 7.6$$

The range of possible true scores for this student is 7.6 to 10.4.

CHECK YOUR UNDERSTANDING

Check your ability to interpret the data presented in Table 4.1 by answering the questions in Activity 4.4.

TABLE 4.1

Split-Half Reliability Coefficients, by Age, for Subtest, Area, and Total-Test Raw Scores from the Fall and Spring Standardization Programs

Subtest/Composite	Program (Fall/Spring)	Age					
		5	6	7	8	9	10
1. Numeration	F	.73	.82	.85	.90	.81	.85
	S	.51	.82	.89	.88	.89	.81
2. Rational Numbers	F	—	.24	.71	.68	.88	.89
	S	—	.27	.42	.86	.82	.86
3. Geometry	F	.63	.81	.79	.77	.82	.80
	S	.80	.81	.76	.77	.80	.75
4. Addition	F	.63	.65	.79	.84	.78	.40
	S	.58	.78	.84	.82	.84	.66
5. Subtraction	F	.25	.68	.64	.85	.89	.86
	S	.30	.70	.85	.90	.92	.85
6. Multiplication	F	.23	.41	.11	.76	.89	.90
	S	.07	.67	.68	.91	.93	.89
7. Division	F	.55	.49	.52	.51	.82	.86
	S	.18	.34	.53	.77	.80	.84
8. Mental Computation	F	—	.78	.68	.80	.85	.88
	S	—	.65	.67	.78	.78	.90
9. Measurement	F	.77	.89	.57	.77	.76	.77
	S	.92	.84	.85	.87	.84	.70
10. Time and Money	F	.50	.61	.73	.89	.87	.93
	S	.38	.70	.84	.89	.92	.86
11. Estimation	F	.44	.43	.50	.74	.86	.72
	S	.59	.50	.53	.85	.76	.84
12. Interpreting Data	F	.41	.86	.81	.80	.88	.85
	S	.32	.79	.83	.85	.88	.87
13. Problem Solving	F	.36	.60	.73	.71	.82	.86
	S	.55	.60	.77	.76	.87	.92
Basic Concepts Area[a]	F	.78	.87	.89	.91	.92	.93
	S	.82	.88	.87	.92	.92	.92
Operations Area[a]	F	.66	.86	.87	.93	.96	.96
	S	.73	.88	.92	.96	.96	.96

Subtest/Composite	Program (Fall/Spring)	Age					
		5	6	7	8	9	10
Applications Area[a]	F	.82	.91	.89	.94	.96	.96
	S	.88	.90	.93	.96	.96	.96
TOTAL TEST[a]	F	.90	.95	.95	.97	.98	.98
	S	.92	.95	.97	.98	.98	.98

Source: KeyMath Revised: A diagnostic inventory of essential mathematics. Copyright © 1990, 1993, 1998 NCS Pearson, Inc. Reproduced with permission. All rights reserved.

[a]Reliability coefficients for the areas and the total test were computed by using Guilford's (1954, p. 393) formula for estimating the reliability of composite scores.

FIGURE 4.5
Calculating the Standard Error of Measurement (*SEM*) for an Instrument with a Standard Deviation of 3

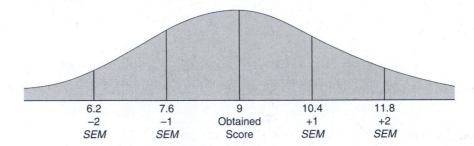

$SEM = 3\sqrt{1 - .78}$

$SEM = 3\sqrt{.22}$

$SEM = 3 \times .4690415$

$SEM = 1.4071245$

CHECK YOUR UNDERSTANDING

Check your accuracy in calculating standard error of measurement by completing Activity 4.5.

Thought to represent a range of deviations from an individual's obtained score, the standard error of measurement is based on normal distribution theory. In other words, by using the standard error of measurement, one can determine the typical deviation for an individual's obtained score as if that person had been administered the same test an infinite number of times. When plotted, the scores form a bell curve, or a normal distribution, with the obtained score representing the mean, median, and mode. As with normal distributions, the range of ±1 standard error of measurement of the obtained score will occur approximately 68% of the times that the student takes the test. This is known as a confidence interval because the score obtained within that range can be thought to represent the true score with 68% accuracy. In the previous example, for instance, the student would score between 7.6 and 10.4 about 68% of the time.

If the teacher wanted 95% confidence that the true score was contained within a range, the band would be extended to ±2 standard errors of measurement of the obtained score. For the example, the extended range would be 6.2 to 11.8. The teacher can assume, with 95% confidence, that the student's true score is within this range.

As seen in Activity 4.5, a test with better reliability will have less error. The best tests for educational use are those with high reliability and a smaller standard error of measurement.

Applying Standard Error of Measurement. Williams and Zimmerman (1984) stated that whereas test validity remains the most important consideration in test selection, using the standard error of measurement to judge the test's quality is more important than reliability. Williams and Zimmerman pointed out that reliability is a group statistic easily influenced by the variability of the group on which it was calculated.

Sabers, Feldt, and Reschly (1988) observed that some, perhaps many, testing practitioners fail to consider possible test error when interpreting the test results of a student being evaluated for special education services. The range of error and the range of a student's score may vary substantially, which may change the interpretation of the score for placement purposes.

In addition to knowing the standard error of measurement for an assessment instrument, it is important to know that the standard error of measurement will actually vary by age or grade level and by subtests. A test may contain less error for certain age or grade groupings than for other groupings. This information will be provided in the technical section of a good test manual.

Table 4.2 is from the *KeyMath—Revised* (Connolly, 1988) technical data section of the examiner's manual. The standard errors of measurement for the individual subtests are low and fairly consistent. There are some differences, however, in the standard errors of measurement on some subtests at different levels.

Consider the standard error of measurement for the subtest on mathematical division at ages 7 and 12 in the spring (S row). The standard error of measurement for age 7 is 2.0, but for age 12 it is 1.0. The larger standard error of measurement reported for age 7 is probably due to variation in the performance of students who may or may not have been introduced to division as part of the school curriculum. Most 12-year-olds, on the other hand, have probably practiced division in class for several years, and the sample of students tested may have performed with more consistency during the test development.

Given the two standard errors of measurement for the subtest on mathematical division at these ages, if a 7-year-old obtained a scaled score (a type of standard score) of 9 on this test ($x = 10$), the examiner could determine with 68% confidence that the true score lies between 7 and 11 and with 95% confidence that the true score lies between 5 and 13. The same scaled score obtained by a 12-year-old would range between 8 and 10 for a 68% confidence interval and between 7 and 11 for 95% confidence. This smaller range of scores is due to less error at this age on this particular subtest.

Consideration of *SEM*s when interpreting scores for students who are referred for a special education evaluation is even more important because a student's scores on various assessments are often compared with each other to determine if significant weaknesses exist. Standard 2.3 of the American Psychological Association's *Standards for Educational and Psychological Testing* addresses the importance of considering *SEM*s when comparing scores:

> When test interpretation emphasizes differences between two observed scores of an individual or two averages of a group, reliability data, including standard errors, should be provided for such differences. (1999, p. 32)

TABLE 4.2

Standard Errors of Measurement, by Age, for Scaled Scores and Standard Scores from the Fall and Spring Standardization Programs

Subtest/Composite	Program (Fall/Spring)	Age							
		5	6	7	8	9	10	11	12
1. Numeration	F	1.3	1.2	1.0	1.0	1.1	1.1	1.2	1.1
	S	1.7	1.1	1.0	1.0	1.0	1.2	1.1	1.0
2. Rational Numbers	F	—	—	—	—	1.2	1.0	1.0	1.0
	S	—	—	—	1.1	1.3	1.1	1.0	0.8
3. Geometry	F	1.5	1.3	1.4	1.4	1.2	1.2	1.3	1.1
	S	1.2	1.2	1.3	1.3	1.4	1.3	1.3	1.1

Subtest/Composite	Program (Fall/Spring)	Age							
		5	6	7	8	9	10	11	12
Addition	F	1.6	1.4	1.4	1.3	1.4	1.7	1.5	1.3
	S	1.8	1.4	1.3	1.4	1.4	1.5	1.3	1.3
4. Subtraction	F	—	1.6	1.5	1.3	1.1	1.1	1.5	1.3
	S	—	1.5	1.3	1.3	1.0	1.1	1.0	1.1
5. Multiplication	F	—	—	—	1.4	1.2	0.9	1.2	1.4
	S	—	—	—	1.0	1.1	1.2	1.1	1.1
6. Division	F	—	—	1.8	1.9	1.6	1.1	1.2	1.0
	S	—	—	2.0	1.6	1.4	1.2	1.1	1.0
7. Mental Computation	F	—	—	—	1.4	1.2	1.1	1.2	1.0
	S	—	—	1.7	1.3	1.2	1.1	1.1	0.9
8. Measurement	F	1.3	1.1	1.5	1.3	1.3	1.2	1.1	1.1
	S	1.2	1.1	1.2	1.1	1.1	1.3	1.1	0.9
9. Time and Money	F	—	1.6	1.3	1.1	1.0	1.0	1.0	1.0
	S	—	1.5	1.2	1.0	0.9	1.0	0.9	0.9
10. Estimation	F	—	1.7	1.8	1.4	1.3	1.3	1.2	1.0
	S	—	1.7	1.7	1.3	1.3	1.2	1.2	1.0
11. Interpreting Data	F	—	—	1.4	1.3	1.1	1.1	1.1	1.1
	S	—	—	1.3	1.2	1.1	1.1	1.1	1.0
12. Problem Solving	F	—	—	1.8	1.6	1.3	1.1	1.2	0.9
	S	—	—	1.6	1.4	1.2	1.1	1.1	0.9
13. Basic Concepts Area	F	5.8	5.3	4.8	4.7	4.0	3.7	3.9	3.3
	S	5.5	4.8	4.8	4.0	4.2	3.9	3.7	3.0
14. Operations Area	F	7.7	5.0	4.8	4.0	3.5	3.0	3.7	3.1
	S	7.1	5.0	4.3	3.5	3.2	3.3	2.9	2.7
15. Applications Area	F	5.8	4.1	4.3	3.6	3.1	2.8	3.0	2.6
	S	5.3	4.4	3.9	3.0	2.9	2.9	2.7	2.3
TOTAL TEST	F	4.1	3.0	2.9	2.5	2.2	1.9	2.2	1.8
	S	3.8	3.0	2.7	2.1	2.1	2.0	1.8	1.6

Source: KeyMath Revised: A diagnostic inventory of essential mathematics. Copyright © 1990, 1993, 1998 NCS Pearson, Inc. Reproduced with permission. All rights reserved.

This is important because the differences found for one individual on two different measures may not be significant differences when the *SEMs* are applied. For example, historically students have been found eligible for special education services for specific learning disabilities because there were significant differences between an obtained IQ score and an academic achievement score. Look at the example below for Leonardo:

IQ score: 103

Reading Achievement Score: 88

FIGURE 4.6 Comparison of Obtained and True Scores

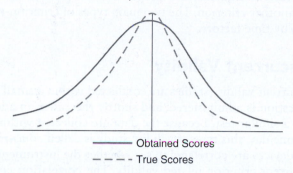

— Obtained Scores
--- True Scores

The difference between these two scores is 15. In some school systems, the difference of 15 points may be considered significant and Leonardo could be found eligible for services for a learning disability. However, look at the range of scores when the *SEM*s are applied:

IQ score: 103; *SEM* 3 Range of Scores: 100–106

Reading achievement score: 88; *SEM* 7 Range of Scores: 81–95

In this example, basing a decision on the performance of this student on these two tests cannot be conclusive because the differences, when considering the range of scores, may not be significant. The student's true scores may actually be 100 on the IQ test and 95 on the reading achievement test, or a difference of only 5 points. This would indicate additional data would be needed to determine if the student required special education support. In practice, however, *SEM*s may not be considered when making decisions for eligibility. When the *SEM*s are not considered, the student may not receive accurate evaluation.

Estimated true scores is another method to examine possible error and the relationship of error to the student's actual score. As seen in Figure 4.6, the estimated true score distribution is closer to the mean than the normal distribution. You can learn more about this method by visiting the Read More About page.

CHECK YOUR UNDERSTANDING

Check your ability to use an *SEM* table to interpret test performance by completing Activity 4.6.

● TEST VALIDITY

To review, *reliability* refers to the dependability of the assessment instrument. The questions of concern for reliability are: (a) Will students obtain similar scores if given the test a second time? (b) If the test is halved, will the administration of each half result in similar scores for the same student? (c) If different forms are available, will the administration of each form yield similar scores for the same student? (d) Will the administration of each item reliably measure the same trait or skill for the same student?

Validity is concerned not with repeated dependable results, but rather with the degree of good results for the purpose of the test. In other words, does the test actually measure what it is supposed to measure? If the educator wants to assess multiplication skills, will the test provide the educator with a valid indication of the student's math ability? Several methods can be used to determine the degree to which the instrument measures what the test developers intended the test to measure. Some methods are better than others, and some of the methods are more easily understood. When selecting assessment instruments, the educator should carefully consider the information on validity.

Criterion-Related Validity

Criterion-related validity refers to a method used for determining the validity of an instrument by comparing its scores with other criteria known to be indicators of the same trait or skill that the test developer wishes to measure. The test is compared with another criterion. The two main types of criterion-related validity are differentiated by time factors.

Concurrent Validity

Concurrent validity studies are conducted within a small time frame. The instrument in question is administered, and shortly thereafter an additional device is used, typically a similar test. Because the data are collected within a short time period, often the same day, this type of validity study is called *concurrent validity*. The data from both devices are correlated to see whether the instrument in question has significant concurrent criterion-related validity. The correlation coefficient obtained is called the *validity coefficient*. As with reliability coefficients, the nearer the coefficient is to ±1.00, the greater the strength of the relationship. Therefore, when students in the sample obtain similar scores on both instruments, the instrument in question is said to be measuring the same trait or a degree or component of the same trait with some accuracy.

Suppose the newly developed *Best in the World Math Test* was administered to a sample of students, and shortly thereafter the *Good Old Terrific Math Test* was administered to the same sample. The validity coefficient obtained was 0.83. The educator selecting the *Best in the World Math Test* would have some confidence that it would measure, to some degree, the same traits or skills measured by the *Good Old Terrific Math Test*. Such studies are helpful in determining whether new tests and revised tests are measuring with some degree of accuracy the same skills as those measured by older, more researched instruments. Studies may compare other criteria as well, such as teacher ratings or motor performance of a like task. As expected, when comparing unlike instruments or criteria, these would probably not correlate highly. A test measuring creativity would probably not have a high validity coefficient with an advanced algebra test, but the algebra test would probably correlate better with a test measuring advanced trigonometry.

Predictive Validity

Predictive validity is a measure of a specific instrument's ability to predict performance on some other measure or criterion at a later date.

Common examples of tests that predict a student's ability are a screening test to predict success in first grade, the *Scholastic Aptitude Test* (SAT) to predict success in college, the *Graduate Record Exam* (GRE) to predict success in graduate school, and an academic potential or academic aptitude test to predict success in school. Much psychoeducational assessment conducted in schools uses test results to predict future success or failure in a particular educational setting. Therefore, when this type of testing is carried out, it is important that the educator selects an instrument with good predictive validity research. Using a test to predict which students should enroll in a basic math class and which should enroll in an advanced algebra course will not be in the students' best interests if the predictive validity of the instrument is poor.

Content Validity

Professionals may assume that instruments reflecting a particular content in the name of the test or subtest have content validity. In many cases, this is not true. For example, on the *Wide Range Achievement Test—Revision 3* (Wilkinson, 1993), the subtest on reading does not actually measure reading ability. It measures only one aspect of reading: word recognition. A teacher might use the score obtained on the subtest to place a student, believing that the student will be able to comprehend reading material at a particular level. In fact, the student may be able to recognize only a few words from that reading level. This subtest has inadequate content validity for measuring overall reading ability.

For a test to have good content validity, it must contain the content in a representative fashion. For example, a math achievement test that has only 10 addition and subtraction problems and no other math operations has not adequately represented the content of the domain of math. A good representation of content will include several items from each domain, level, and skill being measured.

Some of the variables of content validity may influence the manner in which results are obtained and can contribute to bias in testing. These variables may conflict with the nondiscriminatory test practice regulations of Individuals with Disabilities Education Act (IDEA) and the *Standards for Educational and Psychological Testing* (1999) These variables include presentation format and response mode:

1. *Presentation format.* Are the items presented in the best manner to assess the skill or trait? Requiring a student to silently read math problems and supply a verbal response could result in test bias if the student is unable to read at the level presented. The content being assessed may be math applications or reasoning, but the reading required to complete the task has reduced the instrument's ability to assess math skills for this particular student. Therefore, the content validity has been threatened, and the results obtained may unduly discriminate against the student.

2. *Response mode.* Like presentation format, the response mode may interfere with the test's ability to assess skills that are unrelated to the response mode. If the test was designed to assess reading ability but required the student to respond in writing, the test would discriminate against a student who had a motor impairment that made writing difficult or impossible. Unless the response mode is adapted, the targeted skill—reading ability—will not be fairly or adequately measured.

Content validity is a primary concern in the development of new instruments. The test developers may adjust, omit, or add items during the field-testing stage. These changes are incorporated into a developmental version of the test that is administered to samples of students.

Construct Validity

Establishing construct validity for a new instrument may be more difficult than establishing content validity. *Construct*, in psychoeducational assessment, is a term used to describe a psychological trait, personality trait, psychological concept, attribute, or theoretical characteristic. To establish construct validity, the construct must be clearly defined. Constructs are usually abstract concepts, such as intelligence and creativity, which can be observed and measured by some type of instrument. Construct validity may be more difficult to measure than content because psychological constructs are hypothetical and may even seem invisible. Creativity is not seen, but the products of that trait may be observed, such as in writing or painting.

In establishing the construct validity of an instrument, the validity study may involve another measure that has been researched previously and has been shown to be a good indicator of the construct or of some degree or component of the construct. This is, of course, comparing the instrument to some other criterion, which is criterion-related validity. (Don't get confused!) Often in test development, validity studies may involve several types of criterion-related validity to establish different

TABLE 4.3

The *Gray Oral Reading Tests*: Applying Construct Validity to a Reading Instrument

1. Because reading ability is known to be related to age, the GORT–5 Oral Reading Index should be strongly correlated to chronological age and grade level, at least up through the age at which students receive formal instruction specific to reading.
2. Because the GORT–5 subtests measure various aspects of oral reading ability, they should correlate with each other.
3. Because reading ability is known to be an important cognitive ability, the GORT–5 should correlate strongly with tests of intelligence.
4. Because the GORT–5 measures reading ability, its results should correlate strongly with school achievement.
5. Because the GORT–5 measures reading ability, its results should differentiate between groups known to be average in reading and those known to be poor in reading.

Source: From *Gray Oral Reading Tests–5: Examiner's Manual.* By J. L. Wiederholt & B. R. Bryant, 2012. Copyright: Pro–Ed., Austin, Texas. Reprinted with permission.

types of validity. Anastasi (1988) listed the following types of studies that are considered when establishing a test's construct validity:

1. *Developmental changes.* Instruments that measure traits that are expected to change with development should have these changes reflected in the scores if the changeable trait is being measured (e.g., academic achievement).

2. *Correlations with other tests.* New tests are compared with existing instruments that have been found valid for the construct being measured.

3. *Factor analysis.* This statistical method determines how much particular test items cluster, which illustrates measurement of like constructs.

4. *Internal consistency.* Statistical methods can determine the degree with which individual items appear to be measuring the same constructs in the same manner or direction.

5. *Convergent and discriminant validation.* Tests should correlate highly with other instruments measuring the same construct but should not correlate with instruments measuring very different constructs.

6. *Experimental interventions.* Tests designed to measure traits, skills, or constructs that can be influenced by interventions (e.g., teaching) should have the intervention reflected by changes in pretest and posttest scores. (pp. 153–159)

The Gray Oral Reading Tests (GORT) includes an example of the application of construct validity. This is an example that one would use in reviewing the psychometric qualities of an instrument. Table 4.3 illustrates how construct validity is applied.

Validity of Tests versus Validity of Test Use

Professionals in special education and in the judicial system have understood for quite some time that test validity and validity of test use for a particular instrument are two separate issues (Cole, 1981). Tests may be used inappropriately even though they are valid instruments (Cole, 1981). The results obtained in testing may also be used in an invalid manner by placing children inappropriately or by inaccurately predicting educational futures (Heller, Holtzman, & Messick, 1982). For example, an instrument that is valid for assessing reading skills for the general population may not have been validated for use by students with English-learning needs. This means that the reading scores obtained for a student who is an English-language learner may not be representative of this particular student's reading skills. This would not be considered a valid test for this specific student.

When selecting instruments used for assessing a student with exceptional needs, the student's area of disability can make a difference in which tests would be considered valid. If a student has a visual acuity disability, instruments that have a larger font and have been validated for use with individuals with visual impairments would be considered valid based on the level of visual impairment. Other measures, perhaps validated for individuals with visual impairments when administered orally, might be appropriate or a better choice than an instrument with enlarged font. For some students, use of informal curriculum assessments may be more valid for determining academic skill level than standardized norm-referenced tests. These informal measures are presented in Chapter 6.

Some validity-related issues contribute to bias in the assessment process and subsequently to the invalid use of test instruments. Content, even though it may validly represent the domain of skills or traits being assessed, may discriminate against different groups. *Item bias*, a term used when an item is answered incorrectly a disproportionate number of times by one group compared to another group, may exist even though the test appears to represent the content domain. An examiner who continues to use an instrument found to contain bias may be practicing discriminatory assessment, which is failure to comply with IDEA.

Predictive validity may contribute to test bias by predicting accurately for one group and not another. Educators should select and administer instruments only after careful study of the reliability and validity research contained in test manuals. This will assist in the determination of the validity of use of instruments for specific students.

Reliability and Validity Issues of Text Accommodations and Alternative Assessments

As part of the 2001 Elementary and Secondary Education Act and subsequent reauthorizations, schools are required to assess all students for the purpose of educational accountability. These assessments are designed to ensure that students are making adequate progress toward educational standards to meet their grade-level expectations, and all students are required to demonstrate learning on these state-level assessments. These assessment techniques are presented in greater depth in Chapter 5 but the reliability and validity of adapting these instruments is considered here.

For students with significant, exceptional learning needs, the state assessments may be modified for format, time limits, and mode of presentation, without modifying the actual content of the items. These students are expected to demonstrate learning to meet grade-level standards; however; students may be allowed to have accommodations for the administration of the assessment. In addition, students with significant cognitive impairments may be expected to meet alternative standards, rather than general education grade-level standards, and these alternative standards are assessed using alternative assessments.

In order to make certain that students with exceptional learning needs are being instructed and evaluated consistent with the ESEA regulations, educators must administer accountability assessments as designed unless specific modifications are included in the student's IEP. Students who are determined to require accommodations take the exams with specific provisions included in their IEPs. Administration of the exam with accommodations may call to question the reliability and validity

CHECK YOUR UNDERSTANDING

Check your understanding of the concepts of reliability and validity as they apply to research data on a specific achievement test by completing Activity 4.7.

of the administration and the obtained results. Emerging research has found mixed results when applying accommodations for students with and without exceptional learning needs (Finch, Barton, & Meyer, 2009). In other words, accommodations would be expected to provide the opportunity for students with learning difficulties to demonstrate their knowledge without obstacles (e.g., time demands or complex written instructions of the assessment) and therefore be on equal footing with students who do not have learning difficulties. For this reason, Universal Design for learning, or universal accessibility, is also being applied to assessments so that most students will be able to demonstrate their own skills and knowledge on statewide exams.

Alternative assessments, based on alternative standards, may present issues with reliability and validity as well. As these assessments are designed, educators must make certain that these measures are valid in assessing what they are intended to assess: the student's knowledge of content to meet the alternative standards. It is also important that the measures are reliable so that a student who is assessed would be able to demonstrate his or her knowledge on the instrument regardless of who is administering the test. The items on the assessment must also reliably assess representative content included in the alternative standards. Assessment items should be carefully adapted using best practice models reflecting current theory and expectations (Beddow, 2012; Kettler, Elliot, & Beddow, 2009). The classroom teachers provide the assistance to the team when making determinations about appropriate modifications and accommodations. As you watch this video, you will hear how teachers adapt or modify standardized tests for students with exceptional learning needs.

● RELIABILITY VERSUS VALIDITY

A test may be reliable; that is, it may measure a trait with about the same degree of accuracy time after time. However, reliability does not guarantee that the trait is measured in a valid or accurate manner. A test may be consistent and reliable, but not valid. An instrument may consistently result in a score that is not representative of grade-level content or it may not be valid for use with individuals with certain types of disabilities. It is important that a test has received thorough research studies in *both* reliability and validity. It is also important to determine that the specific instrument selected is a valid instrument for the individual student by reviewing the test manual and determining that the instrument is appropriate.

CHAPTER SUMMARY

In this chapter you:

- Learned the types of reliability and validity
- Applied reliability and validity concepts to data
- Analyzed the benefits of reliability and validity for specific types of assessment
- Synthesized the meaning of reliability and validity research in assessment
- Evaluated instruments based on their reliability and validity data

THINK AHEAD

The concepts presented in this chapter will be applied in the remaining chapters of the text. How do you think these concepts help professionals evaluate instruments?

CHAPTER QUIZ

Now complete the Chapter Quiz to measure your understanding of the content in this chapter.

5 An Introduction to Norm-Referenced Assessment

CHAPTER FOCUS

In this chapter you will:

- Learn how norm-referenced assessments are constructed and basic steps in test administration

- Learn about high-stakes assessment

- Apply basic steps in test administraton

- Analyze the benefits of norm-referenced assessments

- Synthesize the meaning of norm-referenced individual and high-stakes assessment

- Evaluate issues in norm-referenced and high-stakes assessment

● HOW NORM-REFERENCED TESTS ARE CONSTRUCTED

Test developers who wish to develop an instrument to assess an educational domain, behavioral trait, cognitive ability, motor ability, or language ability, to name a few areas, will establish an item pool of test items. An item pool is a representation of items believed to thoroughly assess the given area. The items are gathered from several sources. For example, developers may use published educational materials, information from educational experts in the field, published curriculum guides, and information from educational research to collect items for the initial item pool for an educational domain. These items are carefully scrutinized for appropriateness, wording, content, mode of response required, and developmental level. The items are sequentially arranged according to difficulty. The developers consult with professionals with expertise in the test's content area and, after thorough analysis of the items, administer a developmental version to a small group as a field test. During the field-testing stage, the test is administered by professionals in the appropriate discipline (education, psychology, speech–language, etc.). The professionals involved in the study critique the test items, presentation format, response mode requirements, administration procedures, and the actual test materials. At this time, revisions may be made, and the developmental version is then ready to be administered to a large sample of the population for whom it was designed. The steps of test construction are illustrated in Figure 5.1.

Norm-referenced tests allow teachers to compare the performance of one student with the average performance of other students in the country who are of the same age or grade level. Because it is not practical or possible to test every student of that same age or grade level, a sample of students is selected as the comparison group, or norm group. In the norming process, the test is administered to a representative sample of students from across the country. A good representation will include a large number of students, usually a few thousand, who represent diverse groups. Ideally, samples of students from all cultures and linguistic backgrounds who represent the diverse students for whom the test was developed are included in the norming process. The norming process should also include students with various disabilities.

FIGURE 5.1 Steps in Test Development

1. Domain, theoretical basis of test defined. This includes support for construct as well as defining what the domain is not.
2. Exploration of item pool. Experts in the field and other sources of possible items are used to begin collecting items.
3. Developmental version of test or subtests.
4. Field-based research using developmental version of test or subtests.
5. Research on developmental versions analyzed.
6. Changes made to developmental versions based on results of analyses.
7. Standardization version prepared.
8. Sampling procedures to establish how and where persons in sample will be recruited.
9. Testing coordinators located at relevant testing sites representing preferred norm sample.
10. Standardization research begins. Tests are administered at testing sites.
11. Data collected and returned to test developer.
12. Data analyzed for establishing norms, reliability, validity.
13. Test prepared for final version, packaging, protocols, manual.
14. Test available for purchase.

TABLE 5.1			
Analysis of Results from the *Absolutely Wonderful Academic Achievement Test*			
Grade	Average Number of Items Correct	Age	Average Number of Items Correct
K	11	5	9
1	14	6	13
2	20	7	21
3	28	8	27
4	38	9	40
5	51	10	49
6	65	11	65
7	78	12	79
8	87	13	88
9	98	14	97
10	112	15	111
11	129	16	130
12	135	17	137

The development of a norm-referenced test and the establishment of comparison performances usually occur in the following manner. The items of the test, which are sequentially arranged in the order of difficulty, are administered to the sample population. The performance of each age group and each grade group is analyzed. The average performance of the 6-year-olds, 7-year-olds, 8-year-olds, and so on is determined. The test results are analyzed by grade groups as well, determining the average performance of students by grade level. The analysis of test results might resemble Table 5.1.

The average number correct in Table 5.1 represents the arithmetic average number of items successfully answered by the age or grade group of students in the norm sample. Because these figures will later be used to compare other students' performances on the same instrument, it is imperative that the sample of students be representative of the students who will later be assessed. Factors such as background (socioeconomic, cultural, and linguistic), existing disabilities, and emotional environment are variables that can influence a student's performance. The student being assessed should be compared with other students with similar backgrounds and of the same age or grade level.

Although the data in Table 5.1 represent an average score for each age or grade group, test developers often analyze the data further. For example, the average performance of typical students at various times throughout the school year may be determined. To provide this information, the most accurate norming process would include nine additional administrations of the test, one for each month of the school year. This is not practical or possible. Therefore, to obtain an average expected score for each month of the school year, the test developer usually calculates the scores using data obtained in the original administration through a process known as interpolation, or further dividing the existing data (Anastasi & Urbina, 1998).

Suppose that the test developer of the *Absolutely Wonderful Academic Achievement Test* actually administered the test to the sample group during the middle of

TABLE 5.2

Interpolated Grade Equivalents for Corresponding Raw Scores	
Number of Items Correct	Grade
17	2.0
17	2.1
18	2.2
18	2.3
19	2.4
20	2.5
20	2.6
21	2.7
22	2.8
23	2.9
24	3.0
25	3.1
26	3.2
27	3.3
27	3.4
28	3.5
29	3.6
30	3.7
31	3.8
32	3.9
33	4.0
34	4.1
35	4.2
36	4.3
37	4.4
38	4.5
39	4.6
40	4.7
42	4.8
43	4.9

the school year. To determine the average performance of students throughout the school year, the test developer further divides the correct items of each group. In the data in Table 5.1, the average performance of second graders in the sample group is 20, the average performance of third graders is 28, and the average performance of fourth graders is 38. These scores might be further divided and listed in the test manual on a table similar to Table 5.2.

TABLE 5.3

Interpolated Age Equivalents for Corresponding Raw Scores	
Average Number of Items Correct	Age Equivalents
57	11–0
58	11–1
60	11–2
61	11–3
62	11–4
63	11–5
65	11–6
66	11–7
68	11–8
69	11–9
70	11–10
71	11–11
72	12–0

The obtained scores might also be further divided by age groups so that each month of a chronological age is represented. The scores for age 11 might be displayed in a table similar to Table 5.3.

It is important to notice that age scores are written with a dash or hyphen, whereas grade scores are expressed with a decimal. This is because grade scores are based on a 10-month school year and can be expressed by using decimals, whereas age scores are based on a 12-month calendar year and therefore should not be expressed using decimals. For example, 11–4 represents an age of 11 years and 4 months, but 11.4 represents the grade score of the fourth month of the 11th grade. If the scores are expressed incorrectly, a difference of about 6 grades, or 5 years, could be incorrectly interpreted.

● BASIC STEPS IN TEST ADMINISTRATION

Each norm-referenced standardized test has specified directions for the examiner and the examinee. The test manual contains information that the examiner must understand thoroughly before administering the test. The examiner should practice administering all sections of the test several times before using the test with a student. The first few attempts of practice administration should be supervised by someone who has had experience with the instrument. Legally, according to the Individuals with Disabilities Education Act (IDEA), any individual test administration should be completed in the manner set forth by the test developer and should be administered by trained personnel. Both legal regulations and standards and codes of ethics hold testing personnel responsible for accurate and fair assessment.

The examiner should carefully carry out the mechanics of test administration. Although the first few steps are simple, examiners can make careless errors that can result in flawed decisions regarding a student's educational future. The protocol of a standardized test is the form used during the test administration and for scoring and interpreting test results.

Beginning Testing

The following suggestions will help the examiner establish a positive testing environment and increase the probability that the student being assessed will feel comfortable and therefore perform better in the testing situation.

1. Establish familiarity with the student before the first day of testing. Several meetings in different situations with relaxed verbal exchange are recommended. You may wish to participate in an activity with the student and informally observe behavior and language skills.

2. When the student meets with you on test day, spend several minutes in friendly conversation before beginning the test. Do not begin testing until the student seems to feel at ease with you.

3. Explain why the testing has been suggested at the level of understanding that is appropriate for the student's age and developmental level. The student should understand that the testing session is important, although she or he should not feel threatened by the test. Examples of explanations include the following:

   - To see how you work (solve) math problems
   - To see how we can help you achieve in school
   - To help you make better progress in school
   - (If the student has revealed specific weaknesses) To see how we can help you with your spelling (or English, or science, etc.) skills

4. Give a brief introduction to the test, such as: "Today we will complete some activities that are like your other school work. There are some math problems and reading passages like you have in class," or, "This will help us learn how you think in school," or "This will show us the best ways for you to … (learn, read, work math problems)."

5. Begin testing in a calm manner. Make certain that all directions are followed carefully.

During test administration, the student may ask questions or give answers that are very close to the correct response. On many tests, clear directions are given that tell the examiner when to prompt for an answer or when to query for a response. Some items on certain tests may not be repeated. Some items are timed. The best guarantee for accurate assessment techniques is for the examiner to become very familiar with the test manual. General guidelines for test administration, suggested by McLoughlin and Lewis (2001), are presented in Figure 5.2.

As stated in codes of professional ethics and IDEA, tests must be given in the manner set forth by the test developer. Any adaptations to tests must be made judiciously by professionals with expertise in the specific area being assessed who are cognizant of the psychometric changes that will result.

CHECK YOUR UNDERSTANDING

Check your ability to use developmental tables by completing Activity 5.1.

Calculating Chronological Age

Many tests have protocols that provide space for calculating the student's chronological age on the day that the test is administered. Chronological age is typically used to determine the correct norm tables used for interpreting test results.

The chronological age is calculated by writing the test date first and then subtracting the date of birth. The dates are written in the order of year,

FIGURE 5.2 General Guidelines for Test Administration

Test administration is a skill, and testers must learn how to react to typical student comments and questions. The following general guidelines apply to the majority of standardized tests.

STUDENT REQUESTS FOR REPETITION OF TEST ITEMS

Students often ask the tester to repeat a question. This is usually permissible as long as the item is repeated verbatim and in its entirety. However, repetition of memory items measuring the student's ability to recall information is not allowed.

ASKING STUDENTS TO REPEAT RESPONSES

Sometimes the tester must ask the student to repeat a response. Perhaps the tester did not hear what the student said, or the student's speech is difficult to understand. However, the tester should make every effort to see or hear the student's first answer. The student may refuse to repeat a response or, thinking that the request for repetition means the first response was unsatisfactory, answer differently.

STUDENT MODIFICATION OF RESPONSES

When students give one response, then change their minds and give a different one, the tester should accept the last response, even if the modification comes after the tester has moved to another item. However, some tests specify that only the first response may be accepted for scoring.

CONFIRMING AND CORRECTING STUDENT RESPONSES

The tester may not in any way—verbal or nonverbal—inform a student whether a response is correct. Correct responses may not be confirmed; wrong responses may not be corrected. This rule is critical for professionals who both teach and test, because their first inclination is to reinforce correct answers.

REINFORCING STUDENT WORK BEHAVIOR

Although testers cannot praise students for their performance on specific test items, good work behavior can and should be rewarded. Appropriate comments are "You're working hard" and "I like the way you're trying to answer every question." Students should be praised between test items or subtests to ensure that reinforcement is not linked to specific responses.

ENCOURAGING STUDENTS TO RESPOND

When students fail to respond to a test item, the tester can encourage them to give an answer. Students sometimes say nothing when presented with a difficult item, or they may comment, "I don't know" or "I can't do that one." The tester should repeat the item and say, "Give it a try" or "You can take a guess." The aim is to encourage the student to attempt all test items.

QUESTIONING STUDENTS

Questioning is permitted on many tests. If in the judgment of the tester the response given by the student is neither correct nor incorrect, the tester repeats the student's answer in a questioning tone and says, "Tell me more about that." This prompts the student to explain so that the response can be scored. However, clearly wrong answers should not be questioned.

COACHING

Coaching differs from encouragement and questioning in that it helps a student arrive at an answer. The tester must *never* coach the student. Coaching invalidates the student's response; test norms are based on the assumption that students will respond without examiner assistance. Testers must be very careful to avoid coaching.

FIGURE 5.2 Continued

> ### *ADMINISTRATION OF TIMED ITEMS*
>
> Some tests include timed items; the student must reply within a certain period to receive credit. In general, the time period begins when the tester finishes presentation of the item. A watch or clock should be used to time student performance.

Source: McLoughlin & Lewis, *Assessing Students with Special Needs,* "General guidelines for test administration." p. 87, © 2001 by Pearson Education, Inc. Reproduced by permission of Pearson Education, Inc.

month, and day. In performing the calculation, remember that each of the columns represents a different numerical system, and if the number that is subtracted is larger than the number from which the difference is to be found, the numbers must be converted appropriately. This means that the years are based on 12 months and the months are based on 30 days. An example is shown in Figure 5.3.

Notice in Figure 5.3 that, when subtracting the days, the number 30 is added to 2 to find the difference. When subtraction of days requires borrowing, a whole month, or 30 days, must be used. When borrowing to subtract months, the number 12 is added, because a whole year must be borrowed.

When determining the chronological age for testing, the days are rounded to the nearest month. Days are rounded up if there are 15 or more days by adding a month. The days are rounded down by dropping the days and using the month found through the subtraction process. Here are some examples.

	Years	Months	Days	
Chronological age:	7–	4–	17	rounded up to 7–5
Chronological age:	9–	10–	6	rounded down to 9–10
Chronological age:	11–	11–	15	rounded up to 12–0

FIGURE 5.3 Calculation of Chronological Age for a Student Who Is 7 Years, 10 Months, 27 Days Old

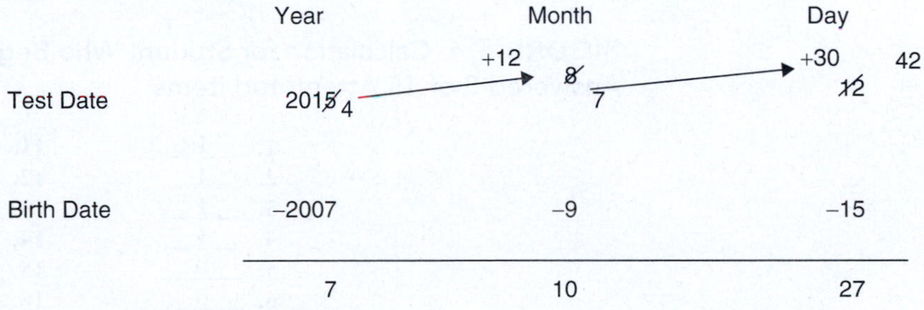

	Year	Month	Day
		+12 8	+30 42 ~~12~~
Test Date	~~2015~~ 4	7	
Birth Date	−2007	−9	−15
	7	10	27

Date of Birth: September 15, 2007

Date of Test: August 12, 2015

Case Study for Determining Chronological Age

Mrs. Luke believed that Sandra was excelling in her math work and needed to be placed in a higher-level class. Mrs. Luke decided to administer a norm-referenced math test to find out how Sandra's math skills compared to a national sample. Once she had administered and scored the test, she discovered that the results were lower than she had expected. Mrs. Luke was confused because she knew that Sandra performed better than her grade peers. Mrs. Luke took another look at the test protocol and discovered some errors in her calculations. Can you identify the errors?

Date of Test	2014	4	15
Date of Birth	2005	7	17
Chronological Age	9	9	28

The correct chronological age should be

8 years	8 months	28 days

The incorrect calculation meant that Mrs. Luke compared Sandra with students who were 9 years–10 months when she should have compared Sandra with 8-year-old students. This error resulted in standard scores that placed Sandra in the low-average range. When the error was corrected and Sandra was compared with the correct age group, her scores were within the high-average range.

Calculating Raw Scores

The first score obtained in the administration of a test is the raw score. On most educational instruments, the raw score is simply the number of items the student answers correctly. Figure 5.4 shows the calculation of a raw score for one student. The student's correct responses are marked with a 1, incorrect responses with a 0. The number of items answered correctly on this test was 8, which is expressed as a raw score. The raw score will be entered into a table in the test manual to determine the derived scores, which are norm-referenced scores expressed in different ways. The administration of this test was stopped when the student missed three consecutive items because the test manual stated to stop testing when this occurred.

Determining Basals and Ceilings

The student whose scores are shown in Figure 5.4 began with item 1 and stopped after making three consecutive errors. The starting and stopping points of a test must be determined so that unnecessary items are not administered. Some tests

CHECK YOUR UNDERSTANDING

Check your understanding of how to calculate chronological age by completing Activity 5.2.

FIGURE 5.4 Calculation for Student Who Began with Item 1 and Correctly Answered 8 of 15 Attempted Items

1.	1		11.	0
2.	1		12.	1
3.	1		13.	0
4.	1		14.	0
5.	0		15.	0
6.	0		16.	
7.	1		17.	
8.	1		18.	
9.	0		19.	
10.	1		20.	

Raw Score: ___8___

contain hundreds of items, many of which may not be developmentally appropriate for all students.

Most educational tests contain starting rules in the manual, protocol, or actual test instrument. These rules are guides that can help the examiner begin testing with an item at the appropriate level. These guides may be given as age recommendations—for example, 6-year-olds begin with item 10—or as grade-level recommendations—for example, fourth-grade students begin with item 25. These starting points are meant to represent a level at which the student could answer all previous items correctly and are most accurate for students who are functioning close to age or grade expectancy.

Often, students referred for special education testing function below grade- and age-level expectancies. Therefore, the guides or starting points suggested by the test developers may be inappropriate. It is necessary to determine the basal level for the student, or the level at which the student could correctly answer all easier items, those items located at lower levels. Once the basal has been established, the examiner can proceed with testing the student. If the student fails to obtain a basal level, the test may be considered too difficult, and another instrument should be selected.

The rules for establishing a basal level are given in test manuals, and many tests contain information on the protocol as well. The basal rule may be the same as a ceiling rule, such as three consecutively correct responses and three consecutively incorrect responses. The basal rule may also be expressed as correctly completing an entire level. No matter what the rule, the objective is the same: to establish a level that is thought to represent a foundation and at which all easier items would be assumed correct.

The examples shown in Figure 5.5 illustrate a basal rule of three consecutive correct responses on Test I and a basal of all items answered correctly on an entire level of the test on Test II.

It may be difficult to select the correct item to begin with when testing a special education student. The student's social ability may seem to be age appropriate, but her or his academic ability may be significantly below expectancy in terms of age and grade placement. The examiner might begin with an item that is too easy or too difficult. Although it is not desirable to administer too many items that are beneath the student's academic level, it is better to begin the testing session with the positive reinforcement of answering items correctly than with the negative reinforcement of answering several items incorrectly and experiencing a sense of failure or frustration. The examiner should obtain a basal by selecting an item believed to be a little below the student's academic level.

FIGURE 5.5 Basal Level Established for Test I for Three Consecutive Correct Responses; Basal Level for Test II Established When All Items in One Level (Grade 1) Are Answered Correctly

TEST I			TEST II		
1.	_____		*Level K*	1.	_____
2.	_____			2.	_____
3.	_____			3.	_____
4.	_____			4.	_____
5.	_____		*Grade 1*	5.	1
6.	1			6.	1
7.	1			7.	1
8.	1			8.	1
9.	0		*Grade 2*	9.	0
10.	1			10.	1
				11.	0
				12.	1

Even when the examiner chooses a starting item believed to be easy for a student, sometimes the student will miss items before the basal is established. In this case, most test manuals contain directions for determining the basal. Some manuals instruct the examiner to test backward in the same sequence until a basal can be established. After the basal is determined, the examiner proceeds from the point where the backward sequence was begun. Other test manuals instruct the examiner to drop back an entire grade level or to drop back the number of items required to establish a basal. For example, if five consecutive correct responses are required for a basal, the examiner is instructed to drop back five items and begin administration. If the examiner is not familiar with the student's ability in a certain area, the basal may be even more difficult to establish. The examiner in this case may have to drop back several times. For this reason, the examiner should circle the number of the first item administered. This information can be used later in interpreting test results.

Students may establish two or more basals; that is, using the five-consecutive-correct rule, a student may answer five correct, miss an item, then answer five consecutive correct again. The test manual may address this specifically, or it may not be mentioned. Unless the test manual states that the examiner may use the second or highest basal, it is best to use the first basal established.

When calculating the raw score, all items that appear before the established basal are counted as correct. This is because the basal is thought to represent the level at which all easier items would be passed. Therefore, when counting correct responses, count items below the basal as correct even though they were not administered.

Just as the basal is thought to represent the level at which all easier items would be passed, the ceiling is thought to represent the level at which more difficult items would not be passed. The ceiling rule may be three consecutive incorrect or even five items out of seven items answered incorrectly. Occasionally, an item is administered above the ceiling level by mistake, and the student may answer correctly. Because the ceiling level is thought to represent the level at which more difficult items would not be passed, these items usually are not counted. Unless the test manual states that the examiner is to count items above the ceiling, it is best not to do so.

Using Information on Protocols

The protocol, or response form, for each test contains valuable information that can aid in test administration. Detailed directions regarding the basal and ceiling rules for individual subtests of an educational test may be found on most protocols for educational tests.

Many tests have ceiling rules that are the same as the basal rules; for example, five consecutive incorrect responses are counted as the ceiling, and five consecutive correct responses establish the basal. Because some tests have different basal and ceiling rules, it is necessary to read directions carefully. If the protocol does not provide basal and ceiling rules, the examiner is wise to note this at the top of the pages of the protocol for the sections to be administered.

The protocols for each test are arranged specifically for that test. Some forms contain several subtests that may be arranged in more than one order. On very lengthy tests, the manual may provide information about selecting only certain subtests rather than administering the entire test. Other tests have age- or grade-appropriate subtests, which must be selected according to the student's level. Some instruments use the raw score on the first subtest to determine the starting point on all other subtests. And, finally, some subtests require the examiner to begin with item 1 regardless of the age or grade level of the student. Specific directions for individual subtests may be provided on the protocol as well as in the test manual.

Educational tests often provide training exercises at the beginning of subtests. These training exercises help the examiner explain the task to the student

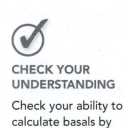

CHECK YOUR UNDERSTANDING

Check your ability to calculate basals by completing Activity 5.3.

and better ensure that the student understands the task before answering the first scored item. The student may be allowed to attempt the training tasks more than once, or the examiner may be instructed to correct wrong answers and explain the correct responses. These items are not scored, however, and a subtest may be skipped if the student does not understand the task. The use of training exercises varies.

Administering Tests: For Best Results

Students tend to respond more and perform better in testing situations with examiners who are familiar with them (Fuchs, Zern, & Fuchs, 1983). As suggested previously, the examiner should spend some time with the student before the actual evaluation. The student's regular classroom setting is a good place to begin. The examiner should talk with the student in a warm manner and repeat visits to the classroom before the evaluation. It may also be helpful for the student to visit the testing site to become familiar with the environment. The examiner may want to tell the student that they will work together later in the week or month. The testing session should not be the first time the examiner and student meet. Classroom observations and visits may aid the examiner in determining which tests to administer. Chances for successful testing sessions will increase if the student is not overtested. Although it is imperative that all areas of suspected disability be assessed, multiple tests that measure the same skill or ability are not necessary.

After the examiner and student are in the testing room, the examiner should attempt to make the student feel at ease. The examiner should convey the importance of the testing situation without making the student feel anxious. As suggested by McLoughlin and Lewis (2001), the examiner should encourage the student to work hard and should reinforce the student's attempts and efforts, not her or his correct responses. Responses that reinforce the efforts of the student may include statements such as "You are working so hard today," or "You like math work," or "I will be sure to tell your teacher [or mother or father, etc.] how hard you worked." If the student asks about performance on specific items ("Did I get that one right?"), the examiner should again try to reinforce effort.

Young students may enjoy a tangible reinforcer upon the completion of the testing session. The examiner may tell the student near the end of the session to work just a few more items for a treat or surprise. Reinforcement with tangibles is not recommended during the assessment because the student may lose interest in the test or no longer pay attention.

During the administration of the test, the examiner must be sure to follow all directions in the manual. As stated in professional standards and IDEA, tests must be given in the manner set forth by the test developer, and adapting tests must be done by professionals with expertise in the specific area being assessed who are cognizant of the psychometric changes that will result.

Cole, D'Alonzo, Gallegos, Giordano, and Stile (1992) suggested that examiners consider several additional factors to decrease bias in the assessment process. The following considerations, adapted from Cole et al. (1992), can help the examiner determine whether the test can be administered in a fair way:

1. Do sensory or communicative impairments make portions of the test inaccessible?

2. Do sensory or communicative impairments limit students from responding to questions?

3. Do test materials or method of responding limit students from responding?

4. Do background experiences limit the student's ability to respond?

5. Does the content of classroom instruction limit students from responding?

CHECK YOUR UNDERSTANDING

Check your ability to calculate basal and ceiling scores by completing Activity 5.4.

CHECK YOUR UNDERSTANDING

Check your ability to calculate a raw score by completing Activity 5.5.

6. Is the examiner familiar to the student?

7. Are instructions explained in a familiar fashion?

8. Is the recording technique required of the student on the test familiar? (p. 219)

Watch this video to observe the administration of a one-on-one norm-referenced assessment.

Obtaining Derived Scores

The raw scores obtained during test administration are used to locate other derived scores from norm tables included in the examiner's manuals for the specific test. Derived scores may include percentile ranks, grade equivalents, standard scores with a mean of 100 or 50, and other standardized scores, such as z scores.

There are advantages and disadvantages to using the different types of derived scores. Of particular concern is the correct use and interpretation of grade equivalents and percentile ranks. These two types of derived scores are used frequently because the basic theoretical concepts are thought to be understood; however, these two types of scores are misunderstood and misinterpreted by professionals (Huebner, 1988, 1989; Wilson, 1987). The reasons for this misinterpretation are the lack of understanding of the numerical scale used and the method used in establishing grade-level equivalents.

Percentile ranks are used often because they can be easily explained to parents. The concept, for example, of 75% of the peer group scoring at the same level or below a particular student is one that parents and professionals can understand. The difficulty in interpreting percentile ranks is that they do not represent a numerical scale with equal intervals. For example, the standard scores between the 50th and 60th percentiles are quite different from the standard scores between the 80th and 90th percentile ranks.

The development of grade equivalents needs to be considered when using these derived scores. Grade equivalents represent the average number of items answered correctly by the students in the standardization sample of a particular grade. These equivalents may not represent the actual skill level of particular items or of a particular student's performance on a test. Many of the skills tested on academic achievement tests are taught at various grade levels. The grade level of presentation of these skills depends on the curriculum used. The grade equivalents obtained therefore may not be representative of the skills necessary to pass that grade level in a specific curriculum.

● TYPES OF SCORES

The concepts of standard scores, percentile ranks, and age and grade equivalents were introduced in Chapter 3. To review briefly, standard scores and percentile ranks are scores used to compare an individual student with the larger norm group to determine relative standing in the areas assessed, such as mathematical skills or IQ. Standard scores include those scores with an average or mean of 100 as well as other scores such as T scores, which have an average of 50, or z scores, which convey the student's standing in terms of standard deviation units. Refer to Figure 3.9 to locate scores. For example, a z score of -1.0 indicates that the student is 1 standard deviation below average, and if this score is converted to a standard score with a mean of 100, the standard score of this student is 85. If the student's z score is converted to T scores, the student's T score is 40 (T score average is 50; SD of 10).

Other scores that may be used to compare the student's standing to the norm group are stanine scores. Stanine scores, like percentile ranks, are not equidistant. Stanines are based on a system of dividing the distribution into nine segments with an average or mean of 5 and a standard deviation of 2. This means that the previously presented student score of 85 and a z score of -1.0 would have a stanine score of 3. The data or student scores within the stanine sections represent large segments of ability and therefore do not convey very precise indications of a student's performance or ability.

● GROUP TESTING: HIGH-STAKES ASSESSMENT

The protocol examples and basal and ceiling exercises presented thus far in this chapter are typical of individually administered norm-referenced instruments. Other instruments commonly used in schools are norm-referenced standardized group achievement tests. These instruments are administered to classroom-size groups to assess achievement levels. Group achievement tests are increasingly used to assess the accountability of individual students and school systems as a result of federal regulations of the Elementary and Secondary Education Act (ESEA) and IDEA. These instruments are also known as *high-stakes tests* because their results often have serious implications of accountability, accreditation, and funding for school systems. States and districts use such instruments to be certain that students are meeting expected academic standards for their grade placement.

Principles to guide the assessment of students for accountability were proposed by Elliott, Braden, and White (2001), who suggested that school systems keep in mind that assessment should be logical and serve the purpose for which it is intended. Elliott and colleagues contended that systems should set their standards or goals before developing assessments. As with individual assessment, these authors argued, no single instrument has the capability of answering all achievement questions, and therefore multiple measures of student progress should be used. Finally, Elliott et al. declared, as with other educational instruments, that high-stakes assessments should be reliable and valid for their specific purpose.

The National Center on Educational Outcomes determined that there are core principles or concepts that should drive the accountability assessment in schools (Thurlow et al., 2008). These core principles are as follows:

> *Principle 1.* All students are included in ways that hold schools accountable for their learning.
>
> *Principle 2.* Assessments allow all students to show their knowledge and skills on the same challenging content.
>
> *Principle 3.* High-quality decision making determines how students participate.
>
> *Principle 4.* Public reporting includes the assessment results of all students.
>
> *Principle 5.* Accountability determinations are affected in the same way by all students.
>
> *Principle 6.* Continuous improvement, monitoring, and training ensure the quality of the overall system. (p. v)

These principles call on educational leaders in school districts to implement accountability assessment that is fair for all learners and to use the data that result from these assessments to make informed curriculum and instructional decisions.

The 1997 IDEA amendments require that students with disabilities be included in statewide and district-wide assessments. The regulations of 2007 further specify how students with disabilities should be included in statewide or district-wide assessments and how students with significant disabilities are to be determined for administration of modified instruments that meet modified standards (Federal Register, 2007). The regulations require educators to decide and include in the IEP process which students would take the general statewide assessments, which students would require accommodations for the statewide assessments, and which students would require modified assessment to meet modified standards.

This decision-making process was detailed in the 2007 regulations, and now the IEP team must determine that there is objective evidence indicating that the student with disabilities has not been able to meet the grade-level expectations in content assessed; that, with appropriate instruction and support, the student will not be able to meet the grade-level expectations even though there may be significant growth during the year of the IEP; and, if the student's IEP includes goals for a subject assessed, these goals must be based on the academic content standards for the grade in which the student is enrolled (Federal Register, 2007). As reviewed in Chapter 4, the modified or alternative instruments must be designed so that they are valid measures of the content or standard being assessed.

Students from culturally and linguistically diverse backgrounds who are considered to be English-language learners (limited English proficiency) may require accommodations to ensure that their academic skills and knowledge are being assessed rather than their English skills. As with assessment to determine eligibility for special education services, students must be assessed in specific areas of content or ability rather than for their English-reading or communication skills. If required, accommodations may be included for the student's language differences (Office of Special Education and Rehabilitative Services, 2000).

Watch this video to learn more about high-stakes testing.

Watch this video to learn more about norm-referenced standardized testing.

Accommodations in High-Stakes Testing

Students who participate in the general education curriculum with limited difficulty most likely will not require accommodations for high-stakes testing. Students who require accommodations in the general education or special education setting—such as extended time for task completion, or use of assistive technology (speech synthesizer, electronic reader, communication board)—to participate in the general curriculum will most likely require accommodations to participate in high-stakes testing. The purpose of accommodations during the assessment is to prevent measuring the student's disability and to allow a more accurate assessment of the student's progress in the general curriculum.

The determination of need for accommodations for classroom instruction and high-stakes testing should be made during the IEP process. The types of accommodations needed must be documented on the IEP. Following statewide or district-wide assessment, teachers should rate the accommodations that proved to be helpful for each specific student (Elliott, Kratochwill, & Schulte, 1998).

The regulations offer some ideas for modification of instruments and accommodations for students. Modifying an assessment might include changing the test so that there are three choices instead of four, replacing the most difficult items with easier items, or changing the administration so that pictures are incorporated into the items or technology is used for the presentation of the items. If the IEP team determines that an alternate test is needed, the assessment, based on modified standards, must be developed so that it meets reliability and validity expectations and will adequately assess the standards upon which it is based. Furthermore, the IEP team is to be instructed to select accommodations and modifications that will not invalidate the test score (Federal Register, 2007).

In the *Accommodations Manual* of the Council of Chief State School Officers (Thompson, Morse, Sharpe, & Hall, 2005), the following adapted list of accommodation categories is described for use in statewide assessment:

> *Presentation accommodations.* For example, a student with a significant reading disability might be provided the content through a means other than reading.
>
> *Response accommodations.* For example, a student who cannot respond in writing might be allowed to respond in another format such as using a communication board or other technology.

CHECK YOUR UNDERSTANDING

To check your understanding of issues related to high-stakes assessment, complete Activity 5.6.

Setting accommodations. For example, if the testing location is inaccessible to a student or the test environment is distracting to a student, an alternate testing site can be used.

Timing and scheduling accommodations. For example, students who require extended time or those who require frequent breaks to sustain attention can be allowed these accommodations.

Issues and Research in High-Stakes Testing

Typically, new concepts and regulations in the assessment of students with special needs have been met with questions that must be considered. The mandate in the 1997 amendments to include all students in high-stakes assessment was added to the law as a measure of accountability. Student progress must be measured to determine if programs are effective. This mandate continues in IDEA 2004. As this mandate has been implemented in schools, problems and concerns have arisen along with what some have seen as positive benefits. Several of these are presented here.

1. Nichols and Berliner (2007) argued that mandatory statewide assessments have resulted in damaging the American educational system for all students and that alternate assessments may not be the best way to measure academic progress.

2. Yeh (2006) found that some teachers reported that high-stakes assessment helped teachers target and individualize instruction, and that their students who disliked reading or had difficulties with academics felt more in control of their own learning.

3. Yovanoff and Tindal (2007) suggested that performance task-based reading alternate tests can be scaled to statewide assessments, although determining their validity and reliability may be difficult.

4. When teachers were surveyed about their perceptions of using alternative or modified accountability tests, teachers with significantly cognitively disabled students expressed greater opposition to the inclusion of their students in the assessment process (Restorff, Sharpe, Abery, Rodriguez, & Kim, 2012). These researchers also found that approximately one-half of the special education teachers surveyed in three states supported statewide assessment and the other half opposed the use of these assessments.

5. Heilig and Darling-Hammond (2008) investigated the results of high-stakes assessment in Texas using longitudinal and qualitative data over a 7-year period. The researchers found that practices on some campuses might result in specific groups of students being encouraged not to attend school on the days of the assessment so that campus data might be more favorable. This finding was discovered as a result of missing data. Moreover, in following the performance and graduation rates of schools in a specific large district in Texas, it was also noted that nearly 40% of the students who should have graduated within a 5-year time period had either dropped out or were otherwise missing from the district. Data derived from assessment results further pointed to large gaps in achievement between various ethnic groups, with African Americans and Latinos having the lowest achievement scores. This study seems to point to the negative impact that high-stakes testing might have in some schools and districts.

6. A study by Bolt and Ysseldyke (2008) found that test items were not comparable across assessments when the modified assessments used for children with various disabilities were analyzed. Moreover, the items varied by disability category.

Universal Design of Assessments

The regulations require that, to the extent possible, states and local school districts apply the principles of Universal Design in the development of assessment instruments for individuals with disabilities. Universal Design is the concept that strives to make all learning materials and assessments fair, accessible, and user friendly for all learners from the beginning rather than attempting to fit a test to a particular student's needs after it has been developed. The principles of Universal Design include consideration of items or administration that would stigmatize any learners or that would make the items not accessible to all students. It is important to also make the items focus on content being assessed rather than providing information that is not needed for accurate assessment of skills or knowledge. Since all learners are being assessed, the instruments must be administered so that they do not require physical or sensory demands beyond the learners' capability.

CHAPTER SUMMARY

In this chapter you:

- Learned how norm-referenced assessments are constructed and the basic steps in test administration

- Learned about high-stakes assessment

- Applied basic steps in test administration

- Analyzed the benefits of norm-referenced assessments

- Synthesized the meaning of norm-referenced individual and high-stakes assessment

- Evaluated issues in norm-referenced and high-stakes assessment

THINK AHEAD

The most frequently used tests in education are achievement tests. In the next chapter, you will use portions of instruments to learn about achievement tests and how they are scored.

CHAPTER QUIZ

Now complete the Chapter Quiz, which includes Figures 5.6 and 5.7, to measure your understanding of the content in this chapter. You will need Figures 5.6 and 5.7 to complete the quiz.

Once you have completed that exercise, assess your progress by completing the Course Progress Monitoring Activity. This activity will let you know if you are moving toward target for course objectives.

FIGURE 5.6 Basal and Ceiling Rules and Response Items for a Subtest from the *Peabody Individual Achievement Test—Revised.*

SUBTEST 2
Reading Recognition

Training Exercises

	Trial 1	Trial 2	Trial 3
Exercise A.	(1) ______	(1) ______	(1) ______
Exercise B.	(3) ______	(3) ______	(3) ______
Exercise C.	(2) ______	(2) ______	(2) ______

Basal and Ceiling Rules
Basal: *highest* 5 consecutive correct responses
Ceiling: *lowest* 7 consecutive responses containing 5 errors

Starting Point
The item number that corresponds to the subject's raw score on General Information.

43. ledge ______ 1
44. escape ______ 1
45. northern ______ 1
46. towel ______ 1
47. kneel ______ 1
48. height ______ 0
49. exercise ______ 1
50. observe ______ 1
51. ruin ______ 0
52. license ______ 1
53. uniforms ______ 0
54. pigeon ______ 1
55. moisture ______ 0
56. artificial ______ 1
57. issues ______ 0
58. quench ______ 0
59. hustle ______ 0
60. thigh ______ 0

READING RECOGNITION
Ceiling Item ______
minus Errors ______
equals RAW SCORE ______

Source: Peabody Individual Achievement Test, Revised (PIAT-R).

FIGURE 5.7 Chronological Age Portion and Numeration Subtest from the *KeyMath—Revised* Protocol

	YEAR	MONTH	DAY
Test date	2014	3	6
Birth date	2005	10	7
Chronological age			

1 NUMERATION

General Directions:

Read Chapter 3 in the *Manual* carefully before administering and scoring the test. The correct procedures for establishing the subtest basal and ceiling are detailed in the chapter. Briefly, the criteria are as follows: *The basal is the 3 consecutive correct responses immediately preceding the easiest item missed; the ceiling is 3 consecutive errors.*

Begin administration at the Numeration item designated as the starting item for the student's grade level. Score items by penciling a 1 (correct) or 0 (incorrect) in the box. Continue administration until a basal and a ceiling have been established for the Numeration subtest. Use the Numeration basal item (the first item of the Numeration basal) to determine the starting points for the remaining subtests; for example, if the student's Numeration basal item is 18, begin the Rational Numbers subtest at item 2, begin the Geometry subtest at item 13, and so on.

The item-score boxes are positioned in columns indicating which domain each item belongs to. When totaling the scores in a domain column, count as *correct* the *un*administered items in that column that *precede* the easiest item administered. The resulting total for the column is the domain score. The sum of the domain scores is the subtest raw score.

GRADE	Item		Numbers 0-9	Numbers 0-99	Numbers 0-999	Multi-digit numbers
K,1 ▸	1.	how many deer	1			
	2.	as many fingers	1			
	3.	read 5, 2, 7	1			
	4.	read in order 5, 2, 7	1			
	5.	how many people	0			
2,3 ▸	6.	fourth person	1			
	7.	____ 20 ____		0		
	8.	read in order 36 15 70 32		1		
	9.	how many rods		0		
4 ▸	10.	how many dots		0		
	11.	order 643 618 305 648			1	
5-7 ▸	12.	blue dot		0		
	13.	729 739 749 ____ ____			0	
	14.	order 3,649 3,581 3,643				0
	15.	how many small cubes				
8,9 ▸	16.	round to nearest hundred				
	17.	how many pencils				
	18.	four-digit number				
	19.	read 6,019,304				
	20.	number in blue box				
	21.	how many small cubes				
	22.	three-digit number				
	23.	less than positive four				
	24.	what does 10^4 represent				

____ CEILING ITEM   DOMAIN SCORES | | | | |

SUBTEST RAW SCORE
(Sum of domain scores) | |

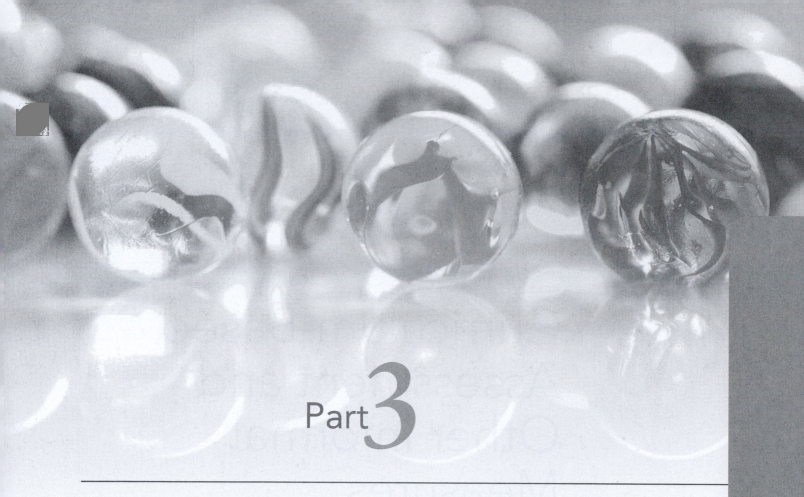

Part 3

Assessing Students

6 Curriculum-Based Assessment and Other Informal Measures

CHAPTER FOCUS

In this chapter you will:

- Learn about the purposes of informal assessment
- Learn about methods used to construct curriclum-based assessment
- Apply data to plot progress of cases
- Analyze scenarios and make intervention decisions
- Synthesize informal assessment methods to apply to case scenarios
- Evaluate informal data-collection case scenarios

● CURRICULUM-BASED MEASUREMENT AND OTHER INFORMAL ASSESSMENT

In Chapter 1, you learned that the traditional assessment model largely employs the use of norm-referenced tests with the goal of determining a student's eligibility for special education support. With the reforms in education and special education, the emphasis is now on prevention strategies. Prevention and early intervention strategies are the focus of the contemporary assessment model (see Chapter 1).

Early intervention methods prevent students from falling behind their peers in expected levels of academic achievement. It is essential that teachers closely monitor the performance of all students, especially the progress of those who appear to be struggling with grade-appropriate academic tasks. In this way, the teacher can implement alternative instructional strategies early and with an eye to meeting specific students' needs. Monitoring the progress of all students during universal instructional activities is consistent with Tier I of the response to intervention (RTI) model introduced in Chapter 1 and covered in depth in Chapter 7. Teachers can check on student progress using a variety of informal methods such as teacher-made tests, checklists, and curriculum-based measurement or CBM. CBM is a method of monitoring instruction regularly. The student's CBM is based on the achievement goal for the school year (Fuchs, 2004). For example, if the goal is to comprehend fourth-grade-level reading material, the CBMs are based on fourth-grade-level reading passages even though at the beginning of the year the student reads at the third-grade level. The monitoring of progress lets the teacher know if the child is making adequate progress under the current educational conditions. This close monitoring, for the purpose of making instructional decisions in the classroom, has been found to result in better academic achievement (Fuchs & Fuchs, 1986; Fuchs, Butterworth, & Fuchs, 1989; Fuchs, Fuchs, Hamlett, & Stecker, 1991).

One reason that curriculum-based measurement is considered the optimal assessment technique for monitoring progress is that it is a formative type of evaluation. An evaluation is considered formative when the student is measured during the instructional period for acquisition of skills to meet goals. This formative evaluation allows the teacher to make observations and decisions about the student's academic performance in a timely manner. Curriculum-based measurement may also be called *progress monitoring* because it is a formative type of evaluation. An evaluation is considered summative if it is a measurement taken at the end of the instructional period. For example, end-of-chapter tests or end-of-year tests are summative. Curriculum-based evaluation is the term used when curriculum-based measurement, curriculum-based assessment, and other informal measures, such as student work, records, and other documentation, are evaluated to make important decisions about instruction when the student has learning problems (Hosp, Hosp, Howell, & Allison, 2014). Curriculum-based measurement, curriculum-based evaluation, and RTI all use a problem-solving process to investigate and reach educational and behavioral decisions to promote student achievement.

To compare curriculum-based measurement, curriculum-based assessment, and commercially produced norm-referenced achievement tests, see Table 6.1.

How to Construct and Administer Curriculum-Based Measurements

In the 1970s, research efforts by the University of Minnesota resulted in the initial development of curriculum-based measures (Deno, 1985; Deno, Marston, & Mirkin, 1982; Deno, Marston, Shinn, & Tindal, 1983). An important result of the research and continuing work in the field of curriculum-based measurement was the identification of measures that have consistently been found to have reliability and

TABLE 6.1

Comparisons of Curriculum-Based Measurement, Curriculum-Based Assessment, and Commercial Academic Achievement Tests

Curriculum-Based Measurements	Curriculum-Based Assessments	Commercial Academic Achievement Tests
1. Repeated measures of same academic skill level based on end-of-year goal (formative)	1. Usually given at end of instructional period (summative)	1. Given to students to determine possible eligibility for special education support
2. Administered one or two times per week during academic period (school year)	2. Each test represents new material	2. Many instruments do not have alternate forms and cannot be repeated frequently for valid results
3. Are standardized and have adequate reliability	3. May be teacher-made and not standardized	3. Have adequate reliability and construct validity but content may not be relevant for specific students
4. Have content validity	4. May not have adequate reliability and validity	4. Are summative measures
5. May be a more fair measure of academic progress for ethnically and linguistically diverse students	5. May or may not be considered more fair for ethnically and linguistically diverse students	5. May be more prone to bias
6. May be administered to groups (spelling and math)	6. May be administered to groups	6. Individual administration (for purposes of determining eligibility)
7. Research supports use in early skills acquisition for elementary and middle grades; some support for use in secondary grades	7. Teacher-made instruments used for summative evaluation; have not been researched	7. Instruments designed to assess all grade levels from preacademic through adult
8. Specific skills assessed for reading fluency, spelling letter sequences, and math skills	8. Assesses mastery of specific content or skill taught during academic period	8. Assesses the broad domain of academic skills and achievement
9. May be used diagnostically for specific skills assessed and rate of learning	9. No true diagnostic capability unless error analysis is completed	9. May have diagnostic capability for a variety of skills
10. Compares student with his or her own performance on skill measured; may be compared to peers in class, compared with local norms, or compared with norms of researched groups	10. Compares student against a standard of mastery (student must pass 80% of items at end of chapter)	10. Compares student with national norm group or with self for diagnostic analysis (strengths and weaknesses across domain)
11. May be part of data collected for eligibility consideration	11. May be part of data collected for eligibility consideration	11. May be part of data collected for eligibility consideration

validity for the measurement of progress in reading, spelling, writing, and mathematics. Deno (1985) pinpointed specific design criteria inherent in effective CBMs:

1. The measures have sufficient reliability and validity so that they can be used confidently by classroom teachers to make educational decisions.

2. The measures are easy to use and understand so that teachers can employ them easily and teach others how to use them.

3. The results yielded by the measures are easy to explain to others, such as parents and other school personnel.

4. Because the measures are used frequently throughout the school year, they have to be inexpensive.

Significant research indicates that there are simple measures that can assist teachers with monitoring progress for the purpose of making data-based educational decisions. According to Shinn, Nolet, and Knutson (1990), most curriculum-based measures should include tasks such as the following: to assess reading, reading aloud for 1 minute to determine how many words are read correctly; to assess spelling, determining the number of correct letter sequences rather than simply counting a whole word incorrect; to assess written language, using a story starter and then assessing for correctness of spelling; and to assess computation, using 2-minute math drills.

Constructing CBMs for Reading. In order to assess reading for a specific grade level, the teacher will need to have a sufficient number of passages to use for two types of activities at least two times per week. In addition to having a student read orally so that the words the student calls correctly can be counted for oral-reading fluency, teachers can use the maze method, which has been found to provide valid assessment results in the area of reading comprehension. The maze method requires that the student read a passage that contains missing words and select the correct word from three choices. Directions for administering both of these types of assessment are presented next.

Oral-Reading Fluency Measure. For this measure, select three grade-level passages from the basal, curricular materials, or other texts of the same readability level. If you are not certain of the readability level of a passage, simply type it into a word-processing program, such as Microsoft Word, that contains a readability calculator. Other methods for determining readability may also be used, such as the readability formulas found in reading textbooks. Research by Hintze and Christ (2004) supports closely controlling readability level for increased reliability of the reading measures. In their study, controlled readability was defined by carefully selecting passages that represented the middle 5 months of the grade-level readability level. This means that all passages for the third grade, for example, ranged from 3.3 to 3.7 in readability level.

You will use these passages to determine baseline data for each student assessed. For the repeated measures for the school year, you will need two passages per week. For example, if the instructional period is 25 weeks, you will need 50 passages in addition to the three passages for the baseline data. It is important that students not be exposed to these passages until the assessment procedure begins. Supply one copy of each passage for the student and one for yourself. On your copy, note the total number of words in each line of each passage. (See Figure 6.1 for an example of a teacher passage.) Have the student read each passage aloud for 1 minute; mark any errors he or she makes on your copy. After 1 minute, have the student stop reading. Calculate the number of words he or she read correctly. The types of errors recorded are presented in Table 6.2.

In order to determine the student's baseline score, have him or her read the three passages orally. Note errors and total the number of words called correctly. Average the scores for the three passages for a baseline score; alternatively, select the median score as the baseline score. Because the data include only three scores, the median score may be more representative of the student's current oral-reading ability.

The literature includes expected levels of progress for the tasks of oral-reading fluency, spelling, written language, and mathematics operations (Deno, Fuchs, Marston, & Shin, 2001; Fuchs, Fuchs, & Hamlett, 1993). The expectations for reading vary by grade level. For example, generally a first-grade student may be expected to increase reading rate by 2 words per week and a fifth-grade student may be

CHECK YOUR UNDERSTANDING

Check your ability to recall the terms and concepts presented thus far in Chapter 6 by completing Activity 6.1.

FIGURE 6.1 Example of Teacher's Passage of a CBM for Oral-Reading Fluency

CBM #4/Grade 1

Student:		Teacher:	
School:		Date:	
Grade:		Examiner:	
# attempted	# of errors		# read correctly

INSTRUCTIONS

You are going to read this story titled Taking Pictures out loud. This story is about when Fox has his picture taken with different friends (place the reading passage in front of the student, face down). Try to read each word. You can use your finger to keep your place. If you come to a word you don't know, I'll tell it to you. You will read for 1 minute. Be sure to do your best reading. Do you have any questions? (Turn the passage right side up.) Put your finger on the first word. Begin.

Taking Pictures

On Monday Fox and Millie went to the fair.	7
"Let's have our picture taken," said Fox.	14
"Oh, yes, let's do," said Millie.	19
"Click," went the camera. And out came the pictures.	28
"Sweet," said Millie.	30
"One for you and one for me," said Fox.	39
On Tuesday Fox and Rose went to the fair.	46
"How about some pictures?" said Fox.	52
"Tee-hee," said Rose.	55
"Click," went the camera and out came the pictures.	64
"Tee-hee," said Rose.	67
"I'll keep mine always," said Fox.	73
On Wednesday Fox and Lola went to the fair.	80
"I don't have a picture of us," said Fox.	89
"Follow me," said Lola.	92
"Click," went the camera. And out came the pictures.	101
"What fun!" said Lola. "I'll carry mine everywhere."	108
"Me too," said Fox.	112

Source: Project AIM Staff, University of Maryland, 1999–2000, which was funded by the Department of Education, Office of Special Education. Deborah Speece, Lisa Pericola Case, and Dawn Eddy Molloy, Principal Investigators.

expected to increase by 0.5 words per week. A student with learning challenges will have somewhat different expectations. A first-grade student with learning problems may be expected to increase 0.83 words per minute, for example. Likewise, gifted students or students with high-level skills in reading would be expected to increase more rapidly, such as a first-grade student increasing by 3 words per week.

TABLE 6.2

Oral-Reading Errors for CBMs

Type of Error	Example of Passage Text	Actual Student Response
Teacher supplies word.	The girl swam in the race.	The girl . . . in the race (teacher supplies *swam*).
Student passes on word.	The girl swam in the race.	The girl . . . pass, in the race.
Student mispronounces word.	The girl swam in the race.	The girl swarm in the race.
Student omits word.	The girl swam in the race.	The swam in the race.
Student reads words out of order.	The girl swam in the race.	The girl swam the in race.
Student substitutes a word.	The girl swam in the race.	The girl swam in the pool.

Source: Adapted from Scott, V. G., & Weishaar, M. K. (2003). Curriculum-based measurement for reading progress. *Intervention in School and Clinic, 38*(3), 153–159.

Once you have determined a student's baseline in oral reading, you can establish a goal (number of words expected to be read by that student by the end of the year), and then plot an aimline to monitor the student's progress in working toward that goal. For example, a second-grade student who obtains a baseline of 55 correctly read words per minute can be expected to increase oral reading by approximately 38 words by the end of the year. This would result in a total of 93 correctly read words per minute. This is calculated in the following manner:

Baseline = 55

Weekly increase in number of words expected for second grade = 1.5 per week

Number of weeks of instruction following baseline period = 25

$$1.5 \times 25 = 38 + 55 = 93$$

In plotting the aimline, begin at the baseline score (55 words) and draw a line to the goal (93 words), as shown in Figure 6.2. To monitor instruction, plot data two

FIGURE 6.2 Oral-Reading Fluency Goal

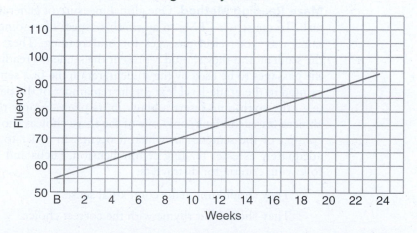

FIGURE 6.3 Calculating Trend Lines

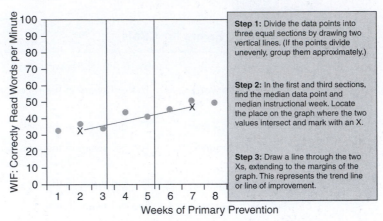

Source: Fuchs, Fuchs, Hintze, & Lembke. (2007, July). *Using curriculum-based measurement to determine response to intervention.* Paper presented at the 2007 Summer Institute on Student Progress Monitoring, Nashville, TN. Retrieved December 17, 2008, from http://www.studentprogress.org/summer_institute/2007/RTI/ProgressMonitoring-RTI2007.pdf.

times per week. When the student falls below the aimline on three to four consecutive measures, or data points, adjust instruction. When the student achieves higher than the aimline on three to four consecutive measures, provide more challenging reading tasks.

Another way to use data points is to construct a trend line (Fuchs, Fuchs, Hintze, & Lembke, 2007). A trend line can provide a quick view of how close the student's performance is to the aimline. If the trend line does not seem to be near the aimline (e.g., if it seems to be flat or above the aimline), adjust your instructional interventions and delivery methods.

To determine the trend line using the Tukey method, divide the data points into thirds. In other words, if there are nine data points, each section would include three data points. Find the median data point for the first and third sections and median week of instruction. As shown in Figure 6.3, draw a line between the two Xs used to note the median data points.

Figure 6.4 presents an example of how curriculum-based measurement can be used to determine when an instructional change is called for. The student in Figure 6.4 failed to make the projected progress in reading words per minute, as can be noted by the lighter-colored data squares. This intervention did not result in making progress along the aimline. A second intervention noted by the darker data squares was more successful, as can be seen by the data points near and passing the aimline.

Maze Reading Method. One global measure of general reading ability is the maze task. To construct CBMs to assess this aspect of reading ability, select passages the same way you select passages for oral reading. These passages must be new to the student and they should represent the student's reading grade level. In preparing the passages to be used by the student, retain the first sentence in each exactly as it is printed in the grade-level text. In the remainder of the passage, delete each *n*th word (e.g., the sixth) and insert a blank in its place. Supply the student with three word choices for each blank; only one of the three choices should "make sense," given the context of the sentence in which it occurs. In order to make certain that the task adequately assesses reading comprehension, Fuchs and Fuchs (1992) proposed the following criteria for distracters:

They should not make contextual sense.

They should not rhyme with the correct choice.

FIGURE 6.4 Curriculum-Based Measurement Data for Two Interventions Used with One Student

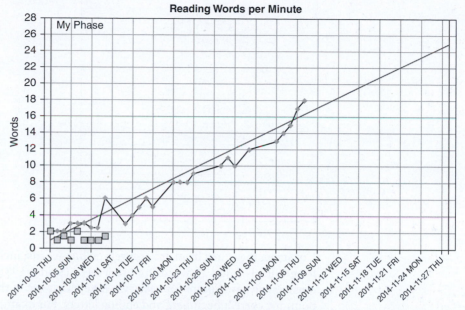

Source: Chart generated using ChartDog Graph Maker from Intervention Central (http://www.interventioncentral.org/teacher-resources/graph-maker-free-online).

They should not sound or look like the correct choice.

They should not be nonsense words.

They should not require the student to read ahead to eliminate a choice.

They should not be challenging in terms of meaning.

In addition, distracters should be of approximately the same length as the correct word.

Caution about Using Expected Growth Rates in Reading

In a study of more than 6,000 students, Silberglitt and Hintze (2007) found that not all student performance was consistent with expected growth rates when using averages of aggregated data. The results of this study suggest that teachers should employ other methods of establishing goals or aimlines that might be more representative of an individual student's ability to respond to interventions in reading. For example, these researchers proposed that the goal can be set using expected growth rates for the student's decile group (students who are ranked within the lowest decile group can be compared with the expected growth rate of that decile group). Another alternative suggestion was for the teacher to establish a criterion-referenced goal rather than comparing students to the average of the aggregated data. Silberglitt and Hintze argue that establishing an expected goal for students based on where they are within the group (rather than comparing students with the average of the group) may offer a method of monitoring progress effectively without the need for interventions provided through special education services. This method appears to be a fair way to measure progress following interventions in reading for students who may be in a lower-achieving group.

Constructing CBMs for Spelling. To assess spelling ability, plot both the number of correct letter sequences (CLSs) and the number of correctly spelled words.

FIGURE 6.5 Analysis of a Spelling Test

Spelling Test
1. ^g^a^t^e^ CLS 5
2. ^s^k^a^t^e^ CLS 6
3. ^c^r^a^t^e^ CLS 6
4. ^c l h i^d^ CLS 3
5. ^l^o^o^k^ CLS 5
6. ^t^o^o^k^ CLS 5
7. ^c^l o k^ CLS 3
8. ^l^o^c^k^ CLS 5
9. ^t^a^k^e^ CLS 5
10. ^s^h^a^k^e^ CLS 6

words correct = 80%
CLS = 49 or 89%

Construct measures from grade-level spelling words; include approximately 12 words for grades 1–3 and 18 words for grades 4–8 (Shinn, 1989). In scoring correct letter sequences, give one point for each two letters that are in the correct sequence. Give one point for correct beginning and ending letters. For example, the number of correct letter sequences for the correctly spelled word *time* is five. One point is scored for the *t*, one point for the correct sequence of *ti*, another point for *im*, another for *me*, and another for the correct ending letter of *e*.

For spelling, a baseline is taken in the same manner as for reading fluency and the aimline is plotted in the same manner, based on the weekly number of correct letter sequences expected. An example of a CBM spelling measure assessing correct letter sequencing is presented in Figure 6.5.

Constructing CBMs for Mathematics. For a math CBM, the problems should be operational (addition, subtraction, multiplication, division). Two-minute math probes should be composed of at least 25 math problems each (Fuchs & Fuchs, 1991). Select or generate 25 grade-level computational problems per probe and construct three math sheets or probes for the baseline score and two probes for each week during the academic period. Have students complete as many problems as they can in the 2-minute period. Count the number of correct digits and plot that number on the student's graph.

Students' rates of expected growth also vary for other skill and subject areas such as spelling and math skills. First-grade students might be expected to improve their spelling skills by increasing the number of correct letter sequences by 1 and fourth-grade students might be expected to gain only 0.45 letter sequences each week.

Computer-Constructed CBM Charts

Computer programs such as Microsoft Word © can be used to make simple CBM graphs. Additional computer-generated graphs are readily available on the Internet through sources such as the Curriculum-Based Measurement Warehouse. Another Internet source for entering data and generating a CBM chart is Chartdog. These online tools make it easy for classroom teachers to quickly enter curriculum-based assessment data each day to monitor student progress.

For assessing increases in mathematics skills, one measure that is frequently used is the number of correct digits on math probes. The number of correct digits expected will be different based on the grade level of the student. A first-grade student might increase by 0.3 correct digits per week and a fifth-grade student might increase by 0.75 digits per week.

CHECK YOUR UNDERSTANDING

Determine a baseline reading score and the aimline for a first-grade student by completing Activity 6.2.

CHECK YOUR UNDERSTANDING

Determine a baseline spelling score and the aimline for a second-grade student by completing Activity 6.3.

Review of Research on Curriculum-Based Measurement

Curriculum-based measurement of progress has been found to noticeably affect academic achievement when the results are used to modify instructional planning. A brief review of many years of research supports the use of curriculum-based measurement for several reasons.

According to Fuchs et al. (1989), when curriculum-based measurement is used for instructional programming, students experience somewhat greater gains in achievement than when it is used for testing purposes alone. These researchers found that effective teachers were sensitive to the results of the assessment data and used those data to adapt or modify their instruction. The use of curriculum-based measurement has been linked to better understanding on the part of students of the expectations for their academic performance (Fuchs, Butterworth, & Fuchs, 1989). Students in this study indicated that they received more feedback from the teacher about their performance than students not participating in curriculum-based measurement. Research has also indicated that teachers using curriculum-based measurement tended to set goals based on higher expectations than did teachers who were not using these methods (Fuchs et al., 1989). Use of curriculum-based measurement, in conjunction with provision of instructional intervention strategies to general education teachers, increased achievement of low-achieving students and students in general education classes with learning disabilities (Fuchs et al., 1994). One study applied curriculum-based measurement in the general education classroom as part of a functional behavioral analysis (Roberts, Marshall, Nelson, & Albers, 2001). In this study, the use of curriculum-based measurement to determine appropriate instructional levels resulted in decreased off-task behaviors. When applied in this manner, curriculum-based measurement allowed instruction to be tailored; it may therefore be viewed as a prereferral strategy.

Curriculum-based measurement has been found effective for use in universal screening of students for early reading acquisition skills (Ardoin et al., 2004; Marchand-Martella, Ruby, & Martella, 2007). A study found that the use of one reading probe was sufficient for predicting overall reading achievement. Clarke and Shinn (2004) found that math CBMs for assessment of early math skills were reliable when used with first-grade students to identify those who might be at risk in mathematics. In a review of the use of CBMs in mathematics, Foegen, Jiban, and Deno (2007) found that there was adequate evidence for use of CBMs in the elementary grades for monitoring the acquisition of problem-solving skills and basic math facts. CBMs have also been found to predict future performance of students on high-stakes state achievement assessments (McGlinchey & Hixson, 2004).

In their study of curriculum-based measurement as one method of screening for special education eligibility, Marston, Mirkin, and Deno (1984) found this form of assessment to be not only accurate but also less open to influence by teacher variables. Its use appeared to result in less bias, as evidenced by more equity in the male–female ratio of referrals (Marston et al., 1984). Canter (1991) supported using curriculum-based measurement to determine eligibility for special education services by comparing the student's progress in the classroom curriculum to the expectations within the average range for the grade level. The student's actual progress may indicate the need for special education intervention.

Curriculum-based measurement has been found useful when the school employs a problem-solving model as the process for interventions (Deno, 1995; Marston, Muyskens, Lau, & Canter, 2003; Shinn, 2002). For this reason, CBM naturally fits within the contemporary assessment model and is consistent with the movement toward assessing learning difficulties by employing response-to-intervention (RTI) strategies. CBM can easily be incorporated in the RTI model that uses tiered instruction. The use of CBM for RTI is presented in Chapter 7.

Curriculum-based measurement has been studied as a possible method of identifying students in special education placements who are ready to move back into the general education setting (Shinn, Habedank, Rodden-Nord, & Knutson, 1993). Using this method may help general education teachers smoothly integrate students from special education environments by providing data to assess progress and use in planning interventions. One study has also suggested that curriculum-based measures might be beneficial in measuring the effects of medication on students with attention disorders (Stoner, Carey, Ikeda, & Shinn, 1994). In this study, Stoner and colleagues replicated another study and found evidence suggesting that CBM may be one measure of determining the effect of methylphenidate on academic performance. Additional research in this area may add insight to the emerging field of effective treatment of students with attention deficit disorder.

One study found that when CBM was combined with peer tutoring, students in a general classroom setting made significantly greater achievement gains (Phillips, Hamlett, Fuchs, & Fuchs, 1993). Another study found substantial overall gains in reading fluency, although at-risk students did not progress at the same rate as their grade peers (Greenwood, Tapia, Abbott, & Walton, 2003). Mehrens and Clarizio (1993) asserted that CBM is helpful in determining when instruction should be adapted, but it does not necessarily provide information about what to change or how to provide the instruction. They advocated using CBM in conjunction with other diagnostic assessments.

Baker and Good (1995) found that CBM used in assessing reading was as reliable and valid when used with bilingual students as when used with English-only students. They also found that CBM was a sensitive measurement of the reading progress made by bilingual students. Kamps et al. (2007) found that the use of progress monitoring of intensive interventions for students who are English-language learners (ELLs) offers effective tier-two interventions. This study suggested that these methods were as effective with ELL students as they were with English-only students. Haager (2007) had inconsistent results when using RTI with ELL students and suggested that students receiving interventions in the first grade might require additional time for reading acquisition skills before they can be expected to meet the reading criteria set for the second grade.

Curriculum-based measurement as a formative evaluation process was also found to predict student achievement on high-stakes assessment (Marcotte & Hintze, 2009). This study determined that the measures for oral fluency, retell fluency, maze, and written retell indicated student performance on tests incorporating a criterion-referenced approach used in high-stakes assessment.

In their sample of fourth-grade students, Fuchs and Fuchs (1996) found that curriculum-based measurement combined with performance assessment provided teachers more in-depth assessment, which resulted in better instructional decisions. Another study found that general education teachers who employed CBM designed better instructional programs and had students who experienced greater gains in achievement than did teachers who did not use CBM (Fuchs et al., 1994). Allinder (1995) found that teachers who used CBM had high teacher efficacy and set high student goals; in addition, their students had significantly greater growth. In the Allinder study, special education teachers using CBM who had greater teaching efficacy set more goals for their students.

Teachers who were asked to compare CBM with norm-referenced assessments rated CBM as a more acceptable method of assessment (Eckert, Shapiro, & Lutz, 1995). Another study suggested that students enjoyed participating in CBM and that their active participation in this process increased their feelings of responsibility for learning (Davis, Fuchs, Fuchs, & Whinnery, 1995).

Researchers are continuing to investigate the use of progress monitoring with CBMs for students with various learning needs. For example, one study investigated the use of progress monitoring for specific learning objectives for students with

CHECK YOUR UNDERSTANDING

Determine a baseline math score and the aimline for a first-grade student by completing Activity 6.4.

cognitive impairments (Wallace & Tichá, 2006). In this study, the researchers found that the use of general outcome measures to assess early and functional reading and academic skills was beneficial for this group of learners. Additionally, CBMs in writing for students with hearing impairments were also useful at the secondary level (Cheng & Rose, 2005). It seems clear that CBMs can provide helpful information to teachers as they monitor the progress of students in skill acquisition.

Cautions

Several researchers have issued statements of caution about employing curriculum-based measurement. Like other types of assessment, curriculum-based measurement may be more useful in some situations and less useful in others. Heshusius (1991) cautioned that curriculum-based assessment might not allow for measurement of some important constructs in education, such as creativity, areas of interest, and original ideas. Hintze, Shapiro, and Lutz (1994) found that CBM was more sensitive in measuring progress when used with traditional basal readers rather than literature samples, indicating that the materials contribute to difficulty in accurate measurement. Mehrens and Clarizio (1993) suggested that CBM should be used as part of comprehensive assessment with other measures because of continuing concerns about the reliability and validity of CBM. Silberglitt and Hintze (2007) cautioned against using average aggregated growth rate expectations to establish reading goals.

When using data from CBMs to make educational decisions, teachers should keep in mind that time of day, presentation format of instruction, and other conditions should be considered (Parette, Peterson-Karlan, Wojcok, & Bardi, 2007). Stecker (2007) reminded educators that there are many variables of student performance and success that are not measurable with CBMs, and that these variables, such as environment and family concerns, should be considered when using CBMs in the decision-making process.

CHECK YOUR UNDERSTANDING

To review your understanding of the CBM literature, complete Activity 6.5.

Online and Computer-Produced Curriculum-Based Measurement

In addition to the teacher-made curriculum-based instruments discussed in the previous sections, computer-produced curriculum-based assessments for progress monitoring are widely used by school districts. Two of the most commonly used products include AIMSWEB (produced by Pearson) and DIBELS (nonprofit by the University of Oregon). These methods include online curriculum probes, and specific data for progress monitoring are generated by the online programs. Both programs include materials for certain skills in English and Spanish. Each of these programs includes a variety of subject areas for assessment and various grade levels.

● CRITERION-REFERENCED ASSESSMENT

Criterion-referenced tests compare the performance of a student to a given criterion. This criterion can be an established objective within the curriculum, an IEP criterion, or a criterion or standard of a published test instrument. The instrument designed to assess the student's ability to master the criterion is composed of many items across a very narrow band of skills. For example, a criterion-referenced test may be designed to assess a student's ability to read passages from the fifth-grade-level reading series and answer comprehension questions with 85% accuracy. For this student, the criterion is an IEP objective. The assessment is made up of several passages and subsequent comprehension questions for each passage, all at the fifth-grade reading level. No other curriculum materials or content items are included. The purpose is to

FIGURE 6.6 Examples of Criterion-Referenced Testing

Items missed	On the Word Attack subtest: the long a–e pattern in nonsense words—*gaked, straced;* the long i–e pattern in nonsense word—*quiles*
Deficit-skill	Decoding words with the long vowel-consonant-silent-*e* pattern
Probe	Decoding words orally to teacher: *cake, make, snake, rake, rate, lake, fake, like, bike, kite*
Criterion	Decode 10/10 words for mastery. Decode 8/10 words to 6/10 words for instructional level. Decode 5/10 words or fewer for failure level; assess prerequisite skill level: discrimination of long/short vowels (vowels: *a, i*).

determine if the student can answer the comprehension questions with 85% accuracy. Criterion-related assessment that uses curriculum materials is only one type of curriculum-based assessment.

Although many criterion-referenced instruments are nonstandardized or perhaps designed by the teacher, a few criterion-referenced instruments are standardized. Some norm-referenced instruments yield criterion-related objectives or the possibility of adding criterion-related objectives with little difficulty. Examples of these instruments are the *KeyMath–3* (Connolly, 2007), *K-TEA–III* (Kaufman & Kaufman, 2014), and the *Woodcock Johnson Tests of Achievement IV* (Woodcock, Schrank, McGrew, & Mather, 2014). Moreover, tests publishers are increasingly providing additional resources such as behavioral objectives, suggestions to guide individualized education program (IEP) goals, and educational strategies (see Chapter 8 for academic norm-referenced tests).

Adapting standardized norm-referenced instruments to represent criterion-referenced testing is accomplished by writing educational objectives for the skills tested. To be certain that the skill or task has been adequately sampled, however, the educator may need to prepare additional academic probes to measure the student's skills. Objectives may represent long-term learning goals rather than short-term gains, determined by the amount of the material or the scope of the task tested by the norm-referenced test. Figure 6.6 illustrates how an item from the WRMT–III (2011) might be expanded to represent criterion-referenced testing.

In addition to adapting published norm-referenced instruments for criterion-related assessment, educators may use published criterion-referenced test batteries, such as the BRIGANCE® inventories, that present specific criteria and objectives. Teachers may also create their own criterion-referenced tests.

The BRIGANCE Comprehensive Inventories

The *BRIGANCE Comprehensive Inventory of Basic Skills* (BRIGANCE, 2010) is a standardized assessment system that provides criterion-referenced assessment at various skill levels. Norms are available, and this set of assessments is aligned with some state assessment requirements. Each battery contains numerous subtests, and each assessment has objectives that may be used in developing IEPs. In addition, the BRIGANCE system includes a variety of assessment screeners and criterion-referenced instruments for age groups ranging from early childhood through transition ages served in special education. These instruments include the *Inventory of Early Development III* (2013), the *Comprehensive Inventory of Basic Skills II Standardized* (2010), and the *Transition Skills Inventory* (2010). In each system, the educator should select only the areas and items of interest that identify specific strengths

FIGURE 6.7 *BRIGANCE® Comprehensive Inventory of Basic Skills II, Examiner Page 96,* B-1 Warning and Safety Signs

Overview

This assessment measures the student's ability to read warning and safety signs.

SKILL

Reads warning and safety signs

ASSESSMENT METHOD

Individual Oral Response

MATERIALS

- Pages S-96 and S-97
- Sheet of 9" × 12" construction paper

SCORING INFORMATION

- **Standardized Record Book:** Page 14
- **Entry:** For grade 1, start with item 1; for grade 2, start with item 8; for grade 3, start with item 20; for grades 4–6, start with item 25.
- **Basal:** 5 consecutive correct responses
- **Ceiling:** 5 consecutive incorrect responses
- **Time:** Your discretion
- **Accuracy:** Give credit for each correct response. **Note:** If a word is mispronounced slightly (for example, the wrong syllable is accented or the word is decoded but not reblended), ask the student to define the word. If the student cannot define the word satisfactorily, mark the sign as incorrect.

BEFORE ASSESSING

Review the Notes at the end of this assessment for additional information.

OBJECTIVES FOR WRITING IEPs

By ___(date)___ , when shown a list of twenty warning and safety signs, __(student's name)__ will read __(quantity)__ of the signs.

Directions for Assessment: Oral Response

Hold up a sheet of construction paper between the student page and this page as a visual barrier.

Point to the warning and safety signs on page S-96, and

Say: These are words of warning we often see on signs. Look at each word carefully and read it aloud.

Point to the first sign, and

Say: Begin here.

If the student does not respond after as few seconds,

Say: You can go on to the next sign.

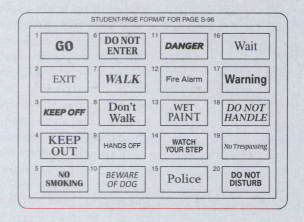

Source: BRIGANCE Comprehensive Inventory of Basic Skills II—Revised. (2010). A. H. Brigance. Curriculum Associates, North Billerica, MA. Reprinted with permission.

and weaknesses. The new inventories have the capability for school personnel to link to an online progress-monitoring system as well as monitor student progress within the classroom using traditional methods.

The BRIGANCE system is composed of large, multiple-ring notebook binders that contain both student and examiner pages. The pages may be turned to resemble an easel format, or the pages to be administered may be removed from the binder. A warning included in the test cautions the examiner to select the necessary subtests and avoid overtesting.

The *Comprehensive Inventory of Basic Skills II Standardized* includes a section for administration of readiness for school and a second section that is designed for students in grades 1 through 6. Figure 6.7 presents an examiner page for the assessment of warning and safety signs to assess the student's ability to recognize common signs. Note the basal and ceiling levels and the objective that may be adapted for a student's IEP. This assessment allows the teacher to use the actual criterion test items to write the IEP. This BRIGANCE® inventory has been standardized, and the publisher's website provides derived scores on a scoring report. Using the website tool, teachers can convert raw scores to scaled scores, quotients, percentile ranks, and age and grade equivalents.

TABLE 6.3

Skills Assessed on the BRIGANCE® Diagnostic Comprehensive Inventory of Basic Skills II Standardized

BRIGANCE® Comprehensive Inventory of Basic Skills II

Basic Reading Skills
Reading Comprehension
Math Calculation
Math Reasoning
Written Language
Listening Comprehension
Information Processing

Source: BRIGANCE® Comprehensive Inventory of Basic Skills II Standardized. (2010). A. H. Brigance. Curriculum Associates, North Billerica, MA.

Teacher-Made Criterion-Referenced Tests

Instead of routinely relying on published instruments, classroom teachers often develop their own criterion-referenced tests. This type of assessment allows the teacher to directly link the assessment to the currently used curriculum. By writing the criterion to be used as the basis for determining when the student has reached or passed the objective, the teacher has created a criterion-referenced test. When the test is linked directly to the curriculum, it also becomes a curriculum-based assessment device and may be referred to as direct measurement. For example, the teacher may use the scope and sequence chart from the reading series or math text to write the objectives that will be used in the criterion-related assessment.

Research supports the use of criterion-referenced assessment in the classroom and other settings (Glaser, 1963; Hart & Scuitto, 1996; McCauley, 1996). The first questions regarding the use of criterion-referenced assessment were raised in the literature in 1963 by Glaser. The issues Glaser raised seemed to be current issues in the debate about better measurement techniques to accurately determine student progress. Glaser stated that the knowledge educators attempt to provide to students exists on a continuum ranging from "no acquisition" to "mastery." He stated that the criterion can be established at any level where the teacher wishes to assess the student's mastery or acquisition. This type of measurement is used to determine the student's position along the continuum of acquisition or mastery.

Hart and Scuitto (1996) concluded that using criterion-referenced assessment is practical, has social validity, and may assist with educational accountability. This type of assessment can be adapted to other areas, such as a child's speech and language development (McCauley, 1996). Criterion-referenced assessment has been shown to be useful in screening entering kindergarten and first-grade students for school readiness (Campbell, Schellinger, & Beer, 1991) and has also been used to determine appropriate adaptations for vocational assessments to assist in planning realistic job accommodations (Lusting & Saura, 1996). In a review of criterion-referenced assessment during the past 30 years, Millman (1994) concluded that to represent a true understanding of the student's ability, this type of assessment requires "item density." He suggested that to accurately assess whether a student has mastered a domain or area, the assessments need to have many items per domain. Teachers who construct their own criterion-referenced assessments should be certain that enough items are required of the student that they can determine accurately the level of mastery of the domain.

One difficulty that teachers may have in constructing criterion-referenced tests is establishing the exact criterion for whether the student has achieved the objective. Shapiro (1989) suggested that one quantitative method of determining mastery would be to use a normative comparison of the performance, such as using a specific task that 80% of the peers in the class or grade have mastered. The teacher may wish to use a criterion that is associated with a standard set by the school grading policy. For example, answering 75% of items correctly might indicate that the student needs improvement; 85% correct might be an average performance; and 95% correct might represent mastery. Or, the teacher might decide to use a criterion that the student can easily understand and chart. For example, getting five out of seven items correct indicates the student could continue with the same objective or skill; getting seven out of seven items correct indicates the student is ready to move up to the next skill level. Often, the teacher sets the criterion using logical reasoning rather than a quantitative measurement (Shapiro, 1989).

Evans and Evans (1986) suggested other considerations for establishing criteria for mastery:

Does passing the test mean that the student is proficient and will maintain the skills?

Is the student ready to progress to the next level in the curriculum?

Will the student be able to generalize and apply the skills outside the classroom?

Would the student pass the mastery test if it were given at a later date? (p. 10)

The teacher may wish to use the following measures for criterion-referenced tests:

More than 95% = mastery of objective

90 to 95% = instructional level

76 to 89% = difficult level

Less than 76% = failure level

Similar standards may be set by the individual teacher, who may wish to adjust objectives when the student performs with 76 to 89% accuracy and when the student performs with more than 95% accuracy. It is important to remember that students with learning difficulties should experience a high ratio of success during instruction to increase the possibility of positive reinforcement during the learning process. Therefore, it may be better to design objectives that promote higher success rates. Figure 6.8 illustrates a criterion-referenced test written by a teacher for addition facts with sums of 10 or less. The objective, or criterion, is included at the top of the test.

CHECK YOUR UNDERSTANDING

In Activity 6.6, you will determine whether the student responses illustrated indicate mastery of the subskill assessed by the *Basic Skills* test. Complete Activity 6.6.

CHECK YOUR UNDERSTANDING

The skills focused on in Activity 6.7 are similar to those that would be included at the beginning level of a reading series. In this activity, you will select the information from one skill to write an objective and construct a short criterion-referenced test. The test should measure the student's mastery of the objective.

FIGURE 6.8 Teacher-Made Criterion-Referenced Test

OBJECTIVE

John will correctly answer 9 out of 10 addition problems with sums of 10 or less.

5	3	8	9	4	6	7	2	4	1
+2	+2	+2	+1	+5	+2	+3	+4	+3	+6

Performance: _____

Objective passed: _____ Continue on current objective: _____

● TASK ANALYSIS AND ERROR ANALYSIS

Teachers often use task and error analyses without realizing that an analysis of student progress has been completed. Task analysis involves breaking down a task into the smallest steps necessary to complete the task. The steps actually reflect subskills, or subtasks, that the student must complete before finishing a task. In academic work, many of these subskills and tasks form a hierarchy of skills that build throughout the school years. As students master skills and tasks, they face new, more advanced curricular tasks that depend on the earlier skills. In mathematics, for example, understanding of numerals and one-to-one correspondence must precede understanding of basic addition facts. A student must conquer addition and subtraction before tackling multiplication and division. Therefore, a thorough task analysis of skill deficits, followed by an informal assessment, may provide the teacher with information about what the student has or has not mastered.

Error analysis is an assessment method that a teacher can use with formal, informal, and direct measures, such as classwork. This is a method of discovering patterns of errors. A teacher may notice that a student who understands difficult multiplication facts, such as those of 11s, 12s, and 13s, continues to miss computation problems involving those facts. With careful error analysis of responses on a teacher-made test, the teacher determines that the student has incorrectly lined up the multiplicands. The student understands the math fact but has made a mistake in the mechanics of the operation.

One way that teachers can perform error analyses is to become familiar with the scope and sequence of classroom curriculum materials. The teacher guides and manuals that accompany classroom materials are a good starting place to develop a thorough understanding of the materials and how to perform an error analysis of student responses. For example, a basal reading series might provide a sequence chart of the sounds presented in a given book at a specific level. Using this sequence chart, the teacher can first determine which errors the student has made and then analyze the possible reason for the errors. Perhaps all of the student's errors involve words with vowel combinations (such as *ea, ie, ee, oa*). The teacher can next perform a task analysis of the prerequisite skills the child needs to master those sounds and be able to decode words with those sounds.

● TEACHER-MADE TESTS

Many of the types of informal assessment described in this chapter are measures that can be designed by teachers. A study by Marso and Pigge (1991) found that teachers made several types of errors in test construction and tended to test items only at the knowledge level. This study also found that the number of years of teaching experience did not make a significant difference in the number and type of errors made in test construction. The types of items developed by teachers in this study included short response, matching, completion, true–false, and multiple choice, with essay items used infrequently. In constructing tests, these teachers made the most errors in matching items, followed by completion, essay, and true–false. Teachers may write test items using different levels of learning, although many teachers use items at the knowledge level because they are easier to write. Such items require the student merely to recall, recognize, or match the material. Higher-order thinking skills are needed to assess a student's ability to sequence, apply information, analyze, synthesize, infer, or deduct. These items may be more difficult and time consuming to construct.

One study found differences and inconsistencies between the content that teachers found important in a secondary textbook and the actual items included on

CHECK YOUR UNDERSTANDING

Check your ability to complete a task analysis in Activity 6.8.

CHECK YOUR UNDERSTANDING

Practice analyzing errors by completing Activity 6.9.

CHECK YOUR UNDERSTANDING

Check your ability to recall the terms introduced thus far in this chapter by completing Activity 6.10.

teacher-made tests of the content (Broekkamp, Van Hout-Wolters, Van de Bergh, & Rijlaarsdam, 2004). This study also found differences between what students thought would be important in a chapter, their expectations for the test content, and the actual demands of the test. It was concluded that in constructing and administering tests at the secondary level, teachers should take care to include sections deemed important and provide assistance in guiding students to prepare for exams as they work through the content.

To learn more about connecting teacher-made tests to academic standards, watch this video and hear teachers discussing developing tests.

Case Study: Teacher-Made Tests

Mr. Smithers is a first-year teacher of fourth-grade students. One of the tasks he has difficulty with is constructing tests. He has several commercially produced tests for many of the textbooks he is using with his students, but he often teaches additional material and writes his own test items. He has noticed that students almost always earn high scores on tests he constructs himself, and although this is exciting for the students, Mr. Smithers is not certain he is accurately measuring their knowledge and skills.

Mr. Smithers decides to ask his mentor teacher, Mrs. Roberts, to assist him. He shows Mrs. Roberts some examples of the items he has written to assess the student's understanding of the concept of division.

1. $4 \div 2 =$
2. $8 \div 2 =$
3. $6 \div 2 =$

Mrs. Roberts points out that the items are the basic division facts that students in the fourth grade are able to learn by simple rote memory. In other words, these items measure a lower leavel of learning—recall—rather than a skill at the conceptual level. Mrs. Roberts suggests that Mr. Smithers look over the scope-and-sequence chart in the curriculum guide to determine the range of concepts in the fourth-grade math curriculum. She also recommends that Mr. Smithers design several problems that assess higher-level thinking and problem-solving skills. She encourages him to write some story or word problems to determine if his students know when the process of division should be used rather than other operations such as addition or subtraction.

Mr. Smithers returns to his classroom and constructs the following problems to assess his students' understanding of the concepts that undergird division:

1. You and four of your friends decide to order two large 10-slice pizzas. You are all hungry and want to be sure everyone gets the same number of slices. How many pieces will each one get?

2. In your art class there are two long tables. Your art teacher tells you that you must all sit around the two tables. There are 16 students in the class. How many students will be at each table?

3. Your dog has been sick and your dad took him to the veterinarian. When he returns with your dog, he tells you that the veterinarian gave your dog a pill and said that he needs to take three more pills evenly spaced over the next 12 hours. How often will you need to give your dog a pill?

In addition to being aware of the level of difficulty of test items, teachers must be aware of types of errors made in constructing items and how the items are associated on a test. Some of the most common types of errors made in Marso and Pigge's (1991) study are presented in Figure 6.9.

FIGURE 6.9 Most Common Test Format Construction Errors

Matching Items
Columns not titled
"Once, more than once, or not at all" not used in directions to prevent elimination
Response column not ordered
Directions do not specify basis for match
Answering procedures not specified
Elimination due to equal numbers
Columns exceed 10 items

Multiple-Choice Items
Alternatives not in columns or rows
Incomplete stems
Negative words not emphasized or avoided
"All or none of above" not appropriately used
Needless repetitions of alternatives
Presence of specific determiners in alternatives
Verbal associations between alternative and stem

Essay Exercises
Response expectations unclear
Scoring points not realistically limited
Optional questions provided
Restricted question not provided
Ambiguous words used
Opinion or feelings requested

Problem Exercises
Items not sampling understanding of content
No range of easy to difficult problems
Degree of accuracy not requested
Nonindependent items
Use of objective items when calculation preferable

Completion Items
Not complete interrogative sentence
Blanks in statement, "puzzle"
Textbook statements with words left out
More than a single idea or answer called for
Question allows more than a single answer
Requests trivia versus significant data

True-False Items
Required to write response, time waste
Statements contain more than a single idea
Negative statements used
Presence of a specific determiner
Statement is not question, give-away item
Needless phrases present, too lengthy

FIGURE 6.9 Continued

Interpretive Exercises
Objective response form not used
Can be answered without data present
Errors present in response items
Data presented unclear

Test Format
Absence of directions
Answering procedures unclear
Items not consecutively numbered
Inadequate margins
Answer space not provided
No space between items

Source: Adapted with permission from Ronald Marso and Fred Pigge, 1991, An analysis of teacher-made tests: Item types, cognitive demands, and item construction errors, *Contemporary Educational Psychology,* 16, pp. 284–285. Copyright 1991 by Academic Press.

● OTHER INFORMAL METHODS OF ACADEMIC ASSESSMENT

Teachers employ many informal assessment methods to monitor the academic progress of students. Some of these methods combine the techniques of error analysis, task analysis, direct measurement, curriculum-based assessment, probes, and criterion-related assessment. These methods include making checklists and questionnaires and evaluating student work samples and permanent products.

Teacher-made checklists may be constructed by conducting an error analysis to identify the problem area and then completing a task analysis. For each subskill that is problematic for the student, the teacher may construct a probe or a more in-depth assessment instrument. Probes might be short, timed quizzes to determine content mastery. For example, a teacher may give 10 subtraction facts for students to complete in 2 minutes. If the teacher uses items from the curriculum to develop the probe, the probe can be categorized as curriculum-based assessment. The teacher may also establish a criterion for mastery of each probe or in-depth teacher-made test. This added dimension creates a criterion-referenced assessment device. The criterion may be 9 out of 10 problems added correctly. To effectively monitor the growth of the student, the teacher may set criteria for mastery each day as direct measurement techniques are employed. As the student meets the mastery criterion established for an objective, the teacher checks off the subskill on the checklist and progresses to the next most difficult item on the list of subskills.

Other informal methods that have been designed by teachers include interviews and questionnaires. These can be used to assess a variety of areas. Wiener (1986) suggested that teachers construct interviews and questionnaires to assess report writing and test taking. For example, a teacher may wish to find out additional information about how students best can complete assignments such as reports or projects. A questionnaire may be designed to ask about student preferences for teacher instructions, previous experiences with these types of tasks, and how assignments should be evaluated. A teacher may want to determine how students plan or think about their projects and what steps they have found useful in the past to complete these tasks.

CHECK YOUR UNDERSTANDING

Check your ability to correct errors in the items of a teacher-made test by completing **Activity 6.11.**

Interviews and questionnaires can be written to determine students' study habits. Questions might include the type of environment the student prefers, what subjects are easier for the student to study independently, and which subjects are more problematic.

Teachers can also gather helpful information by informally reviewing students' work samples—actual samples of work completed by the student. Samples can include independent seatwork, homework, tests, and quizzes. Work samples are one kind of permanent product. Other permanent products evaluated by the teacher include projects, posters, and art.

Informal Assessment of Reading

Comprehension, decoding, and fluency are the broad areas of reading that teachers assess using informal methods. *Comprehension* is the ability to derive meaning from written language, whereas *decoding* is the ability to associate sounds and symbols. *Fluency* is the rate and ease with which a student reads orally.

Howell and Morehead (1987) presented several methods to informally assess comprehension. For example, students might be asked to answer comprehension questions about the sequence of the story and details of events in the story. Other techniques might include asking students to paraphrase or tell the story or events in their own words, answer vocabulary items, or complete cloze or maze tasks.

A study by Fuchs and Fuchs (1992) found that the cloze and story-retelling methods were not technically adequate and sensitive enough to measure the reading progress of students over time. The maze method, however, was determined to be useful for monitoring student growth. This seems to suggest that the story-retelling and cloze methods may be best used for diagnostic information or as instructional strategies rather than as a means to monitor progress within a curriculum.

Barnes (1986) suggested using an error analysis approach when listening to students read passages aloud. With this approach, the teacher notes the errors made as the student reads and analyzes them to determine whether they change the meaning of the passage. The teacher then notes whether the substituted words look or sound like the original words.

Decoding skills used in reading can also be assessed informally. The teacher may design tests to measure the student's ability to (1) orally read isolated letters, blends, syllables, and real words; (2) orally read nonsense words that contain various combinations of vowel sounds and patterns, consonant blends, and digraphs; and (3) orally read sentences that contain new words. The teacher may sample the reader used by the student to develop a list of words to decode, if one has not been provided by the publisher. A sample may be obtained by selecting every 10th word, selecting every 25th word, or, for higher-level readers, randomly selecting stories from which random words will be taken. Proper nouns and words already mastered by the student may be excluded (e.g., *a, the, me, I*).

Fluency is assessed using a particular reading selection to determine a student's reading rate and accuracy. Reading fluency will be affected by the student's ability to decode new words and by the student's ability to read phrase by phrase rather than word by word. The teacher may assess oral-reading fluency of new material and previously read material. Howell and Morehead (1987) suggested that the teacher listen to the student read a passage, mark the location reached at the end of 1 minute, and then ask the student to read again as quickly as possible. The teacher may note the difference between the two rates as well as errors.

Teachers can also measure students' reading skills using informal reading inventories, which assess a variety of reading skills. Inventories may be teacher-made instruments that use the actual curriculum used in instruction or commercially prepared devices. Commercially prepared instruments contain passages and word lists and diagnostic information that enable the teacher to analyze errors.

CHECK YOUR UNDERSTANDING

Check your skill in constructing informal reading assessments by completing Activity 6.12.

Considerations When Using Informal Reading Inventories

The cautions about grade levels and curriculum verification stated in the previous section should be considered when using any commercially prepared informal reading inventory. Moreover, teachers should be concerned about the specific characteristics of the informal reading inventory when selecting one for classroom use (Flippo, Holland, McCarthy, & Swinning, 2009). These authors stress that teachers determine the specific reading behaviors that are being assessed, examine the type of reading passages for interest and purpose, and make certain that the passages do not assume a high level of background knowledge in order to understand the passage. In addition, the authors advise that teachers understand the manner in which to interpret the results provided from the administration of the informal reading inventory.

In a review of informal reading inventories by Nilsson (2008), it was noted that these instruments vary widely in the level of reading and thinking assessed, in the format of the instruments, and in the reliability and validity of the inventories. The author suggested that teachers review the features of the inventory to determine if it is a good match for the purpose intended and for the students in the setting.

The results of reading inventories, along with other informal and formal measures of reading, can be compared across instruments to evaluate students' consistency in reading skills. For example, Rubin (2011) suggested comparing a student's ability by applying the ranking of a 1 for frustration level, a 2 for instructional level, and a 3 for independent reading level. By assigning these rankings, a teacher can determine if a student is consistently reading at the frustration level across all measures or only in comprehension on an informal reading inventory or other measure. The author provided the example of a frustration level on an informal reading inventory score of <7 on a 10-question instrument. This same student may be performing at an independent reading level on reading recognition; therefore, the teacher could determine that the student's difficulty might be in the comprehension assessed on the inventory rather than across all reading skills.

Informal Assessment of Mathematics

The teacher may use curriculum-based assessment to measure all areas of mathematics. The assessment should be combined with both task analysis and error analysis to determine specific problem areas. These problem areas should be further assessed by using probes to determine the specific difficulty. In addition to using these methods, Liedtke (1988) suggested using an interview technique to locate deficits in accuracy and strategies. Liedtke included such techniques as asking the student to create a word problem to illustrate a computation, redirecting the original computation to obtain additional math concept information (e.g., asking the student to compare two of the answers to see which is greater), and asking the student to solve a problem and explain the steps used in the process.

Howell and Morehead (1987) suggested several methods for assessing specific math skills. Their techniques provide assessment of accuracy and fluency of basic facts, recall, basic concepts, operations, problem-solving concepts, content knowledge, tool and unit knowledge, and skill integration. These authors also suggested techniques for assessing recall of math facts and correct writing of math problems. For example, they suggested asking the student to respond orally to problems involving basic operations rather than in writing. The responses should be scored as correct or incorrect and can then be compared with the established criterion for mastery (e.g., 90% correct). When a student responds to written tasks, such as copying numbers or writing digits, the student's ability to write the digits can be evaluated and compared with the student's oral mastery of math facts. In this way, the teacher is better able to determine if the student's ability to write digits has an impact on responding correctly to written math problems.

Informal Assessment of Spelling

A common type of informal spelling assessment is that the teacher states the word, uses the word in a sentence, and repeats the word. Most elementary spelling texts provide this type of direct curriculum-based assessment. The teacher may wish to assign different words or may be teaching at the secondary level, where typical spelling texts are not used. The teacher may also need to assess the spelling of content-related words in areas such as science or social studies. Or, the teacher may use written samples by the student to analyze spelling errors.

Informal Assessment of Written Language

A student's written language skills may be assessed informally using written work samples. These samples may be analyzed for spelling, punctuation, correct grammar and usage, vocabulary, creative ability, story theme, sequence, and plot. If the objective of instruction is to promote creativity, actual spelling, punctuation, and other mechanical errors should not be scored against the student on the written sample. These errors, however, should be noted by the teacher and used in educational planning for English and spelling lessons. Guerin and Maier (1993) provided guidance on scoring informal written language by suggesting that teachers check for substitutions, omissions, additions, and errors in sequencing in spelling and also in writing of words. These authors also suggest that teachers pay particular attention in comparing what a student hears with what the student writes. For example, a student may hear the word "purchase" but write "purchasing," which would indicate an error of addition. An example of a substitution of a word would be that a student hears "ring" but writes "bell," indicating a linguistic substitution.

Analysis of Spelling Errors Used in Informal Assessment

Shapiro also suggested creating local (schoolwide) norms to compare students. The number of words that are correct can be used as a baseline in developing short-term objectives related to written expression. This informal method may be linked directly to classroom curricula and may be repeated frequently as a direct measure of students' writing skills. Writing samples may also be used to analyze handwriting. The teacher uses error analysis to evaluate the sample, write short-term objectives, and plan educational strategies.

Handwriting should also be analyzed in addition to analysis of written language. Guerin and Maier (1983) suggested analyzing the handwriting products of students by considering letter formation to determine if the letters are written below the line, if the student writes the letters counterclockwise, if the size of the letters is uniform, and also if the spacing between letters and words is correct. These authors further suggest that teachers should also note the length of time the student requires to write the letters and words and if there are discrepancies between lower- and uppercase letters.

Performance Assessment and Authentic Assessment

In performance testing, the student creates a response from his or her existing knowledge base. The U.S. Office of Technology Assessment defines performance assessment as "testing methods that require students to create an answer product that demonstrates their knowledge or skills" (1992, p. 16). The teacher may use a variety of formats in performance assessment, including products that the student constructs. Harris and Graham (1994) state that performance assessment stresses the constructivist nature of the task the student undertakes in demonstrating his or her knowledge.

The types of tasks that teachers require a student to complete in performance assessment might include the student's explanation of process as well as the student's perception of the task and the material learned. This type of assessment involves several levels of cognitive processing and reasoning, and allows educators to tap into areas not assessed by more traditional modes of assessment. When considering performance assessment as an alternative for making educational placement decisions, Elliott and Fuchs (1997) cautioned that it should be used in conjunction with other types of assessment because of insufficient knowledge regarding psychometric evidence and the lack of professionals who are trained to use this type of assessment reliably. Glatthorn suggested criteria for educators to use in the evaluation of performance tasks (1998).

Authentic assessment differs from performance assessment in that students must apply knowledge in a manner consistent with generalizing into a "real-world" setting or, in some instances, students complete the task in the "real world." Archbald (1991) stated that authentic assessment requires a disciplined production of knowledge using techniques that are within the field in which the student is being assessed. The student's tasks are instrumental and may require a substantial amount of time to complete. The student may be required to use a variety of materials and resources and may need to collaborate with other students in completing the task.

Portfolio Assessment

One method of assessing a student's current level of academic functioning is through **portfolio assessment.** A portfolio is a collection of student work that provides a holistic view of the student's strengths and weaknesses. The portfolio collection contains various work samples, permanent products, and test results from a variety of instruments and methods. For example, a portfolio of reading might include a student's test scores on teacher-made tests, including curriculum-based assessments, work samples from daily work and homework assignments, error analyses of work and test samples, and the results of an informal reading inventory with miscues noted and analyzed. The assessment of the student's progress would be keyed to decoding skills, comprehension skills, fluency, and so on. These measures would be collected over a period of time. This type of assessment may be useful in describing the current progress of the student to his or her parents (Taylor, 1993).

Watch this video on portfolio assessment to see how a teacher reviews a student's progress in written language.

When evaluating a student's performance on the submitted portfolio, teachers should assess the portfolios by determining the student's level of engagement and the evidence provided of the skills and abilities using multiple products or modes of responding to the portfolio requirements (Glatthorn, 1998). It will be beneficial to apply scoring rubrics that measure the level of mastery of the tasks included in the portfolio assignment and to assess the progress or improvement across time.

The essential elements of effective portfolio assessment were listed by Shaklee, Barbour, Ambrose, and Hansford (1997, p. 10). Assessment should realize the following:

Be authentic and valid.

Encompass the whole child.

Involve repeated observations of various patterns of behavior.

Be continuous over time.

Use a variety of methods for gathering evidence of student performance.

Provide a means for systematic feedback to be used in the improvement of instruction and student performance.

Provide an opportunity for joint conversations and explanations between students and teachers, teachers and parents, and students and parents.

Ruddell (1995, p. 191) provided the following list of possible products that could be included in a portfolio for assessing literacy in the middle grades:

Samples of student writing

Story maps

Reading log or dated list of books student has read

Vocabulary journal

Artwork, project papers, photographs, and other products of work completed

Group work, papers, projects, and products

Daily journal

Writing ideas

Reading response log, learning log, or double-entry journal or writing from assigned reading during the year

Letters to pen pals; letters exchanged with teacher

Out-of-school writing and artwork

Unit and lesson tests collected over the grading period or academic year

Paratore (1995) reported that establishing common standards for assessing literacy through the use of portfolio assessment provides a useful alternative in the evaluation of students' reading and writing skills. Hobbs (1993) found portfolio assessment useful in providing supplemental information for eligibility consideration that included samples of the quality of work that was not evident in standardized assessment.

Portfolio data were also found to provide information to teachers that was more informative and led to different decisions for instructional planning (Rueda & Garcia, 1997). This study found that the recommendations were more specific and that student strengths were more easily identifiable using this form of assessment.

● INFORMAL AND FORMAL ASSESSMENT METHODS

In Chapter 7, you will be introduced to norm-referenced testing. These tests are useful in assessing factors that cannot be reliably or validly assessed using informal measures. There are some difficulties with using norm-referenced tests, however, and this has led to the shift to the response-to-intervention method and problem-solving method, and the increased use of informal measures, such as CBMs, to collect data.

Some of the difficulties with the use of norm-referenced assessment are presented in the next section.

● PROBLEMS RELATED TO NORM-REFERENCED ASSESSMENT

The weaknesses attributed to norm-referenced assessment include problems specific to the various instruments and problems with test administration and interpretation. Norm-referenced tests may not adequately represent material actually taught in a specific curriculum (Shapiro, 1996). In other words, items on norm-referenced tests may include content or skill areas not included in the student's curriculum. Salvia and Hughes (1990) wrote:

> The fundamental problem with using published tests is the test's content. If the content of the test—even content prepared by experts—does not match the content that is taught, the test is useless for evaluating what the student has learned from school instruction. (p. 8)

Good and Salvia (1988) studied the representation of reading curricula in norm-referenced tests and concluded that a deficient score on a norm-referenced reading test could actually represent the selection of a test with inadequate content validity for the current curriculum. Hultquist and Metzke (1993) determined that curriculum bias existed when using standardized achievement tests to measure the reading of survival words and reading and spelling skills in general.

In addition, the frequent use of norm-referenced instruments may result in bias because limited numbers of alternate forms exist, creating the possibility of "test wiseness" among students (Fuchs, Tindal, & Deno, 1984; Shapiro, 1996). Another study revealed that norm-referenced instruments are not as sensitive to academic growth as other instruments that are linked more directly to the actual classroom curriculum (Marston, Fuchs, & Deno, 1986). This means that norm-referenced tests may not measure small gains made in the classroom from week to week.

According to Reynolds (1982), the psychometric assessment of students using traditional norm-referenced methods is fraught with many problems of bias, including cultural bias, which may result in test scores that reflect intimidation or communication problems rather than ability level. These difficulties in using norm-referenced testing for special education planning have led to the emergence of alternative methods of assessment.

CHAPTER SUMMARY

In this chapter you:

- Learned about the purposes of informal assessment
- Learned about methods used to construct curriculum-based assessment
- Applied data to plot progress of cases
- Analyzed scenarios and made intervention decisions
- Synthesized informal assessment methods to apply to case scenarios
- Evaluated informal data-collection case scenarios

THINK AHEAD

When a student has academic difficulty and does not respond to the intensive interventions employed in a general education setting, it is important to use specific measurement techniques to analyze if enough progress has been made. Chapter 7 presents additional measurement techniques to use with interventions that aid educators in understanding if sufficient progress has been made.

CHAPTER QUIZ

Now complete the Chapter Quiz to assess your understanding of the content in this chapter.

7 Response to Intervention and Progress Monitoring

CHAPTER FOCUS

In this chapter you will:

- Learn the models of response to intervention (RTI)
- Apply progress-monitoring decisions to case scenarios
- Analyze cases to determine when response to intervention is successful
- Synthesize the RTI process into the comprehensive evaluation process
- Evaluate case scenarios illustrating the RTI decision process

● RESPONSE TO INTERVENTION

In Chapter 1, you were introduced to the three-tier model of intervention presented in Figure 1.4. This model forms the framework for the response-to-intervention (RTI) structure. As depicted in the introduction, RTI is a way of organizing instruction across a campus. RTI is also mentioned in the federal regulations and is one method to use in the determination of learning disabilities.

The first tier represents general instruction provided to all students in the school in all subject areas. Moreover, the first tier includes the typical behavioral strategies, such as classroom- and campus-level behavior management, that address the behavior of most children. Conceptually, the first tier includes methods that should meet the needs of approximately 80–85% of all students (Council of Administrators of Special Education, 2006). In other words, with the typical research-based behavior management and academic instruction practices on a campus, at least 80–85% of students will likely achieve as expected for their age or grade group and their behaviors will not interfere with this academic progress. Because these methods meet the needs of most students, these methods are called *universal methods*.

In order to make certain that instructional and behavior management practices are working, schools typically use universal screening measures to provide information about student achievement. The same universal screening methods will inform school personnel about students who are not experiencing the success expected. At this point, when students are screened and found to lack the progress expected, RTI begins. An important part of the RTI process is monitoring progress. Progress monitoring will inform the teacher when a student's current educational program needs to be changed. Progress monitoring assists with the process of RTI and the decisions that are made in the RTI framework.

RTI is designed to remediate or provide requisite learning at the acquisition stage of learning in the general education setting. The goal of RTI is to prevent a child from lagging behind peers in academic or behavioral expectations. RTI is not a vehicle to use simply to engage in a special education referral process. One of the main objectives of RTI is to prevent special education referrals unless the student does not respond to intensive interventions as expected. McCook (2006) identified the following components of an RTI model: (a) universal screening of all students; (b) baseline data collection for all students, using measureable terms when evaluating student progress and setting goals; (c) inclusion of an accountability plan that includes measureable terms and how and when the interventions will occur; (d) development of a progress-monitoring plan used for data collection; and (e) inclusion of a data-based decision-making plan used to determine whether progress has been made.

Tier I

Tier I includes all students who are receiving traditional instruction in the general education setting. As mentioned previously, this will likely include from 80 to 85% of students in the school. For example, Tier I students receive reading instruction based on the traditional curriculum, often set by the state's educational agency. This curriculum is typically taught in group format, with students reading assigned texts, orally and silently, interacting with new vocabulary contained in the text, and then responding to specific questions measuring literal, inferential, and critical comprehension of textual matter. In middle and high school, the academic content areas are taught in the general education program using general curricular materials. General education teachers monitor their students' progress as they move through the school year and note when specific students need interventions because their academic progress is not occurring as expected.

In Chapter 6, you learned that curriculum-based measurement (CBM) and curriculum-based assessment may be used to monitor the progress of students in the general education setting. It is important to make the connection between the RTI process and the use of CBMs or other informal measures to monitor progress. Students who seem to be struggling in the general education setting may benefit from a closer look at their progress to determine exactly where and why their learning breaks down. Used skillfully, CBMs can be sensitive measurements of how students respond to instruction. The student who is not making progress as expected might be considered for Tier II.

Tier II

Tier II interventions represent a different set of instructional strategies that are used for individual students who are not experiencing success in the general education program. These strategies differ from traditional modes of instruction in that they are more *intensive* and *intentional*: that is, more time is spent in the teaching of a specific concept or skill, alternative pedagogies are used to deliver instruction, and students are given more guided and independent practice in carrying out the tasks that demonstrate that learning has occurred. Tier II interventions are typically presented to small groups of students *in addition to* the instruction they receive in the general education setting. Students who are in general elementary class for reading, language arts, or math instruction, and who are not making the progress expected as noted by careful progress monitoring, are provided with Tier II interventions. For reading, Tier II interventions might include small-group instruction for fluency, decoding, or comprehension. For language arts, additional small-group instruction might be provided for spelling or written language. In math, Tier II interventions might include small-group instruction in numeration or number values, or in basic operations such as math, subtraction, multiplication, or division, and so on. Tier II interventions can be delivered and monitored by teachers, paraeducators, reading or math specialists, or other school staff.

Tier III

Tier III interventions are more intensive than Tier II interventions. They may be delivered by specialists, including the special education teacher, and are usually delivered in very small groups or even in a one-on-one setting. For example, Byron, a first-grade student, was having difficulty in reading. His teacher provided him with Tier II interventions that included additional small-group instruction in fluency and vocabulary. When Byron continued to struggle in these areas, his teacher arranged for additional instructional time for him, intensifying her Tier II interventions. Using progress monitoring and trend analysis, she noted that Byron still failed to make the progress she had anticipated he would. She then arranged for Byron to receive Tier III interventions—in this case, one-on-one teaching during reading class time. Byron received individualized instruction 5 days each week from the reading specialist. The specialist monitored his progress throughout the Tier III interim and determined that one-on-one instruction resulted in Byron's making satisfactory gains in the reading skills that caused him greatest difficulty. Byron's classroom teacher and other members of the RTI committee decided to continue with the Tier III interventions rather than refer him for an evaluation for special education.

Students who do not respond to Tier II and III interventions (in other words, data do not indicate improvement) may be referred for special education evaluation. A student in Tier III may or may not be eligible for special education. A discussion in a later section of this chapter provides information about using RTI to obtain data that may be used in conjunction with other assessments to determine a need for special education.

RTI and Educational Policy

The implementation of RTI, which was addressed in both the Individuals with Disabilities Education Act (IDEA, 2004) and the Elementary and Secondary Education Act (ESEA, 2001) came about partly as a result of discontent with the measures used to assess students with mild learning and behavioral challenges. For example, research found that the cognitive characteristics of low- and slow-achieving students and students with reading disabilities were difficult to differentiate (Lyon et al., 2001). Moreover, difficulties with a disproportionality of minority students in the mild-learning and behavior-disorder categories may have been a function of the traditional assessment methods used to determine eligibility.

Even though addressing students' needs through the use of research-based interventions has been included in federal regulations for both IDEA and ESEA, the implementation of the RTI process has been varied across school systems and states' educational policies. For example, Zirkel and Thomas (2010) found that some states incorporated the requirements into state law while other states addressed the requirements in policy manuals alone. Moreover, RTI was operationalized differently across states, with some states requiring the use of RTI for determining learning disabilities, others requiring the earlier method of discrepancy analysis, and still others requiring both or neither. Discrepancy analysis compares a student's cognitive ability with his or her academic achievement to determine if a significant difference between the two exists. Additionally, some state policies contained deadlines for implementation and others did not have a timeline in place. The authors noted that schools might be in jeopardy if their implementation of RTI procedures were based on state education policy manuals rather than state law. In other words, regardless of what is in a state policy manual, school districts should comply with federal and state regulations rather than state policy manuals alone: Districts that do otherwise may risk being noncompliant with federal regulations.

It is imperative that teachers and other school personnel understand the process of RTI and be able to document efforts to improve student progress as required in the federal regulations. Therefore, teachers need a level of understanding of how effectiveness of interventions can be measured and how to determine and document the use of research-based interventions and scientifically research-based interventions. These concepts are presented in following sections.

● IMPLEMENTATION OF RTI AND PROGRESS MONITORING

Important conceptual foundations are found in a classroom in which RTI is implemented. Instructional foundations that support RTI include the use of (1) research-based teaching methods as required by the federal regulations of ESEA and (2) differentiated instruction. Research-based methods are those that have met specific criteria, such as interventions that have been studied with large samples of students and been found to effect change or progress in academics or behavior. For example, in language arts instruction, the Kaplan Spell/Read program has been found to be effective in developing fluency and comprehension (What Works Clearing House, n.d.). This determination was made because more than 200 students in first through third grades responded to this strategy in research studies. Likewise, the Saxon Middle School Math program was found to have positive effects on mathematics achievement in studies that involved 53,000 middle school students in 70 different schools across six states. Any instructional strategy categorized as "research-based" must meet rigorous requirements established by the What Works Clearinghouse of the U.S. Department of Education Institute of Education Sciences (What Works Clearinghouse, n.d.). These requirements include such components

FIGURE 7.1 Differentiated Instruction: Content, Process, Product

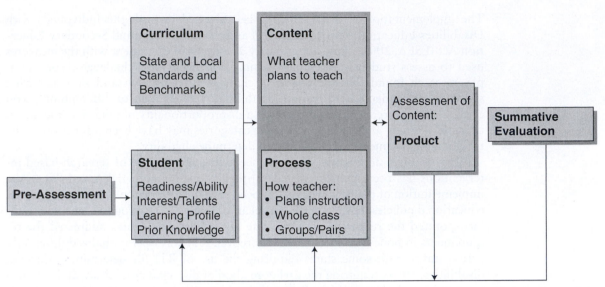

Source: Adapted from Oaksford, L., & Jones, L., (2001). *Differentiated instruction abstract.* Tallahassee, FL: Leon County Schools.

as randomly selected students for participation in the research study and meeting effectiveness standards.

The second conceptual foundation that is needed for an RTI classroom—differentiated instruction—is illustrated in Figure 7.1. Briefly, teachers who differentiate instruction vary their teaching according to student needs. Instruction may be differentiated (1) by adapting or changing *content* to reflect student interests and learning levels, (2) by adapting or changing the *process* of instruction, or (3) by adapting or changing the *product* expected of the student.

RTI Models

In order for a campus to implement RTI, school leadership, teachers, and staff must all understand and agree with the RTI process that will be used. Although federal laws do not specify how the process should take place or mandate a model to follow, two RTI models are currently implemented in schools. One RTI model, the *standard protocol model* or *standard model*, uses similar interventions for all students with similar academic and behavioral challenges. Students are often placed into groups with readily available interventions. For example, a school using a standard protocol model will likely implement academic interventions and monitor progress through a commercially produced curriculum or published interventions, and likely will use commercially produced progress-monitoring systems such as AIMSweb (AIMSweb, n.d.) and the Dynamic Indicators of Basic Early Literacy Skills (DIBELS) (Good & Kaminski, 2002). In the standardized model, first-grade readers who do not respond to universal instruction in one general education reading classroom of a campus receive the same or very similar interventions as other struggling readers in another first-grade classroom. In this model, students receiving intensive interventions are monitored using the same progress-monitoring program.

The second RTI model is a problem-solving model. In this model, each student who does not respond to universal instruction is analyzed by the teacher and perhaps an RTI committee to determine possible interventions that might address his or her specific needs. The general education teacher, along with other members of the RTI committee, evaluate the student's performance through permanent products, grades, attendance, and information from parents and school records to determine (a) the intervention that will be most effective, (b) who will carry out the intervention, and (c) what materials will be used. Progress monitoring yields data about student performance in response to specific interventions.

Progress Monitoring

Implementation of RTI procedures requires that general and special education teachers understand the importance of compiling and interpreting student data. Progress-monitoring programs such as AIMSweb and DIBELS may be used to monitor a student's progress throughout an intervention. Although some commercially produced progress-monitoring programs include data interpretation that is readily available for teachers, all academic skills may not be included in them; in fact, many students have skill or behavioral challenges for which commercially produced, data-driven, progress-monitoring programs simply do not exist. Therefore, special education teachers, general education teachers, and other educational personnel may find themselves relying on curriculum-based measurement tools in collecting and interpreting data for educational decision making.

School personnel may find that new roles and responsibilities emerge as they implement the conceptual framework of RTI. One survey of special education administrators in one state found that 92% of respondents believed that special education teachers, general education teachers, and reading teachers should determine when students are nonresponders to instructional interventions (Werts, Lambert, & Carpenter, 2009). In the same survey, 87% of respondents indicated that school psychologists should collect data, and 80% agreed that special education teachers who work with the students should also be involved with data collection. Fuchs (2007) proposed that educators will likely need to engage in collaboration and consultation in order to make a successful transition to the RTI framework. Mitchell, Deshler, and Lenz (2012) found that special educators were largely involved with managerial tasks, explaining results to RTI teams, discussing assessment results, and collaborating on effective instruction. Suggested roles and responsibilities for RTI team members are presented in Figure 7.2.

Decisions in RTI

School professionals collaborate in making decisions about when a student requires a Tier II or Tier III intervention. Data must be reviewed and understood by the decision makers. In order to make instructional decisions, team members need to agree on the criteria they will use in making those decisions. For example, they must agree about what criteria they will use in determining whether a student has made enough progress to be moved back to Tier I or whether a student needs to be moved to Tier III. Before they reach their decisions, teachers and other school personnel must understand measurement of progress. Progress can be measured in a variety of ways. Gresham (2005) presented RTI measurement methods school personnel should consider. These measurement methods are in addition to the methods, such as trend lines, presented in Chapter 6. School personnel must determine if the changes revealed by the data are reliable and, if so, how much change is needed to make a decision. Measurement methods that Gresham (2005) alludes to include absolute change, reliable change index, percent of nonoverlapping data points (PNDs), percent change, and visual inspection.

Absolute change is a simple way to examine change in an individual student (Gresham, 2005). Teachers can make a determination about a student's progress using absolute change by comparing the student's performance pre- and post-intervention. Measuring absolute change requires simply comparing a baseline

FIGURE 7.2 RTI Roles and Responsibilities

Task	Responsibility
Collecting screening data using existing data or individually administered brief assessments on all students	Teachers and trained aides
Interpreting screening data	Special educators and school psychologists
Ensuring the quality of general education	Curriculum specialists at the school or district level, school psychologists, teachers, and parents
Collecting continuing progress-monitoring data	Teachers and trained aides
Interpreting progress-monitoring data	Special educators and school psychologists
Designing Tier II and beyond programs that incorporate validated intervention protocols	Special educators and school psychologists
Implementing Tier II and beyond programs with fidelity	Trained aides under the supervision of special educators and school psychologists
Conducting the Step 4 evaluation	Special educators and school psychologists

Source: Fuchs, L. S. (2007). NRCLD updated on responsiveness to intervention: Research to practice. [Brochure]. Lawrence, KS: National Research Center on Learning Disabilities.

performance with performance at the end of the intervention period. For example, if the student was completing math probes with 11 digits correct at baseline and had 16 digits correct at the end of intervention, the absolute change would be 5. It is important for the RTI team to establish a criterion for absolute change rather than relying on a simple raw data number. For example, the team might set a criterion of 16 out of 20 items correct in a math probe, for an accuracy level of 80%, before declaring instructional intervention successful. Similarly, in determining whether an intervention has been successful for a student struggling in reading, an RTI team might set a criterion for the student of 85% accuracy in reading fluency and comprehension on several measures of performance. When the criterion of 85% has been reached, according to progress monitoring, the teacher has evidence that the student has reached an absolute change. In a behavior-related example, a teacher might wish to see a student's acting-out behaviors decrease from 15 incidents per day to 2. When the student exhibits problematic behavior only twice a day following the intervention, and the student's improvement in behavior has been consistent over time, the teacher may determine that absolute change in behavior has occurred. And finally, when a student's pre-intervention score is compared with post-intervention and the performance is what the teacher expected on the post-inervention, the teacher can determine that absolute change has occurred. For example, the teacher may decide that the post-intervention score should be 90 on a specific measure. When the student reaches this level of performance, absolute change has occurred.

CHECK YOUR UNDERSTANDING

Complete Activity 7.1 to assess your understanding of the RTI terms presented.

Reliable change index (RCI) is another method used to examine data. This method is more complex and involves knowledge of the standard error of the difference score of the pre- and posttest scores, similar to a standard deviation score and a standard error of measurement score (Gresham, 2005; Jacobson, & Truax, 1991). This standard error of difference score is used to divide difference scores calculated by subtracting a student's posttest score from the pretest score. For example, if a student's posttest score was 88 and her pretest score was 35, the difference is −53. When this is divided by a standard error of the difference score, the reliable change index is determined. If the standard error of the difference is 2, for example, the resulting RCI = −26.5.

$$\text{Reliable Change Index} = \frac{\text{Postest} - \text{Pretest}}{\text{Standard Error of Difference}}$$

The standard error of the difference is calculated by using the following information:

$$\text{Standard error of the difference} = \sqrt{2} \, (\text{standard error})^2$$

As noted, this measure of change is more complex and requires more time to caculate than many classroom teachers can provide. Therefore, when using interventions that require documentation to determine change in behavior or academic performance, other methods such as percent change or percent of nonoverlapping data points may be preferable.

Percent of nonoverlapping data points (PNDs) is based on the idea that the data points that are plotted after the intervention begins that are not represented during the baseline or pre-intervention days are the points that indicate if the intervention is effective. To calculate the PNDs, first determine the highest data point achieved during the baseline period. Next, count the data points that are above the highest baseline point and divide that total by the number of data points during the intervention. Then multiply this number by 100. For example, if the student's highest point of baseline data was 20 and the number of data points above 20 during intervention was 15, and the total number of data points during the intervention was 22, the PND would be calculated as follows:

$$\frac{15}{22} = .68 \times 100 = 68\%$$

The result of 68% indicates that 68% of the data points are above the highest data point during the period before the intervention began. Guidelines for the interpretation of PNDs were provided by Scruggs and Mastropieri (1998): 90% of the points above the highest baseline point or greater indicate very effective interventions, between 70% and 90% indicate effective interventions, between 50% and 70% indicate treatment that appears to be effective but may be open to question, and below 50% indicate that the interventions are not effective. If the PNDs of the previous example had been above 70%, it would have been considered an effective intervention.

Another measure that uses percent is percent change. This measure uses the mean or average of the baseline and compares this with the average of the intervention. The percent change is calculated as follows:

Mean of baseline − Mean of intervention/Mean of baseline = Percent change

An example of this calculation is provided below. In this example, a student had 11 incidents per day of noncompliance. Following the intervention, the number had decreased to 4. The calculation is:

$$11 - 4/11 = 63\% \text{ to } 11 - 4/11 = 63.6\% \text{ or } 64\%$$

Cut-off points may be determined by the RTI committee or classroom teacher. This is a score or number that the student must reach in order for the determination to be made that progress is occurring as a result of intervention. This is similar to a criterion, but may also be a score, such as a score of 85% on a weekly test. For example, the RTI committee might set the measure of 85% on weekly tests for a period of several weeks to make certain the performance is consistent. Once the student has scored at 85% or higher for the set number of weeks, the committee may decide to move the student back to Tier I.

A method that is easy and quick for teachers is visual inspection. The teacher simply inspects the student's data graphs to determine whether (1) the data are moving in the right direction and (2) that positive movement is consistent over time. For example, if the objective is to increase reading fluency and the data points continue to rise consistently across weeks, indicating an increase in fluency, simple visual inspection could be used to determine that interventions have been effective. If the objective is to decrease a problematic behavior and the data points continue to decrease, visual inspection can be used to determine that interventions are meeting with success. While this method seems to be the easiest to use in examining data, it is likely not as accurate and may be more subjective.

Another form of visual inspection is informal observation. A teacher can informally observe whether a student is making noticeable progress in the classroom during Tier II and III interventions. If the student is able to perform a task when required in the classroom or his or her behavior has noticeably improved in the setting in which it was once interferring with learning, it can be determined that interventions have been successful. This is discussed further in the next section on decisions about RTI. The measurement methods used to determine if a change has occurred or if there has been a response to a specific intervention are summarized in Table 7.1.

Decisions about Intervention Effectiveness

As noted previously, guidelines exist to determine if an intervention is effective for some measures, such as PNDs. RTI committee members may also collaboratively establish criteria for effectiveness. For example, for percent change, the team may decide that 70% change is enough to indicate that an intervention is effective. Likewise, the team may decide to set a criterion related to the performance of a particular skill, such as decoding 9 out of 10 pseudowords correctly. The RTI team might determine that interventions are effective and a student will be moved to a "lower" tier when the student's data show improvement over multiple interventions. A student who is receiving Tier II interventions might remain in that tier until such time as he or she demonstrates progress in fluency, comprehension, and decoding, for example. A student who is receiving Tier II interventions for behavior might remain in that tier until he or she demonstrates improvements in behavior across several settings and over a predetermined number of weeks.

Teachers and other members of the RTI committee are charged with the responsibility of making decisions about the effectiveness of a specific intervention.

CHECK YOUR UNDERSTANDING

Complete Activity 7.2 to check your understanding of Section 504 and Tiers I and II.

TABLE 7.1

Measures of Change

Indication of Change	Advantages	Disadvantages
1. Absolute change	1. Easy to calculate; may be changed to percentage or other criteria	1. May be difficult to generalize to other settings or skills
2. Reliable change index	2. May detect change more accurately than absolute change	2. Difficult to calculate quickly; need to compare with change across settings or skills
3. Percentage of nonoverlapping points	3. Fairly easy to calculate	3. May overestimate change; need to compare with change across settings or skills
4. Percent change	4. Easy to calculate	4. May need to establish guidelines for noticeable change; need to compare with change across settings or skills
5. Cut-off points	5. Easy to set	5. May not be as sensitive to change that occurs below the cut-off point; need to compare across settings or skills
6. Visual inspection	6. Quick and easy	6. Less precise; subjective; need to compare with change across settings or skills

CHECK YOUR UNDERSTANDING

Complete Activity 7.3 to determine your level of understanding of the concepts presented in this chapter.

They determine effectiveness based on the data collected during multiple probes, tests, or observations not only in the intervention setting, but in other settings as well, most particularly the general education classroom. The team is interested in determining whether improvements effected by interventions generalize to other academic tasks or to behaviors in different environments. The question of generalization is educationally and socially the most important question for teachers in the RTI process. If a student has mastered an isolated skill or can demonstrate an appropriate behavior in the intervention setting but is not yet able to transfer that learning to a more complex academic task or is not able to transfer that appropriate behavior to other settings, the student may require additional interventions or changes in the intervention.

The use of RTI to make educational decisions about when and how to provide interventions to students who are struggling is an emerging practice that continues to be researched. Vanderheyden (2011) cautions educators to consider the accuracy of the decisions made using the RTI approach. For example, the criteria and cut-off scores used to make decisions may vary in validity and reliability based on the specific school population. In schools where there are large numbers of struggling students, the application of RTI may be different than in schools with large numbers of higher-achieving students and low numbers of struggling students. If the set criteria are the same across both schools, the numbers of students found to need Tier II interventions will be different. Should the schools use different criteria, a student who may be found to require Tier II interventions in the school with high-achieving students may not be found to require interventions in the school with large numbers of struggling students. In addition, some predictive models used in determining cut-off scores may miss large numbers of students who need intervention or may falsely identify other students as needing intervention who, in fact, do not. These measurement issues continue to be researched but in practice may result in inaccuracies when only one screening measure is used to determine which students should receive interventions.

In reaching decisions about the effectiveness of interventions, O'Connor and Klingner (2010) warned that not only the outcome effectiveness should be examined from the student perspective, but the teacher must also be considered. A student receiving instruction from a highly skilled teacher who implements the interventions with integrity and fidelity may have greater gains than a student receiving interventions provided by a less skilled teacher or provided in a less reliable manner. This underscores the need for multiple methods of evaluating the struggling student.

For example, Fuchs, Fuchs, and Compton (2012) found that the use of both cognitive and reading measures was more predictive in the identification of students with true reading difficulties than the use of single reading measures. The results of this research point to the need for multiple gating to determine more accurately the students who require interventions. The application of multiple gating to reach decisions is consistent with Vanderheyden's (2011) conclusions of technical adequacy in how educators can reach decisions in RTI. In other words, teachers should not accept only one universal screening measure as an indication that a student requires Tier II or even Tier III interventions. Best practice in assessment in RTI requires multiple measures and perhaps from multiple sources.

CHECK YOUR UNDERSTANDING

Complete Activity 7.4 to evaluate when a student needs additional intervention.

● THE ROLE OF RTI AND SPECIAL EDUCATION COMPREHENSIVE EVALUATIONS

IDEA 2004 did not specifically require that RTI be included in the assessment of all students referred for special education evaluation. The focus on RTI in the assessment process is to provide another means of collecting data that may be used in making special education referral and eligibility decisions. In other words, RTI data can be added to that derived from other assessments to provide a complete picture of the student's functioning in school. One of the requirements of special education placement is that a student's disability, weakness, or disorder must be significant enough that general education alone will not meet his or her educational needs. RTI data can offer evidence that within a general classroom setting, even with interventions that are based on researched strategies, the student is not making progress and may need special education support. A student may be referred for special education assessment for many reasons. For example, a kindergartener may lag significantly behind her peers in language, processing and responding to classroom instruction, self-help skills such as toileting, demonstrating preacademic skills, and functioning in a school environment. This student's behavior may be indicative of cognitive or developmental delays that require special education support. A thorough evaluation of this student will necessarily include cognitive assessment, preacademic readiness assessment, speech and language assessment, motor-skills assessment, and adaptive behavior assessment. Assessment results drive educational decisions and interventions. As required by law, students who are suspected of having a disability should be evaluated in all areas of suspected disability. In this case, RTI alone will not provide the information needed to meet the student's educational needs.

Data derived from RTI are particularly important in those cases where a mild disability such as a learning or behavioral disability is suspected. As noted by Hale, Kaufman, Naglieri, and Kavale (2006), in order to be identified as having a learning disability, a student must meet the criterion in the federal definition of *learning disability* that refers to a processing disorder that manifests in a specific academic skill area. Linking a processing deficit to weakness in a particular academic area cannot occur without cognitive and academic assessments. The information yielded by RTI data can be used as evidence that a student's difficulty in the general education curriculum does not stem from a lack of intensive and intentional instruction using research-based methods; however, RTI will not replace correct identification of specific learning disabilities through the use of appropriate, valid, and reliable formal and informal assessment.

Likewise, using RTI in isolation to identify a behavioral disability (sometimes referred to as *emotional disturbance*) is inappropriate. When a student evinces behavioral difficulties and the implementation of RTI resolves those issues, it is likely that the child does not have significant behavioral or emotional challenges that impede learning. When a student does not respond to RTI strategies at all tiers, parents, teachers, and other educational personnel become involved in the collection of data to determine if a behavioral disability or emotional disturbance exists. These measures are presented in Chapter 9. The determination that a behavioral disability or emotional disturbance exists must be based on thorough assessment that will drive specific, intensive interventions and support from special education staff.

Research and Practice of the Integration of RTI and Comprehensive Assessment for Special Education

As you read through the information in this chapter and previous chapters, you might be wondering how the RTI process and special education assessment practices fit together. As noted in Chapter 1, all assessment is for the purpose of determining when a student might need additional supports or interventions. In a school that has fully implemented RTI as a framework for instruction, most students who are served in Tier II would be returned to Tier I once the interventions have been found to result in change. The change would need to be significant, as determined when the student met criteria set by the RTI committee and the classroom teacher, and the change would be noted in other settings or skills linked to the intervention. In other words, behavioral interventions are successful when they result in noted changes in behavior across settings, and academic interventions are successful as indicated by data and as applied in classroom tasks within the general education curriculum.

Those students (typically 3 to 5%) who do not experience school success even when Tier III interventions are implemented may eventually be referred for full individual comprehensive assessment to determine if they require special education support. These students may be identified as have a learning disability in a processing area, they may be found to have impairments in cognitive functioning, or they may be found to have a behavioral disability or emotional disorder. Since the initial implementation of RTI, case law indicates there continues to be confusion about the role of RTI within the eligibility process (Daves, & Walker, 2012; Zirkel, 2012). The U.S. Department of Education has made it clear that parents may continue to request an evaluation for their child to determine a possible disability even without going through the RTI process first. Moreover, they cautioned educators to refrain from using the RTI process as a delay to assessment. To read more about this statement, visit the Read More About page.

The way in which school districts use RTI data in the eligibility process remains an unanswered question, although it is being examined in research (Ball & Christ, 2012; Hoover, 2010). Researchers call for additional study of the use of RTI to address the academic needs of students from diverse backgrounds (Finch, 2012) and students with attention problems (Haraway, 2012). RTI has been found an effective method of addressing needs of schools (Burns & Scholin, 2013), in addressing schools with difficult-to-each students with both reading and behavioral challenges (Algozzine et al., 2012), in reading remediation in secondary students (Pyle & Vaughn, 2012), and in improving services and increasing communication between students and teachers in rural schools (Sheperd & Salembier, 2011). RTI has also been proposed as a method to meet the needs of students who are gifted and also have learning disabilities (Yssel, Adams, Clarke, & Jones, 2014). Clearly, RTI can be applied in many learning scenarios that may benefit students and promote success.

Typically, for students who are not successful even with Tier III interventions, a referral for a comprehensive evaluation is made. Those students who are referred for special education services will be assessed in multiple ways with a variety of instruments. The wealth of data yielded by assessment provides the evaluation team with important information that can be used to answer questions like the following:

1. Has the student had consistent instruction that included research-based methods?

2. Has the student had frequent absences or other interference with the consistent instruction?

3. Are there specific patterns of performance that can be noted by looking at progress-monitoring data and classroom performance? If so, how would this relate to the selection of the specific instruments and methods to be used in the comprehensive assessment?

4. Does the student have specific difficulties in one area of academic achievement and classroom performance, or is the student struggling across multiple areas or skills?

When the team meets to discuss the referral, information obtained from the child's performance in the RTI process can assist the team in determining who will be involved in the assessment and which types of assessment will be used. Together with information provided by the parents and teachers who work with the student, an assessment plan can be put in place and the evaluation can be designed to assess all areas of suspected disability as stated in federal regulations. RTI data become part of the comprehensive evaluation data that are incorporated into the assessment results report to provide background information, reason for referral, and classroom performance.

CHAPTER SUMMARY

In this chapter you:

- Learned the models of response to intervention (RTI)

- Applied progress-monitoring decisions to case scenarios

- Analyzed cases to determine when response to intervention is successful

- Synthesized the RTI process into the comprehensive evaluation process

- Evaluated case scenarios illustrating the RTI decision process

THINK AHEAD

When students continue to have academic difficulties, what other measures may be useful to examine students' strengths and weaknesses? In the next chapter, you will learn about academic achievement methods to use for more comprehensive assessments.

CHAPTER QUIZ

Now complete the Chapter Quiz to measure your understanding of the content in this chapter.

8 Academic Assessment

CHAPTER FOCUS

In this chapter you will:

- Learn content assessed by several commonly used achievement instruments
- Apply basal and ceiling rules to raw score data
- Analyze scores to determine academic skill strengths and weaknesses
- Synthesize score profiles and interpret results
- Evaluate case scenarios to select appropriate achievment tests

● ACHIEVEMENT TESTS

Used in most schools, achievement tests are designed to measure what the student has learned. These tests may measure performance in a specific area of the educational curriculum, such as written language, or performance across several areas of the curriculum, such as math, reading, spelling, and science. Brief tests containing items that survey a range of skill levels, domains, or content areas are known as screening tests. Screening tests assess no single area in depth. Rather, they help the educator determine a student's weak areas—those that need additional assessment in order to determine specific skill mastery or weaknesses.

Aptitude tests contain items that measure what a student has retained but also are designed to indicate how much the student will learn in the future. Aptitude tests are thought to indicate current areas of strength as well as future potential. They are used in educational planning and include both group and individually administered tests. Diagnostic tests are those used to measure a specific ability, such as fine-motor ability. Adaptive behavior scales measure how well students adapt to different environments. In comprehensive assessment, achievement tests are used along with aptitude, diagnostic, cognitive, and, often, adaptive behavior scales. This chapter focuses on norm-referenced academic achievement batteries, academic screening instruments, and diagnostic academic tests. Together, these will provide educators with a comprehensive view of a student's academic functioning.

Standardized Norm-Referenced Tests versus Curriculum-Based Assessment

Norm-referenced tests as measures of academic achievement help educators make both eligibility and placement decisions. When selected and administered carefully, these tests yield reliable and valid information. As discussed in the previous chapter, norm-referenced instruments are researched and constructed in a systematic way and provide educators with a method of comparing a student with a peer group evaluated during the standardization process. Comparing a student to a norm-referenced group allows the educator to determine whether the student is performing as expected for her or his age or grade. If the student appears to be significantly behind peers developmentally, she or he may qualify for special services.

● REVIEW OF ACHIEVEMENT TESTS

This text is designed to involve you in the learning process and to help you develop skill in administering and interpreting tests. Because you will likely use only several of the many achievement tests available, this chapter presents selected instruments for review. These have been chosen for two primary reasons: (1) they are used frequently in schools and (2) they have been shown to be technically adequate. The following are individually administered academic achievement tests used frequently by educators.

1. *Woodcock–Johnson IV Tests of Achievement (WJ IV)*. The assessment battery is now made up of three separate forms: Form A, Form B, and Form C. Together, these three batteries make up the extended battery. In addition to the achievement tests, the WJ IV also includes a cognitive battery and an oral language battery. The linking of these three instruments (cognitive, achievement, and oral language batteries) allows the examiner to obtain a comprehensive view of the student and integrate these three major areas together.

2. *Kaufman Test of Educational Achievement III*. This instrument assesses academic achievement and includes norms for students of ages 4 years to 25 years

and 11 months. The latest revision of this instrument adds new fluency subtests for math, writing, and silent reading and a new reading vocabulary test. This instrument allows the examiner to test basic academic skills and screens oral language.

3. *Peabody Individual Achievement Test–4.* This test was listed as one of the most frequently used by professionals in Child Service Demonstration Centers (Thurlow & Ysseldyke, 1979), by school psychologists (LaGrow & Prochnow-LaGrow, 1982), by special education teachers who listed this as one of the most useful tests (Connelly, 1985), and by teachers who are in both self-contained and resource classrooms for students with learning disabilities (German, Johnson, & Schneider, 1985).

4. *Wechsler Individual Achievement Test, Third Edition.* This revised instrument was designed to be used in conjunction with the Wechsler intelligence scales or other measures of cognitive ability and assesses the academic areas specified in special education regulations.

These tests, which represent several academic areas, are discussed in the following sections. Their reliability and validity are presented in an effort to encourage future teachers to be wise consumers of assessment devices.

Woodcock–Johnson IV Tests of Achievement (WJ IV)

This edition of the *Woodcock–Johnson Tests of Achievement IV* (Woodcock, McGrew, & Mather, 2014), presented in easel format, is composed of three parallel forms, A, B and C, that allow the examiner to retest the same student within a short amount of time with less practice effect. In addition to the three parallel forms of the Standard Tests, an additional Extended Test Book provides additional subtests to tap the variety of specific skills and abilities that are consistent with the Cattell-Horn-Carroll (CHC) theory that forms the basis of the instrument. The battery of subtests allows the examiner to select the specific clusters of subtests needed for a particular student, and a variety of clusters are available. The WJ IV is based on the CHC theory, and considerable research resulted in a reconfiguration of some of the clusters, the addition of new clusters, and the addition of new individual subtests. The new arrangement of clusters for the achievement batteries includes: Reading, Broad Reading, Reading Comprehension, Reading Comprehension Extended, Reading Fluency, Reading Rate, Basic Reading Skills, Broad Written Language, Written Expression, Basic Writing Skills, Mathematics, Broad Mathematics, Math Calculation Skills, Math Problem Solving, Academic Skills, Academic Applications, Academic Fluency, Academic Knowledge, Phoneme-Grapheme Knowledge, Brief Achievement, and Broad Achievement.

Information on the standardization and norm sample provided by the authors indicates the national sample included a total of 7,416 participants for the development of the WJ IV batteries. The WJ IV Achievement Tests were conormed with the Oral Language and Cognitive Batteries. The Achievement Tests may be used with the Oral Language and Cognitive Batteries or each may be used independently. The batteries were designed to be used with individuals of ages 2 to 90 years. Forty-six states were represented in the sample and the grade levels included preschool through university level and an additional adult sample. Clinical validity studies included samples of individuals with learning disabilities in reading, math, and writing; individuals with traumatic brain injury; and individuals with language delay, autism spectrum disorders, attention deficit hyperactivity disorder (ADHD), and cognitive disabilities. A sample of gifted individuals was also included in the clinical validity research.

1. Basal and ceiling levels are specified for individual subtests, and timed tests do not require specific basal and ceiling rules. For some of the subtests, when the

student answers six consecutive items correctly, the basal is established; when the student answers six consecutive items incorrectly, the ceiling is established. Other subtests require basal and ceiling levels to be established when the five lowest items are answered correctly for the basal, and the five highest items are answered incorrectly for the ceiling. Examiners should study the basal and ceiling rules and refer to the protocol and the examiner's manual for specific rules.

2. Derived scores can be obtained for each individual subtest for estimations of age and grade equivalents only. Other standard scores are available using the online scoring program.

3. The norm group ranged in age from 2 years to older than 90 years and included students at the college/university level through graduate school. The use of extended age scores provides a more comprehensive analysis of children and adults who are not functioning at a school grade level.

4. How examinees offer responses to test items varies. Some subtests require the examinee to respond using using paper and pencil; some are administered via audio CD, requiring an oral response. Icons on the test protocol denote when the test response booklet or the CD player is needed as well as which subtests are timed.

5. The examiner's manual includes useful interpretive information to assist the examiner when analyzing the results and writing reports. For example, the manual provides an analysis of task difficulty by subtest areas. To illustrate, for the math tests, problem-solving tasks included on the Applied Problems and Number Matrices subtests are rated as the more complex tasks while the math facts tasks on the Calculation subtest are rated among the less complex tasks.

6. The online scoring program includes an option for determining the individual's cognitive–academic language proficiency (CALP) level. The clusters that will provide the CALP levels are Reading Clusters (Reading, Basic Reading Skills, Reading Comprehension, Reading Comprehension-Extended), Writing Clusters (Written Language, Basic Writing Skills, Written Expression), and Cross-Domain Clusters (Academic Skills, Academic Applications, Academic Knowledge, and Brief Achievement).

7. A test session observation checklist is located on the front of the protocol for the examiner to note the examinee's behavior during the assessment sessions and individual Qualitative Observation checklists are provided for each individual subtest that are specific to the task demands.

8. Accommodation suggestions and guidelines are provided within the manual. Accommodation suggestions for setting, timing, presentation, and scheduling are presented. Additional guidelines for use of the instrument with young children; English Language Learners; and individuals with reading challenges, attention/behavioral challenges, hearing impairments, visual impairments, and physical impairments are included in the manual along with lists of specific subtests that may be considered useful for the specific learning challenges.

The WJ IV is organized into subtests that are grouped into broad clusters to aid in the interpretation of scores. The examiner may administer specific clusters to screen a student's achievement level or to determine a pattern of strengths and weaknesses. For example, a student who gives evidence of having difficulty with math problem solving might be administered the subtests of Math Matrices and Applied Problems. A student who has had difficulty with beginning reading skills might be given the phoneme/grapheme cluster that includes Word Attack and Spelling of Sounds.

Standard Battery. The following paragraphs describe the subtests in the Standard Battery.

Letter-word identification. The student is presented with letters to match for the easier items and words to read aloud for subsequent items. The basal and ceiling levels are, respectively, the six lowest consecutive items that are correct and the six highest items that are incorrect.

Applied problems. The examiner reads a story math problem, and the student must answer orally. Picture cues are provided at the lower levels. The test is administered by complete pages so that the basal is established when the student obtains five of the lowest-level items correctly or, if needed, until the first page of items is completed and the ceiling is the five highest-level items obtained correctly, or until the final page of the subtest is administered. An item may be repeated to the student on this subtest if the student requests.

Spelling. This subtest assesses the individual's ability to write words that are presented orally by the examiner. The early items include tracing lines and letters, and the more advanced items include multisyllabic words with unpredictable spellings. The basal and ceiling levels are, respectively, six consecutive correct and six consecutive incorrect items.

Passage comprehension. The examiner shows the student a passage with a missing word; the student must orally supply the word. The basal and ceiling levels are, respectively, the six lowest consecutive correct items and the six highest consecutive incorrect items.

Calculation. The student solves a series of math problems in paper-and-pencil format. The problems include number writing on the early items and range from addition to calculus operations on the more advanced items. The basal and ceiling levels are, respectively, the six lowest consecutive correct items and the six highest consecutive incorrect items.

Writing samples. This subtest requires the student to construct age-appropriate sentences meeting specific criteria for syntax, content, and the like. Test administration is conducted by blocks of items. The items are scored as 2, 1, or 0 based on the quality of the response given. The examiner's manual provides a comprehensive scoring guide.

Word attack. The student is asked to read aloud nonsense words or words that are not commonly used. Initial items require the student to sound out single letters and the subsequent items use the nonsense or infrequently used words. This subtest measures the student's ability to decode and pronounce new words. The basal is established when a student answers six consecutive items correctly, and the ceiling is six consecutive incorrect responses.

Oral reading. This subtest requires the student to read sentences aloud that increase in difficulty. Students who are believed to be functioning at the first-grade level and higher are administered this test. Students are scored for the following: mispronunciation, omission, insertions, substitutions, hesitation, repetition, and transportation, and for not observing punctuation within the passages read aloud. The basal and ceiling rules are not used on this subtest since the items are administered in blocks.

Sentence-reading fluency. This subtest is administered for a period of 3 minutes. All students are administered the practice items and students who are able to correctly complete only two sample items or less do not continue with the test. The student reads statements and determines if they are true or not true. The subtest assesses how quickly the student reads each sentence presented, makes a decision about its validity, and circles the correct response.

Math facts fluency. This subtest is included in the student's response book-let. The student is required to solve problems utilizing the basic operations of addition, subtraction, multiplication, and division. This subtest is timed: The student solves as many problems as possible within 3 minutes.

Sentence-writing fluency. This paper-and-pencil subtest consists of pictures paired with three words. The examiner directs the student to write sentences about each picture using the words. The student is allowed to write for 7 minutes. Correct responses are complete sentences that include the three words presented.

Extended Achievement Test

Reading recall. This subtest requires the student to read a short story silently and then to tell the examiner as much of the story as can be recalled. This subtest is administered by blocks and does not use basal and ceiling rules. The scoring is based on the number of story elements recalled.

Number matrices. This quantitative test assesses both quantitative-reasoning and fluid-reasoning skills. When presented with a numerical matrix, the student tells the examiner which number is missing. The basal and ceiling levels are, respectively, the six lowest consecutive correct items and the six highest consecutive incorrect items.

Editing. This subtest requires the student to proofread sentences and passages and identify errors in punctuation, capitalization, usage, or spelling. The student is asked to correct errors in written passages shown on the easel page. The basal and ceiling levels are, respectively, the six lowest consecutive correct items and six highest consecutive incorrect items.

Word reading fluency. This timed subtest requires the student to read rows of words and mark through the two words that are similar in each row. Sample and practice items are provided. The ceiling and basal rules do not apply since this is a timed test.

Spelling of sounds. The examiner presents the first few items of this subtest orally; the remaining items are presented via audiotape. The examinee is asked to write the spellings of nonsense words. This requires that she or he be able to associate sounds with their corresponding written letters. The basal and ceiling levels are, respectively, the six lowest consecutive correct items and the six highest consecutive incorrect items.

Reading vocabulary. This subtest contains two sections: Part A, Synonyms; and Part B, Antonyms. Both sections must be completed in order to obtain a score for the subtest. The student is asked to say a word that means the same as a given word in Part A and to say a word that has the opposite meaning of a word in Part B. Only one-word responses are acceptable for the subtest items. The examiner obtains a raw score by adding the number of items that are correct in the two subtests. The basal and ceiling levels are, respectively, the five lowest consecutive correct items and the five highest consecutive incorrect items.

Science. For the Science test, the examiner orally presents open-ended questions covering scientific content. The basal and ceiling levels are, respectively, the six lowest consecutive correct items and the six highest consecutive incorrect items. Picture cues are given at the lower and upper levels.

Social studies. The Social Studies test orally presents open-ended questions covering topics about society and government. The basal and ceiling levels are, respectively, the six lowest consecutive correct items and the six highest consecutive incorrect items. Picture cues are given at the lower level.

CHECK YOUR UNDERSTANDING

Complete Activity 8.1 to assess your understanding of the Woodcock-Johnson IV.

Humanities. The questions in the Humanities test cover topics the student might have learned from the cultural environment. The basal and ceiling levels are the same as for the Science and Social Studies subtests.

Peabody Individual Achievement Test–Revised (PIAT–R NU)

The *PIAT–R NU* (Markwardt, 1989, 1998) is contained in four easels, called *Volumes I, II, III,* and *IV.* For this revision, the number of items on each subtest has been increased. The subtests are General Information, Reading Recognition, Reading Comprehension, Mathematics, Spelling, and Written Expression. Descriptions of these subtests follow.

General information. Questions in this subtest are presented in an open-ended format. The student gives oral responses to questions that range in topic from science to sports. The examiner records all responses. A key for acceptable responses is given throughout the examiner's pages of the subtest; this key also offers suggestions for further questioning.

Reading recognition. The items at the beginning level of this subtest are visual recognition and discrimination items that require the student to match a picture, letter, or word. The student must select the response from a choice of four items. The more difficult items require the student to pronounce a list of words that range from single-syllable consonant-vowel-consonant words to multisyllabicwords with unpredictable pronunciations.

Reading comprehension. This subtest is administered to students who earn a raw score of 19 or better on the Reading Recognition subtest. The items are presented in a two-page format. The examiner asks the student to read a passage silently on the first page of each item. On the second page, the student must select from four choices the one picture that best illustrates the passage. The more difficult-to-read items also have pictures that are more difficult to discriminate.

Mathematics. Math questions are presented in a forced-choice format. The student is orally asked a question and must select the correct response from four choices. Questions range from numeral recognition to trigonometry.

Spelling. This subtest begins with visual discrimination tasks of pictures, symbols, and letters. The spelling items are presented in a forced-choice format. The student is asked to select the correct spelling of the word from four choices.

Written expression. This subtest allows for written responses by the student; level 1 is presented to students who are functioning at the kindergarten or 1st-grade level, level II to students functioning in the 2nd- to 12th-grade levels. Basal and ceiling levels do not apply.

Scoring. The examiner uses the raw score on the first *PIAT–R NU* subtest, General Information, to determine a starting point on the following subtest, Reading Recognition. The raw score from the Reading Recognition subtest then provides a starting point for the Reading Comprehension subtest, and so on throughout the test. The basal and ceiling levels are consistent across subtests. A basal level is established when five consecutive items have been answered correctly. The ceiling level is determined when the student answers five of seven items incorrectly. Because the Written

CHECK YOUR UNDERSTANDING

Check your understanding of the *PIAT–R NU* protocol by completing Activity 8.2. Use Figure 8.1 to complete the activity.

Expression subtest requires written responses by the student, basal and ceiling levels do not apply.

The *PIAT–R NU* yields standard scores, grade equivalents, age equivalents, and percentile ranks for individual subtests and for a Total Reading and a Total Test score. The manual provides for standard error of measurement for obtained and derived scores. The raw score from the Written Expression subtest can be used with the raw score from the Spelling subtest to obtain a written language composite. Scoring procedures are detailed in Appendix I of the *PIAT–R NU* examiner's manual.

Markwardt, F. (1989, 1997). Peabody Individual Achievement Test–Revised–Normative Update (PIAT-R/NU). San Antonio, TX: Pearson Clinical.

FIGURE 8.1 Basal and Ceiling Rules and Response Items for a Subtest from the *Peabody Individual Achievement Test–Revised*

SUBTEST 2
Reading Recognition

Training Exercises

	Trial 1	Trial 2	Trial 3
Exercise A.	(1) _____	(1) _____	(1) _____
Exercise B.	(3) _____	(3) _____	(3) _____
Exercise C.	(2) _____	(2) _____	(2) _____

Basal and Ceiling Rules
Basal: *highest* 5 consecutive correct responses
Ceiling: *lowest* 7 consecutive responses containing 5 errors

Starting Point
The item number that corresponds to the subject's raw score on General Information.

43.	ledge	1
44.	escape	1
45.	northern	1
46.	towel	1
47.	kneel	1
48.	height	0
49.	exercise	1
50.	observe	1
51.	ruin	0
52.	license	1
53.	uniforms	0
54.	pigeon	1
55.	moisture	0
56.	artificial	1
57.	issues	0
58.	quench	0
59.	hustle	0
60.	thigh	0

READING RECOGNITION

Ceiling Item _____
minus Errors _____
equals RAW SCORE [ ]

Kaufman Test of Educational Achievement, 3rd Edition (KTEA-3)

The KTEA-3 (Kaufman & Kaufman, 2014) is an individually administered achievement battery for children of ages 4 years and 0 months to college/adult students 25 years and 11 months. The KTEA-3 was linked with the *Kaufman Assessment Battery for Children, Second Edition (K–ABC–II)* (Kaufman & Kaufman, 2004) and the WISC-V (2014). This revised instrument is scored using the Q-Global platform available through the publisher (Pearson). Brief descriptions of the K TEA-3 subtests are presented in Table 8.1.

TABLE 8.1

Brief Description of KTEA-3 Subtests*

Subtest	Range	Description
Phonological Processing	PK–12+	This subtest includes a variety of tasks that require the student to rhyme, match, blend, segment, and delete sounds. The audio CD is used for examiner training but not during the actual administration of the deleting sounds and blending items. Students are generally not penalized for dialect or regional speech patterns.
Math Concepts and Applications	PK–12+	The examinee responds orally to test items that focus on the application of mathematical principles to real-life situations. Skill categories include number concepts, operation concepts, time and money, measurement, geometry, data investigation, and higher math concepts. Visual stimuli include pictures, graphs, and charts as well as numerically represented problems for advanced-level items.
Letter & Word Recognition	PK–12+	The student identifies written letters and words by orally responding to examiner prompts (e.g., "What word is this?"). The items increase in difficulty from the identification of single letters to multisyllablic words.
Math Computation	K–12+	The student writes solutions to math problems printed in the student response booklet. Skills assessed include addition, subtraction, multiplication, and division operations; fractions and decimals; square roots; exponents; signed numbers; and algebra.
Nonsense-Word Decoding	1–12+	The student applies phonics and structural analysis skills to decode invented words of increasing difficulty. The nonsense words are provided in written format and the student is asked to pronounce each one.
Writing Fluency	2–12+	The examinee is provided with pictures and asked to write a sentence for each one. The student must write in the response booklet as many sentences as possible within the time limit.
Silent-Reading Fluency	1–12+	The examinee silently reads sentences in the response booklet and marks yes or no indicating if the sentence is true or not true. The student completes as many as possible within the time limit.
Math Fluency	1–12+	This timed subtest requires the student to complete as many math problems as possible in the student response booklet. The items begin with simple addition and subtraction facts and become increasingly more difficult with division and multiplication problems.
Reading Comprehension	PK–12+	Initial items at the lower level of the subtest ask the student to match a symbol or word to the correct picture. As items increase in difficulty, students are required to read and respond to instructions and later to read sentences and place them into a paragraph and answer questions about the paragraph.

Written Expression	PK–12+	Prekindergarten and kindergarten children trace and copy letters and write letters from dictation. At grade 1 and higher, the student completes writing tasks in the context of an age-appropriate storybook format. Tasks at those levels include writing sentences from dictation, adding punctuation and capitalization, filling in missing words, completing sentences, combining sentences, writing compound and complex sentences, and, starting at spring of grade 1, writing an essay based on the story the student helped complete.
Associational Fluency	PK–12+	The examiner provides a specific category and asks the student to provide as many words as possible in that category.
Spelling	K–12+	The student writes words dictated by the examiner in the response booklet. Early items require students to write single letters that represent sounds. The remaining items require students to spell regular and irregular words of increasing complexity.
Object-Naming Facility	PK–12+	The examinee is shown a page of rows of pictures and asked to name the pictures as quickly as possible. The task is repeated using a second page of the same pictures.
Reading Vocabulary	1–12+	The lower-level items present three words and the examinee selects the one that represents a picture. Later items include sentences that the student reads aloud or silently; the student then selects a word in the sentence that matches the meaning of the target word.
Letter-Naming Facility	K–12+	The student is asked to name letters as quickly as possible when provided with written uppercase and lowercase letters.
Listening Comprehension	PK–12+	The initial items are read to the examinee by the examiner and later items are presented on a CD. The examinee responds orally to questions asked by the examiner about the sentences. Questions measure literal and inferential comprehension.
Word-Recognition Fluency	1–12+	The student reads isolated words as quickly as possible for two 15-second trials.
Oral Expression	PK–12+	The examinee is shown photographs and asked to describe them using complete sentences. More difficult items require that the student use target words to begin the response.
Decoding Fluency	3–12+	The examinee is shown nonsense words and is asked to read as quickly as possible for two 15-second trials.

*Adapted from KTEA-3 Administration Manual (Pearson, 2014).

The K TEA-3 Q-Global scoring provides standard scores, age and grade equivalents, percentile ranks, normal curve equivalents, and growth score values. The scoring will also allow the examiner to obtain error analyses on the student's performance, score comparisons, and make suggestions for educational interventions. The examiner should carefully read and adhere to administration procedures.

Some of the subtests of the K-TEA-3 require the use of an audio CD for administration and others require the examiner to listen to the audio CD to hear how to administer specific items such as the deleting sounds portion of the Phonological Processing subtest; but the CD is not used during the administration of those specific items. Other subtests require the examiner to read the items aloud at the beginning and then to use the audio CD later in the administration of the subtest. It is imperative that the examiner follow all of the standardized instructions during

CHECK YOUR UNDERSTANDING

To check your understanding of the **KTEA-3**, complete Activity 8.3.

CHECK YOUR UNDERSTANDING

To experience scoring a math achievement test, complete Activity 8.4.

CHECK YOUR UNDERSTANDING

Check your ability to calculate and determine significant differences in comparing composites of an achievement test by completing Activity 8.5.

the administration in order to obtain a valid representation of the student's academic ability.

The student's responses are scored as pass or fail (0 or 1), and the specific pronunciations are noted by the examiner. The raw score is determined and the errors are then analyzed on a separate form that allows the examiner to complete a within-item error analysis. The results of the error analysis within the items can be used to determine the educational needs of the student. These needs are the basis for writing educational objectives, designing teaching strategies, and identifying which specific skills will be monitored through other classroom assessment methods, such as curriculum-based assessment.

Wechsler Individual Achievement Test, Third Edition (WIAT–III)

The *WIAT–III* (Psychological Corporation, 2009) is an individually administered achievement test made up of 16 subtests. Students of ages 4–0 to 19–11 or in grades pre-K (age 5) through high school may be administered this instrument. Not all subtests are administered to all age groups. For example, pre-K students are administered the following subtests: Listening Comprehension, Early Reading Skills, Math Problem-Solving, Alphabet Writing Fluency, and Oral Expression. This third edition of the *WIAT* contains changes in individual items, subtests, and scoring. Moreover, the third edition has the following new subtests: Early Reading Skills, Oral Reading Fluency, Math Fluency for addition, Math Fluency for subtraction, and Math Fluency for multiplication. The *WIAT–III* includes two methods of determining learning disabilities. The first method is the traditional ability–achievement discrepancy method. The second method is the determination of a pattern of strengths and weaknesses with the determination of processing strengths and processing weaknesses and how these relate to achievement. The *WIAT–III* test format includes easels, paper-and-pencil tasks, separate reading cards, and an oral-reading fluency booklet. Starting points and ceiling rules, which vary by subtests, are presented in the manual and on the protocol form. Some items are timed and cues are provided to the examiner in the protocol. Examiners are also provided rules for reverse administration in the examiner's manual and on the protocol if the student does not establish a basal.

The *WIAT–III* includes subtests in the areas of oral expression and listening comprehension. These areas may not be included in other academic achievement tests and may offer the educator useful information for determining a possible disability and for intervention. This test provides skill information on the protocol of the math subtests that can easily be adapted to write educational objectives. The protocol includes a qualitative observation section at the end of the protocol. Additional information regarding each subtest follows.

Listening comprehension. This subtest presents two tasks. The first task asks the student to point to a picture that represents a word read to the student. The second task asks the student to remember sentences read to her or him and to respond to questions about the specific sentence or passage heard.

Early reading skills. This subtest presents a variety of reading tasks, including alphabetic awareness, identification of words with the same beginning sounds and ending sounds, and matching letters and sounds.

Reading comprehension. This test presents a variety of passages and text in different formats. The student reads the passages and responds to questions about them. The questions measure literal and inferential comprehension.

Math problem solving. These applied math items assess basic skills in concepts, geometry, everyday math problems, and algebra.

Alphabet-writing fluency. On this subtest, children in pre-K through grade 3 are asked to write the letters of the alphabet within a 30-second time limit. Students may write in print or cursive, and any order of the letters is acceptable.

Sentence composition. This two-part subtest asks that the student first combine two sentences into one sentence that conveys the meaning of the original two sentences. For the second task, the student is asked to write a sentence that contains a specific word and that complies with the context provided.

Word reading. This revised subtest requires that the student read a list of words in an untimed format. The examiner notes the progress of the student after 30 seconds, and the student continues with the subtest until the "discontinue" has been reached.

Essay composition. The student is required to write an essay within a 10-minute time limit to assess spontaneous writing skills.

Pseudoword decoding. This subtest is presented on a reading card and is administered to students in grade 1 and above. The student's responses are recorded exactly using correct pronunciation or phonetic symbols. Although the student is not told to read quickly, decoding fluency is assessed by noting the pseudowords read within the first 30 seconds.

Numerical operations. Items for pre-K students include number recognition, number sequencing (1–10), dictation of specific numbers, and counting. Additional items require the student to respond in writing to solve calculation problems. More difficult items involve geometry, percent, decimals, and simple algebraic equations.

Oral expression. This subtest includes expressive vocabulary, oral word fluency, and sentence repetition. To assess expressive vocabulary, the student is asked to provide a word for the picture stimulus. The oral word fluency task requires the student to provide as many words as possible for a specific category. The final task, sentence repetition, asks the student to repeat sentences of increasing length.

Oral-reading fluency. This subtest assesses the student's ability to read passages aloud and to respond to questions asked about the content of the passages. Speed, accuracy, fluency, and prosody are assessed.

Spelling. The student responds in writing to letters, sounds, or words dictated by the examiner. The spelling test includes the presentation of the word, the use of the word in a sentence, and a repetition of the word. The student responds in writing.

Math fluency–addition. This 60-second math test assesses how quickly and accurately the student can solve addition problems.

Math fluency–subtraction. This 60-second math test assesses how quickly and accurately the student can solve subtraction problems.

Math fluency–multiplication. This 60-second math test assesses how quickly and accurately the student can solve multiplication problems.

CHECK YOUR UNDERSTANDING

Check your understanding of the *WIAT–III* by completing Activity 8.6.

Scoring. Directions for scoring the *WIAT–III* are provided in the protocol for each subtest. Specific rules, such as when to discontinue or when to reverse the administration process, are provided. The examiner must become familiar with each subtest's scoring rules. To assist in scoring the Alphabetic Fluency, Sentence Combining, Sentence Building, Essay Composition Content and Organization, and Essay Composition Grammar and Mechanics items, a separate scoring workbook is provided. Examiners can review item examples and determine how to score an examinee's work. This workbook also features a practice scoring exercise examiners can complete before attempting to score an actual protocol.

● SELECTING ACADEMIC ACHIEVEMENT TESTS

The tests reviewed in this chapter are the more commonly used instruments in public school assessment. One instrument may be preferable to another in a particular situation. Strengths and weaknesses of these tests are summarized in Table 8.2.

● DIAGNOSTIC TESTING

Teachers often need additional information to make the correct decisions for educational interventions. Instruments that can yield more detailed information for making such decisions are known as diagnostic tests. The tests presented here are among those most commonly used by teachers; they have also been selected because of existing research that supports their use. Diagnostic assessment of the basic skill areas of reading, mathematics, spelling, and written language is presented in this chapter.

KeyMath–3 Diagnostic Assessment (KeyMath–3 DA)

The *KeyMath–3 DA* (Connolly, 2007) is presented in an easel format and consists of two equivalent forms, A and B. This instrument is aligned with the Standards of the National Council of Teachers of Mathematics (NCTM, 2000), and the matrix reflecting this alignment is included in the appendix of the test manual. The alternate forms may be administered every 3 months to monitor progress of the student in mathematics. The third edition of this diagnostic mathematics battery includes computer-scoring software and progress-monitoring capability. The software program provides a functional analysis of the student's responses on the instrument and will yield the specific items that require intervention. The functional analysis provides behavioral objectives that may be used to drive the math intervention process. The instrument may be administered to students who are 4 years and 6 months of age through students who are 21 years of age who are within the skill levels provided by the instrument. The estimated administration time ranges from 30 to 90 minutes.

On the *KeyMath–3 DA,* many of the items are presented orally by the examiner. The computation items for the basic math operations of addition, subtraction, multiplication, and division are presented as paper-and-pencil tasks. This test includes subtests that are grouped into three areas: Basic Concepts, Operations, and Applications. Table 8.3 presents the areas, domains, and content of the revised *KeyMath–3 DA.* Additional information is presented here.

Basic concepts. In this content area, items presented assess the student's conceptual understanding of numeration, algebra, geometry, and measurement. Items also relate to analysis and interpretation of data.

Numeration. These items sample the student's ability to understand the number system and the functional application of that system. Items include tasks such as counting, identifying numbers, identifying missing numbers in a sequence, understanding concepts of *more* and *less,* and reading multidigit numbers.

Algebra. This subtest measures understanding of the concepts and skills used in prealgebraic problems and includes items such as number sentences, functions, and equations.

Measurement. Items range from recognition and identification of units of measurement to problems that involve application and changing of the various units of measurement. Items related to time and money are also included.

Geometry. These items range from understanding spatial concepts and recognizing shapes to interpreting angles and three-dimensional figures.

Operations. This content area includes computation problems using paper and pencil and mental computation items that are presented in the easel format.

Academic Achievement Tests

Name of Instrument	Purpose of Test	Constructs Measured	Standardization Information	Reliability Information	Validity Information
Woodcock–Johnson Tests of Achievement, Fourth Edition (WJ IV)	Comprehensive assessment of academic areas and oral language applying a processing-strengths-and-weaknesses model through clusters	Reading, oral language, math, written language, academic fluency, academic applications, oral language, brief and broad achievement	More than 7,416 persons of ages 2 to over 90 years Variables included race, sex, Hispanic/non-Hispanic, occupation, level of education, and community size; 46 states and D.C. represented	Test–retest, interrater reliability, alternate forms reliability, and internal consistency; most reliability coefficients for internal reliability in the 0.90s	Concurrent validity researched with other measures such as the KTEA II, OWLS-WE, and WIAT III; multiple clinical samples included in validity research
Woodcock–Johnson Tests of Achievement– Form C/Brief	A shorter battery that assesses basic achievement	Basic and broad measures of reading, math, and written language	Normative sample based on 2005 census; included more than 8,000 students	Test–retest, interrater reliability, alternative forms reliability ranged from adequate to high	Validity update provides evidence of content and assessment validity with clinical samples
Kaufman Test of Educational Achievement, Third Edition (KTEA-3)	Comprehensive assessment of academic areas	Reading, reading-related composites, math, written language, oral language	Sample of 2,400 students in grades K–12; variables included ethnicity, educational level of parents, geographic region, sex	Internal consistency reliability for subtests and composites; most in the 0.90s; alternate forms reliability; interrater reliability	Construct validity, concurrent validity studies with the WJ-III, and PIAT–R NU; confirmatory factor analysis
Wechsler Individual Achievement Test, Third Edition	Assessment of academic achievement	Reading, written expression, math, listening comprehension, oral expression	Included 2,775 students in grades pre-K through 12 and ages 4–19; variables included race/ethnicity, sex, geographic area, parents' educational level; fall and spring testing periods	Reliability research included internal consistency measures, test–retest, and interscorer reliability; coefficients ranged from 0.81 to 0.99	Construct validity, content validity, and criterion-related validity research included in manual

TABLE 8.3

Content Specification of *KeyMath–3 DA:* Subtests and Content of Domains

Areas	Basic Concepts	Operations	Applications
Strands and Domains	*Numeration* Early number awareness Place value and number sense Magnitude of numbers Fractions Decimals Percentages Exponents, integers, multiples, and factors	*Mental Computation and Estimation* Early awareness of mental computation Mental computation chains Mental computation with whole numbers Mental computation with rational numbers Estimation and whole numbers Estimation and rational numbers	*Foundations of Problem Solving* Analysis of problems Word problems *Applied Problem Solving* Numerations Algebra Geometry Measurement Data analysis and probability
	Algebra Early algebraic awareness Algebraic uses of numbers and geometry Symbolic representation Ratio and proportion Coordinate graphing	*Addition and Subtraction* Algorithms to add and subtract whole numbers Algorithms to add and subtract rational numbers Integers Algebra	
	Geometry Early geometric awareness Two-dimensional shapes Three-dimensional shapes Lines and angles Formulas Grids and coordinate planes	*Multiplication and Division* Algorithms to multiply and divide rational numbers Integers Algebra	
	Measurement Early awareness of measurement Standard units Time Money Data analysis and probability Early awareness of data and probability Charts, tables, and graphs Graphical representation Statistics Probability		

Source: Adapted from *KeyMath–3 DA* (Appendix E, pp. 341–345) by A. J. Connolly, 2007, NCS Pearson, Inc. Minneapolis, MN: Pearson Assessments. Reprinted by permission.

Mental computation. This orally administered subtest includes math operations problems and more difficult problems that require several steps and operations to complete.

Addition and subtraction. This subtest assesses the student's ability to perform addition and subtraction computation problems.

Multiplication and division. This subtest is presented in the same format as the addition and subtraction subtests and includes simple grouping problems (sets) and more difficult multiplication of mixed numbers and fractions. The items cover a range of difficulty levels and contain some multistep, or "long" division, computations, addition and subtraction of fractions, and beginning algebraic computations.

Application. This content area includes problems that are representative of how mathematics is used in everyday life.

Foundations of problem solving. These items assess a student's early ability or "readiness" to complete application problems.

Applied problem solving. On these items, the student is presented with math problems of daily living, such as calculating sales tax or categorization of objects.

Scoring. Grade-level starting points are provided on the protocol. The basal is established when a student responds correctly to at least three items in the set before missing an item. If the student incorrectly responds to an item, the items are presented in reverse order until the student successfully answers three consecutive items correctly. The basal level is the three items prior to the first incorrect response. The ceiling is established when a student incorrectly answers four consecutive items. Once the raw scores for each subtest are calculated, they are used to locate the standard scores in the examiner manual.

The *KeyMath–3 DA* provides scale scores for the individual subtests. These scores have a mean of 10 and a standard deviation of 3. Each of the three areas and the total test score are presented as standard scores with a mean of 100 and a standard deviation of 15 for all age and grade groups. Norm tables are included for fall and spring for standard scores and percentile ranks. Age- and grade-equivalent developmental scores are also provided. Areas can be compared so that it may be determined if a student is significantly strong or weak in a specific math area.

Tables provide information regarding a student's functional range according to the subtest raw scores. Tables also indicate which items are focus items that the student missed that fall below the student's functional range, pointing to skills deficits that may be in particular need of intervention. A table also indicates the items that the student answered correctly that were above the student's functional level.

Another score is provided to assist with measurement of ongoing progress. This is called the *growth scale value* or GSV. An example of the graphing of the GSV is presented in Figure 8.2.

The examiner uses the raw scores to locate scaled scores for each subtest and then sums the raw scores of the subtests for the area raw score. The area raw scores are used to determine area standard scores, percentile ranks, and age or grade equivalents.

Comparing Area Standard Scores for Significance. The examiner compares the standard scores obtained on the three areas in the section of the protocol titled Area Comparisons, shown in Figure 8.6. The examiner writes the standard scores in the appropriate spaces and writes >, <, or = on each of the lines between the boxes. The standard score differences are determined by subtracting the scores. To determine significance level, the examiner refers to a table in the manual that lists the differences that are considered significant. If the difference is listed as significant at the 0.05 level, this means that the chances are 95 out of 100 that a true difference exists

CHECK YOUR UNDERSTANDING

Check your skill in scoring a portion of the *KeyMath–3 DA* by completing Activity 8.7. You will need to use Figures 8.3, 8.4, 8.5, and 8.6 to complete Activity 8.7.

FIGURE 8.2 Graphical Display of the KeyMath–3 DA Progress Report

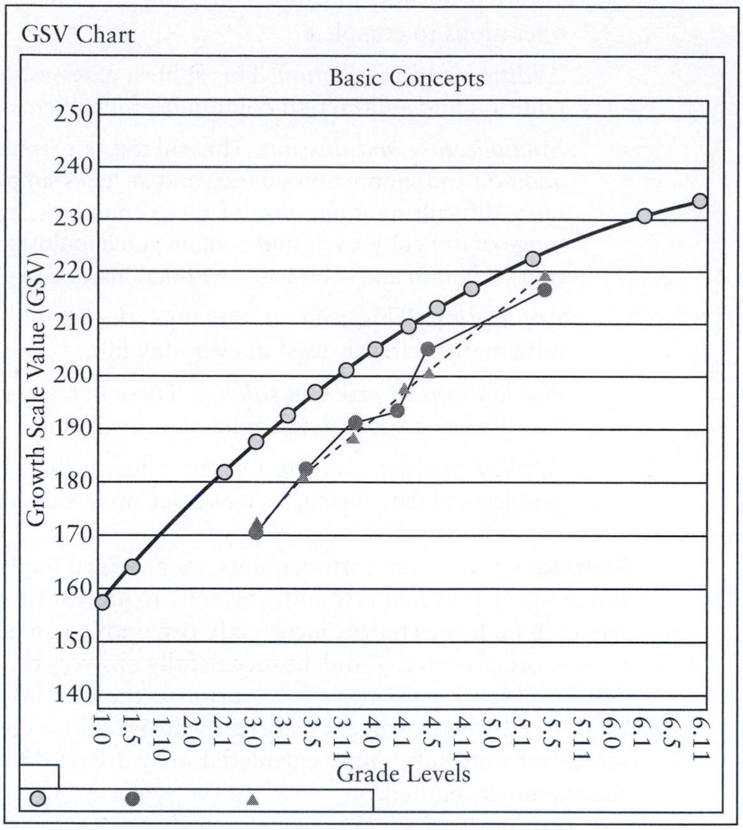

GSV Chart

Source: KeyMath–DA, by J. A. Connolly, 2007. Page 32 of the examiner's manual, NCS Pearson, Inc. Minneapolis, MN. Reprinted with permission.

and there are only 5 chances out of 100 that the difference is by error or chance. The level of 0.01 means that the difference exists with only 1 possibility out of 100 that the difference is by error or chance.

It is recommended that the frequency of such a difference also be determined. For example, how often would a student have such a difference between areas happen? To determine this, the examiner refers to a table in the examiner's manual.

The *KeyMath–3 DA* was normed on 3,630 people of ages 4 years and 6 months through 21 years and 11 months. Persons who participated in the norming process were English proficient. The norm sample was representative of the population of the United States in race/ethnicity, sex, parent's educational level, and geographic location. The norm sample reflected the U.S. population based on the 2004 survey of the U.S. Bureau of Census.

The examiner's manual provides evidence of internal reliability, including split-half reliability for subtests, area, and total test scores. Additional reliability information is provided for alternate forms and test–retest reliability. Information regarding construct validity, content validity, and concurrent criterion-related validity is also contained in the manual. Children with attention-deficit hyperactivity disorder, children with learning disabilities in reading, in math, and in reading and math, and students with mild intellectual disabilities were among the clinical samples used to establish the test's validity. A study with a sample of gifted students provided evidence of discriminant validity with that sample of students who, on average, earned points that were consistently one standard deviation above the mean of the instrument on both scale scores and standard scores.

FIGURE 8.3 Addition and Subtraction

Addition and Subtraction

Note: Skip this subtest if the examinee's Numeration ceiling item is 6 or below.
See Chapter 2 in the KeyMath–3 DA manual for details.

OPERATIONS

Numeration Ceiling Item	Item	Score	Description	Correct Response
4–19 ►	1.	(1) 0	1 + 2	3
	2.	(1) 0	0 + 5	5
	3.	(1) 0	6 − 0	6
20, 21 ►	4.	(1) 0	7 + 2	9
	5.	(1) 0	4 − 2	2
	6.	1 (0)	8 − 8	0
22–25 ►	7.	(1) 0	9 + 5	14
	8.	1 (0)	14 − 7	7
	9.	1 (0)	21 + 7	28
26–29 ►	10.	1 (0)	14 + 6	20
	11.	1 (0)	56 − 5	51
	12.	1 0	13 + 47	60
30–34 ►	13.	1 0	50 − 9	41
	14.	1 0	45 + 59	104
	15.	1 0	305 + 97	402

Ceiling Item [ ] − Errors [ ] = Raw Score* [ ]

*Read the scoring instructions on page 10 of this record form before calculating the subtest raw score.

FIGURE 8.4 Determine the Area Scores

Mental Computation and Estimation	Addition and Subtraction	Multiplication and Division	Foundation of Problem Solving	Applied Problem Solving	Scale Score
37–40	30–35	22–31	26–27	32–35	19
35–36	29	21	25	30–31	18
33–34	—	20	—	29	17
31–32	28	18–19	24	27–28	16
29–30	27	17	23	26	15
27–28	26	15–16	21–22	24–25	14
24–26	25	14	20	23	13
22–23	24	13	19	21–22	12
21	23	11–12	17–18	20	11
19–20	22	—	15–16	18–19	10
17–18	20–21	9–10	14	16–17	9
15–16	18–19	8	12–13	14–15	8
12–14	16–17	7	11	12–13	7
10–11	14–15	5–6	9–10	10–11	6
7–9	12–13	4	7–8	8–9	5
5–6	9–11	2–3	5–6	6–7	4
3–4	6–8	1	4	5	3
2	4–5	0	3	3–4	2
0–1	0–3	—	0–2	0–2	1
1.0	1.4	0.9	1.2	1.2	68% CI

FIGURE 8.5 Locate the Total Score

Standard Score	Basic Concepts	Operations	Applications	Total Test
85	77	39	24	140–142
84	75–76	38	—	137–139
83	73–74	37	23	133–136
82	71–72	36	22	129–132
81	70	35	—	126–128
80	68–69	34	21	123–125
79	67	32–33	20	120–122
78	65–66	31	—	116–119
77	63–64	30	19	112–115
76	61–62	28–29	18	109–111
75	60	27	17	105–108
74	58–59	25–26	16	101–104
73	56–57	24	—	97–100
72	54–55	23	15	93–36
71	52–53	22	—	89–92
70	50–51	20–21	14	84–88
69	47–49	19	13	80–83
68	45–46	18	12	76–79
67	42–44	17	11	73–75
66	40–41	16	—	68–72
65	37–39	14–15	10	64–67
64	34–36	13	9	60–63
63	31–33	12	—	56–59
62	29–30	11	8	52–55
61	26–28	10	7	48–51
60	24–25	9	—	45–47
59	22–23	8	6	42–44
58	20–21	7	—	39–41
57	19	—	5	36–38
56	18	6	—	33–35
55	0–17	0–5	0–4	0–32
90% CI	5	7	8	4

FIGURE 8.6 Calculating the Operations Standard Score

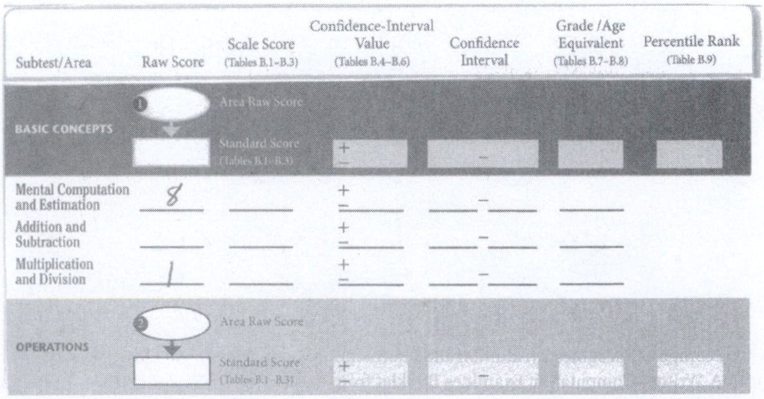

Process Assessment of the Learner II-Diagnostic Assessment for Math (PAL-II-M)

The PAL-II- M (Berninger, 2007) was developed for assessing math skills and related processing skills for students in grades K–6. Some of the specific intermediate and higher-level subtests are not administered to kindergarten and first-grade students. The purpose of the instrument is to find the target skills that are causing the student's difficulties in math and to assist in planning of instruction and interventions to remediate those skill areas. The test author notes that the instrument may be used at all three tier levels of instruction, from screening to the diagnosis of specific math difficulties for students who are not able to make sufficient progress in Tier I and Tier II. The test provides standard scale scores with a mean of 10 for individual subtests, and percentile equivalent scores. General recommendations for interventions are provided in the examiner's manual. The skills assessed on the PAL-II-M range from oral counting to spatial working memory. Descriptions of the specific subtests are featured below.

Numerical writing. The student is required to write numerals from memory.

Oral counting. The student is required to follow a variety of counting instructions, such as counting forward and backward, in a timed format. Each item has a 45-second time limit. Tasks begin with counting forward and end with counting forward by 7s.

Numeric coding. The student is asked to view a visual set of numbers for a short period of time, and then to look at the next set to determine if the numbers are the same. The student must be able to discriminate if the numbers are exactly the same, including if the same numbers are in the exact same sequence.

Fact retrieval. This subtest is administered to students in grades 1–6. The examinee is provided with written problems to solve in the Response Booklet. The problems range from simple addition facts to mixed multiplication and division facts. The student is not allowed to erase mistakes but must cross out any errors and correct them. In this way, the examiner can note the kinds of errors that were made.

Computation operations. This subtest is administered to students in grades 1–6. This assesses the student's ability to line up digits correctly and perform the tasks of spatial alignment, verbal explanation, and problem solving.

Place Value. This subtest is not administered to kindergarten students.

This subtest assesses the student's ability to indicate understanding of place value when presented with visual stimuli. Students must first respond orally and then, on the second task, the student writes the correct number to represent the visual stimuli. The final items require the student to write the number and then write what the number would be when x (number) is added to, or subtracted from, the original number.

Part-whole relationships. Kindergarten-level students are not given this subtest. The child responds orally to items about size, parts, wholes, fractions, mixed numbers, and time. Lower-level items use pictures as the visual stimuli and the upper-level items include oral items about time.

Finding the bug. This subtest is not administered to students in kindergarten and first grade. The student is provided with problems that have been solved and is asked to find the mistakes and indicate the errors by circling the problem.

Multistep problem solving. This subtest is administered to grades 2 to 6. This subtest presents short story math problems and the student is asked to identify the correct sequence of operations used in the problem. For example, if the story includes an addition statement and then a multiplication statement, the sequence identified is + x =. The most difficult items require a sequence of four steps to solve the problem.

CHECK YOUR UNDERSTANDING

Check your understanding of the PAL-II-M by completing Activity 8.8.

Quantitative-working memory. This subtest is not administered to students in kindergarten. The examinee is asked to listen to a sequence of oral instructions that include counting, counting back, and adding, and then to tell the examiner the final number. The student must retain the number mentally and add, subtract, or do both in a sequence, and then tell the examiner the ending number.

Spatial working memory. This subtest is not administered to kindergarten-level examinees. The examinee is shown visual stimuli and asked to draw the same number of dots in his or her response booklet from memory.

RAN-digits. This subtest is not administered to students in kindergarten. The student is required to name visually presented numbers as quickly as possible.

RAS. This subtest is not administered to kindergarten students. The examinee is shown a stimulus page with numbers and words and asked to read the numbers and words as quickly as possible.

Fingertip writing. This subtest is not administered to students in kindergarten. This assesses the student's ability to identify a number written by the examiner on the child's fingertip while the child's eyes are closed. This measures the child's ability to integrate sensory perception without visual stimuli.

Test of Mathematical Abilities–2 (TOMA–2)

The *TOMA–2* (Brown, Cronin, & McEntire, 1994) was designed to assess areas of math functioning that might not be addressed by other instruments. This test, now in its second edition, is used with students who range in age from 8 years to 18 years 11 months. The test's authors present the following questions, not answered by other instruments, as their rationale for developing the TOMA.

1. What are the student's expressed attitudes toward mathematics?
2. What is the student's general vocabulary level when that vocabulary is used in a mathematical sense?
3. How knowledgeable is the student (or group of students) regarding the functional use of mathematical facts and concepts in our general culture?
4. How do a student's attitudes, vocabulary, and general math information compare with the basic skills shown in the areas of computation and story problems?
5. Do the student's attitudes, vocabulary, and level of general math knowledge differ markedly from those of a group of age peers? (Brown, Cronin, & McEntire, 1994, p. 1)

The *TOMA–2* consists of five subtests, with the fifth subtest, Attitude toward Math, considered supplemental. The remaining subtests are Vocabulary, Computation, General Information, and Story Problems. The subtests yield standard scores with a mean of 10, a math quotient with a mean of 100, age equivalents, and percentile ranks. The examiner's manual cautions against misinterpretation of test scores and encourages further diagnostic assessment if a math disability is suspected.

The test's authors list three diagnostic questions that the *TOMA–2* may help educators answer:

1. Where should the student be placed in a curriculum?
2. What specific skills or content has the student mastered?
3. How does this student's overall performance compare with that of age or grade peers? (Brown, Cronin, & McEntire, 1994, p. 1)

Woodcock–Johnson III Diagnostic Reading Battery (WJ III DRB)

The *WJ III DRB* (Schrank, Mather, & Woodcock, 2004) consists of 10 subtests taken from the *Woodcock-Johnson Tests of Achievement III* that measure the skills and abilities required for reading. The subtests, presented next, include subtests administered in the standard fashion, with the examiner reading directions and prompts to the student; subtests that require audio presentations with headphones; and timed subtests.

Subtests. The following subtests of the *Woodcock–Johnson III Tests of Achievement (WJ III)* are included in the *WJ III DRB*:

Letter–Word Identification

Passage Comprehension

Word Attack

Reading Vocabulary

Reading Fluency

Spelling of Sounds

Sound Awareness

Sound Blending

Oral Vocabulary

Oral Comprehension

Scoring. The *WJ III DRB* is scored in the same way the *WJ III* is scored. The computerized scoring program produces percentile ranks, standard scores, predicted and actual scores, and difference scores. The scoring program will also generate a W Difference Score that indicates the difference between the student's performance and the performance of the typical individual in the same age or grade group. The Relative Proficiency (RP) provides a measure of where the student's performance falls compared to her or his grade or age group. The Test Observation Checklist on the front of the protocol allows the examiner to note qualitative observations about the testing session.

Theoretical Model of Reading Performance. The Comprehensive Manual of the WJ III DRB provides a model of how a student's reading scores relate to her or his reading performance in a classroom setting. As noted in the manual, the student's reading performance in class is likely the result of many contributing factors. For example, reading performance is the integration of many of the student's aptitudes in areas such as phonemic awareness and oral vocabulary, which then contribute to decoding and reading comprehension. The WJ III DRB provides a measurement of some of these factors or abilities and a means of understanding how specific reading weaknesses already measured may result in a specific reading disability when linked to processing abilities. This method of determining learning disabilities is explained in more detail in Chapter 13.

CHECK YOUR UNDERSTANDING

Check your understanding of the *WJ III DRB* by completing Activity 8.9.

Woodcock Reading Mastery Test, Third Edition (WRMT-III)

The WRMT-III (Woodcock, 2011) provides a single easel test of nine subtests that can be grouped as four clusters: Readiness, Basic Skills, Reading Comprehension, and Total Reading. The WRMT-III has two equivalent forms of the instrument and the manual states that the revised instrument reflects the Standards for the Assessment of Reading and Writing (2009) of the International Reading Association and the National Council of Teachers of English. The instrument includes assessment of the skills that are effective indicators of reading achievement: phonemic awareness, vocabulary, fluency, and comprehension. The instrument can be administered to individuals from preschool through college level and to adults. Specific subtests are targeted for preschool ages (ages 4 years 6 months who are not yet in kindergarten): letter identification, phonological awareness, and rapid automatic naming. The strength of the instrument is the specific error analysis that guides the teacher in making instructional decisions. The examiner manual provides guidance in error analysis categories and examples of scoring.

Process Assessment of the Learner–Second Edition: Diagnostic Assessment for Reading and Writing (PAL-II-RW)

The PAL-II-RW is designed to assess the processes used in initial and emerging reading and writing skills as well as the skills expected during the intermediate grades in school (through grade 6). The PAL-II-RW can be used to assess students who are having difficulties with the acquisition of the skills needed in reading and writing and may be used for determining when a student requires Tier II interventions. This instrument can easily be linked to interventions provided using additional resources by the same author. A brief description of each subtest is presented in the following section.

Alphabet writing. This subtest requires the student to write as many letters of the alphabet from memory as possible under a timed format.

Copying. There are two tasks on this subtest. Task A requires the student to copy a sentence and Task B requires the student to copy a paragraph.

Receptive coding. The child is asked to read a word and then is asked to view other visual stimuli and determine if the stimuli, words, letters, or groups of letters match the previously read word.

Expressive coding. Students are asked to view a stimulus word and then write either the word, letter, or group of letters upon request.

Rhyming. This subtest assesses the student's ability to provide rhymes for spoken words.

Syllables. The task requires students to understand and manipulate the deletion of syllables they hear and say.

Phonemes. The student is asked to repeat words said by the examiner, and then say the words without a specific phoneme.

Rimes. Students manipulate and then say words in which they delete a sound.

Are they related? The student must decide if one word is part of or taken from another word and must also determine if the meanings are similar.

Does it fit? The student must determine which pseudoword fits a sentence based on the grammatically correct suffix.

Sentence structure. The student selects the group of words that represents a sentence based on the order of the words.

Pseudoword decoding. This subtest is for students in grades 1–6. Students are asked to read nonsense words.

Find the true fixes. The student distinguishes between spelling patterns that represent morphemes such as prefixes and suffixes.

Morphological decoding fluency. The student must use a provided word and add suffixes as quickly as possible.

Word choice. This subtest assesses the student's ability to discriminate between words with correct written spellings and incorrect written spellings.

Sentence sense. Students are required to read and discriminate which sentence, in sets of three sentences, makes sense.

Compositional fluency. The student is required to write compositions for 5 minutes.

Expository note taking. Students read passages and take notes for a passage and then write a short report based on their notes.

Letters. The child is asked to say specific letters, such as the letter after or before a given letter.

Words. The student is required to remember words, reverse spell the words, and identify the position of specific letters within words.

Sentences: Listening. The student is asked to remember and manipulate words.

Sentences: Writing. Students must remember a sentence and write new sentences that are related to the given sentence.

Rapid automatic naming (RAN). Students are asked to name letters, groups of letters, or words correctly as quickly as possible.

RAS. This subtest requires the student to switch naming letters and numbers quickly.

Oral motor planning. The student alternates between saying the same syllable over again or saying different syllables over again to determine the difference in time between executing repetitions and planning and saying different syllables.

Finger sense. This subtest is administered to students in grades K–6. Students must physically respond to finger-sequencing tasks and respond to tasks that require them to have adequate sensation within their fingers.

This revised assessment instrument offers a variety of subtests that tap into the individual skills needed to read and write in school successfully. This test is not a comprehensive assessment of reading comprehension, but it offers a format in which to assess other skills needed, such as memory, sequencing, association, and fluency of the visual, aural, and motor abilities required for reading and written language skills.

Figure 8.7 provides a sample of a scored section of the Reading-Related Processes of the PAL-II-RW. As noted on the protocol, scale scores are used with an average of 10 and a standard deviation of 3.

● OTHER DIAGNOSTIC TESTS

The remainder of this chapter summarizes several other tests frequently used in the classroom. Some of these tests will not require the lengthy test administration time required by tests presented in the first section of the chapter. Some of these tests may be administered, in part or in their entirety, to groups of students. These tests are included here because they provide useful information to the educator for diagnosing deficits in specific academic areas and aid in educational planning.

Gray Oral Reading Tests–Fourth Edition (GORT–5)

The *GORT–5* provides the teacher with a method of analyzing oral reading skills. This instrument is a norm-referenced test that may be administered to students of ages 6 through 23 years 11 months. The *GORT–5* has equivalent forms so that students may be reassessed using the same instrument. On this instrument, the student reads stories aloud to the teacher, who scores rate, accuracy, fluency, comprehension, and overall reading ability called the *Oral Reading Index.* The comprehension score is derived from answers to questions asked by the teacher following each story. Oral reading miscues may be analyzed in the following areas: meaning similarity, function similarity, graphic/phonemic similarity, multiple sources (of errors), and self-correction. The authors state that the purposes of the *GORT–5* are to identify students with

FIGURE 8.7 Example of a Completed Score Profile Page from the *PAL Test Battery for Reading and Writing* Administration and Scoring Manual, p. 24

Name: *Susy Sample* Grade: *2* Age: *7* Test Date: *9/15/07*

Sex: *F* Handedness: *R* Examiner: *Linda Tester* School: *Oak Elementary*

Part 2: Reading-Related Processes

PAL-II Domain, Subtest, and Scores	Raw Score / Sum of Scaled Scores	Scaled Score (A.1) / Composite Scaled Score (A.3)	%ile (Table 2.2)	Cum. % (A.2)	Base Rate (A.9–A.13)
Orthographic Coding (OR)					
Receptive Coding (RC) Total	50	8	25		
Expressive Coding (EC) Total	—	—	—		
Orthographic Coding Composite (ORC)	—	—	—		
Phonological Coding (PL)					
Rhyming (RY) Total	—	—	—		
Syllables (SY) Total	11	11	63		
Phonemes (PN) Total	25	11	63		
Rimes (RI) Total	5	10	50		
Phonological Coding Composite (PLC)	32	10	50		
Morphological /Syntactic Coding (MSC)					
Are They Related? (RR) Total	32	12	75		
Does It Fit? (DF) Total	4	11	63		
Sentence Structure (ST) Total	5	10	50		
Morphological/Syntactic Coding Composite (MSCC)	33	11	63		
RAN/RAS					
RAN—Letters Total Time (RAN—LTT)	24	15	95		
RAN—Letter Groups Total Time (RAN—LGTT)	25	13	84		
RAN—Words Total Time (RAN—WTT)	35	12	75		
RAN—Letters + —Letter Groups + —Words Rate Change Total (RAN—L—LG—WRC)	35	14	91		
RAN—Letters + —Letter Groups + —Words Total Errors (RAN—L—LG—WTE)	4				<5
RAN—Letters + —Letter Groups + —Words Total Time Composite (RAN—L—LG—WC)	40	14	91		
RAS—Words and Digits Total Time (RAS—WDTT)	50	12	75		
RAS—Words and Digits Rate Change (RAS—WDRC)	12	15	95		
RAS—Words and Digits Total Errors (RAS—WDTE)	0				>25
Oral Motor Planning					
Oral Motor Planning Total Time (OMT)	59	8	25		
Oral Motor Planning Errors (OME) Total	2				26–50
Finger Sense					
Finger Localization (FSL) Total	10				>25
Finger Recognition (FSRC) Total	10				>50
Verbal Working Memory (WMV)					
Letters (WML) Total	4	8	25		
Words (WMW) Total	9	8	25		
Letters + Words Composite (WML—WC)	16	8	25		
Sentences: Listening (WMSL) Total	15	7	16		
Sentences: Writing (WMSW) Total	7	7	16		
Sentences: Listening + Sentences: Writing Composite (WMSL—SWC)	14	6	9		
Verbal Working Memory Composite (WMVC)	30	6	9		

Source: Process Assessment of the Learner, Second Edition (PAL-II). Copyright © 2007 NCS Pearson, Inc. Reproduced with permission. All rights reserved.

problems and to determine the significance or degree of the reading problem, to determine strengths and weaknesses, to document progress made in intervention, and to conduct research using the *GORT–5* (Wiederholt & Bryant, 2012, p. 3). Subtest scale scores are provided with a mean of 10 and the Oral Reading Index is a standard score with a mean of 100. Percentile ranks are also provided for the obtained raw scores.

Test of Reading Comprehension–Third Edition (TORC–4)

The five subtests of the *TORC–4* assess reading comprehension. Those subtests are Relational Vocabulary, Sentence Completion, Paragraph Construction, Text

Comprehension, and Contextual Fluency (Brown, Wiederholt, & Hammill, 2009). Skills are assessed using a variety of task formats and include multiple-choice items, fill-in-the-blank items, open-ended questions, and items that require the student to separate words that have been run together in lines.

Test of Written Language–4 (TOWL–4)

The fourth edition of the *TOWL* includes two alternate forms test booklets (A and B) and is organized into three composites: Overall Writing, Contrived Writing, and Spontaneous Writing (Hammill & Larsen, 1999). The *TOWL–4* contains seven sub-tests; scores on two of those subtests are calculated from a story the examinee writes spontaneously. The student completes all test items in the student response booklet. This instrument may be administered in small groups, although, for optimal monitoring of written responses, individual administration appears to be best. A description of each subtest follows.

Vocabulary. The student is provided a stimulus word and required to use the word in a sentence.

Spelling. The student is required to write sentences that are dictated and must comply with spelling rules.

Punctuation. The student writes dictated sentences and must punctuate sentences and capitalize properly.

Logical sentences. The student is provided an illogical sentence and is required to edit it so that it is more logical.

Sentence combining. The student is presented two or more sentences per item and must combine them into one meaningful and grammatically correct sentence.

Contextual conventions. The student is provided a stimulus picture and asked to construct a story. The story is scored for punctuation, spelling, and grammar.

Story Composition. This subtest scores the written story for quality of elements such as plot, character development, and so on.

Test of Written Spelling–5 (TWS–5)

A standardized spelling test, the *TWS–4* (Larsen, Hammill, & Moats, 2013) consists of two alternate forms that can be administered to individual students or to groups of students of ages 6–0 to 18–11. The examiner's manual includes directions for determining starting points and basal and ceiling levels. The manual provides information about the revision of the instrument, and the authors report improvements in the lower-level items so that a more accurate assessment of students in the early grades can be obtained. The norm sample included 1,634 students ranging from 1st through 12th grades and the sample was designed to reflect the U.S. Census data of 2011.

During administration of this test, the student begins at the appropriate entry level and continues until the ceiling has been reached. The ceiling is established when the student misspells five consecutive words. Once the ceiling has been reached, the examiner checks to see that the basal of five consecutive words spelled correctly was obtained. For students who do not establish a basal, the examiner administers items in reverse order until five consecutive items are spelled correctly, or until the student reaches item 1. All items below the established basal are scored as correct. Raw scores are entered on tables for standard scores with a mean of 100, percentile ranks, age equivalents, and grade equivalents.

This revision of the *TWS* includes more elaboration for examiners regarding the theoretical bases of the test and a discussion of the skills of spelling in English. The authors also provide a useful chapter on additional assessment methods of spelling and other related skills, such as the assessment of phoneme awareness. These additional assessment methods offer the use of this instrument as part of a total evaluation effort, in which teachers would use additional methods and perhaps an alternate form of the *TWS* for measuring gains following interventions.

● ASSESSING OTHER LANGUAGE AREAS

The ability to understand and express ideas using correct language is fundamental for school achievement. Language assessment, through tests that measure a student's understanding and use of language, is presented in this section. Tests administered by speech clinicians in an effort to diagnose and remediate speech disorders (articulation, voice, or fluency disorders) are beyond the scope of this text. Effective remediation of language disorders is considered a shared responsibility of the clinician, teacher, and parent, each of whom must be familiar with the tests to diagnose and monitor these skills. These tests assess a student's receptive language vocabulary, oral expressive language, and written language skills. Teachers also conduct informal assessment of written language in the classroom, as discussed in Chapter 6.

Peabody Picture Vocabulary Test–4 (PPVT–4)

The *PPVT–4* (Dunn & Dunn, 2007) measures the student's verbal comprehension skills by presenting a series of four visual stimuli and requesting the student to discriminate the stimulus that best represents the orally stated word. An example of this format is illustrated in Figure 8.8. Two equivalent forms of this individually administered language test, form A and form B, allow retesting to monitor progress. The test package includes an easel test, examiner's manual, norms booklet, and protocol. Derived scores include standard scores, percentile ranks, normal curve equivalents, stanines, age equivalents, and growth scale values (GSVs). Scoring is fairly easy, and the basal level is determined when the student correctly answers all of the items in a set or misses only one item in the set. The ceiling is determined when the student incorrectly answers at least eight items in the set. The examiner's manual provides easy examples and cases to illustrate scoring procedures and interpretation of raw scores. The examiner's manual also includes an analysis worksheet to determine if the student has more difficulty with the receptive vocabulary of nouns, verbs, or attributes. This may assist with planning interventions for promoting language development.

The examiner is cautioned to use this instrument with children who are English speakers because the *PPVT–4* was normed on students who were proficient in English. The examiner's manual provides evidence of internal consistency, alternate forms reliability, test–retest reliability, content validity, concurrent criterion-related validity, and discriminant validity comparing clinical groups with nonclinical groups. The *PPVT–4* was conormed with the *Expressive Vocabulary Test–2*.

Expressive Vocabulary Test–2

This instrument was conormed with the receptive language measure, the *PPVT–4*. This instrument was normed on persons from ages 2 years and 6 months to those older than 90 years. There are two forms of this measure, A and B. The student's expressive vocabulary is assessed by asking the student to name a picture or to provide a synonym for a picture. Specific directions with acceptable prompts are provided in the examiner's manual. Children are not penalized on this measure for mispronunciations or articulation errors if the word is recognizable. The examiner's manual includes worksheets that will assist the examiner in determining if the child has weaknesses in expressive vocabulary used at home or at school. An additional

FIGURE 8.8 Example of Visual Stimuli Presented to Measure Verbal Comprehension Skills in the *PPVT™–4*

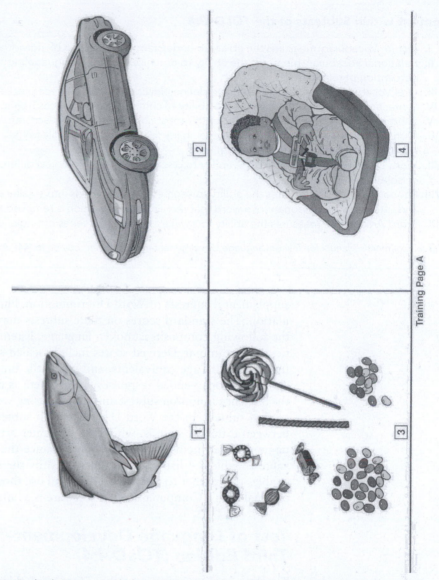

worksheet is provided for an analysis of parts of speech for each item of the instrument. Therefore, it can be determined that the student has a strength in nouns but has difficulty with verbs or attributes, for example. These analyses may provide useful information to assist with language development interventions.

Test of Language Development–Primary: Fourth Edition (TOLD–P:4)

The *TOLD–P:4* (Newcomer & Hammill, 2008) was designed for use with students ranging in age from 4–0 to 8–11 years. The theoretical structure is based on a two-dimensional language model, described in the manual. *TOLD–P:4* contains the following subtests: Picture Vocabulary, Relational Vocabulary, Oral Vocabulary, Syntactic Understanding, Sentence Imitation, Morphological Completion, and the

Content within Subtests of the *TOLD–P:4*

   I. *Picture Vocabulary* measures the ability to understand the meaning of individual words when they are spoken.

  II. *Relational Vocabulary* measures the ability to organize incoming language into categories that permit the perception of relationships.

 III. *Oral Vocabulary* measures the ability to define individual stimulus words precisely.

 IV. *Syntactic Understanding* measures the ability to comprehend sentences having differing syntactic structures.

  V. *Sentence Imitation* measures the ability to repeat complex sentences accurately.

 VI. *Morphological Completion* measures the ability to complete a partially formed sentence by supplying a final word that has a proper morphological form.

VII. *Word Discrimination* measures the ability to discern subtle phonological differences between two words spoken in isolation.

VIII. *Phonemic Analysis* measures the ability to segment spoken words into smaller phonemic units by remembering and uttering the component of a word that remains after a portion is removed from the original stimulus word.

 IX. *Word Articulation* measures the ability to say (i.e., articulate) a series of single words properly.

Source: Examiner's Manual for Test of Language Development–Primary: Third Edition (p. 44). Austin, TX: Pro–Ed. 1997.

supplemental subtests of Word Discrimination, Phonemic Analysis, and Word Articulation. The standard scores on these subtests may be used to obtain quotients for the following composites: spoken language, listening, organizing, speaking, semantics, and grammar. Derived scores include scaled scores (mean = 10), index scores (mean = 100), age equivalents, and percentile ranks. Subtests call for both forced-choice and open-ended responses. The student is also asked to repeat sentences on the Sentence Imitation subtest and fill in missing words for the Morphological Completion subtest. In the Word Discrimination subtest, the student must discriminate between different sounds, which the examiner articulates orally. The student must name pictured items and correctly pronounce the names in the Word Articulation subtest. Table 8.4 lists the skills measured by the subtests; understanding the skills enables the teacher to interpret results and use those interpretations to develop educational plans. Computer-scoring software is available from the publisher.

Test of Language Development–Intermediate: Third Edition (TOLD–I:4)

The Intermediate edition of the *TOLD–I:4* (Hammill & Newcomer, 2008) was constructed to aid in the diagnosis of students with language problems. The theoretical structure of the *TOLD–I:4* is similar to the two-dimensional model of the *TOLD–P:4*. The following subtests are used to assess language skills for students of ages 8 through 17 years 11 months: Sentence Combining, Picture Vocabulary, Word Ordering, Generals, Morphological Comprehension, and Multiple Meanings. The examiner presents all subtests orally; items include forced-choice and open-ended questions. Derived scores of the *TOLD–I:4* are scaled scores (mean = 10), index scores (mean = 100), and percentile ranks by age norms. Age equivalents are also available. Computer-scoring software is available from the publisher.

Test of Adolescent and Adult Language, Fourth Edition (TOAL-4)

The TOAL-4 (Hammill, Brown, Larsen, & Wiederholt, 2007) is an assessment of written and oral language skills especially designed for ages of 12 years to 24 years and 11 months. The three composites available on this instrument are

(1) Spoken Language composite, made up of the Word Opposites, Word Derivations, and Spoken Analogies; (2) Written Language composite, made up of the Word Similarities, Sentence Combining, and Orthographic Usage subtests; and (3) General Language composite, which includes all six subtests. Each student assessed begins with item 1 for each subtest and the ceiling is reached when the student responds with consecutive incorrect answers. The instrument provides scale scores, percentile ranks, and index scores. The authors report that the assessment can be completed in about 1 hour.

The norm sample included 1,671 persons in 35 states and the sample was designed to reflect U.S. Census data of 2004. Demographic categories of the sample included gender, region of the United States, ethnicity (White, Black/African American, American Indian/Eskimo, Asian/Pacific Islander, Other), Hispanic status, disability or no disability, educational level of parents, income, and age. Reliability studies of the instrument included coefficient alpha ranging from 0.87 to 0.97 (averages across subtests and composites), clinical sample and demographic group coefficient alpha ranging from 0.84 to 0.98, and test–retest reliability ranging from 0.78 to 0.97. Validity studies provided in the examiner's manual include content-description validity, item analysis, differential item functioning, criterion-prediction validity, construct validity, and confirmatory factor analysis. Validity ranged from moderate to very high.

Brief Screening of Academic Skills and Assessing for Accommodations

When a teacher is concerned that a student may need additional interventions or may need to be referred for an evaluation, a brief screening instrument may assist in the decision. For example, the WJ IV provides a brief assessment by using the first three subtests; or a teacher may use a screening instrument such as the *Wechsler Fundamentals: Academic Skills* (2008). This would provide a brief assessment of skills such as word reading or word recognition, math computation, and spelling. This information may guide the teacher in determining if a Tier II intervention is needed or if other more intense intervention is required.

The *Dynamic Assessment of Test Accommodations*, or *DATA* (Fuchs, Fuchs, Eaton, & Hammlett, 2003), is a method of assessing testing skills across the conditions: Large Print, Extended Time, Read Aloud, Calculator Condition, and No Accommodations. In this assessment, the teacher provides the assessment of Reading Comprehension, Math Calculations, and Math Applications across the various conditions. For example, the Math Computation assessment is administered as No Accommodation and then again as Extended Time condition. The Math Application assessment is administered as No Accommodation, Calculator condition, and Reader condition. The assessment is to be conducted over a 3-week period. DATA was developed to be used with students from second to seventh grades. The assessment can be administered individually or to a group of students in order to determine which students might require accommodations during a statewide assessment or for instruction.

● SELECTING DIAGNOSTIC INSTRUMENTS

The instruments presented in this chapter are among those most used by educators to determine academic difficulties. Some instruments are recommended for specific academic areas or skills. Thus, an examiner may appropriately select one instrument because it contains subtests that will yield information necessary for academic planning and intervention. Table 8.5 presents a summary of the instruments discussed in Chapter 8.

TABLE 8.5

Test Review

Name of Test	Purpose of Test	Constructs Measured	Standardization Information	Reliability Information	Validity Information
KeyMath–3 DA	Comprehensive and diagnostic assessment of math skills	Basic math concepts, math operations, math applications	Sample included 3,630 persons of ages 4 years 6 months to 21 years 11 months; variables considered were geographic region, ethnicity, socioeconomic status, parents' educational level	Alternate forms reliability coefficients 0.96–A 0.97–B for total test split-half reliability	A variety of research supporting evidence for content validity, construct validity, concurrent criterion-related validity in manual
Test of Mathemati-cal Abilities–Second Edition	Assesses aspects of math not found on other measures	Math vocabulary, attitude toward math, general math information	Sample included more than 2,000 students from 26 states; variables consid-ered were race, community, disability status	Internal consistency coefficients and group coefficients ranged from 0.73 to 0.98; test–retest ranged from 0.66 to 0.93	Concurrent criterion-related validity ranged from low to adequate; construct validity supported
Process Assessment of the Learner: Test Battery for Reading and Writing	Assesses the processes involved in reading and writing	Prereading and writing processes such as receptive and expressive coding, alphabet writing, phonemic awareness skills, acquisition of written symbols, short-term memory of visual and oral symbols and sounds associated with reading, fluency of recall or rapid automatic naming	Sample included 868 students of ages 5–13 years; variables considered included race/ethnicity, geographic region, and parents' educational level; sample approximated 1998 U.S. Census representation	The manual includes reliability studies of internal consistency of alpha coefficients, test–retest reliability, and interscorer reliability; coefficients ranged from adequate to high	Evidence of content and construct validity provided; concurrent criterion-related validity information provided with other diagnostic and reading/writing measures; strong support for clinical discriminant validity provided
Woodcock-Johnson III Diagnostic Reading Battery	Assesses the skills of reading	Reading decoding skills, reading comprehension skills	Sample included more than 8,000 persons from grade K to 12; variables considered were age, sex, race, geographic region, size of community, parents' educational level	Intercorrelations for subtests and clusters were adequate to high; test–retest 0.50s to 0.90s	Content and construct validity studies; independent studies for concurrent validity research
Gray Oral Read-ing Tests–Fourth Edition	Assesses oral reading skills	Accuracy, fluency, comprehension, and overall oral reading ability	Sample included more than 1,600 persons from four geographic regions; variables considered were race, ethnicity, family income and educational status, age	Alternative forms reliability, interscorer reliability, and test–retest reliability with coefficients ranging from 0.85 to 0.99	Content validity, differential item functioning, criterion-related validity research supports test validity

Test	Assessment	Areas Assessed	Sample	Reliability	Validity
Test of Reading Comprehension–Fourth Edition	Assesses reading comprehension skills	Reading comprehension, vocabulary from content-related areas	Sample included more than 1,900 students; variables considered were age, sex, race, ethnicity, and geographic region	Internal consistency, interscorer, content and time sampling were considered with reliability coefficients ranging from 0.79 to 0.98	Information provi r content, construct, and criterion-related validity; information provided for discriminant validity for specific groups
Test of Written Language–Fourth Edition	Assessment of various written language skills	Written language, spelling skills, vocabulary	Sample included more than 2,000 students; variables considered were sex, race and ethnicity, community type, disability, and geographic region	Interscorer, coefficient alpha, split-half reliability, and test–retest reliability ranged from adequate to high	Concurrent criterion-related validity, factor analysis information provided and considered adequate
Test of Language Development–Primary: Fourth Edition	Assesses various aspects of language development of young children	Vocabulary, grammatical and syntactic understanding, articulation of words and phonemic analysis	The sample included 1,000 students of ages 4–0 to 8–11; variables considered were sex, community size, race, ethnicity, parents' educational level, family income, and geographic region	Reliability coefficients ranged from 0.77 to 0.99 for content sampling, internal consistency measures, time sampling, and interscorer reliability studies	Content validity, construct validity, and criterion-related validity studies included in the manual, with coefficients ranging from 0.52 to 0.97
Test of Language Development–Intermediate: Fourth Edition	Assessment of general language skills of children of ages 8–0 through 17–11	Vocabulary, grammatical comprehension	A portion of the sample was included from previous studies with a sample size of 779; variables considered were sex, community size, race, ethnicity, parents' occupation, and geographic area	Internal consistency using coefficient alpha, content sampling, and interscorer reliability presented in the manual, with coefficients ranging from 0.83 to 0.97	Criterion-related validity, construct validity, item validity, and factor analysis information included in the manual
Test of Adolescent and Adult Language–Fourth Edition	Assessment of written and spoken language skills	Spoken Language—word opposites, word derivations, spoken analogies; Written Language—word similarities, sentence combining, orthographic usage	Sample size of 1,671 individuals of ages 12 to 24 years and 11 months; representative of U.S. Census data	Reliability coefficients were adequate to large across multiple measures of reliability, including criterion-related, internal consistency, and test–retest reliability	Validity coefficients for content, construct, confirmatory factor analysis ranged from moderate to very large
Test of Written Spelling–Fifth Edition	Assessment of spelling skills	Spelling skills	Sample included over 4,000 students; variables considered were race, sex, ethnicity, and geographic region	Internal reliability coefficients were high, ranging from 0.93 to 0.99; test–retest reliability studies were adequate, although the sample sizes of the studies for reliability were small	Content, criterion-related validity information, and construct validity research included and based on developmental gains
Peabody Picture Vocabulary Test–Third Edition	Assessment of vocabulary skills through equivalent forms	Receptive vocabulary, expressive vocabulary, ability to name pictures and provide synonyms	Sample included 3,540 persons ranging in age from 2 years to 90+ years; variables considered sex, ethnicity, age, educational level of person or parents, and geographic region; representation based on 2004 U.S. Census survey data; conormed with the PPVT–4 (see above for standarization sample)	Internal consistency studies included split-half and alternate forms; test–retest information included All coefficients ranged from the 0.83s to 0.90s for both forms; split-half reliability ranged from 0.88 to 0.97	Examiner's manual provides various research studies providing evidence of construct, criterion-related, and content validity; evidence provided for clinical discriminant validity with clinical samples
Expressive Vocabulary Test-2	Assesses expressive vocabulary				

● RESEARCH AND ISSUES

Research is emerging on the newly revised versions of the tests presented in this chapter, but is scant on the newly developed instruments, such as the *KTEA 3 and the WJ IV Tests of Achievement*. A brief review of selected research on these instruments and issues of academic assessment follows.

1. In a presentation of the use of the WJ IV Tests of Achievement by one of the test authors, it was stated that the revised instrument now makes it possible to link cognitive abilities, achievement, and oral language measures to assist in the determination of a significant learning disability (Mather, 2014). This allows diagnosticians to determine specific learning disabilities by looking for discrepancies between and among abilities and by examining processing strengths and weaknesses between and among the abilities and skills assessed.

2. The revised WJ IV batteries allow the clinicians to examine a variety of abilities and link the cognitive processes to academic skills to better target areas that require intervention (McGrew, 2014). The new instrument provides reorganized clusters for some skills and processing abilities that may result in greater specification in cognitive, academic, and linguistic abilities.

3. One study of the KeyMath–3 for second-grade English learners administered the subtest items in English first and then Spanish for the items that the students missed (Alt, Arizmendi, Beal, & Hurdato, 2013). In all subtests, students' scores increased when the items were administered in Spanish. These differences were significant for the Basic Concepts and the Applications subtests. Although the sample was small, this research poses an interesting question for examiners to consider when administering items to English learners who, while perhaps proficient in English, may continue to benefit from item follow-up administration in their primary language.

4. Berninger (2006) suggested that instruments such as the *Process Assessment of the Learner: Test Battery for Reading and Writing (PAL–RW)* and the *Wechsler Individual Achievement Test, Third Edition (WIAT–III)* should be used in combination with intensive interventions for reading and written language for students who are at risk for developing written language disabilities. This may offer an advantage over using CBM-type progress monitoring alone, as the student would be assessed and compared with age norms.

5. Canivez (2013) investigated the criterion validity of the Wechsler Adult Intelligence Scale-IV (WAIS-IV) and the WIAT- II and WIAT–III and determined that the performance on the WIAT-II and WIAT-III subtests and composite score variance was predicted by the individuals' performances on the WAIS-IV. This indicates that these instruments are correlated: Individuals who do well on the cognitive measure will also do well on the academic achievement measure.

6. Fuchs, Fuchs, and Capizzi (2005) suggested that the use of additional measures, such as the DATA instrument for accommodations, assists in making accurate decisions about specific accommodations, especially for students with learning challenges. These authors call for additional research to determine usefulness in day-to-day practice.

7. Vladescu (2007) reviewed the KTEA–II and stated that internal consistency for the test was not adequate for the Oral Language subtest. Furthermore, this reviewer noted that skills may not be assessed adequately: Other instruments assess each skill with more items and subtests. Vladescu also argued that an insufficient number of items at the floor or beginning levels of the instrument make it difficult to assess younger students and students with lower skills. Vladescu cautioned against using this instrument alone to design academic interventions.

8. Peterson, Martinez, and Turner (2010) reviewed the *Process Assessment of the Learner: Test Battery for Reading and Writing (PAL–RW)* and noted its strength in linking the assessment process with interventions that might be used in a tiered intervention approach.

9. Cascella (2006) noted that some language assessments provide normative data on students with intellectual disabilities. This might be helpful to educators in determining if a student should receive additional speech and language therapy in the school setting. In this review, it was noted that the *TOAL,* the *TOLD,* the *TOLD–P,* the *PPVT–3,* and the *EVT* provide such norms.

10. In an older review of the *PIAT–R*, Allinder and Fuchs (1992) cautioned that the format of the test might encourage guessing. These reviewers also cautioned that information obtained from multiple-choice items is diagnostically different from information obtained when a response must be produced independently by the student. They reminded consumers that this instrument was designed as a wide-range screening instrument and should therefore not be used in educational decision making involving placement, eligibility, or planning. Another study found that changing the visual stimuli associated with the *PIAT–R* Written Expression subtest resulted in significantly higher scores for structure (Cole, Muenz, Ouchi, Kaufman, & Kaufman, 1997).

CHAPTER SUMMARY

In this chapter you:

- Learned content assessed by several commonly used achievement instruments
- Applied basal and ceiling rules to raw score data
- Analyzed scores to determine academic skill strengths and weaknesses
- Synthesized score profiles and interpreted results
- Evaluated case scenarios to select appropriate achievement tests

THINK AHEAD

How do you think student behaviors influence a student's ability to make successful progress in school? In the next chapter, you will learn a variety of methods used to study and assess behavior in a school setting.

CHAPTER QUIZ

Now complete the Chapter Quiz and assess your understanding of the legal regulations for the practice of assessment of learners with special needs and learning challenges.

9 Assessment of Behavior

CHAPTER FOCUS

In this chapter you will:

- Learn about legal aspects of individuals with behavior challenges
- Apply behavioral concepts to observational data
- Analyze results of behavioral observations
- Synthesize data and case scenarios to target behaviors for interventions
- Evaluate case scenarios to select interventions

● TIER I BEHAVIORAL INTERVENTIONS

Behavioral challenges, like educational challenges, are to be addressed within the three-tier structure in the school setting. This means that prior to a student being referred for special education, teachers and staff must indicate the interventions that have been implemented and document that these interventions were not successful. As presented in Chapter 7, students who need educational interventions may be moved to Tier II to receive academic interventions. Students who have behavioral challenges for which the universal supports, such as schoolwide behavioral expectations, rules, and consequences, are not sufficient, may require Tier II interventions. As with educational interventions, these behavioral interventions are to be implemented consistently and with integrity. A well-known strategy to address the three-tier model is schoolwide positive behavioral support systems. These systems are structured by the local school and provide consistent schoolwide positive behavioral expectations. All adults consistently implement all school rewards, rules, and consequences. The implementation of such programs is most successful when all teachers and staff believe in and support the school's goals for improving behavior. This is considered a Tier I intervention. The behavioral tiers are presented in Figure 9.1.

Tier II behavioral interventions include small-group interventions and some specific intensive efforts for students at risk. Examples of these interventions include mentoring, classroom opportunities for the at-risk student to be successful and earn rewards, and discussion with the student about expectations, rewards, and consequences. When students fail to respond to these interventions, data may be collected through techniques such as functional behavioral assessments, behavioral analysis, or frequency counts to determine baselines of behavior, to attempt interventions, and to observe increases in positive behavior or increases in negative behavior. These techniques are presented following the discussion of legal requirements.

● REQUIREMENTS OF THE 1997 IDEA AMENDMENTS

The behavioral assessment and behavioral planning mandates of the 1997 IDEA amendments were included to ensure procedural safeguards for students with

FIGURE 9.1 Three Tiers for Behavioral Interventions

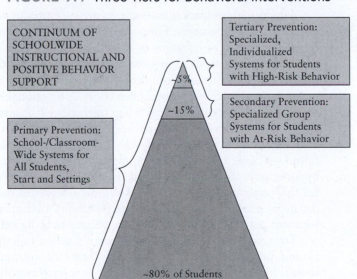

Source: From OSEP Center on Positive Behavioral Interventions and Supports, www.pbis.org. Used with permission.

behaviors that interfere with educational success. Prior to the amendments, the application of discipline procedures for students with disabilities and students without disabilities was inconsistent (Yell, Drasgow, & Ford, 2000). Special education students who were repeatedly suspended from school for several days each time or who were expelled from school were no longer receiving free, appropriate education. In addition, these punitive types of disciplinary procedures often resulted in more harm to the student or caused the student's negative behaviors to escalate (Kubick, Bard, & Perry, 2000).

Seeking to make schools safe for all learners, Congress provided educators with the means to discipline students fairly (Drasgow & Yell, 2001). To ensure that students requiring special education support were assisted with their behavioral needs rather than merely punished for behaviors, the 1997 and 2004 amendments to the Individuals with Disabilities Education Act (IDEA) required schools to determine if the behaviors were the result of or manifested by the student's existing disability using a procedure called manifestation determination. This procedure is required before a student receiving special education services can be suspended for more than 10 school days. To read the federal requirements for behavior, functional behavioral assessments (FBAs), and manifestation determination, click on the link below.

Manifestation determination must be completed as quickly as possible and comply with federal regulations. One requirement of manifestation determination is confirming that the student's IEP was appropriately written and followed. The IEP must include the present levels of educational performance and behavioral functioning. In addition, the student exhibiting the behaviors must have a behavioral intervention plan in place that is based on a functional behavioral assessment (FBA). The student's present levels of behavioral functioning are to be based on information obtained in the functional behavioral assessment and should be written in clear, understandable language (Drasgow, Yell, Bradley, & Shriner, 1999). The regulations require that the behavioral intervention plan include strategies for positive behavioral support and interventions that provide the student with acceptable replacement behaviors.

The focus of the manifestation determination is for the members of the student's individualized education program (IEP) team to decide if the behavior under consideration is a manifestation of the student's disability. If the parents, teacher, and other school personnel on the team agree that the behavior is a manifestation of the disability, the team must decide if the behavioral intervention plan is addressing the student's needs or must conduct another FBA and revise the intervention plan. The student is also then returned to the setting from which he or she was removed when the behavior occurred.

Functional behavioral assessments are measures to determine the function or purpose of a child's behavior. Functional behavioral assessment does not aim to describe or label the type of behavior or disorder (e.g., describing hitting or labeling depression), but rather seeks to answer the question of why the inappropriate behavior is occurring. Once this has been determined, interventions can be developed to promote positive, acceptable replacement behaviors. A functional behavioral assessment defines the target behavior, determines when the behavior occurs and when it does not occur, and generates hypotheses about the possible function of the behavior. Once these have been determined, the hypotheses are tested or tried so that the exact function can be found (O'Neill, Horner, Albin, Sprague, Storey, & Newton, 1997). The testing out of hypotheses is also called functional behavioral analysis. Personnel who are responsible for this phase of the functional behavioral assessment should receive additional training in its procedures because of the possibility that manipulating the student's environment may result in more negative behaviors being exhibited (O'Neill et al., 1997).

Drasgow and Yell (2001) summarized when functional behavioral assessments *should* be conducted and when they *must* be conducted. For example, students should have an FBA when their behavior interferes with their progress on their IEP or when their behavior may present a threat to others. Students must have an FBA when their behavior includes bringing drugs or weapons to school.

Federal regulations require that both special education personnel and general education personnel participate in the functional behavioral assessment along with the student's parents (Conroy, Clark, Gable, & Fox, 1999). Initial efforts to apply functional behavioral assessments may have resulted in schools treating the requirements as merely a compliance issue (Gable, Hendrickson, & Smith, 1999). In other words, schools may not have completed extensive functional behavioral assessments but rather completed the minimal amount of paperwork needed to comply with the mandates. This resulted in numerous due process hearings brought by parents who believed that their children were not appropriately served or assessed prior to suspensions or other disciplinary actions (Drasgow & Yell, 2001). Most of these hearings found in favor of the parents as a result of inadequate or nonexistent functional behavioral assessments. It is necessary to fully understand the functional behavioral assessment process in order to fully comply with the law.

● FUNCTIONAL BEHAVIORAL ASSESSMENTS

Information to determine why a student displays a specific behavior can be obtained through three broad methods of assessment (O'Neill et al., 1997; Witt, Daly, & Noell, 2000). The first method of assessment is indirect. It includes techniques such as interviewing the classroom teacher and parents, reviewing data in school records, and completing behavioral rating scales and checklists. These methods are presented later in the chapter. Another method used in functional behavioral assessment is direct observation, also referred to as the *descriptive observational method*. This requires that the student be observed in the environment in which the behaviors are occurring. During this part of the assessment, several techniques may be employed, such as event recording, interval recording, anecdotal recording, duration recording, latency recording, interresponse time, and interviews with parents, school personnel, and, when appropriate, the student. These techniques are presented in following sections of the chapter. The third broad method of assessment is the functional behavioral analysis method. During both the indirect assessment and the direct observation phases of the assessment, hypotheses are generated regarding the purpose or function of the behavior. In the functional behavioral analysis portion of the assessment, the variables believed to be triggering the behavior and the possible consequences following the behavior are manipulated. By this manipulation, it can be determined exactly why the student is using the behavior. For example, following the initial phases of the functional behavioral assessment, it is hypothesized that the reason a student is calling out in class is to receive peer attention. During the functional behavioral analysis, the hypothesis of peer attention is tested. Students in the class are directed to ignore the calling-out behavior, and the calling out decreases. When students react to the calling-out behavior, such as turning to look at the target student when calling out occurs, the calling out increases. Thus, the function of the calling out is to receive peer attention. Following the functional behavioral analysis and additional assessment, the students in the class are directed to ignore all calling-out behavior and to reinforce appropriate hand raising by paying attention to the target student. This manipulation of the consequence (peer attention) resulted in decreasing the calling out and in an appropriate replacement behavior (raising hand).

Education personnel may need to use functional assessment interviews with teachers, parents, and the target student (Gresham, Watson, & Skinner, 2001). During these interviews, the goal is to obtain information that will assist in formulating a hypothesis about the function of the target behavior. These interviews will provide information concerning how the student functions in various environments. When interviewed, the student can share feelings and concerns about school and other areas of life.

Direct Observation Techniques

The first step in the intervention of behavioral problems is the identification of target behaviors. Once the exact behavior or behaviors have been identified, direct observations can begin. In direct observation, the teacher notes how often a particular behavior occurs, thereby establishing a baseline that will be used to monitor the student's progress during and after intervention. Direct observation also allows the teacher to note antecedent events that might trigger the target behavior or increase the likelihood that it will occur.

Behavioral observations can be completed by the teacher or by another objective professional or trained paraeducator. Behaviors may be observed for frequency, duration, intensity, or for the length of time between responses—what has been termed *interresponse time* (Gresham et al., 2001). The observer should remember two important guidelines for effective behavioral observation: Be objective and be specific. The observer should be fair and nonjudgmental and should precisely pinpoint or identify problem behaviors. The identified behaviors should be stated exactly so that two observers would be able to agree about whether the behavior is or is not occurring.

Antecedents

Antecedents may be actual events that increase the probability of target behaviors occurring. For example, a teacher may place a demand on a student such as completing a math task that results in the student displaying defiant behavior. Other events may happen, of which the teacher is not aware, that may increase the likelihood of a behavior occurring. These events, called setting events, may have an influence on the student's behavior before another antecedent event happens in school. For example, a setting event may be that a student has an argument at home with an older sibling before coming to school. This antecedent may increase the probability that the student will exhibit externalizing target behaviors within the school environment. So, this student may become defiant when the teacher places a difficult task demand on the student.

Other events that increase the probability that a target behavior will occur are those that make a consequence more attractive. For example, a student may be more anxious to receive an edible reward as a consequence when the student is hungry. This may increase the probability that a student will behave in a specific way, such as stealing another student's lunch. This type of event is known as an establishing operation, or EO (Michael, 2000).

Anecdotal Recording

Behavioral intervention strategies are based on a clear understanding of why a behavior occurs. The behavioristic principle is founded in the theory that behaviors are maintained or increased by the reinforcing events that follow the event or behavior; that is, events that happen prior to the target behavior increase the likelihood that the behavior will be exhibited. Conditions occurring prior to the exhibited behavior are known as *antecedents*. The teacher may recognize when a behavior occurs but not be able to identify the reinforcing event or the antecedent event. One behavioral observation technique that will enable the teacher to hypothesize about the exact antecedent event and reinforcing event, or consequence, is called *anecdotal recording*.

In the anecdotal recording method, the teacher observes the student in a particular setting—usually the classroom—and writes down everything that occurs in that setting. The teacher or other professional observes the student during a specific time period, usually when the behavior seems to occur most frequently. The teacher may wish to observe during a particular academic subject time, such as math class, or during a nonacademic time when the behavior occurs, such as at lunch or during recess.

An anecdotal recording might look like this:

Name: Micah

Observation Time

9:30 A.M.	Language Arts—Micah enters the classroom and walks around the room twice, then sits in his chair. He looks out of the window.
9:32 A.M.	Micah speaks out: Teacher, can I go to the office?
	Teacher responds: Micah, get your workbook out and turn to page 56.
9:33 A.M.	Micah gets workbook out and begins to look at the pictures on several of the pages. Continues for quite some time.
9:45 A.M.	Micah speaks out: What page, teacher?
	Teacher responds: Page 56.
9:47 A.M.	Micah speaks out: Teacher, can I use a pencil?
	Teacher responds: Here is a pencil, Micah.

Using the anecdotal format for observation provides a basis for analyzing the antecedent, behavior, and consequence. The antecedent is the event preceding the behavior, and the consequence is the event following the behavior. The antecedent may actually trigger the behavior, whereas the consequence is thought to maintain or reinforce the behavior. In the preceding example, the antecedent, behavior, and consequence analysis, or A–B–C, might look like this:

A	B	C
Micah enters room, sits in chair and looks at the teacher	walks around talks out	allowed to walk freely teacher responds
looks at pages in workbook,	talks out	teacher responds then looks at teacher
looks at the teacher	talks out	teacher responds

This analysis provides information that will help the teacher plan a behavioral intervention strategy. It appears that the reinforcing event for Micah's talking out is the teacher's responding to him. It also seems that the teacher has not provided an organizational intervention plan that will convey to Micah the behaviors expected of him when beginning academic work or instruction. Through this observation, two behaviors have been targeted for intervention: organizational behaviors (preparing for work) and talking out. The organizational behaviors expected can be broken down into specific behaviors for intervention: student in chair, paper and pencils ready, books out.

Event Recording

Event recording assesses the frequency with which behaviors occur. The teacher simply marks or tallies the number of times a specific behavior occurs. This information—the initial recording of data—creates a baseline for the teacher to use as a comparison following intervention. This type of recording is useful for observing easily detectable behaviors for short periods of time. Examples of this type of behavior include time on task, talking out, and hitting. One illustration of frequency counting, another term for event recording, is shown in Figure 9.2.

Observations using event recording are typically completed for an entire class period or continuously for a specified amount of time. Other methods for observing behaviors intermittently or for short periods of time are time sampling and interval recording.

CHECK YOUR UNDERSTANDING

Check your ability to analyze an anecdotal recording and a functional assessment interview by completing Activity 9.1.

FIGURE 9.2 An Example of Event Recording (Frequency Counting)

	Mon.	Tues.	Wed.
Name _Joe_			
Target behavior: _Out of seat_			
9:00 – 10:00	~~THL~~ ~~THL~~	~~THL~~ ~~THL~~ ||	~~THL~~ ~~THL~~ |
10:00 – 11:00	||	|	|||
11:00 – 12:00	|	|||	||

Time Sampling

Time sampling uses frequency counting to determine how often behaviors are occurring. The collection of data, or counting of behaviors, can be conducted by checking to see if the behavior is occurring or not occurring every 5 to 10 seconds. The observer may simply check or tally if the behavior occurs. This type of time sampling is called partial-interval recording. In whole-interval recording, the teacher would indicate if the behavior occurred for an entire interval. This enables the teacher to observe more than one student or more than one behavior throughout the day. An example of a time-sampling observation is shown in Figure 9.3.

Interval Recording

Interval recording is used when the teacher wants to observe several students or behaviors at one time, record intermittently throughout the day or class period, or record behaviors that occur too frequently to record each event, such as stereotypical behaviors (Kerr & Nelson, 2002). During interval recording, the teacher notes whether the behavior is occurring or not occurring. Observation intervals might be very brief (e.g., 1 or 2 minutes). During this time, the teacher notes every 30 seconds whether or not the behavior is occurring. An example of interval recording is shown in Figure 9.4.

Duration Recording

Duration recording is used when the length of the behavior is the target variable of the behavior. For example, a student may need to increase the amount of time spent

FIGURE 9.3 Sample Chart for Time Sampling of On-Task and Off-Task Behaviors

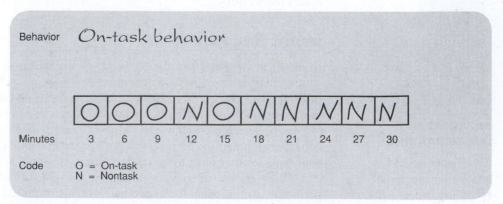

Behavior	_On-task behavior_									
	O	O	O	N	O	N	N	N	N	N
Minutes	3	6	9	12	15	18	21	24	27	30
Code	O = On-task N = Nontask									

FIGURE 9.4 Sample Interval-Recording Form

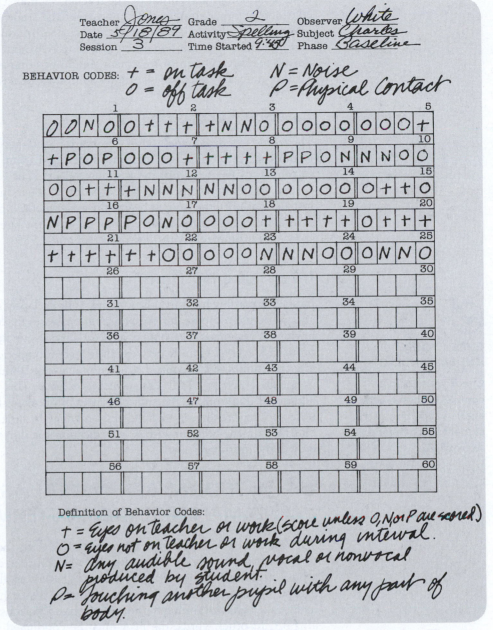

Source: From *Strategies for Addressing Behavior Problems in the Classroom* (4th ed., p. 97) by M. M. Kerr and C. M. Nelson, 1989, Upper Saddle River, NJ: Merrill/Prentice Hall. Copyright 2002 by Prentice Hall. Reprinted by permission.

on task. The teacher will record how long the student remains on task following the directive to do so. Duration recording might look like this:

Name: Robbie

Task: Writing assignment

On Task	Off Task
2 min	60 s
60 s	2 min
60 s	60 s

On-task/off-task ratio is 4:8 min = 50% on task

This brief duration recording reveals that Robbie is on task only 50% of the expected time. Following intervention by the teacher, such as a prompting signal, behavioral contract, or other strategy, it is hoped that the student's on-task time will increase while off-task time will decrease. Reinforcement for on-task time increases the probability that Robbie will remain on task longer. A duration recording of on-task time during the intervention or treatment should be compared with the baseline data of 50% to note the effectiveness of intervention strategies.

Latency Recording

The latency recording method of observation also involves the element of time. This is an observation in which the time is recorded from the moment a stimulus (e.g., a command) is given until the response occurs. The element of elapsed time is recorded. For example, the time is recorded from the moment the teacher gives spelling instructions until the student begins the assignment. If the student must be prompted several times during the completion of the task, the latency is recorded each time the student is prompted (Evans, Evans, & Schmid, 1989).

Interresponse Time

CHECK YOUR UNDERSTANDING

Check your ability to complete a behavioral analysis for a fifth-grade student by completing Activity 9.2.

Latency recording measures the amount of time elapsed between the specific stimulus and the actual response. Interresponse time assesses the length of time between the behaviors or responses (Gresham et al., 2001). For example, a student may be distracted or off task every 2 minutes between the observation period of 2:00 to 3:00 P.M., which is social studies, but become distracted only every 20 minutes during the observation period of 10:00 to 11:00 A.M., which is science. This assessment would then pose additional questions: Is the subject matter more interesting or easier in the morning observation? Are there more hands-on activities? Is the student tired in the afternoons? Has the student been prescribed a medication for distractibility that is administered only in the morning?

● FUNCTIONAL BEHAVIORAL ASSESSMENTS AND MANIFESTATION DETERMINATION

The law clearly indicates that when a student with special needs violates the code of conduct of the school, the student is to be considered as other students are when school personnel implement punishment. The law is also clear that a student with exceptional learning needs must be following his or her own IEP, and if that IEP includes a behavioral intervention plan, that plan must be followed and based on an FBA. In other words, the FBA must be conducted first and the results used to formulate the behavioral modification program. This means that if school personnel find that the student's behavior is maintained or reinforced as a result of peer or adult attention, or that the behavior is maintained by the student's being allowed to avoid or escape the demands of school, the behavioral intervention plan (BIP) must be written to address the student's behavior by changing either the antecedent or changing the consequence the student is seeking. Therefore, a child who behaves in a certain way to obtain peer attention can participate in a plan in which the antecedent—what triggers the behavior—is changed so that the student no longer exhibits the behavior and therefore would not be reinforced by his or her peers. For example, if a student is assigned a seat near the instruments in music class and always pounds the drums as he walks past them, the antecedent is changed by assigning the student to a different seat. Similarly, if a student misbehaves after recess when he is assigned math seatwork, the antecedent can be manipulated by the teacher's issuing the math assignment prior to recess with the condition of earning recess when the assignment is complete. In these examples, the antecedent and the consequence have been manipulated to address the behavior.

A behavior intervention plan must include instruction in positive behaviors to replace the negative behaviors. In the previous examples, the positive behaviors that the students must learn might include showing respect for property (musical instruments) and completing assigned work according to teacher directives when prompted to do so. For the math example, the positive behavioral instruction might focus on academic engagement. Following instructions for math, the student is reinforced for working on the math assignment and the student is also reinforced for positive behaviors that happen during the remainder of the day. This communicates that positive behaviors should happen throughout the day rather than only when the behaviors are prompted.

When a student has violated a school conduct code, such as by engaging in a fight on school grounds or at a school-sponsored activity, and the student has been receiving special education support services, the student must be disciplined in the same way as other students. If the school's practice is to suspend students for 3 days when they participate in a fight, the student receiving special education must be suspended. However, if the student has been suspended numerous times throughout the year for similar behaviors, and the days add up to 10, school personnel must conduct a manifestation determination to decide if the misbehaviors are the result of the student's disability. As noted previously, an appropriate IEP must be in place and must be followed. Moreover, for the child who has numerous behavioral infractions, the committee conducting the manifestation determination must determine that the IEP has been followed and that the FBA that is in place is appropriate and has been followed. When the school has not followed either the IEP or the FBA, the student cannot be suspended. The reasoning here is that the behaviors are the result of the disability and the school has been negligent in implementing the correct interventions for the behaviors.

CHECK YOUR UNDERSTANDING

Check your ability to determine when a student must have a manifestation determination and if the student's behavior is the result of a disability by completing Activity 9.3.

● STRUCTURED CLASSROOM OBSERVATIONS

Observation methods discussed so far in this chapter may be teacher-made, informal instruments that can be used for prereferral, assessment, and intervention of behavioral problems. A structured classroom observation form called the *Direct Observation Form* (Achenbach, 1986) is one part of the *Child Behavior Checklist (CBCL)* system, a multiaxial system for assessment of behavioral and emotional problems. Other forms in this system are described throughout the chapter in the appropriate topical sections.

Child Behavior Checklist: Direct Observation Form, Revised Edition

The *Direct Observation Form* (Achenbach, 1986) is four pages in length, including general instructions and guidelines. The first page consists of the student's identifying information (name, date of birth, observation settings, etc.) and general administration directions. The inside pages of the form comprise three parts: an observation rating scale on which to mark observed behaviors and rate their intensity or severity, a space for anecdotal recording of all events during the observation period, and an interval recording form. The observer makes several observations of the target student across several different settings. The observer compares the target student with two grade and gender peers. When comparing the target student with peers, the observer ascertains whether the student is significantly different from the two control students in on-task behavior. This method is often used to assess behavioral disorders such as attention deficit disorder. Often, the criterion for indicating

FIGURE 9.5 Behavior Checklist

	Yes	No
1. Student is prepared for work each period.	_____	_____
2. Student begins assignment on request.	_____	_____
3. Student stays on task with no distractions.	_____	_____
4. Student completes tasks.	_____	_____
5. Student stays on task but is sometimes distracted.	_____	_____
6. Student complies with teacher requests.	_____	_____
7. Student raises hand to speak.	_____	_____
8. Student talks out inappropriately.	_____	_____
9. Student completes homework.	_____	_____
10. Student is aggressive toward peers.	_____	_____
11. Student is disruptive during class.	_____	_____
12. Student talks out of turn.	_____	_____
13. Student is verbally aggressive.	_____	_____
14. Student has damaged property belonging to others.	_____	_____

possible attention problems is that the target student's off-task behavior score is 1.5 or 2 standard deviations above the control students' scores. The observer marks the items on the rating scale if the target child exhibits the behaviors during the observation. Figure 9.5 illustrates the types of items presented on the *Direct Observation Form*. These items are then scored, as are the other rating scales and interviews of the multiaxial *CBCL* system, for significant behavioral problems. The behaviors are defined on two broad bands: (1) externalizing (acting out); and (2) internalizing (turning inward), which includes problems such as anxiety or withdrawal. In addition, the system notes the occurrence of several clinical behavioral syndromes, such as social problems, somatic complaints, aggressive behavior, and attention problems. The other components of the *CBCL* are scored along the same broad and narrow bands of behavioral and emotional functioning.

OTHER TECHNIQUES FOR ASSESSING BEHAVIOR

Some techniques for assessing behavior do not involve direct observation. These techniques include checklists, questionnaires, interviews, sociograms, and ecological assessment. These methods rely on input from others such as parents, teachers, or peers rather than on direct observation of behavior. When these indirect methods are used with direct observation, the teacher can plan effective behavioral intervention strategies.

Checklists and Rating Scales

A checklist is a list of questions that the respondent completes by checking the appropriate responses. The respondent may answer yes or no or check off the statements that apply to the student. Teachers, parents, or both may complete the checklist. Figure 9.5 presents an example of a behavioral checklist.

A rating questionnaire is similar in content to a checklist, but the respondent indicates his or her response along a rating scale. For example, the respondent might rate the frequency of certain student behaviors as *never, almost never, sometimes, somewhat often, frequently,* or *almost always.* This format allows for interpretation of the extremes. For example, a student's behavior might be rated as almost never completing assignments, but frequently being verbally aggressive and sometimes damaging property. This information helps the teacher pinpoint areas that need observation and further evaluation.

Elliot, Busse, and Gresham (1993) suggested that the following issues be considered when using rating scales:

1. Ratings are summaries of observations of the relative frequency of specific behaviors.

2. Ratings of social behavior are judgments affected by one's environment and the individual rater's standards for behavior.

3. The social validity of the behaviors one assesses and eventually treats should be understood.

4. Multiple assessors of the same child's behavior may agree only moderately.

5. Many characteristics of a student may influence social behavior; however, the student's sex is a particularly salient variable.

Several rating forms are commonly used in the assessment of behavioral problems. Many of these include forms for teachers and parents. Common examples include the *Teacher Report Form* (Achenbach, 1991b) and the *Child Behavior Checklist* (Achenbach, 1991a), the *Behavior Rating Profile–2* (Brown, & Hammill, 1990), and the *Conners Teacher Rating Scales* and *Conners Parent Rating Scales* (1997). These forms and scoring systems ask a variety of questions about the student, and the parent or teacher rates the student on each item.

Achenbach System of Empirically Based Behavior Assessment (ASEBA) Parent, Teacher, and Youth Report Forms

The *Achenbach System of Empirically Based Behavior Assessment (ASEBA),* also known as the *Child Behavior Checklist* (Achenbach, 1991a; Achenbach & Rescorla, 2001), includes a *Parent Report Form* and companion forms such as the *Teacher Report Form* (Achenbach, 1991b; Achenbach, & Rescorla, 2001) and the *Youth Self-Report* (Achenbach, 1991c). (The system's *Direct Observation Form* and interview form are discussed in other sections of this chapter.) This system also includes a preschool version with an informal language survey (Achenbach & Rescorla, 2000).

The Achenbach system allows for the student to be rated on both positive, or adaptive, behaviors and behavioral syndromes. In 1991, the author revised the system to allow the profiles to be scored consistently across the parent, teacher, and youth scales (McConaughy & Achenbach, 1993). The parent form includes, in addition to the rating scales, some open-ended questions, such as: What concerns you most about your child?

Two *ASEBA* forms are available to parents: one for children aged 1/2–5 years and another for students aged 6–18 years. The *Teacher Report Form* is for students aged 6–18. Items on these instruments are closely related so that both parents and teachers are rating the student on similar dimensions. An example of a *Teacher Report Form* profile is shown in Figure 9.6.

In addition to the teacher and parent forms, a self-rating form is available for students aged 11–18. The *Youth Self-Report* (Achenbach, 1991c; Achenbach & Rescorla, 2001) covers many of the same topics as the teacher and parent forms. This instrument calls for responses that can be analyzed qualitatively to determine the student's self-perceptions. The student also answers items concerning current

FIGURE 9.6 Syndrome Profile from TRF Completed for Alicia Martinez by Her Teacher, Ms. Segovia

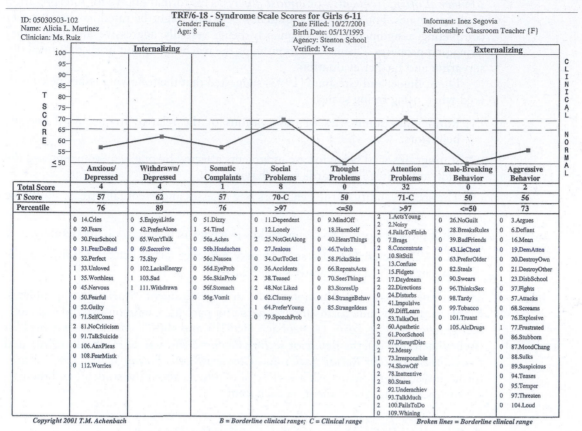

Source: Copyright T. M. Achenbach and L. A. Rescorla. Reproduced by permission.

academic achievement and rates himself or herself on social dimensions such as getting along with family members.

Examiner manuals address the issues of validity and reliability for each of the individual parts of the multiaxial *ASEBA* system by Achenbach (1991a, 1991b, 1991c; Achenbach & Rescorla, 2000, 2001). The examiner is provided with detailed information about content and criterion-related validity and the discriminant validity of using cutoff scores to identify students with specific behavioral problems. Test–retest, testing across time, and reliability of raters are presented, and the technical quality of the systems appears to be adequate or above on all measures.

Behavior Assessment System for Children, Second Edition (BASC–2)

This assessment system includes rating scales for parents to complete, rating scales for teachers to complete, a developmental history form for parents, and self-reports for students ages 8–25 years. This system includes an observation form for recording observations in the classroom. The *BASC–2* system was developed to be used with students 2 to 25 years of age. The system provides a method for distinguishing students with attention deficit disorder, depression, other behavioral concerns, and social maladjustments. Scores indicate students who are within a clinical range of significance or at risk for having difficulties. The *BASC–2* also indicates how well students are adapting in a positive manner. Scores on the adaptive scales are noted to be *very high*, *high*, *average*, *at risk*, and *clinically significant*. The *BASC–2* includes an audiotape provided for students who have difficulty reading the self-report form in English but who understand spoken English. The student self-report form is presented in a true–false format. The instrument may be hand scored, and computer scoring provides additional information such as the validity of the specific test administered. The *BASC–2* provides a means of comparing the student with both the norm sample and clinical samples. This may be helpful in determining the severity of behavioral difficulties.

The examiner's manual provides information regarding the standardization and norm samples for all components of the *BASC–2*. The total number of students and parents for the norm samples was 4,650 for the *Teacher Rating Scale*, 4,800 for the *Parent Rating Scale*, and 3,400 for the *Self-Report of Personality*. The samples were representative geographically, and gender and race/ethnicity approximated U.S. population estimates.

The manual presents reliability and validity information for all scales. Ample technical data for internal consistency, test–retest reliability, interrater reliability, standard error of measurement, factor structure of scales, and concurrent validity data are presented.

Behavior Evaluation Scale, Third Edition (BES-3)

The BES-3 (McCarney & Arthaud, 2005) includes a short or long form for rating behaviors of students ages 4 to 19 years. Like the ASEBA, this instrument has versions to be completed at home and school. Among the types of indices on the instrument, students may be rated for interpersonal difficulties, unhappiness or depression, inappropriate behaviors, and learning problems. Unlike the ASEBA, there is no scale for assessing adaptive behaviors. The standardization samples for the instrument included nearly 5,000 students for the home version and slightly over 5,000 for the school version. This scale may be used best to screen for the presence of possible behavioral challenges that require additional assessment to determine the specific target behaviors or the possible existence of an emotional disturbance.

Behavior Rating Profile–2

The *Behavior Rating Profile–2* (Brown & Hammill, 1990) includes forms for the student, parent, and teacher. The student completes the rating by marking that items are true or false about himself or herself. The teacher and parents rate the student by marking that the items are *very much like* the student, *not like* the student, *like* the student, or *not at all like* the student. This system allows the examiner to compare how the student, teacher, and parent perceive the student. It also categorizes the student's perceptions into the various environments of the student's life: school, home, and peer relationships. This enables the examiner to determine whether the student has more positive feelings about school, relationships with peers, or relationships with parents. The instrument is scored using a standard score with a mean of 10 and a standard deviation of 3. The examiner can plot a profile that presents a view of how the student, parent, and teacher perceive the student.

The manual provides reliability and validity information that includes studies conducted with relatively small samples. The internal consistency and test–retest coefficients seem to be adequate, with many reported to be in the 0.80s. Validity studies include criterion-related research, with reported coefficients ranging from below-acceptable levels to adequate. The authors provide discussion of content and construct validity.

Conners Rating Scales–Revised

The Conners system (Conners, 1997) includes the following scales:

Conners Parent Rating Scale–Revised: Long Version

Conners Parent Rating Scale–Revised: Short Version

Conners Teacher Rating Scale–Revised: Long Version

Conners Teacher Rating Scale–Revised: Short Version

Conners-Wells Adolescent Self-Report Scale: Long Version

Conners-Wells Adolescent Self-Report Scale: Short Version

Auxiliary Scales

Conners Global Index–Parent

Conners Global Index–Teacher

Conners ADHD/DSM–IV Scales–Parent

Conners ADHD/DSM–IV Scales–Adolescent

The revised version of this instrument includes several substantial changes. The author states that the revised version provides multidimensional scales that assess attention deficit hyperactivity disorder (ADHD) and other disorders that may coexist with attention disorders. The new version includes additional methods for assisting mental health professionals in making diagnoses according to the *Diagnostic and Statistical Manual of Mental Disorders*, Fourth Edition (DSM-IV; American Psychiatric Association, 2000). The former edition of the *Conners* included a hyperactivity index, which is now called the *Conners Global Index.*

The *Conners Rating Scales–Revised* was developed with a large standardization sample (more than 8,000 persons) with representative samples in the United States and Canada. In addition to representative norms, several studies are included in the manual that compare ethnic differences in samples of the following groups: African American/Black, Asian, Caucasian, Hispanic, Native American, and Other. These studies are presented in adequate detail in the manual, with main-effect differences by ethnic group provided for each scale. Consumers of this instrument are encouraged to read this section of the manual carefully when using the instrument for diagnostic purposes with the mentioned ethnic groups.

Behavioral dimensions assessed by the *Conners* include oppositional, cognitive problems/inattention, hyperactivity, anxious-shy, perfectionism, social problems, and psychosomatic. Although these dimensions are addressed on the *Conners*, it is best used to screen for these disorders and to follow up with multiple measures to determine if other behavioral, learning, or emotional disorders exist.

The special "Quick Score" paper included with the rating scales enables the teacher or other member of the multidisciplinary team to score the short form in minutes. The long versions of the various rating scales involve much more effort to score, and hand scoring using the profile sheets is difficult because of the large number of columns included on the page. Computer scoring is available.

Reliability studies included internal reliability. Internal consistency for the various scales ranged from 0.72 to 0.95. Some variability exists on some scales with different age groups. For example, teacher ratings were more consistent for the younger and older age groups than for other age groups.

Validity studies in the *Conners* examiner's manual address factorial validity, convergent validity, divergent validity, discriminant validity, and concurrent validity. Information concerning this research is much more extensive than that presented in the previous edition and seems to range from below acceptable levels to adequate. Many of the studies included small samples. The author states that research in this area is continuing.

Questionnaires and Interviews

The questions found on questionnaires are similar to the items on checklists, but the respondent is encouraged to describe the behaviors or situations where the behavior occurs. The respondent answers with narrative statements. For example, the questions might appear as follows.

1. How well is the student prepared for class each day?
2. Describe how the student begins assignments during class.
3. How does the student perform during distractions?
4. How often does the student complete homework assignments?
5. How does the student respond during class discussions?

Respondents should provide objective responses that describe as many variables of the behavior as possible. Interviews are completed using questions similar to those used on questionnaires. The evaluator orally asks the respondent the questions and encourages objective, detailed information. The interview format may also be used with the student to obtain information about the student's feelings and perceptions about the target behaviors. Figure 9.7 illustrates how an interview could be adapted so that both parents and the student could provide answers.

Child Behavior Checklist: Semistructured Clinical Interview

Interviews may be conducted by different members of the multidisciplinary team. Often, these interviews are unstructured and informal. Achenbach and McConaughy (1989, 1990) developed a semistructured interview and observation form to be used with students aged 5–11. This interview assesses the student's feelings about school, family, and peers as well as his or her affect or emotional functioning. The examiner is provided with, in addition to the interview, an observation form to rate behaviors of and comments by the student observed during the interview. The student is asked open-ended questions and guided through the interview process. This interview can be useful in determining current social and emotional issues affecting the student.

Sociograms

The sociogram method of behavioral assessment enables the teacher to obtain information about group dynamics and structure within the classroom. This information can be interpreted to determine which students are well liked by their peers,

FIGURE 9.7   Interview Questions Adapted for Both Parent and Student

Parent Interview	Student Interview
1. How do you think your child feels about school this year?	4. Tell me how you feel about school this year.
2. Tell me how your child completes homework assignments.	5. Describe how you go about finishing your homework.
3. Describe the responsibilities your child has at home.	6. What type of things are you expected to do at home? Do you think you complete those things most of the time?

which students are considered to be the leaders in the group, and which students are believed to be successful in school. A sociogram is presented in Figure 9.8a and b.

A sociogram is constructed by designing questions that all members of the class will be asked to answer. These questions might include: Whom would you select to be in your group for the science project? or Whom would you invite to the movies? The answers are then collected and interpreted by the teacher. The diagram in Figure 9.8a illustrates a sociogram; Figure 9.8b lists questions asked of a class of fourth-grade students.

FIGURE 9.8 Sociogram (a) and Sociogram Questions (b)

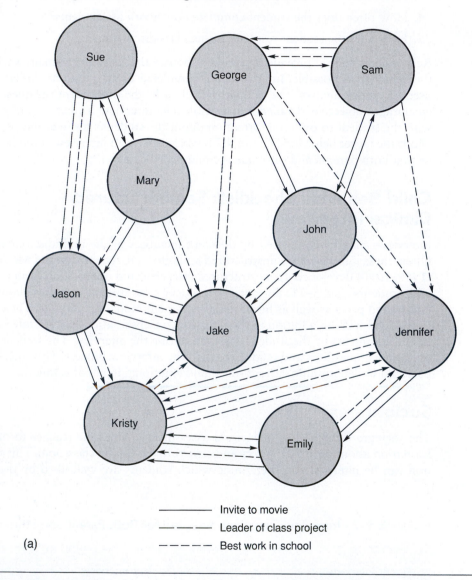

(a)

— Invite to movie
– – – Leader of class project
- - - Best work in school

Sociogram questions.

1. Name two students in our class whom you would most like to invite to a movie (or other activity).

   a. _____

   b. _____

2. In our class, whom would you like to be the leader of our class project? _____

3. Name two students in our class who do the best work in school.

   a. _____

   b. _____

(b)

Data are analyzed to determine whom the class members perceive as being the class stars, the social isolates, and so on. The teacher can also determine where mutual choices exist (where two students share the same feelings about each other) and can identify cliques and persons who are neglected. The teacher can then use this information to intervene and structure social and academic situations that would promote fair social skills. Role-playing, class projects, and school social activities could be used to increase the interpersonal interaction opportunities for social isolates and neglectees. Caution should be used when employing a sociogram technique so that students do not feel that they are not perceived in a positive way by their peers. The data are therefore not shared with the students but rather used to consider interventions to improve social skills or to assist in designing collaborative instructional groups that may indirectly improve social skills and interactions within the classroom.

Ecological Assessment

Ecological assessment analyzes the student's total learning environment. This analysis includes the student's interactions with others (peers, teachers, paraeducators, parents, and other persons who are directly involved with the student's learning process); the teacher's interactions with other students in the classroom; the methods of presentation of materials; materials used in the classroom; the physical environment; and the student's interactions with others in different settings, such as the playground or lunchroom. All of the informal behavioral assessment methods presented thus far may be used as a part of ecological assessment.

The teacher variable is one area that can be assessed by direct observation and other techniques such as questionnaires. Guerin and Maier (1983) suggested surveying teachers to determine their level of teacher competency. This would include assessing areas such as level of instruction, teaching strategies, types of instruction, media used in the classroom, and general communication and interaction with students and parents. These types of questionnaires can be completed by the teacher or by an objective observer. Educational materials, also a part of classroom ecology, should be evaluated for their appropriateness for the individual student. The level of difficulty of the materials, their format, and their mode of presentation and expected student response are important considerations. Overton (1987) suggests that the following questions be considered when assessing educational materials:

1. Are the objectives of the materials appropriate for the student?
2. Do the ability/readability levels match the current instructional level of the student?
3. Is the interest level appropriate for the student?
4. Does the method of presentation match the student's learning strength?
5. Are prerequisite steps needed before the student can attempt the task?
6. Does the format of the material contain extraneous stimuli that can confuse or distract the student?
7. Does the material contain information not necessary for task completion?
8. Are too many tasks contained on one page?
9. Is the student capable of completing the task in the amount of time allowed?
10. Does the task need to be broken down into smaller tasks?
11. Is the student capable of responding with relative ease in the manner required by the materials?
12. Can the criterion level for success be reduced?

CHECK YOUR UNDERSTANDING

Check your ability to analyze a sociogram of a classroom by completing Activity 9.4.

13. Does the material allow the student to self-check or self-correct?

14. Does the material allow the student to observe progress? (pp. 111–115)

Case Study Mr. Blackburn notices that one of his second-grade students, Gracelyn, is enthusiastic during morning classes but has difficulty in the afternoon. She disturbs other students and generally seems to be unhappy in class. Sometimes Gracelyn says things to her peers that result in an argument, and he has to ask her to leave the classroom. Mr. Blackburn collects the following data for afternoon classes:

	Off-Task Behaviors	Inappropriate Remarks to Peers
Monday	5	2
Tuesday	6	3
Wednesday	1	0
Thursday	6	3
Friday	7	3

After he has collected the data, he notices that Gracelyn's behavior was markedly better on Wednesday than on the other days of the week. He begins to analyze all the variables in the environment: academic tasks, lunchroom behavior, seating arrangements. He concludes that the only variable that was different on Wednesday was that another student, Joyce, who typically joined the class in the afternoons, was absent. Mr. Blackburn decides his next step will be to discuss this with Gracelyn. When he speaks with her, Gracelyn explains that she and Joyce had been friends last year, but now Joyce has a new best friend and she is afraid that Joyce does not like her anymore. After his data analysis and discussion with Gracelyn, Mr. Blackburn is able to intervene and assist Gracelyn with the social skills she needs to resolve this issue.

CHECK YOUR UNDERSTANDING

Check your ability to analyze a case study in a classroom by completing Activity 9.5.

● PROJECTIVE ASSESSMENT TECHNIQUES

The measures presented in this section are measures that are scored more subjectively; they are often referred to as *projective techniques*. These measures include sentence completion tests, drawing tests, and apperception tests, which require the student to tell a story about some stimulus, such as picture cards. These instruments are most likely administered by the school psychologist, school counselor, or other professional such as a clinical psychologist who has the training and experience required to administer such instruments. Teachers and other members of the multidisciplinary team may be required to make eligibility and planning decisions based on the results of these instruments. The school psychologist will write interpretations of the results of these instruments that will be considered in addition to other data, to make decisions about a possible emotional disturbance. It is beneficial to teachers, therefore, to understand the nature of the instruments and how they might be used in the assessment process.

Sentence Completion Tests

Sentence completion tests provide stems or beginnings of sentences that the student is required to finish. The stems have been selected to elicit comments from the student on such topics as relationships with parents and friends and feelings about oneself. The examiner analyzes the comments written by the student for themes rather than analyzing each sentence independently. The *Rotter Incomplete Sentence Test k* (Rotter & Rafferty, 1950) is an example of this type of instrument. Figure 9.9 presents stems similar to those on sentence completion tests.

FIGURE 9.9 Sample Items from a Sentence Completion Test

1. Sometimes I wish _____.
2. I wish my mother would _____.
3. I feel sad when _____.
4. My friends always _____.
5. My father _____.

Drawing Tests

Drawing tests attempt to screen the student's feelings about self, home, and family. Each of these instruments follows a simple format. The student is presented with a form or a piece of plain paper and is asked to draw a picture of: self; a house, a tree, and a person; or family members doing something together. These tests are commonly known as the Draw-a-Person, Human-Figure Drawing, House-Tree-Person, and Kinetic Family Drawings. An examiner who has had training and experience in this type of assessment scores the drawings. More empirically based scoring systems are also available: the *Kinetic Family Drawing System for Family and School* (Knoff & Prout, 1985), the *Draw-a-Person: Screening Procedure for Emotional Disturbance* (Naglieri, McNeish, & Bardos, 1991), and the *Human-Figure Drawing Test* (Koppitz, 1968). The *Draw-a-Person* can be scored developmentally using a system like that developed by Naglieri (1988) or Harris (1963).

The newer versions of scoring systems include standardization information and developmental information. The *Kinetic Family Drawing System for Family and School* includes questions that the examiner asks the student about the drawings. For example, one question is: What does this person need most? (Knoff & Prout, 1985, p. 5). The scoring booklet provides various characteristics that the student may have included in the drawings. The examiner checks to see whether a characteristic, such as the omission of body parts, is present in the student's drawing. Guidelines for interpreting these characteristics are provided in the manual through a listing of relevant research on drawing analysis. The examiner analyzes themes that exist within the drawing on such dimensions as figure characteristics and actions between figures. Several case studies are provided for the examiner to use as guidelines for learning how to interpret the drawings.

The scoring system of the *Draw-a-Person: Screening Procedure for Emotional Disturbance* uses scoring templates and a norm-referenced method of scoring the drawings. The instrument is a screening device used in determining whether the student needs further emotional or behavioral assessment. The manual features case studies that include exercises in using the templates and scoring system. Derived scores include *T* scores with a mean of 50 and a standard deviation of 10 and percentile ranks. The scores are interpreted as follows (Naglieri et al., 1991, p. 63):

Less than 55   Further evaluation is not indicated.

55 to 64   Further evaluation is indicated.

65 and above   Further evaluation is strongly indicated.

Figure 9.10 presents an example of the template scoring system from the manual.

The standardization information and technical data provided in the Naglieri et al. (1991) manual is fairly extensive and impressive for a projective drawing instrument. The sample included 2,260 students, ages 6 to 17 years. Approximately 200 students were represented in each age group. Consideration was given for age, sex, geographical region, population of community, ethnicity, race, occupation of parent, and socioeconomic status. Internal consistency was researched using the

FIGURE 9.10 Example of the Naglieri et al. Template Scoring System for the *Draw-a-Person* Test

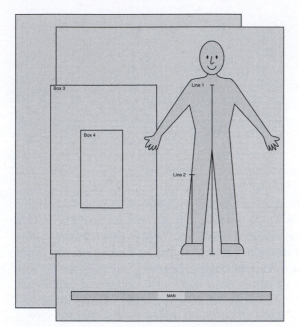 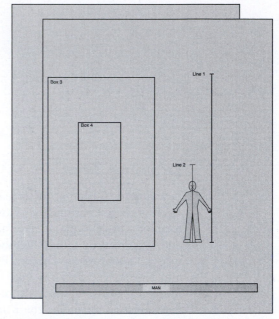

Source: From *Draw a Person: Screening Procedure for Emotional Disturbance, Examiner's Manual* (p. 23) by J. A. Naglieri, T. J. McNeish, and A. N. Bardos, 1991, Austin, TX: Pro-Ed. Copyright 1991 by Pro–Ed, Inc. Reprinted by permission.

coefficient alpha, and coefficients were adequate, ranging from 0.67 to 0.78. The standard error of measurement is approximately 5 for all ages. The test–retest information gives a coefficient of 0.67, although the sample for this study was fairly small ($n = 67$). Both intrarater and interrater agreement were studied and resulted in coefficients of 0.83 and 0.84, respectively. This study was also small, using 54 cases and 2 raters.

Descriptive statistics are included for validity studies that used the scoring system to compare students who had been clinically diagnosed with emotional or behavioral problems to students without such problems. The scoring system did discriminate between the groups, at least at the .05 significance level. Construct validity is supported by discriminant validity studies of intelligence testing and the Naglieri et al. *Draw-a-Person* scoring system. The research presented indicates that two separate areas are assessed by the *Draw-a-Person* and intelligence tests.

Apperception Tests

Apperception tests consist of a set of picture or story cards that have been designed to elicit responses about emotional issues. These instruments must be administered and interpreted only by professionals with the training and experience required by the test developers. Most of these projective techniques require that the examiner possess advanced graduate-level training in psychological assessment. Because apperception tests may contribute information used by the multidisciplinary team to determine educational and behavioral interventions, teachers should understand what these instruments attempt to measure and how they are interpreted. Two commonly used instruments are the *Children's Apperception Test* (Bellak & Bellak, 1949, 1952; Bellak, & Hurvich, 1965) and the *Roberts Apperception Test for Children* (Roberts, 1982).

Roberts–2

The *Roberts–2* (Roberts & Gruber, 2005), like its original version, the *Roberts Apperception Test for Children* (McArthur & Roberts, 1982), presents story-picture cards of human figures engaged in situations with family members and peers. The second edition may be used with students ranging in age from 6 through 18 years. Of 27 stimulus cards, the student responds to 11 cards that are specific to the student's gender, as well as to five gender-neutral cards. This instrument has Hispanic cards and cards representing African American children as well as Caucasian children. The examiner uses the cards to elicit comments from the examinee about her or his feelings about fear, parental relationships, dependency, peer and racial interaction, and so on. The examiner instructs the student to tell a story about what happened before, during, and after each scene pictured and to tell what the characters are doing, saying, and thinking. The examiner scores responses according to guidelines set forth in the manual, which gives information about adaptive indicators, clinical problems such as aggression or anxiety, and measures such as social-cognitive functioning.

The manual includes information about the standardization of the instrument as well as studies comparing students within the normal range of emotional functioning with several different clinical samples. Reliability information includes interrater reliability and test–retest reliability studies. Median interrater reliability correlations ranged from 0.43 to 1.00. The validity information included in the manual presents several studies of the factors measured, as well as the instrument's ability to discriminate clinical from nonclinical groups. Generally, the information presented appears to be adequate for this type of behavior instrument.

● COMPUTERIZED ASSESSMENT OF ATTENTION DISORDERS

Computerized instruments have been developed for the assessment of sustained focused attention and impulsive responding patterns. Difficulty with these behaviors is believed to be characteristic of students with attention deficit disorders. This type of difficulty may be manifested as distractibility, impulsivity, and overactivity in classroom situations. These instruments should not be used as a single measure of attention problems, but rather should be used in combination with other measures, particularly classroom observations. Two such computerized systems currently used in clinical practice and research are the *Continuous Performance Test* (Gordon, 1983) and the *Conners Continuous Performance Test* (Conners, 1993). All tests of this general type are known as CPTs.

Continuous Performance Test

In Gordon's (1983)*Continuous Performance Test,* the student must discriminate between visual stimuli presented for a period of 9 minutes. The stimuli are numbers that appear at the rate of one per second. The scoring program computes the number of correct responses, omissions, and commissions. This instrument has been widely researched, and the author reports reliability coefficients ranging from 0.66 to 0.80.

Conners Continuous Performance Test, Third Edition

The *Conners Continuous Performance Test-3* is presented in much the same manner as Gordon's version (Conners, 1993; Conners, 1997, 2014). This CPT, however, lasts for 14 minutes, and the visual stimuli—letters—appear at varying rates throughout administration. The student must maintain focus, and the number of targets hit is calculated to determine impulsivity and loss of attention. Interpretive, computer-generated reports give derived scores for hit rate, reaction time, pattern for standard error or variability, omissions, commissions, attentiveness, and response tendencies such as risk taking. Students ages 8 years and older may take this test. The normative sample ranged in age from 8 to 60-plus years of age. Data included in the manual and from computer reports compare the student with age and gender peers in a clinical group of students with attention deficit disorders. Scores are reported as T-scores and the ranges of performance include *very high, high, moderate,* and *minimal.*

● DETERMINING EMOTIONAL DISTURBANCE

According to federal regulations, students may be found to be eligible for interventions under the category of emotional disturbance if they meet one or more of the following criteria:

An inability to learn that cannot be explained by other factors (such as a sensory or learning disorder)

Difficulty in establishing and maintaining relationships with peers and adults

Behaviors that are inappropriate for the circumstances

A persistent mood of unhappiness or depression

Physical symptoms manifested as the result of fears or concerns about school or other problems

It is important to note that even though a student may be experiencing emotional difficulties, he or she may not be eligible for special education services. For example, a student may be depressed; however; if there is no documented need for special education support, the student will not be found eligible for services. Students who manifest only mild behavioral problems without a coexisting emotional disorder will also not likely be served under special education. For many students with such behavioral issues, it is simply a matter of poor learning or social maladjustment. It is also noteworthy that most students with attention deficit disorders or physiologically based disorders such as Tourette's syndrome will be served under the category of Other Health Impaired. The reasoning for this distinction is that although these disorders have behavioral manifestations, they are not the result of an emotional disorder. This distinction may be difficult to ascertain without additional assessment data from the school psychologist.

One instrument that may be used to assist in making such determinations, in combination with other behavioral and developmental data from parents and teachers, is the *Scale for Assessing Emotional Disturbance* (Epstein & Cullinan, 1998). The measures on this instrument are consistent with the five requirements of the federal regulations. The classroom teacher and other educators working with the student may be asked to complete a variety of questionnaires and checklists to assist in the determination. Students who are found to have emotional disturbance must manifest these behaviors across environments and in social interactions with a variety of peers and adults. The use of multiple checklists provides information about these multiple settings and social encounters.

● RESEARCH AND ISSUES

The assessment of emotional and behavioral problems is by nature more ambiguous than other types of assessment, such as assessment of intellectual ability or academic achievement. The techniques range from systematic observations and computer assessment to projective techniques, such as telling stories about picture cards. Voluminous research on each of these methods exists. The following list summarizes results of more recent studies using the instruments often employed in settings that serve children and youth. Other measures, such as the Rorschach inkblot test (Rorschach, 1921, 1942), are more often used in clinical settings and therefore are not included in this text.

1. Gable, Park, and Scott (2014) noted in their review of functional behavioral assessment (FBA) that school personnel may not yet have the training needed to write effective behavioral plans based on the function of the target behaviors.

2. Zirkel (2011) noted that special education state laws do not include specific definitions and processes and that the way in which FBAs and behavior intervention plans (BIPs) are constructed and implemented lacks reliability and does not reflect professional literature or best practice.

3. In a review of literature about functional behavioral assessment (FBA), it was found that FBA has largely studied high-rate behaviors in students with low-incidence

disabilities, such as self-injurious behaviors in children with mental retardation (Ervin et al., 2001). Additional research is needed on low-rate behaviors (e.g., aggressive acts) in students with high-incidence disabilities, such as learning disabilities.

4. Northup and Gulley (2001) reviewed research that applied functional behavioral assessment in samples of students with attention deficit hyperactivity disorder and found that it is a useful technique in determining the interaction and effectiveness of medication with various environmental stimuli.

5. Curriculum-based assessment used as part of a functional behavioral assessment was found to be an effective strategy in identifying escape-motivated behaviors of students within a general education classroom (Roberts, Marshall, Nelson, & Albers, 2001).

6. Information gained from functional behavioral assessments in preschool students at risk for attention deficit hyperactivity disorder was found to be useful in identifying specific strategies that decreased problematic behaviors (Boyajian, DuPaul, Handler, Eckert, & McGoey, 2001).

It is evident from the small sample of research reviewed in this chapter that many factors are to be considered in the assessment of students exhibiting behavioral and emotional challenges. It is important that multiple measures and multiple informants be used and that the individual student's environment be assessed as well (Clarizio & Higgins, 1989). In a review of relevant research on assessment of attention and behavioral disorders, Schaughency and Rothlind (1991) stressed the need for a variety of methods, such as interviews, teacher ratings, observations, and peer nominations. These techniques may aid in determining whether the difficulties are reactions to the environment or reactions to current stress within the student's world. As with all assessment, a holistic view of the complete student and her or his environment is necessary.

CHAPTER SUMMARY

In this chapter you:

- Learned about legal aspects of individuals with behavioral challenges
- Applied behavioral concepts to observational data
- Analyzed results of behavioral observations
- Synthesized data and case scenarios to target behaviors for interventions
- Evaluated case scenarios to select interventions

THINK AHEAD

The assessment of cognitive abilities—intelligence—remains a part of the assessment process in determining the need for special education intervention. Chapter 10 presents the most commonly used measures of intelligence and adaptive behavior.

CHAPTER QUIZ

Now complete the Chapter Quiz and assess your understanding of the legal regulations for the practice of assessment of learners with special needs and learning challenges.

10 Measures of Intelligence and Adaptive Behavior

CHAPTER FOCUS

In this chapter you will:

- Learn about constructs of intelligence assessment

- Apply learning to case scenarios

- Analyze how intelligence assessment informs instructional planning

- Synthesize data from intelligence assessment and adaptive behavioral assessment

- Evaluate how intelligence assessment results and adaptive behavioral assessment inform educational decisions

● MEASURING INTELLIGENCE

The measurement of intelligence has been a controversial issue in educational and psychological assessment for the past several years. Even though professionals in the field disagree to some extent about the definition of the term *intelligence* and about the fairness and importance of intelligence testing, the assessment of intellectual ability is mandated by the Individuals with Disabilities Education Act (IDEA) for the diagnosis of many disabilities. This federal law also requires the assessment of adaptive behavior, or how a student functions within her or his environment, for the diagnosis of mental retardation.

This chapter presents a review of several measures of intelligence and adaptive behavior that commonly are used in schools to diagnose students with learning or emotional disabilities. Group intelligence tests may be administered in school systems to students in the regular education curriculum; for special education diagnostic purposes, however, group IQ tests are not appropriate. Tests constructed to be administered in an individual setting are commonly used to measure cognitive abilities. Although teachers will not be responsible for administering intelligence tests, special education teachers should possess an understanding of the interpretation of intelligence test results and their possible implications for educational planning. A general discussion of intelligence testing and the court cases that have influenced current practice are presented before the review of intelligence tests.

● THE MEANING OF INTELLIGENCE TESTING

The results of intelligence tests are usually reported in the form of a standardized intelligence quotient (IQ) score. The IQ score is a quotient that was historically derived in the following manner:

$$IQ = MA/CA \times 100$$

In this calculation, *MA* means the mental age of the student and *CA* is the chronological age of the student. Using this formula, a child with a mental age of 9 and a chronological age of 11 would have an IQ of around 82. A student with a mental age of 14 and a chronological age of 10 would have an IQ of 140. This way of calculating IQ scores was not always a good estimate of cognitive abilities since it was difficult to apply accurately to adults. This method of calculating IQ was replaced with a method that uses a deviation IQ or a determination of an individual's standing when compared with an average of the age group.

It is important for the special education professional to understand what an IQ score is and is not. To possess a basic understanding of IQ scores, the professional educator should consider what is measured by IQ tests, that is, the content and presentation of the items on an IQ test and what the items represent. It is a commonly believed myth that IQ scores are measurements of potential that is innate in a person. The following statements illustrate some current views about intelligence and intelligence testing expressed in the literature:

> "The IQ does not reflect a global summation of the brain's capabilities and is certainly not an index of genetic potential, but it does predict school achievement effectively" (Kaufman, 1979, p. 9).
>
> "Ultimately, intelligence is not a kind of ability at all, certainly not in the same sense that reasoning, memory, verbal fluency, etc., are so regarded. Rather it is something that is inferred from the way these abilities are manifested under different conditions and circumstances" (Wechsler, 1974, p. 5).
>
> "Intelligence—unlike height and weight, but like all psychological constructs— must be measured indirectly; it must be inferred from intelligent behavior, past and present" (Hopkins, Stanley, & Hopkins, 1990, p. 374).
>
> "Measurement of current intellectual performance has become confused with measurement of innate potential. Intelligence tests do not assess potential;

they sample behaviors already learned in an attempt to predict future learning" (McLoughlin & Lewis, 1990, p. 187).

"Child-standardized intelligence performance provides a quantitative index of developmental status, but does not provide information on those functions that have not developed or on the route by which the child arrived at his or her current developmental state" (Swanson, & Watson, 1989, p. 93).

"Historically, intelligence has been an enigmatic concept. It is a much-valued construct or quality that is extremely difficult to define. Is intelligence the same as verbal ability? Analytical thinking? Academic aptitude? Strategic thinking? The ability to cope? Different theorists might argue for each, or a combination of these abilities. Similarly, they might ask whether intelligence is, or should be, defined in the same way for individuals of different cultural, ethnic, or social backgrounds" (Taylor, 1993, pp. 185–186).

Wasserman and Tulsky (2005) note that "Over 100 years of debate have failed to lead to a consensus definition of this core psychological construct" (p. 14). The theories upon which these tests are based influence their use and interpretation. As the development of intelligence tests continues, and that development is based on researched theories, the measurement and interpretation of intelligence test results will continue to be more meaningful for interventions (Kamphaus, Winsor, Rowe, & Kim, 2005). There is increasing evidence that the results of cognitive measures are useful indicators of students' strengths and weaknesses that can inform educational planning, goals, and strategies (Decker, Hale, & Flanagan, 2013).

The use of IQ tests or cognitive assessment instruments may result in bias when used to categorize and label students as students with exceptional learning needs (Reschly, 1981). The outcomes of early eligibility and classification of students into disability categories raised concerns, including questioning using the same measures of intelligence for individuals of all cultures because the outcomes of using these instruments raised concerns that minority students were overrepresented in special education classrooms (Heller et al., 1982; Taylor, 1993). Specifically, early data trends of students supported through special education indicated that African-American students have been overrepresented in classrooms for students with intellectual disability (Heller et al., 1982; Tucker, 1980), and Hispanic students have been increasingly determined eligible for the category of learning disabilities (Mick, 1985; Tucker, 1980). With federal regulations focused on decreasing disproportionality, it is even more important to make certain that formal assessment measures are free from ethnic, cultural, and linguistic bias.

Salvia and Ysseldyke (1988) underscored the importance that culture and background have on intellectual assessment:

Acculturation is the single most important characteristic in evaluating a child's performance on intelligence tests. . . . The culture in which a child lives and the length of time that the child has lived in that culture effectively determine the psychological demands a test item presents. (p. 149)

The issues of innate potential, learned behaviors, environmental influence, and acculturation and their influence on intelligence testing have fueled the fire of many professional debates (Herrnstein & Murray, 1994). Intelligence testing, however, like all testing in education, is simply examining the way that a student responds to a set of stimuli at a specific point in time. Reynolds et al. (1982) reviewed and summarized the general problems with bias in assessment; these include bias that may exist due to the examiner being from a different culture than the examinee and bias in the actual cultural differences in content and language. Some of the problems of intelligence testing stem from content validity, construct validity, predictive validity (Messick, 1980), and the mean differences obtained by groups of different cultural or ethnic backgrounds (Reschly, 1981), as well as problems that affect all types of standardized testing, such as examiner familiarity (Fuchs & Fuchs, 1989) or examiner bias and inconsistency (McDermott, Watkins, & Rhoad, 2014).

● ALTERNATIVE VIEWS OF INTELLECTUAL ASSESSMENT

The use of traditional intelligence tests in schools has been criticized for producing different results for different groups (Canter, 1997). The movement toward change in special education assessment, accountability, and educational reform in schools has also had an influence on the use of traditional assessment methods. As a result of these trends, it is likely that assessment personnel along with researchers will seek alternative types of assessment models and methods of determining intellectual ability. Canter stated that "intelligence testing as we practice it today seems increasingly out-of-step with the needs of tomorrow's schools" (1997, p. 256). Dissatisfaction with the traditional psychometric approach has stimulated research and theoretical exploration of additional definitions and techniques used to assess intellectual ability. For example, Gardner (1993) presents a model with seven intelligences:

> But there is an alternative vision that I would like to present—one based on a radically different view of the mind and one that yields a very different view of the school. It is a pluralistic view of mind, recognizing many different and discrete facets of cognition, acknowledging that people have different cognitive strengths and contrasting cognitive styles. . . . One such approach I have called my "theory of multiple intelligences." (1993, pp. 6–7)

The original seven types of intellectual ability proposed by Gardner are linguistic intelligence, logical–mathematical intelligence, spatial intelligence, musical intelligence, bodily–kinesthetic intelligence, interpersonal intelligence, and intrapersonal intelligence. Gardner stresses the need for fair intellectual assessment that would assess all areas rather than only the linguistic and logical–mathematical assessments included in traditional intellectual assessment instruments. Since his earlier theory, he has proposed additional types of intelligences or additional areas for consideration, including naturalist intelligence and existentialist intelligence (Gardner, 2008). A student with strong naturalist intelligence can apply comparisons and find similarities to species that occur in nature, and the existentialist would show strength in reasoning about the larger questions about existence in the world and life.

Carroll (2005) proposed a theory of intelligence based on three levels or stratums. According to this theory, a general or overarching intelligence influences the abilities included within the other two levels. Level 2 includes more specific abilities than the *g* or general factor of intelligence, and level 3 includes very specific abilities. This theory has been expanded and enhanced in the CHC theory, which is a combination and expansion of intelligence by Cattell, Horn, and Carroll (Flanagan & Harrison, 2012). Tests assessing cognitive abilities that have incorporated this theoretical framework into the development of the assessment instrument include the *Woodcock–Johnson IV Cognitive Tests*, the *Differential Ability Scales–Second Edition*, and the *Kaufman Assessment Battery–II*.

The concept of dynamic assessment is another area of current research in the quest for alternate assessment models. This model uses the assessment experience to measure the precise task of learning. The tasks used in dynamic assessment are those in which the learner is presented with interventions to determine how the learner responds to those strategies or interventions. The learner begins a task and is assisted by the examiner rather than merely observed by the examiner. Lidz (1997) pointed out the differences between traditional and dynamic assessment:

> Most of our (traditional) procedures provide information only about the learner's independent level of performance and infer future from previous functioning. . . . Dynamic assessment begins where traditional psychometric assessment ends. Instead of terminating the procedure with the establishment of a ceiling, the dynamic assessor views the ceiling as an area of functioning that warrants assessment. (1997, pp. 281–282)

Others caution against the rapid adoption of alternative measures of intelligence without scientific basis for the changes (Lopez, 1997). Additional researchers call for the use of cross-battery assessment of cognitive abilities, noting that the use of multiple measures can better account for the variety of abilities that must be measured (Flanagan & Ortiz, 2001). Brown, Reynolds, and Whitaker (1999) argued that although many alternate assessment measures of IQ have been proposed, professionals should rely on research-based methods, including traditional standardized assessment instruments. Therefore, in most states, traditional IQ tests continue to be used as a part of the assessment process. Based on the individual student's measured performance on tasks on these IQ tests, team members infer the student's intellectual ability (Turnbull, Turnbull, Shank, Smith, & Leal, 2002).

Even though IQ testing has received much criticism, MacMillan and Forness reminded assessment personnel that traditional IQ scores derived from traditional methods serve a function in schools today:

> What IQ tells us is that if nothing is done and the child remains in general education with no adjustment to instructional strategies, the child with a low score is likely to experience failure—the lower the score, the greater the probability and the greater the degree of failure that the child will encounter. (1998, p. 251)

The most important consideration for school personnel using or interpreting IQ assessment data is that the data obtained from these assessments are only a small part of the information employed in the decision-making process (Prifitera, Saklofske, & Weiss, 2005). Therefore, it is most important to select measures that will provide useful information and assist in making appropriate educational and behavioral interventions.

Litigation and Intelligence Testing

The issues of intelligence testing and the overrepresentation of minorities in special education classrooms led to litigation that has affected current practice in the field, including the decreased use of intelligence tests by some state and local education agencies for the diagnosis of disabling conditions (Bersoff, 1981). Major court cases that have involved the assessment of intellectual ability are *Larry P. v. Riles* (1984) and *PASE v. Hannon* (1980). Other cases have involved assessment and placement procedures: *Diana v. State Board of Education* (1990) and *Lora v. New York City Board of Education* (1984). These cases are summarized in Figure 10.1.

As a result of recent litigation involving the testing of intelligence as well as the information included in the assessment sections of IDEA, a movement toward more objective testing practices is currently under way in the assessment field. In addition, professionals are reminded to follow the *Standards for Educational and Psychological Testing* (see Chapter 2) by the Joint Committee on Testing Practices and the standards set forth by the American Educational Research Association (AERA) (1999).

● USE OF INTELLIGENCE TESTS

The use of intelligence tests remains controversial in part because of inappropriate use in the past. Revised instruments, alternative testing practices, and understanding of the ethnic or cultural differences that may occur are promising improvements in the assessment of intelligence. Intelligence testing is likely to remain a substantial part of the assessment process because of the known correlation between performance on IQ tests and school achievement (Reschly & Grimes, 1995). Kaufman (1994), a strong advocate for the intelligent use of intelligence tests, contended that intelligence tests should be used "as a helping agent rather than an instrument for placement, labeling, or other types of academic oppression" (p. 1). McGrew and Flanagan (1998) stated that, to have a complete picture of a person's true intellectual

FIGURE 10.1 Summary of Court Cases Involving IQ Assessment

Larry P. v. Riles (1984). This case resulted in the court's finding that schools could no longer use standardized but unvalidated IQ tests for the purpose of identifying and placing black children into segregated special education classes for children designated as educable mentally retarded (EMR) (Turnbull, 1990, p. 92).

PASE v. Hannon (1980). Although PASE (Parents in Action on Special Education) found that some of the items in the tests were discriminatory, the court upheld that the tests were generally nondiscriminatory. More important, it found that the tests were not the sole basis for classification and that the school district therefore was complying with the Education of the Handicapped Act, EHA, which requires multifaceted testing (Turnbull, 1990, p. 95).

Diana v. State Board of Education (1970). In this case, the state board of education of California agreed to test students in their native language, to omit unfair test items of a verbal nature, to construct tests that would reflect the culture of Mexican American students, and to provide tests that would be standardized for Mexican Americans (Ysseldyke & Algozzine, 1982).

Lora v. New York City Board of Education (1984). This case required that the school system use objective and improved referral and assessment methods and multidisciplinary evaluations to reach decisions for diagnosis of students with emotional disturbance. The court found that the method previously in use was racially discriminatory and ruled that the school system could no longer consider school monetary problems or availability of services as reasons to place or not to place students in special education (Wood, Johnson, & Jenkins, 1990).

CHECK YOUR UNDERSTANDING

Complete Activity 10.1 to assess your knowledge of concepts of intelligence and legal issues related to the measuring of intelligence.

ability, a cross battery or multiple measures of intelligence tests should be used. Given that IQ tests will continue to be used, educators must promote fair and appropriate use of intelligence measures.

Reschly and Grimes (1995) provided guidelines for appropriate use of IQ tests. For example, these authors remind examiners that these instruments should be used in a manner that addresses the initial reason for referral and that other types of assessments should be used to provide a comprehensive picture of the student's abilities. They caution examiners to include strengths and weaknesses in abilities within the interpretation of the test scores. Reschly and Grimes further note that examiners should protect students by making certain the information gathered through the assessments should be used in the manner for which they were designed.

Special education professionals can obtain meaningful information from IQ test results if they understand the types of behavior that are assessed by individual subtests and items. Readers should take notice of the possible areas of testing bias as well as previous court decisions as they study the tests reviewed in this chapter.

● REVIEW OF INTELLIGENCE TESTS

This chapter reviews some of the tests most commonly used by schools to measure cognitive ability or intelligence. Perhaps the best-known intelligence measures are the Wechsler scales, three separate tests designed to assess intellectual functioning at different age levels. The *Wechsler Preschool and Primary Scale of Intelligence–Fourth Edition (WPPSI–IV)* was developed for use with children aged 2–6 to 7–3; it is reviewed in Chapter 11, "Special Considerations of Assessment in Early Childhood." The *Wechsler Adult Intelligence Scale–Fourth Edition (WAIS–IV)* (discussed later) is used with youth 16 years of age through adulthood. The *Wechsler Intelligence Scale for Children–Fifth Edition* assesses school-aged children ranging in age from 6 through 16–11.

The revised *Kaufman Assessment Battery for Children, Second Edition (K–ABC–II)* has an even stronger theoretical base than the original version (Kaufman & Kaufman, 2004). It allows the examiner to score the test based on one of two theoretical viewpoints, with one theoretical framework yielding a composite score that is not as heavily influenced by language or linguistic differences. This instrument will no doubt receive attention in those schools where an increasingly larger percentage of students whose primary language is not English are enrolled.

Other measures of intelligence are commonly used with school-aged children. The following are reviewed briefly in this chapter: the *Woodcock–Johnson Tests of Cognitive Ability–Fourth Edition,* the *Stanford–Binet Intelligence Scale–Fifth Edition,* and the *Differential Ability Scales–Second Edition.* Like the Wechsler scales and the *K–ABC–II,* these tests may not be administered by classroom teachers; however, test results provided by the psychologist or diagnostician can be useful to the teacher and are often considered in the determination of eligibility for special education.

Wechsler Intelligence Scale for Children–Fifth Edition

The *WISC–V* (Wechsler, 2014) is designed to assess the global intellectual ability and processing ability of children ages 6–0 through 16–11. This revision of the WISC provides both a traditional version of the instrument and a digital format. The test is scored using the Web-based scoring platform, Q-Global. The structure of the scoring system is based on the supported factor structure of the test. Therefore, test results are presented with a Full Scale IQ score, General Ability Index, and several index or processing scores. The factors, measured by indexes, are presented in Table 10.1, indicating that each index score is derived from the student's performance on two subtests. The Full Scale IQ and Cognitive Ability Indexes are presented in Table 10.2. In addition to the information presented in these tables, combinations of various

TABLE 10.1

Subtests and Indexes of the WISC–V

Subtests of Specific Indexes	Index Name
Similarities	Verbal Comprehension Index
Vocabulary	
Information	
Comprehension	
Block Design	Visual Spatial Index
Visual Puzzles	
Matrix Reasoning	Fluid Reasoning Index
Figure Weights	
Picture Concepts	
Arithmetic	
Digit Span	Working Memory Index
Picture Span	
Coding	Processing Speed Index
Symbol Search	

TABLE 10.2	
Subtests, Full Scale, and Cognitive Index	
Subtests for Specific Scores	Cognitive Indexes
Similarities	Full Scale IQ
Vocabulary	
Block Design	
Matrix Reasoning	
Figure Weights	
Digit Span	
Coding	
Similarities	General Ability Index
Vocabulary	
Block Design	
Matrix Reasoning	
Figure Weights	

subtests also provide a Nonverbal Index and a Cognitive Proficiency Index. Subtests are included within each index cluster. A discussion of each subtest is presented in the following section. As you read through the subtests and index descriptions, think about how student performance on these measures might be useful when developing instructional goals and strategies.

Subtests of the *WISC–V*. The following subtests are grouped by index scores. For example, the Similarities, Vocabulary, Comprehension, Information, and Word Reasoning subtests all support the factor structure of the Verbal Comprehension Index score. This means that research using the scores obtained during the standardization process indicates that these subtests all contribute to the Verbal Comprehension Index. In other words, a student who scores high on these subtests is likely to have strength in the area of verbal comprehension. We would anticipate that students with strength in this area would be able to score consistently across subtests. When a student scores very low on one or two subtests included on an index, the psychologist might conduct additional testing to determine if this is a true weakness. The psychologist might also complete cross-battery assessment or collect additional data when a student scores lower on one index than on others.

Verbal Comprehension Index. The following subtests support the construct of verbal comprehension. These subtests are heavily weighted in the ability to understand language concepts.

> *Similarities.* On this subtest, students are required to compare two words read by the examiner to determine how the two words are alike. The responses may be scored as a 0, 1, or 2.

> *Vocabulary.* The student is asked to define common words. For the younger child, pictures serve as the stimulus for the item. For children aged 9 to 16 years, words are presented as stimuli.

Information. These items assess information that may also be obtained from experiences or education. Items may include questions similar to the number of legs a cat has or the number of weeks in a month. In other words, this information is likely to have been learned prior to test administration and the student is simply using recall to respond to the question.

Comprehension. The items on this subtest assess the student's knowledge of common concepts learned incidentally or from experiences or the environment. For example, some questions tap into understanding of social issues, such as keeping your word to a friend; other items assess information for everyday functioning such as paying bills or maintaining good health. Such items reflect the influence of environment on learning, that environment is limited or enriched.

Visual Spatial Index. This index includes subtests that assess the ability to use visual stimuli, such as patterns or shapes, to solve novel problems. Visual processing skills are measured by these subtests.

Block design. On this subtest, students are required to manipulate and copy a pattern of red and white blocks. This is a timed subtest and students are awarded additional points when the pattern is copied quickly and accurately. The task requires that students use visual–motor responses and that they have the visual–perceptual ability to understand and reproduce the stimulus.

Visual puzzles. On this subtest, the examiner presents a completed visual image and a variety of choices of other visual images from which the student is asked to select the three pieces that would form the completed image. The examiner may provide information to the students such as indicating the shapes or images that might need to be turned in order to fit into the completed image.

Fluid Reasoning. These subtests assess the ability of students to use new stimuli to solve novel tasks. The stimuli provided are both visual and auditory and, for some items, the student is integrating and applying multiple stimuli, visual and auditory, to solve the problems. Students are required to hold the new information as they reason and apply the various stimuli to solve the problem. Some of these items may not depend much on previous learning experiences.

Matrix reasoning. This subtest presents visual stimuli that represent incomplete matrices. The student is asked to select the representation that would complete the matrix. There are different types of tasks presented on this subtest, such as pattern completion and serial reasoning.

Figure weights. On this subtest, students are asked to examine a scale with objects on one side of the scale and select the items that would be the same weight on the other side of the scale. For example, if there are three triangles on one side, the student should select the choice of three triangles from the choices provided.

Picture concepts. The student is presented with one picture and several rows of pictures. The student must select pictures from the rows of pictures to form a common concept. This task requires the student to use abstract verbal reasoning skills.

Arithmetic. On this subtest, the student is presented with math problems that must be solved mentally. This subtest requires working memory and some knowledge of math operations and reasoning.

Working Memory Index. When an item is presented that requires the student to hold on to the stimuli for a period of time in order to solve the task, it is referred to as a *working memory item*. These items may require visual or auditory working memory.

Digit Span. On this subtest, the examiner says a series of numbers to the student that the student must repeat as a series. The series become increasingly longer. The series of numbers are presented forward and backward.

Picture span. The student examines pictures on one page for a specific period of time and then must point to the pictures in order on the next page. This requires the student to use visual sequential memory ability.

Letter–number sequencing. On this subtest, the student hears a series of letters with numbers and is required to recall the numbers in ascending order and also the letters in alphabetical order. Children 6 and 7 years old perform the simpler tasks of counting and reciting part of the alphabet.

Processing Speed Index. The subtests included in this index score assess how quickly a person can complete a task. The subtests included in the index require visual–motor processing and fine-motor skills to respond to the items. All subtests in this index are timed.

Coding. On this subtest, the student is required to copy visual symbols that correspond to visually presented numbers.

Symbol Search. The student is presented with an initial symbol or with two symbols at the beginning of each row of symbols. The child must scan the row of symbols and determine if one of the initial symbols is present in that row. The task requires visual discrimination and memory.

Cancellation. On this subtest, the student is presented with a page of small pictures and asked to mark all animals. The subtest has two formats of presentation: random and organized.

Scores Obtained on the *WISC–V*. Subtests yield raw scores that are converted to derived scaled scores. The scaled scores have a mean of 10. A score is obtained for each of the indices along with the Full Scale Intelligence Quotient (FSIQ). The index scores and the FSIQ score are based on the standard score with a mean of 100 and a standard deviation of 15. Additional process scores may be obtained; however, these are obtained from data collected by the administration of the existing subtests and are used primarily for diagnostic purposes. For example, data collected during the administration of the Digit Span subtest can be used to obtain the Digit Span Forward and Digit Span Backward scaled scores.

Figure 10.2 illustrates a profile of scores obtained on the WISC–V. This illustration shows the student's scaled scores, index scores, and the FSIQ. The index scores, which are based on the mean of 100, are related to the normal distribution. The subtest scores, or scale scores, have a mean of 10. As you review the scores, think about how these might inform your instruction as you complete Activity 10.2.

Additional subtests are included on the WISC–V that may be used when the examiner needs further information, when one of the subtests administered is not thought to have been a valid administration (e.g., a fire drill went off during the administration or the student was ill that day), or when the student's performance indicated inconsistent scores on subtests for the same index. These additional measures are useful for determining information to inform the examiner and the teacher about the student's cognitive abilities.

Wechsler Adult Intelligence Scale–Fourth Edition (WAIS–IV). The *Wechsler Adult Intelligence Scale–Third Edition (WAIS–IV)* was published in 2008 and is

CHECK YOUR UNDERSTANDING

Check your knowledge of the terms presented in association with the Wechsler scales by completing Activity 10.2. Use Figure 10.2 to respond to the questions.

FIGURE 10.2 Profile of Student's Scores on WISC–V

Subtests	Subtest Scale Scores	Index Name	Index Scores
Similarities	12	Verbal Comprehension Index	110
Vocabulary	11		
Information	13		
Comprehension	11		
Block Design	7	Visual Spatial Index	78
Visual Puzzles	8		
Matrix Reasoning	8	Fluid Reasoning Index	88
Figure Weights	8		
Picture Concepts	7		
Arithmetic	10		
Digit Span	12	Working Memory Index	90
Picture Span	7		
Letter-Number Sequencing	10		
Coding	8	Processing Speed Index	92
Symbol Search	8		

appropriate for individuals ages 16 years and 0 months to 90 years and 11 months. Many of the same subtests of the children's version are included on the scales for adults. The *WAIS–IV* includes subtests that assess verbal comprehension, perception, working memory, and processing speed. New subtests on this instrument that are different from the subtests included on the children's scale include Visual Puzzles and Figure Weights that are designed to assess perceptual reasoning without requiring the examinee to use fine-motor abilities to respond to the stimuli. This instrument is appropriate for individuals who are 16 years of age or older; clinical studies have been completed on samples of individuals with cognitive impairments, autism, and learning disabilities.

The fourth edition of the *WAIS* provides additional items on the lower end and additional practice items on some of the subtests. This instrument is clinically more user friendly for examinees who are functioning significantly below the average. These additional items may allow examinees at the lower end to respond to more items before reaching a ceiling, providing the clinician with a better picture of an examinee's ability. This edition includes additional supplemental subtests that assess each of the four domains.

Kaufman Assessment Battery for Children, Second Edition (K–ABC–II)

The *Kaufman Assessment Battery for Children, Second Edition (K–ABC–II)* assesses the cognitive ability of children aged 3–0 to 18–11. This newly revised instrument includes a revised method of scoring and interpretation. Although this instrument cannot be administered by classroom teachers, an understanding of the theoretical bases of the scoring will assist the teacher in interpreting the results and developing interventions.

Before the test is administered, the psychologist must decide which theoretical base will be used to administer and score the instrument. A brief explanation of each theoretical base follows.

One theoretical base, Luria's neurological processing theory, is quite extensive; however, one of the major premises of the theory is that the brain functions using two modes of processing: simultaneous and sequential. The *K–ABC–II* includes subtests that assess a student's ability to perceive and process information that is presented sequentially. This means that each stimulus that the student processes is linked to the previous stimulus and must be processed sequentially in order to perform the task or solve the problem. Other subtests include items that must be processed simultaneously, that is, stimuli must be processed and integrated at the same time in order to perform the task.

The *K–ABC–II,* using the Luria model, yields scale index scores for sequential processing, simultaneous processing, learning, planning, and mental processing for the general measure of cognitive ability.

The other theoretical base for scoring is the Cattell-Horn-Carol (CHC) theory of intelligence. This theory is founded on three levels, or stratums, of intellectual ability. The first level is general intellectual functioning, commonly called the *g* factor. The next level is composed of broad cognitive abilities, and the final level is made up of narrow abilities of cognitive functioning. The original CHC theory included *broad fluid* and *crystallized* abilities as the two main components or types of processing in cognitive ability or intelligence. The *K–ABC–II* yields a Fluid Crystallized Index score for the global cognitive score.

Additional scale indexes include Gsm for short-term memory, Gv for visual processing, Glr for learning, Gf for fluid reasoning, and Gc for crystallized ability. Tasks that assess Gsm processing include those that require short-term and working memory. Tasks that assess Gv are those that require, for example, visual memory, spatial relations, spatial screening, and visualization. Tasks that measure Glr require long-term memory and recall. Tasks scored on the Gf scale require fluid reasoning or adapting and solving novel problems or figuring out how to do something one has not been exposed to in the past. The Gc scale assesses general information learned from the environment or previous experiences.

Another index used to score the *K–ABC–II* is the Nonverbal Index. This index includes subtests that do not rely heavily on language skills or learned verbal concepts. For example, the examinee might be asked to solve problems that require copying visual patterns using manipulatives or to imitate hand movements. This scale is especially appropriate for students who may not have mastery of the English language or who may have other language difficulties. It can be used to provide an estimate of cognitive functioning without using subtests that are heavily weighted in language or verbal concepts.

For very young children, only a general cognitive score is available. Either the Fluid Crystallized Index or the Mental Processing Index scores may be obtained.

Stanford–Binet Intelligence Scales, Fifth Edition

The fifth edition of the *Stanford–Binet Intelligence Scales* is administered to persons ages 2 to 85+ years (Roid, 2003b). This instrument consists of 10 subtests and yields a full scale IQ score, a nonverbal IQ score, and a verbal IQ score. The factors assessed on this instrument include fluid reasoning, knowledge, quantitative reasoning, visual–spatial reasoning, and working memory. Within each factor or area, various tasks are presented. Figure 10.3 features a brief description of the tasks and their performance requirements. For example, note that the visual–spatial processing factor is assessed verbally and nonverbally. For the nonverbal task requirement, the student works puzzles that are solved using visual–perceptual motor skills. For the verbal task requirement, the student must respond to questions and problems verbally. The problems for this task involve directional terms or prepositions for correct responses. Yet both the verbal and nonverbal tasks are concerned with visual–spatial processing.

FIGURE 10.3   Organization of the *Stanford–Binet V*

		Domains	
		Nonverbal (NV)	Verbal (V)
Factors	Fluid Reasoning (FR)	*Nonverbal Fluid Reasoning** Activities: Object Series/Matrices (Routing)	*Verbal Fluid Reasoning* Activities: Early Reasoning (2–3), Verbal Absurdities (4), Verbal Analogies (5–6)
	Knowledge (KN)	*Nonverbal Knowledge* Activities: Procedural Knowledge (2–3), Picture Absurdities (4–6)	*Verbal Knowledge** Activities: Vocabulary (Routing)
	Quantitative Reasoning (OR)	*Nonverbal Quantitative Reasoning* Activities: Quantitative Reasoning (2–6)	*Verbal Quantitative Reasoning* Activities: Quantitative Reasoning (2–6)
	Visual-Spatial Processing (VS)	*Nonverbal Visual-Spatial Processing* Activities: Form Board (1–2), Form Patterns (3–6)	*Verbal Visual-Spatial Processing* Activities: Position and Direction (2–6)
	Working Memory (WM)	*Nonverbal Working Memory* Activities: Delayed Response (1), Block Span (2–6)	*Verbal Working Memory* Activities: Memory for Sentences (2–3), Last Word (4–6)

Note: Names of the 10 subtests are in bold italic. Activities include the levels at which they appear. * = Routing subtests

Source: Figure 2.1, page 24 from the *Stanford–Binet Intelligence Scales, Fifth Edition* (SB-5) Kit by Gale H. Roid, 2003, Austin: PRO-ED. Used with permission.

CHECK YOUR UNDERSTANDING

To assess your understanding of measures of intelligence discussed in this section, complete Activity 10.3.

Case Study Using the Stanford–Binet V (SB–V) The following scores were obtained for a fourth-grade student who was referred for learning difficulties following several interventions. Examine the scores and answer the questions about the student's performance. Refer to your text as needed for information about the *SB–V.*

	Domains	
	Nonverbal	Verbal
Fluid Reasoning	11	9
Knowledge	9	9
Quantitative Reasoning	12	8
Visual–Spatial Processing	14	10
Working Memory	7	7

Composite Profile

Nonverbal	IQ	108
Verbal	IQ	93
Full Scale	IQ	101
Fluid Reasoning		100
Knowledge		92
Quantitative Reasoning		99
Visual–Spatial Reasoning		109
Working Memory		80

Woodcock–Johnson IV Tests of Cognitive Abilities

The tests of *Woodcock–Johnson IV Tests of Achievement* are administered to assess skills in general academic areas such as reading, math, and written language. Students may also be assessed in oral language on the Oral Language Battery. The *Woodcock–Johnson IV Tests of Cognitive Abilities* assess areas such as general intellectual ability, cognitive factors like visual processing, short-term working memory, cognitive processing speed, and fluid reasoning. Supplement subtests, such as those measuring perceptual speed, quantitative reasoning, number facility, and vocabulary, provide additional measures for specific processing areas. Together these batteries provide a comprehensive assessment of cognitive abilities, language abilities, and academic skills. These are consistent with an expansion of CHC theory and are interpreted using this expanded theoretical model. The examiner's manual provides information for accommodations during administration and special considerations about the appropriateness of administering the subtests to individuals with the following disabilities or concerns: young children, English Language Learners, learning or reading difficulties, attention or behavior difficulties, hearing impairments, visual impairments, and physical impairments. When the instrument is administered to students with these challenges, the examiner should address any specific accommodations or concerns in the test interpretation report. These accommodations and the results obtained using these may be useful to the teacher as accommodations are discussed in planning for educational interventions and future statewide testing.

The cognitive subtests included in the standard and extended batteries are presented in Table 10.3. Descriptions of the standard battery subtests are provided in the following section. As you review these descriptions, consider how information about a student's skills and abilities on these measures would inform instructional decisions.

The *WJ IV Tests of Cognitive Abilities*, like their counterpart achievement tests, are computer scored. The scoring program is easy to use, yielding comparative data for age and grade norms, confidence intervals, standard scores, and percentile ranks.

Kaufman Brief Intelligence Test (KBIT)

Designed as a screening instrument, the *KBIT* (Kaufman & Kaufman, 1990) should not be used as part of a comprehensive evaluation to determine eligibility or placement. According to the manual, the test serves to screen students who may be at risk for developing educational problems and who then should receive a comprehensive evaluation. The test takes about 15–30 minutes to administer and consists of two subtests: Vocabulary and Matrices. The vocabulary subtest has two parts: Expressive and Definitions. These two subtests are designed to measure crystallized intelligence (Vocabulary) and fluid intelligence (Matrices).

CHECK YOUR UNDERSTANDING

Use the information from Figure 10.3 and the case study above to apply the test results of the *Stanford–Binet V* to complete Activity 10.4.

Woodcock–Johnson IV Tests of Cognitive Abilities Standard Subtest Descriptions
Brief descriptions are provided for the subtests.

Oral Vocabulary. This subtest includes the assessment of understanding of the English language by asking the student to provide responses for items measuring knowledge of synonyms and antonyms.

Number Series. The student is presented with a number series with one missing number. The student must provide the missing number to complete the series.

Verbal Attention. This subtest requires the student to listen to a mix of verbal stimuli without knowing the specific question that will be asked following the series of verbal stimuli. A mixture of words, numbers, and animals may be presented, with the question focusing on one specific aspect of the stimuli (e.g., what was the third animal?).

Letter-Pattern Matching. This is a timed subtest in which the student is asked to discriminate between and match series of letters in a pattern.

Phonological Processing. This subtest comprises three separate tasks that provide information about the student's ability to process and produce sounds or phonemic elements as parts of words or missing parts of words.

Story Recall. Students listen to recordings of stories that gradually increase in detail and complexity and are asked to provide as many details as they can recall.

Visualization. The student must complete two types of tasks. One task assesses the ability to determine which pieces would form a complete shape presented in the stimulus and the other task requires a student to select which block patterns match the specific pattern presented in the item.

General Information. These items tap into a student's general knowledge about his or her own experiences and environment. An item might ask where a specific object would be found and other items ask how a specific object is used.

Concept Formation. This subtest presents several items that the student must examine and determine a rule for the set of stimuli. For example, a set of stimuli might be presented in a series and the student is asked what would go in the empty box, with the correct figure or shape completing the series. A student might also be asked what is different about the shape in a box compared with the other shapes, with the correct response being that the shape in the box is larger or smaller than the other shapes.

Numbers Reversed. On this subtest, a student listens to taped series of numbers and is required to remember and then say the numbers in reverse order.

Nonverbal Intelligence Tests

Some of the commonly used measures—the *Universal Test of Nonverbal Intelligence,* the *Comprehensive Test of Nonverbal Intelligence,* the *Nonverbal Test of Intelligence, Third Edition,* and the *Wechsler Nonverbal Scales*—are reviewed here to provide examples of this type of assessment.

Differential Ability Scales–Second Edition

The *Differential Ability Scales–Second Edition (DAS–II)* (Elliot, 2007), is composed of 20 different subtests that are categorized by age of examinee. Children who are between the years of 2 years 6 months and 3 years 5 months are administered the lower Early Years subtests and children who are between 3 years 6 months and 6 years 11 months are administered the upper Early Years subtests. Children who are ages 7 years 0 months to 17 years and 11 months are administered the School Years subtests. The author clearly indicates that the General Conceptual Ability (GCA) score is similar to an IQ score; however, it is not made up of a total of all contributing subtests but rather only the subtests that tap into the general conceptual reasoning abilities. This test was designed to measure strengths and weaknesses based on individual subtest scores or combinations of subtests. An example of how individual subtests are combined to assess differential abilities is presented in Figure 10.4. As noted in the figure, diagnostic subtests can provide information about the student's working memory or processing speed.

The *DAS–II* includes a special nonverbal composite that is used to score the reasoning abilities of individuals whose verbal skills are compromised, such as those with hearing impairments or those who are learning the English language.

CHECK YOUR UNDERSTANDING

Check your understanding of instruments measuring cognitive ability by completing Activity 10.5.

FIGURE 10.4 *Differential Ability Scales–Second Edition* School Age Battery

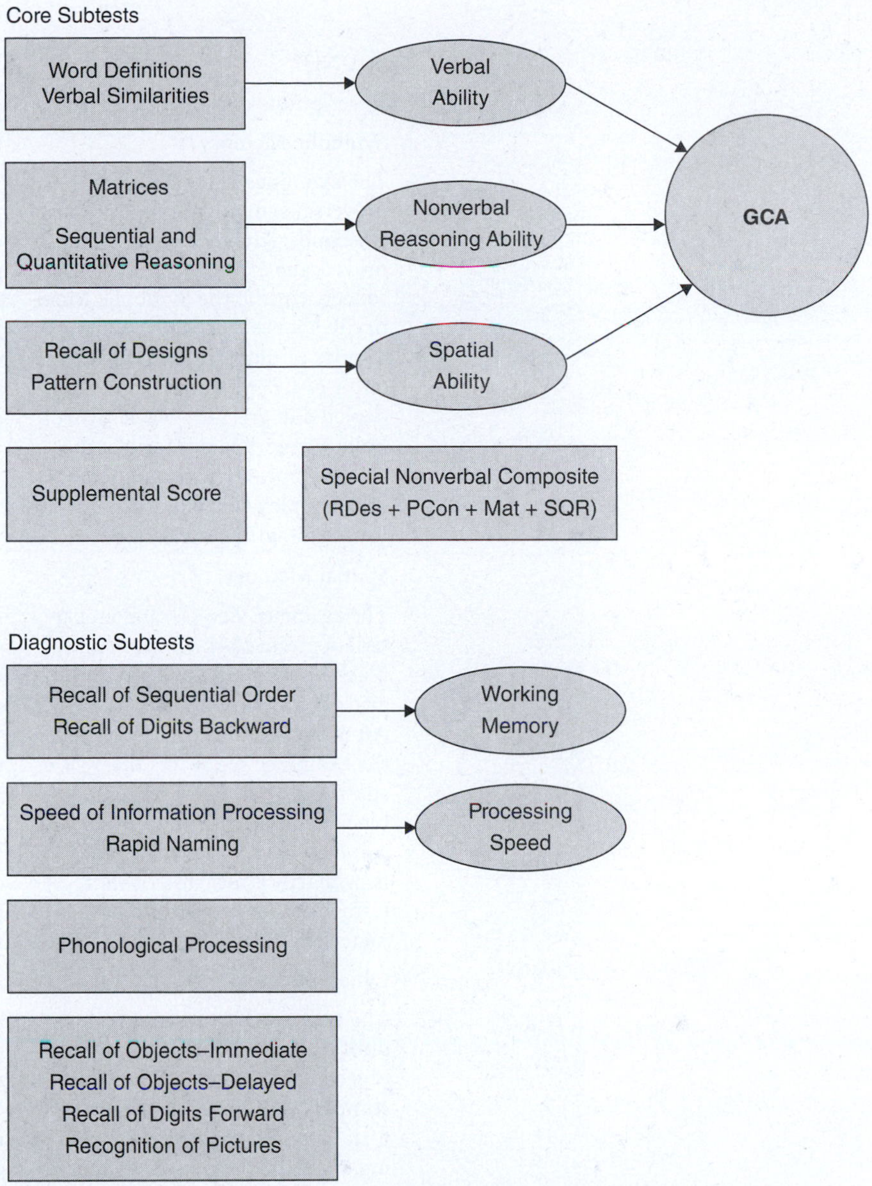

Core Subtests

```
┌──────────────────────┐           ╭─────────╮
│ Word Definitions     │─────────▶ │ Verbal  │
│ Verbal Similarities  │           │ Ability │
└──────────────────────┘           ╰─────────╯
                                                    ╭─────╮
┌──────────────────────┐           ╭────────────╮   │ GCA │
│ Matrices             │           │ Nonverbal  │─▶ ╰─────╯
│ Sequential and       │─────────▶ │ Reasoning  │
│ Quantitative Reasoning│          │ Ability    │
└──────────────────────┘           ╰────────────╯

┌──────────────────────┐           ╭─────────╮
│ Recall of Designs    │─────────▶ │ Spatial │
│ Pattern Construction │           │ Ability │
└──────────────────────┘           ╰─────────╯

┌──────────────────────┐   ┌──────────────────────────────┐
│ Supplemental Score   │   │ Special Nonverbal Composite   │
│                      │   │ (RDes + PCon + Mat + SQR)     │
└──────────────────────┘   └──────────────────────────────┘
```

Diagnostic Subtests

```
┌──────────────────────────┐       ╭──────────╮
│ Recall of Sequential Order│─────▶ │ Working  │
│ Recall of Digits Backward │       │ Memory   │
└──────────────────────────┘       ╰──────────╯

┌──────────────────────────────┐   ╭────────────╮
│ Speed of Information Processing│─▶ │ Processing │
│ Rapid Naming                  │   │ Speed      │
└──────────────────────────────┘   ╰────────────╯

┌──────────────────────────────┐
│ Phonological Processing       │
└──────────────────────────────┘

┌──────────────────────────────┐
│ Recall of Objects–Immediate   │
│ Recall of Objects–Delayed     │
│ Recall of Digits Forward      │
│ Recognition of Pictures       │
└──────────────────────────────┘
```

Source: Adapted by permission. Copyright © by the Secretary of State for Education and Science (England). Revised edition Copyright © by Colin D. Elliott. Second edition copyright © 1996 by Colin D. Elliott. *Differential Ability Scales, Second Edition* (DAS-II). Copyright © 2007 NCS Pearson, Inc. Reproduced with permission. All rights reserved. Normative date copyright © 2007 NCS Pearson, Inc. "DAS" is a trademark, in the United States and/or other countries, of Pearson Education, Inc. or its affiliate(s).

The Universal Nonverbal Intelligence Test

The *Universal Nonverbal Intelligence Test (UNIT)* is an intellectual assessment measure for children ages 5 years through 17 years 11 months. It includes six subtests and may be given as a standard battery, abbreviated battery, or extended battery (Bracken & McCallum, 1998). The most typical administrations are the standard battery, which includes four subtests, and the extended battery, which includes all subtests. The abbreviated battery of two subtests is given for screening rather than diagnostic purposes. The test measures reasoning and memory skills through the nonverbal presentation of the subtests. The subtest descriptions are presented in Figure 10.5.

FIGURE 10.5 Descriptions of *UNIT* Subtests

Overview of the UNIT

Table 1.1   Descriptions of the UNIT Subtests

Symbolic Memory

The examinee views a sequence of universal symbols for a period of 5 seconds. After the stimulus is removed, the examinee re-creates the sequence using the Symbolic Memory Response Cards. Each item is a series of universal symbols for *baby*, *girl*, *boy*, *woman*, and *man*, depicted in green or black. Symbolic Memory is primarily a measure of short-term visual memory and complex sequential memory for meaningful material.

Spatial Memory

The examinee views a random pattern of green, black, or green and black dots on a 3 × 3 or 4 × 4 grid for a period of 5 seconds. After the stimulus is removed, the examinee re-creates the spatial pattern with green and black circular chips on the blank response grid. Spatial Memory is primarily a measure of short-term visual memory for abstract material.

Object Memory

The examinee is presented a random pictorial array of common objects for 5 seconds. After the stimulus is removed, a second pictorial array is presented, containing all of the previously presented objects and additional objects to serve as foils. The examinee recognizes and identifies the objects presented in the first pictorial array by placing response chips on the appropriate pictures. Object Memory is primarily a measure of short-term recognition and recall of meaningful symbolic material.

Cube Design

Cube Design involves the presentation and direct reproduction of two-color, abstract, geometric designs. While viewing the stimulus design, the examinee reconstructs the design directly on the stimulus book or response mat, using green and-white 1-inch cubes. Cube Design is primarily a measure of visual–spatial reasoning.

Analogic Reasoning

Analogic Reasoning presents incomplete conceptual or geometric analogies in a matrix format and requires only a pointing response. The items feature either common objects or novel geometric figures. The examinee completes the matrix analogies by selecting from four response options. Analogic Reasoning is primarily a measure of symbolic reasoning.

Mazes

The examinee uses paper and pencil to navigate and exit mazes by tracing a path from the center starting point of each maze to the correct exit, without making incorrect decisions en route. Increasingly complex mazes are presented. Mazes is primarily a measure of reasoning and planful behavior.

Source: Table 1.1, p. 3 from examiner's manual from the UNIT™ (UNIT) Kit by Bruce A. Bracken and R. Steve McCallum, 1998, Austin: PRO-ED. Used with permission.

FIGURE 10.6 Palm Rolling

Palm Rolling
With one or both hands held out and
with palms up and fingers together,
the wrists are rotated toward the
body so that the hands inscribe small
circles in the air.
This gesture communicates
"Go ahead" or "You try it now."

Palm Rolling

Source: Figure 4.5, p. 49 from examiner's manual from the UNIT™ (UNIT) Kit by Bruce A. Bracken and R. Steve McCallum, 1998, Austin: PRO-ED. Used with permission.

The test developers designed this instrument to be a fair measure of intellectual ability for children and adolescents for whom it might be difficult to obtain an accurate estimate of ability using tests that are heavily weighted with verbal content (e.g., children and adolescents who have hearing impairments, who are from culturally or linguistically diverse environments, or who have not mastered the English language). This instrument may also yield a fairer estimate of intellectual ability for students with mental retardation and for students with other disorders that impact verbal communication, such as autism.

In order to present a nonverbal assessment in a manner that does not require spoken language, several gestures for communication during the administration are provided in the manual. For example, palm rolling conveys a message to the student to "Continue," "Keep going," or "Take your turn now." These gestures are illustrated in the manual; the gesture called *palm rolling* is presented in Figure 10.6.

The *UNIT* yields scores for the various subtests, scaled scores, and a ful scale IQ score. The scaled scores are for the four scales of memory, reasoning, and symbolic and nonsymbolic concepts. The memory scale relates not only to the storing of information, but also to the skills and abilities needed for memory, such as attending, encoding, and organization. The reasoning subtest taps into problem-solving ability. The symbolic scale assesses abilities that are believed to be precursors to understanding and using language, and the nonsymbolic scale assesses processing, perception, and integration of information. The symbolic and nonsymbolic scales both assess mediation, or what one does cognitively with material as it is processed, associated, and retained or used to solve problems.

Subtest scores have a mean of 10, and the scales have quotients with a mean of 100. Standard scores are interpreted according to the following guidelines:

Very superior	>130
Superior	120–130
High average	110–120
Average	90–110
Low average	80–90
Delayed	70–80
Very delayed	<70

Case Study: Intellectual Assessment

Read the following background information about Lupita, a second-grade student.

Name: Lupita Garcia

Date of Birth: February 1, 1996

Date of Evaluation: April 6, 2004

Age: 8–2

Grade Placement: 2.8

BACKGROUND AND REFERRAL INFORMATION

Lupita is currently enrolled in the second grade at Wonderful Elementary School. She has been attending this school since October of the current school year. There was a delay in receiving her school records from another state, and therefore it was not known for several months that Lupita had been in the referral process at her previous school. School records from her previous school indicate that she has attended three schools since she entered kindergarten about 3 years ago.

Lupita lives with her mother and father, who until recently were migrant farm workers. Her parents now have full-time employment in the city and plan to make this community their home. Lupita has two older sisters.

Information provided through a home study reveals that all family members speak both English and Spanish. Lupita's mother, who was born in the United States, reports that she learned English while growing up because in school she was not allowed to speak Spanish as her parents did at home. Lupita's father was raised in Mexico, where he attended school until he was 12 years of age. At that time, he stopped going to school in order to work the field with his parents. Mr. Garcia reports that his English is not as good as his wife's, and therefore she helps Lupita with all of her homework assignments.

Mrs. Garcia indicates that she has taught her three children to speak English first because she knows that having facility with the English language is important for school. Although Mrs. Garcia has emphasized English in the home, Mr. Garcia usually speaks to the children in Spanish. Mr. Garcia is very proud of his daughters' ability to speak and write English so well because he often must rely on them to translate for him when they are in the community.

Lupita has been referred because of difficulty in learning to read. The child study team has met four times to plan and implement interventions to assist Lupita. Lupita has been receiving additional assistance from the school system's bilingual program. As part of the referral process, Mrs. Garcia has completed a home language assessment. The results of that assessment indicate that while both languages are spoken in the home, English is the primary language and is used in approximately 75% of communication within the home. Despite these findings, team members are not certain that Lupita has mastered English, particularly at the level required for academic learning and especially in the area of reading.

At the last meeting of the team, members agree, at the urging of Mrs. Garcia, to complete a comprehensive evaluation. Given background information about Lupita, team members decide that the *K–ABC–II* Nonverbal Index and the *UNIT* will yield the fairest and most accurate estimate of Lupita's intellectual ability.

Comprehensive Test of Nonverbal Intelligence–Second Edition (CTONI 2)

The CTONI 2 may be used with persons ages 6–0 to 89–11 years of age (Hammill, Pearson, & Wiederholt, 2009). Six subtests comprise this instrument:

Pictorial Analogies, Geometric Analogies, Pictorial Categories, Geometric Categories, Pictorial Sequences, and Geometric Sequences. The administration of all subtests will yield a nonverbal intelligence composite, the administration of the pictorial subtests will provide a pictorial nonverbal composite, and administration of the geometric subtests will provide a geometric nonverbal intelligence composite.

According to the authors, the *CTONI 2* has three principal uses. It can be used with persons for whom other instruments assessing intelligence would be inappropriate or biased; it can be used to make comparisons between verbal measures and nonverbal intelligence; and it can be used for research. This instrument was developed using multiple theoretical bases rather than a single theory. The *CTONI 2* may be administered orally or via pantomime. The second edition includes tests administration in languages other than English.

Test of Nonverbal Intelligence–Third Edition (TONI–3)

This instrument assesses a single cognitive process: solving novel abstract problems (Brown, Sherbenou, & Johnsen, 1997). The authors state that the *TONI–3* is a language- and motor-reduced instrument that also reduces cultural influence. It may be used with students ages 6–0 to 89–11. The test package includes two equivalent forms, A and B. The examiner gives directions via pantomime. Administration time is approximately 45 minutes.

Wechsler Nonverbal Scale of Ability

The *Wechsler Nonverbal Scale of Ability* (Wechsler & Nagliari, 2006) assesses cognitive ability using nonverbal subtests. It may be used with individuals aged 4–0 to 21–11. Examinees aged 4–0 to 7–11 are administered the Matrices, Coding, Object Assembly, and Recognition subtests; examinees aged 8–0 to 21–11 are administered the Matrices, Coding, Spatial Span, and Picture Arrangement subtests. The examiner uses gestures and gives oral instructions for items. The examiner manual provides instructions in the following languages: English, French, Spanish, Chinese, German, and Dutch. The gestures used are similar to those used in other nonverbal measures and include sweeping the hand, pointing, and dragging a finger across the stimulus.

● RESEARCH ON INTELLIGENCE MEASURES

Many of the most popular intelligence measures have recently been revised, and research continues to emerge in the literature. Some research studies on earlier editions and test reviews are summarized here.

1. After an extensive review of evidence in the literature and other sources, Schrank and Flanagan conclude that the *WJ–III Tests of Cognitive Ability* are well grounded in the CHC theory, or Three Stratum Theory, proposed by Carroll (2003).

2. Miller (2007) reports that the theoretical structure of the *WJ–III Tests of Cognitive Ability* makes this instrument useful in assessing persons referred for school neuropsychological assessment. The abilities assessed on this instrument fall within an assessment model employed in the field of school neuropsychology.

3. Decker, Hale, and Flanagan (2013) report that a greater emphasis on using cognitive assessments for identifying strengths and weaknesses needs to be reflected in day-to-day practice. These authors reviewed and supported research indicating that the profiles and narrow ability scores can provide meaningful information to teachers and assessment personnel as they design effective educational strategies for improving student achievement.

4. Prewett (1992) found that the *KBIT*'s correlation with the *WISC–III* supports its use as a screening instrument. Prewett and McCaffery (1993) contended that the *KBIT* should be interpreted as only a rough estimate of the IQ that can be obtained using the *Stanford–Binet*. Kaufman and Wang (1992) found that the differences in means obtained by blacks, Hispanics, and whites on the *KBIT* are in agreement with mean differences found on the *WISC–R*. Canivez (1996) found high levels of agreement between the *KBIT* and the *WISC–III* in the identification of students with learning disabilities using discrepancies between these measures and the *WJ–R*.

5. Differences in scores were found between Asian and white children on the *K–ABC* (Mardell-Czudnowski, 1995). In this study, Asian children scored higher on the sequential processing scale but showed no differences on the mental processing scales. Achievement-scaled scores were higher for children who had lived in the United States for at least 4 years.

6. Roid and Pomplin (2005) found that differential diagnosis between clinical groups, such as students with mental retardation and students with low-functioning autism, could not be made using the *Stanford–Binet IV* alone. Additional assessment measures were needed.

7. In a concurrent validity study, Canivez (1995) found similarities in *WISC–III* and *KBIT* scores. However, he suggested that the *KBIT* be reserved for screening with more comprehensive measures used for detailed interpretations of ability. Other researchers have also found that the *KBIT* may be suitable for screening but not for determining more comprehensive information (Parker, 1993; Prewett & McCaffery, 1993).

● ASSESSING ADAPTIVE BEHAVIOR

Adaptive behavior is a term used to describe how well a student adapts to the environment. The importance of this concept was underscored by the passage of PL 94–142, which contained the requirement of nondiscriminatory assessment—specifically, the mandate to use more than one instrument yielding a single IQ score for diagnosis (Federal Register, 1977). The measurement of adaptive behavior must be considered before a person meets the criteria for mental retardation. A student who functions within the subaverage range of intelligence as measured by cognitive assessment but who exhibits age-appropriate behaviors outside the classroom should not be placed in a setting designed for students with cognitive impairments.

Adaptive behavior measurement is also viewed as a method of promoting non-biased assessment of culturally different students (Mercer, 1979; Reschly, 1982). Use of adaptive behavior scales in the assessment of students with learning problems can add another perspective that may be useful in planning educational interventions (Bruininks, Thurlow, & Gilman, 1987; Horn & Fuchs, 1987). Other researchers have found the assessment of adaptive behavior useful in educational interventions for students with learning disabilities (Bender & Golden, 1988; Weller, Strawser, & Buchanan, 1985). Adaptive behavior scales typically consist of interviews to be answered by a parent, teacher, or other person familiar with the student's functioning in the everyday world. The questions on the scale elicit information about the student's independent functioning level in and out of school. The items focus on self-reliance and daily living skills at home and in the community.

Reschly (1982) reviewed the literature on adaptive behavior and determined that several common features were presented. The measuring of adaptive behavior had the common concepts of (a) developmental appropriateness, (b) cultural context, (c) situational or generalized behaviors, and (d) domains. Reschly found that definitions of adaptive behavior and the measurement of that behavior were based on expectations of a particular age, within the person's culture, in given or general situations, and that the behaviors measured were classified into domains.

Harrison (1987) reviewed research on adaptive behavior and drew the following conclusions:*

1. There is a moderate relationship between adaptive behavior and intelligence.

2. Correlational studies indicate that adaptive behavior has a weak relationship with school achievement, but the effect of adaptive behavior on achievement may be greater than the correlations indicate and adaptive behavior in school may have a greater relationship with achievement than adaptive behavior outside school.

3. There is typically a moderate to a moderately high relationship between different measures of adaptive behavior.

4. Adaptive behavior is predictive of certain aspects of future vocational performance.

5. There is a possibility that the use of adaptive behavior scales could result in the declassification of individuals with cognitive impairments, but no evidence was located to indicate that this is actually happening.

6. There are few race and ethnic group differences on adaptive behavior scales.

7. There are differences between parents' and teachers' ratings on adaptive behavior scales.

8. Adaptive behavior scales differentiate among different classification groups such as typical, individuals with cognitive impairments, and students with learning and emotional challenges.

9. Adaptive behavior scales differentiate among individuals with cognitive impairments in different residential and vocational settings.

10. Adaptive behavior is multidimensional.

11. Adaptive behavior can be increased through support in settings that focus on training in adaptive behavior skills.

12. Adaptive behavior scales exhibit adequate stability and interrater reliability.

Although earlier research found that there were differences between parent and teacher ratings on adaptive behavior, Foster-Gaitskell and Pratt (1989) found that when the method of administration and familiarity with the adaptive behavior instrument were controlled, differences between parent and teacher ratings were not significant. Assessing adaptive behavior requires that the examiner have training in the specific interview procedures and that the examiner assists parents in understanding the specific meaning of the items and how to differentiate between the independence level of skills and other levels of independence of the student's ability.

The formal measurement of adaptive behavior began with the development of the *Vineland Social Maturity Scale* (Doll, 1935). The assessment of adaptive behavior as a common practice in the diagnosis of students, however, did not occur until litigation found fault with school systems for the placement of minority students in special education programs based only on IQ results (Witt & Martens, 1984). As PL 94–142 mandates were carried out, some researchers argued that the assessment of adaptive behavior in students being evaluated for special education eligibility should not be required by law until further research on adaptive behavior instruments occurred (Kamphaus, 1987; Witt & Martens, 1984). After reviewing several adaptive behavior scales, Evans and Bradley-Johnson (1988) cautioned examiners to select instruments carefully because of their generally low reliability and validity.

---

* Adapted from "Research with Adaptive Behavior scales" by P. Harrison, 1987, *The Journal of Special Education,* 21, pp. 60–61. Copyright by 1987 by PRO-ED, Reprinted by permission.

Measurement of Level of Support and Adaptive Behavior Scales

In addition to examination of existing scales, teachers should also be aware that there are methods that may be used during assessment that will provide information about exactly how much support a student may require. For example, students with intellectual disabilities may require more support in one area than in another in order to be successful in school. Students with autism spectrum disorders may require more assistance in communication, for example, than in academic work, or more assistance in social skills than in communication. Adaptive behavior scales can provide this type of information. Other sources that may provide this type of information include the Supports Intensity Scale (SIS) available from the American Association on Intellectual and Developmental Disabilities. On this measure, information about the student's level of needed support for daily living skills (e.g., using the toilet, caring for clothes), community functioning (e.g., shopping or accessing resources), or being able to advocate for and participate in the education process are evaluated. The sections of the SIS are Home Living, Lifelong Learning, Employment, Health and Safety, and Social.

One of the methods used by clinical professionals, such as independent practitioners in psychology and psychiatry, is to determine diagnostic categories by using the Diagnostic and Statistical Manual revised in 2013 (American Psychiatric Association, 2013). Within the diagnostic categories of neurodevelopmental disorders such as autism and intellectual disability, criteria are included to determine the level of severity for planning the level of support. This information may be included in reports from outside evaluators or may also be used and included in reports by school psychologists. For the category of intellectual disability, clinicians rate the severity level for the conceptual domain, social domain, and practical domain. Within each domain, the student would be rated based on criteria to determine if the level of impairment is mild, moderate, severe, or profound. For example, a student who requires significant support in the area of self-care such as toileting, bathing, and feeding would likely be found to have a profound impairment level in the practical domain.

Similarly, a student with an autism disorder would also be rated for severity level and intellectual impairment. So, a student with an autism disorder might be found to have an intellectual impairment that has profound implications in the practical domain, and, due to the neurodevelopmental disability of autism, the student may be determined to need very substantial support in the social communication domain and the restricted, repetitive behaviors domain. The clinician would rate students with autism disorders as requiring support, requiring substantial support, or requiring very substantial support on the social communication domain and the restricted, repetitive behaviors domain.

CHECK YOUR UNDERSTANDING

Check your understanding of general adaptive behavior and level of supports by completing Activity 10.6.

● REVIEW OF ADAPTIVE BEHAVIOR SCALES

The adaptive behavior scales reviewed in this chapter are the *Vineland Adaptive Behavior Scales* (Survey Form, Expanded Form, and Classroom Edition), the *AAMR Adaptive Behavior Scale—School, Second Edition*, the *Adaptive Behavior Inventory* (*ABI* and *ABI Short Form*), and the *Adaptive Behavior Inventory for Children*. As stated previously, examiners should be cautious in selecting the scale appropriate for the student's needs. Some scales have been normed using special populations only; some scales have been normed using both special and normal populations; and some scales contain items for assessing maladaptive behavior as well as adaptive behavior. The size of the samples used during standardization and the reliability and validity information should be considered.

Vineland Adaptive Behavior Scales, Second Edition (Vineland–II)

A revision of the original *Vineland Social Maturity Scale* (Doll, 1935) and the *Vineland Adaptive Behavior Scales* (Sparrow, Balla, & Cicchetti, 1984), this edition of these adaptive behavior scales contains additional items at the lower levels and is consistent with the recommendations of the American Association on Mental Deficiency (Sparrow, Cicchetti, & Balla, 2005). The scales include the Survey Interview Form, the Parent/Caregiver Form, and the Teacher Rating Form. The Parent Form is available in Spanish. The Interview Form and the Parent Rating Form assess the same skills; however, the Parent Form is in a rating scale format.

The Survey and Parent Forms may be used to obtain information about individuals who range in age from 0 to 90 years. The Teacher Form was designed for students ages 3 to 21 years and 11 months. The areas assessed include communication, daily living skills, socialization, motor skills, and an optional maladaptive behavior scale. Computer scoring is available. Scores that are provided using the *Vineland–II* include scaled scores, percentile ranks, standard scores, age equivalents, and domain and adaptive behavior composite scores.

AAMR Adaptive Behavior Scale–School, Second Edition (ABS–S2)

Test developers constructed the *ABS–S2* as one method to determine whether persons meet the criteria for the diagnosis of mental retardation (Lambert, Nihira, & Leland, 1993). The *ABS–S2* is divided into two parts: (a) independent living skills and (b) social behavior. The domains assessed in each are listed in Figure 10.7.

The person most familiar with the student may administer the scale by completing the items, or a professional who is familiar with the child may complete the items. The information is plotted on a profile sheet to represent the student's adaptive behavior functioning. Standard scores, percentile ranks, and age equivalents are provided in the manual.

FIGURE 10.7 Areas Assessed by the *AAMR Adaptive Behavior Scale–School, Second Edition*

Part I: Independent Living Domains	Part II: Social Behavior Domains
Independent Functioning	Social Behavior
Physical Development	Conformity
Economic Activity	Trustworthiness
Language Development	Stereotyped and Hyperactive Behavior
Numbers and Time	Self-Abusive Behavior
Prevocational/Vocational Activity	Social Engagement
Self-Direction	Disturbing Interpersonal Behavior
Responsibility	
Socialization	

Adaptive Behavior Assessment System (ABAS–II)

This instrument measures the adaptive ability of individuals aged birth to 89 years (Harrison & Oakland, 2003). For children aged birth to 5, rating forms are provided for the parent or primary caregiver. A teacher or daycare worker form is provided for children aged 2 years to 5 years. A parent form and a separate teacher form are provided for subjects aged 5 years to 21 years. Adaptive behavior in the areas of communication, motor skills, self-help, safety, leisure, and other similar areas is assessed. In addition, Conceptual, Social, and Practical Composites and a total General Adaptive Composite (GAC) can be calculated.

Case Study Using Intelligence Measures, Adaptive Behavior, and Levels of Support

Read the following case study **for Mario** and use the information to complete Activity 10.7.

Mario, a 6-year-old student, was evaluated for developmental disabilities at the age of 3. At that time, it was difficult to determine specific strengths and weaknesses. Mario was provided with support services through a special education early childhood classroom. Mario was with the same teacher for 3 years and, at the age of 6, he was re-evaluated to determine a more exact picture of the types of support he would need in school and at home. At the conclusion of the evaluation, the following information was provided to the individualized education program (IEP) team as they met to plan Mario's next year in school.

Mario's cognitive ability was found to be approximately 75, with strength noted in visual spatial skills (standard score of 95) and weakness noted in verbal comprehension and oral language areas (standard scores ranged between 70 and 78).

The Vineland II was administered and the results indicated that Mario demonstrated weakness in Communication and Social Skills, with scores ranging between 68 and 71. Examination of communication indicated that his relative strength was in receptive language, with significant weakness in expressive language skills. Daily Living Skills and Motor Skills scores were found to represent relative strengths, with standard scores of 82 and 88. Within the Daily Living Skills Domain, it was noted that Interpersonal Relationships was a weakness.

CHECK YOUR UNDERSTANDING

Check your understanding of this case study applying general adaptive behavior and level of supports by completing

Activity 10.7.

● INTELLIGENCE AND ADAPTIVE BEHAVIOR: CONCLUDING REMARKS

Refer to Tables 10.4 and 10.5 for a summary of the instruments presented in Chapter 10. Intelligence tests for diagnosis of learning problems should be used with caution. In addition to the many issues surrounding the use of intelligence tests, the interpretation of test results is largely dependent on the training of the individual examiner. Some professionals believe that appropriate classification can occur only after numerous formal and informal assessments and observations. Others rely on only quantitative test data. Some professionals may use a factor analysis approach to determine learning disabilities, whereas others use informal and curriculum-based achievement measures.

The determination of the classification of mild mental retardation or educational disability is complicated by many social and legal issues. In a review of the problems and practices in the field for the past 20 years, Reschly (1988a, 1988b) advocated the need for a change of focus in the diagnosis and classification of students with mental retardation:

TABLE 10.4

IQ Test Review

Instrument	Purpose	Constructs Measured	Standardization Information	Reliability Information	Validity Information
Wechsler Intelligence Scale for Children–IV	Assess overall intellectual ability of children aged 6–0 to 16–11	Verbal comprehension, perceptual reasoning, working memory, processing speed, full scale IQ	Sample based on U.S. Census of 2000; variables considered were geographic region, ethnicity, gender, age, parental education level	Adequate to high evidence of split-half reliability, test–retest reliability SEMs, interscorer reliability	Evidence provided for content validity, construct validity, confirmatory factor analysis
Wechsler Adult Intelligence Scale–IV	Assess overall intellectual ability of adults	Same abilities as indexed in children's scales	Standardization sample included 2,200 individuals from all regions of the United States; variables considered were age, sex, race/ethnicity, educational level, and geographic region	Reliability research included internal consistency coefficients for subtests, process, and composites; testre–test reliability; and interrater or interscorer reliability with adequate evidence provided	Evidence provided for content validity; intercorrelation coefficients support convergent and discriminant validity; confirmatory factor analysis supports constructs of instrument; concurrent validity supported
Kaufman Assessment Battery for Children–II	Assess processing and cognitive abilities of children ages 3–18	Fluid/crystalized intelligence factors and mental processing factors	Total sample of 3,025 children ages 3–18; variables considered were sex, age, ethnicity, parental education level, and geographic region	Evidence of test–retest reliability, internal consistency, SEMs, reliability of nonstandard administration, differences by ethnicity, sex, and parental education level	Evidence of construct validity, factor analytic data, concurrent criterion-related validity data
Stanford–Binet V	Assess general and specific cognitive and processing abilities	Fluid reasoning, knowledge, quantitative reasoning, visual–spatial processing, working memory	Total sample of 4,800 persons in norming and standardization process; variables considered were sex, age, community size, ethnicity, socioeconomic status, geographic region	Internal consistency SEM, test–retest reliability, and interscorer reliability research	Evidence of content, construct, and concurrent criterionrelated validity; factor analysis also supports validity

(Continued)

TABLE 10.4

IQ Test Review (Continued)

Instrument	Purpose	Constructs Measured	Standardization Information	Reliability Information	Validity Information
Woodcock–Johnson III Tests of Cognitive Ability	Measures cognitive factors, clinical clusters, intracognitive discrepancies; instrument designed to be used with the WJ III Tests of Achievement	Global cognitive ability, specific processing clusters, predicted academic achievement	More than 8,000 persons included in sample; variables included ethnicity, community size, geographic region; adult sample included educational and occupational variables	Information regarding test–retest reliability, interrater reliability, alternate forms reliability, and internal consistency reliability included; most reliability coefficients for internal consistency are reported to be in the .90s	Evidence of criterion-related, construct, and content validity
Differential Ability Scale, Second Edition	General conceptual reasoning and strengths and weaknesses of individual abilities	General cognitive, verbal ability, nonverbal reasoning ability, spatial ability, special nonverbal composite, working memory, processing speed	Total sample of 3,480 persons representative of U.S. population in the five regions of Midwest, North East, South, and West; demographic variables considered were gender, rural or urban community, race (white, black, other), ethnicity (African American, Hispanic, Asian, or other), family income, educational attainment of parents	Internal consistency coefficients calculated for all three age groups for subtests, clusters, and composites; wide range of coefficients, with most in upper .80s to .90s; internal reliability calculated for special groups, including those with attention deficit hyperactivity disorder (ADHD), learning disabilities, giftedness, language disorders, hearing impairments, developmental disorders, limited English proficiency; test–retest and interscorer reliability adequate	Internal, confirmatory factor analysis, criterion-related, and construct validity supported and presented by subtest
Universal Nonverbal Intelligence Test	Assesses nonverbal reasoning and cognitive abilities	Memory, reasoning, symbolic mediation, nonsymbolic mediation	Standardization sample included more than 2,000 students; variables considered were sex, age, race, Hispanic origin, region, parental educational level, and general or special education placement	Sample of 1,765 children participated in reliability studies; evidence of internal consistency in general, clinical, and special samples; test-retest reliability	A sample of 1,765 children participated in validity studies; evidence of content, confirmatory factor analysis, concurrent, criterion-related validity

Test	Purpose	Measures	Norming Sample	Reliability	Validity
Comprehensive Test of Nonverbal Intelligence	Assesses various nonverbal cognitive abilities	Nonverbal analogies, categories, and sequences	Norming sample included 2,901 persons in 30 states; variables considered were geographic area, gender, race (white, black, other) urban/rural residence, ethnicity (Native American, Hispanic, Asian, African American, other), family income, and parental educational level	Reliability information provided for internal consistency, standard error of measurement, test–retest reliability, and interrater reliability; all coefficients within adequate to high range	Validity information for content validity, including analyses of the content validity of other measures of nonverbal intelligence, relationship to theories of intelligence, item analysis, and differential item functioning analysis
Test of Nonverbal Intelligence–Third Edition	Brief measure of nonverbal cognitive ability	Abstract problem-solving skills of nonverbal items	Norming sample of 3,451 persons representing 28 states; demographic considerations based on the 1997 *Statistical Abstracts of the United States* (U.S. Bureau of the Census, 1997); factors included geographic region, gender, race (white, black, other), residence (urban/rural), ethnicity (Native American, Hispanic, Asian, African American, and other), disability status (no disability, speech-learning disability, speech-language disorder, mental retardation, other disability); parental income and educational level, educational level of adult subjects	Evidence of reliability includes internal consistency measures using coefficient alpha and standard error of measurement, alternate forms reliability, testre–test reliability, and interrater reliability; all reliability coefficients within the .90s	Evidence of content, criterion-related, and construct validity
Wechsler Nonverbal Scale of Ability	Brief measure of nonverbal cognitive reasoning	Nonverbal reasoning using perceptual and some fine-motor perceptual abilities	Norming sample included 1,323 persons in the United States and 875 in Canada; variables considered were age, sex, race, educational level of parents, geographic region	Internal consistency coefficients range generally from .70s to .90s; test–retest reliability adequate	Convergent and discriminant validity research conducted with adequate evidence to support instrument; factor analysis and concurrent validity resulted in adequate results

TABLE 10.5

Adaptive Behavior Assessment Instrument Review

Instrument	Purpose	Constructs Measured	Standardization Information	Reliability Information	Validity Information
Vineland–II	Assess adaptive behavior for persons ranging in age from 0 to 90	Communication skills, daily living skills, socialization, motor skills, and maladaptive behavior	Standardization sample included 3,695 persons ranging in age from birth to 18–11; variables considered were sex, geographic region, parental educational level, race or ethnic group, community size, and educational placement and age. Additional clinical groups included students with ADHD, emotional disturbance, learning disabilities, mental retardation, noncategorical developmentally delay, speech and/or language impairments, and others (such as other health impairment, multiple disabilities)	Evidence of split-half, test–retest, and interrater reliability; reliability coefficients range from adequate to high	Information includes construct validity, content validity, and criterion-related validity studies; construct validity based on developmental progression and factor analysis of domains and subdomains; content validity information also provided
Vineland Adaptive Behavior–Expanded Form	Expanded form of adaptive behavior assessment	More detailed assessment of communication skills, daily living skills, socialization skills, motor skills, and maladaptive behavior	Same norming sample used for expanded form	Reliability studies used split-half, test retest, and interrater reliability measures; split-half reliability coefficients were in the .80s for standardization sample and the .80s and .90s for supplementary norms; information for test–retest and interrater reliability based on survey	Information includes construct, content, and criterion-related validity; studies based on survey form; discussion of estimating coefficients for expanded form included
AAMR–Adaptive Behavior Scale–2	Assessment of adaptive behavior	Independent living skills and social skills	Normed on sample of 2,074 persons with mental retardation and 1,254 persons who were nondisabled; variables of race, gender, ethnicity, urban and rural residence, geographic region, and age (3–18) were considered	Information on interrater reliability, internal consistency, and test–retest reliability presented in manual; all coefficients presented range from adequate to high	Examiner's manual addresses construct and item validity for students with and without mental retardation
Adaptive Behavior Assessment System	Assessment of adaptive behavior for ages birth to 89 years	Independent living skills, including self-help, leisure, communication, social skills, school, practical, and others	Normed on sample of 1,045 parents, 980 teachers, and 1,406 completed parent, teacher, and adult forms; variables considered included sex, race (white, Hispanic, African American, and other), and education level; clinical cases of developmental disabilities included in sample	Reliability research included internal consistency, test–retest, interrater reliability, and cross-form consistency; coefficients adequate	Validity research includes content validity, intercorrelations of domains, and concurrent validity; adequate correlations

The classification system reforms advocated would place more emphasis on three dimensions: (1) severe, chronic achievement deficits; (2) significantly deficient achievement across most if not all achievement areas; and (3) learning problems largely resistant to regular interventions. The students meeting these criteria will be virtually the same as the current population with MMR; however, their classification will not carry the stigma of comprehensive incompetence based on biological anomaly that is permanent. (p. 298)

The American Association on Intellectual and Developmental Disabilities (AAIDD; 2010) advocates that students with cognitive impairments and other developmental disabilities receive universal education, positive behavior support, and educational supports that are consistent with individual levels of need. Moreover, this organization reminds all educators and related professionals that students with cognitive impairments are guaranteed by law appropriate IEPs and interventions based on accurate assessment of their cognitive abilities and adaptive behaviors. In summary, AAIDD recommendations are consistent with federal regulations for students with special education needs within a response-to-intervention (RTI) framework.

CHAPTER SUMMARY

In this chapter you:

- Learned about the constructs of intelligence assessment

- Applied learning to case scenarios

- Analyzed how intelligence assessment informs instructional planning

- Synthesized data from intelligence assessment and adaptive behavioral assessment

- Evaluated how intelligence assessment results and adaptive behavioral assessment inform educational decisions

THINK AHEAD

This text is concerned primarily with the assessment of school-age students—those typically from about age 6 to 18. Students who require special education services often begin receiving those services during their preschool years and have additional needs for postsecondary years. The assessment of students in the years of early childhood and in the years requiring special considerations for transition to adulthood are presented in Chapter 11.

CHAPTER QUIZ

Complete the Chapter Quiz for Chapter 10 to assess your understanding of intelligence testing and adaptive behavior assessment.

11 Special Considerations of Assessment in Early Childhood

CHAPTER FOCUS

In this chapter you will:

- Learn the legal history and regulations for early childhood special education
- Apply knowledge of early childhood evaluation techniques to interventions
- Analyze evaluation results to determine developmental strengths, weaknesses, and needs
- Synthesize evaluation results to plan effective interventions
- Evaluate case scenarios to select appropriate evaluation techniques

● LEGAL GUIDELINES FOR EARLY CHILDHOOD EDUCATION

Public Law 99–457 set forth many of the guidelines and provisions governing services to infants and toddlers. Many of these guidelines were incorporated into the 1997 amendments; now, the Individuals with Disabilities education Act (IDEA) includes mandates for early childhood special education. The assessment of infants and young children raises several concerns, many of which are related to the age of the child. For example, young children must be evaluated in domains and areas that are not based on school-related competencies such as academic achievement. These children are evaluated in other areas: physical challenges, developmental motor skills, functional communication skills, behaviors in specific situations, and developmental competence. The assessment of young children and infants also includes the unique component of family needs and a family plan for appropriate intervention.

IDEA provides for educational intervention for children beginning at age 3. Part C of the IDEA amendments of 1997 authorizes funding to states for intervention for infants and toddlers with special needs. Part C and Part B of IDEA address serving infants, toddlers, and preschool children who are experiencing developmental differences. The elements of IDEA that pertain to the assessment of infants, toddlers, and preschool children are presented in the following section.

● INFANTS, TODDLERS, AND YOUNG CHILDREN

Federal regulations define the population of children eligible to be served, define the methods of assessment, provide procedural safeguards, and outline procedures to be used for intervention based on the family's needs.

Eligibility

Infants and toddlers from birth to age 2 who are experiencing developmental delays in one or more of the following areas are eligible for services: cognitive development, physical development (includes vision and hearing), communication development, social or emotional development, and adaptive development. Infants and toddlers may also be eligible for services if they have a diagnosed physical or mental condition that is likely to result in developmental delay. The law gives the individual states discretion to determine the lead agency to provide services for infants and toddlers with special needs. The states also have the option to provide services for children 3 years of age and younger considered to be at risk for developmental delay unless the child has appropriate interventions.

Children eligible for early childhood services are those with the same disabilities enumerated and defined for school-aged children: autism, deaf-blindness, deafness, hearing impairment, mental retardation, multiple disabilities, orthopedic impairment, other health impairment, serious emotional disturbance, specific learning disability, speech or language impairment, traumatic brain injury, and visual impairment. Infants and toddlers who have a diagnosed physical or mental condition that is known to have a high probability of resulting in developmental delay are also eligible (IDEA amendments, 1997).

Although not all states choose to serve infants and toddlers who are at risk for developmental delays, many states do provide intervention services. Katz (1989) lists as biological risk factors "prematurity associated with low birth weight, evidence of central nervous system involvement (intraventricular hemorrhage, neonatal seizures), prolonged respiratory difficulties, prenatal maternal substance use or abuse" (p. 100). These risk factors may not always result in an early diagnosed physical condition, but may prove problematic as the child develops.

In addition to biological risk factors, environmental risk factors often exist. The most often cited environmental risk factors found by Graham and Scott (1988) included poor infant/child interaction patterns, low maternal educational level, young maternal age, disorganization or dysfunction of the family, and few family support networks. Suggestions for assessing infants at risk are given later in this chapter.

● EVALUATION AND ASSESSMENT PROCEDURES

The 1997 IDEA amendments define *evaluation* as the ongoing procedures used by qualified personnel to determine the child's eligibility for special services and continued eligibility while the child is served under this law.

The regulations require that an **individual family service plan (IFSP)** be developed for each infant or toddler and his or her family. According to the amendments (pp. 62–63), the IFSP must include each of the following components:

1. A statement of the infant's or toddler's present levels of physical development, cognitive development, communication development, social or emotional development, and adaptive development, based on objective criteria

2. A statement of the family's resources, priorities, and concerns relating to enhancing the development of the infant or toddler with a disability

3. A statement of the major outcomes expected to be achieved for the infant or toddler and the family, and the criteria, procedures, and timelines used to determine the degree to which progress toward achieving the outcomes is being made and whether modifications or revisions of the outcomes or services are necessary

4. A statement of specific early intervention services necessary to meet the unique needs of the infant or toddler and the family, including the frequency, intensity, and method of delivering services

CHECK YOUR UNDERSTANDING

Check your ability to define terms used in the discussion of serving infants and toddlers by completing Activity 11.1.

As the toddler reaches early childhood age, the child will transfer to the settings and interventions appropriate for children included under IDEA. To prepare for this transition, the child's IFSP will include a transition plan. For additional information about the transition time period and the evaluation procedures, read the federal regulations.

In addition, this plan must include a statement detailing how services will be provided in the child's natural environment and to what extent any services will not be provided in the child's natural environment. The plan must also include anticipated dates for services to begin and a statement about the expected duration of those services. The coordinator of the services must be named, and the steps that will be taken to transition the child to preschool or other services must be outlined (IDEA amendments, 1997).

The amendments require that the IFSP be reviewed every 6 months (or more frequently as appropriate) and the family given the review of the plan. The IFSP must be evaluated at least once a year.

The assessment of infants and young children must also follow IDEA's regulations concerning nondiscriminatory assessment, parental consent, confidentiality, and due process procedural safeguards. The multidisciplinary team for this process must include at least one parent and at least two professional providers from different disciplines with one of the providers being the service coordinator. The law requires annual evaluation of progress, but notes that because of the rapid development of the child during this period of his or her life, some evaluation procedures may need to be repeated before the annual review.

Federal law mandates all states to serve children ages 3 to 5 years; at their discretion, states can provide services to children 2 years of age and younger. The IFSP for children ages 3 to 5 must include statements about the child's natural environment as well as educational statements that address the child's school readiness, preliteracy skills, language, and numeracy skills.

● ISSUES AND QUESTIONS ABOUT SERVING INFANTS AND TODDLERS

A goal of PL 99–457, the initial law for early childhood education for children with disabilities or at risk of disabilities, was to involve families as much as possible in the assessment and planning processes integral to the provision of services. Since the law's passage in 1986, many concerns have been raised by clinical practitioners working with these regulations. Of chief concern is the role of the parents in the assessment and planning process (Dunst, Johanson, Trivette, & Hamby, 1991; Goodman & Hover, 1992; Katz, 1989; Minke, & Scott, 1993).

The issues raised by Goodman and Hover include confusion with the interpretation and implementation of the family assessment component. The regulations may be misunderstood as requiring *mandatory assessment of family members* rather than *voluntary participation by the parents*. The family's strengths and needs as they relate to the child, not the parents themselves, are the objects of assessment. Furthermore, these authors contended that a relationship based on equal standing between parents and professionals may not result in a greater degree of cooperation and respect than the traditional client–professional relationship. When parents and professionals are viewed as equal partners, the professional surrenders the role of expert. Goodman and Hover suggested that the relationship be viewed as reciprocal rather than egalitarian. An assessment process directed by his or her parents may not be in a child's best interest because parents retain the right to restrict professional inquiry.

Katz (1989) observed that the family's view of the child's most important needs takes precedence over the priorities perceived by professional team members. In some instances, parents and professionals must negotiate to agree on goals for the child. The family will be more motivated to achieve those goals they perceive as important.

The law clearly states that the IFSP be developed with parent participation. This provision must be upheld whether or not the family participates in the assessment process. In practice, parental participation varies, according to a study of the development of IFSPs in three early childhood intervention programs (Minke & Scott, 1993). This study found that parents do not always participate in goal setting for their children, that they play a listening role without soliciting input from professionals, that they appear to need better explanations by professionals, and that they may become better advocates for their child with early participation. These issues are similar to those associated with parental participation during eligibility meetings for school-aged children (refer to Chapter 2).

Differences in the implementation of regulations designed to meet the needs of children who are preschool age or younger may be the result of state-determined policies and procedures. One area of difference seems to be in the interpretation of how families should be involved in the early intervention process. Dunst et al. (1991) described the family-centered program and the family-focused program as paradigms representing two such interpretations. In the family-centered program paradigm, family concerns and needs drive assessment, anything written on the IFSP must have the family's permission, and the family's needs determine the actual roles played by case managers. The family-focused program paradigm restricts assessment to the family's needs only as they relate to the child's development, goals are agreed on mutually by professionals and parents, and the case manager's role is to encourage and promote the family's use of professional services.

In addition to involvement of the family in the assessment process, the Division of Early Childhood (DEC) of the Council for Exceptional Children (CEC) recommends that all assessment be developmentally appropriate, include familiar

CHECK YOUR UNDERSTANDING

Check your ability to answer questions about IFSPs and serving infants and toddlers by completing Activity 11.2.

environments and people, and be functional (Sandall, Hemmeter, Smith, & McLean, 2005). An assessment is considered functional when data is collected in situations that commonly occur in the child's daily routine. This type of assessment will result in more reliable and valid information.

RTI, Progress Monitoring, and Accountability

In the education of young children with exceptional learning needs, response to intervention (RTI) can prevent children from being classified into special education by focusing on emerging skills (Jackson, Pretti-Frontczak, Harjusola-Webb, Grisham-Brown, & Romani, 2009). These authors suggested that ongoing assessment be conducted in the tiers so that all students are assessed universally, and so that children who do not have the developmental skills expected receive specific interventions as their progress is monitored. For example, children who do not yet have mastery of alphabetic knowledge would receive focused interventions to assist in the acquisition of these skills. These authors note that educational professionals should work in a collaborative manner to collect information and data from multiple sources using multiple methods. In addition, Grisham-Brown, Hallam, and Brookshire (2006) suggest using authentic assessment of classroom activities to monitor progress in early childhood. An example of authentic assessment in an early childhood curriculum is presented in Figure 11.1.

According to Hebbeler, Barton, and Mallik (2008), early childhood assessment provides methods of accountability by enabling professionals to determine the effectiveness of interventions and instruction. Downs and Strand (2006) contended that data collected through assessment of performance on learning activities can assist in educational planning and decisions. Moreover, the implementation of universal behavioral and academic interventions and assessment in early childhood can be beneficial to students and to their teachers (Benedict, Horner, & Squires, 2007). By monitoring the progress of young children in the curriculum, teachers can make necessary changes in instruction quickly and redirect interventions to increase the likelihood of skill acquisition.

● METHODS OF EARLY CHILDHOOD ASSESSMENT

As previously noted, many states serve children who are considered at risk for developmental disabilities. The discussion of assessment methods presented in this text applies to children with existing developmental disabilities as well as to those who may be at risk for developmental disabilities if they do not receive early childhood intervention.

Regulations require that qualified personnel assess children in many developmental areas; for example, assessments of vision, hearing, speech, and medical status are part of a multifactored evaluation. Detailed assessment in these areas is beyond the scope of this text. Measures presented include behavior questionnaires, observations, interviews, checklists, and measures of cognitive and language functioning. Techniques used in the assessment process are also presented.

● ASSESSMENT OF INFANTS

Documenting developmental milestones and health history is primarily the responsibility of health professionals. Infants may be suspected of having developmental delays or of being at risk for developmental delays if there are clinical indications of

FIGURE 11.1 Sample Activity for Preschool Authentic Assessment

Activity: Play Dough

Student Child's Name _____ DOB ____ Date ____

A _____ ____ ____

B _____ ____ ____

C _____ ____ ____

D _____ ____ ____

E _____ ____ ____

F _____ ____ ____

Observer: _____

Behavior Code:
2 = can do/meets criterion in note column
1 = can do with assistance or meets part of the criterion
0 = cannot do

Materials Needed: Art shirts for each child; play dough in several colors; shape, alphabet, and number cookie cutters; nesting cookie cutters

Area / Strand	Item	Notes	Children A	B	C	D	E	F
Fine Motor A	G1. Uses two hands to manipulate objects.	Buttons art shirt before activity begins.						
	1.1 Holds object with one hand while the other hand manipulates.	Opens can of play dough.						
Adaptive C	G1. Unfastens fasteners on garments.	If scores for 1.1–1.3 are all 2, then score 2 here. If a combination of 0, 1, 2, score 1 here. If all were 0, score 0 here.						
	1.1 Unfastens buttons/snaps/Velcro fasteners on garments.	Unfastens art shirt (buttons, snaps, or Velcro).						
	1.2 Unties string-type fasteners.	Unfastens art shirt (e.g. tie).						
	1.3 Unzips zipper.	Unfastens zippers on art shirt.						
	G3. Fastens fasteners on garments.	If scores for 3.1–3.3 are all 2, then score 2 here. If a combination of 0, 1, 2, score 1 here. If all were 0, score 0 here.						
	3.1 Ties string-type fastener.	Fastens art shirt (buttons, snaps, Velcro, zipper, tie).						
	3.2 Fastens buttons/snaps/Velcro fasteners.	Fastens art shirt (buttons, snaps, Velcro, zipper, tie).						
	3.3 Threads and zips zipper.	Fastens art shirt (e.g., zipper).						
Cognitive A	G1. Demonstrates understanding of color, shape, and size concepts.	If scores for 1.1–1.3 are all 2, then score 2 here. If a combination of 0, 1, 2, score 1 here. If all were 0, score 0 here.						
	1.1 Demonstrates understanding of eight different colors.	Child follows directions, answers questions, or identifies objects, people, or events using at least eight different terms that describe color. Ex. Knows 8 colors (colors of play dough and utensils).						
	1.2 Demonstrates understanding of five different shapes.	Child follows directions, answers questions, or identifies objects, people, or events using at least five different terms that describe shape. Ex. Knows five shapes (circle, square, triangle, diamond, star "cookies").						
	1.3 Demonstrates understanding of six different size concepts.	Child follows directions, answers questions, or identifies objects, people, or events using at least six different terms that describe size. Ex. Knows six size concepts (long/short "snake"; fat /skinny "cookie"; big/ little "snowman"; thick/thin, large/small, tiny/huge).						
Cognitive G	G2. Demonstrates understanding of printed numerals.	Child correctly discriminates numerals from letters and uses number symbols to represent quantity. Ex. Locates "number" cookie cutters.						
	2.1 Labels printed numerals.	Labels numbers on cookie cutters (up to 10).						
	2.2 Recognizes printed numerals.	Discriminates "number cookies" from "letter cookies."						

Source: From Grisham-Brown, Hallam, & Brookshire. (2006). "Using Authentic Assessment to Evidence Children's Progress toward Early Learning Standards," in *Early Childhood Education Journal, 34*(1), 45–51. With kind permission from Springer Science Business Media.

concern. Mayes (1991, p. 445) cited the following indications of need for an infant assessment:

1. *Regulatory disturbances.* Sleep disturbances, excessive crying or irritability, eating difficulties, low frustration tolerance, self-stimulatory or unusual movements.

2. *Social/environmental disturbances.* Failure to discriminate mother, apathetic, withdrawn, no expression of affect or interest in social interaction, excessive negativism, no interest in objects or play, abuse, neglect, multiple placements, repeated or prolonged separations.

3. *Psychophysiological disturbances.* Nonorganic failure to thrive, recurrent vomiting or chronic diarrhea, recurrent dermatitis, recurrent wheezing.

4. *Developmental delays.* Specific delays (gross motor, speech delays); general delays or arrested development.

The prenatal, birth, and early neonatal health history is an important component of the evaluation of infants and is required by PL 99–457. Following the careful history taking of the infant's health factors, Greenspan (1992, pp. 316–317) organized the infant/toddler/young child assessment using the following factors:

1. Prenatal and perinatal variables

2. Parent, family, and environmental variables

3. Primary caregiver and caregiver/infant–child relationship

4. Infant variables: physical, neurologic, physiologic, and cognitive

5. Infant variables: formation and elaboration of emotional patterns and human relationships

Of particular concern in assessing the infant are regulatory patterns, or how the infant reacts to stimuli in the environment and processes sensory information (Greenspan, 1992; Mayes, 1991). These include how the infant interacts with and reacts to caregivers and the infant's sleeping habits, level of irritability, and so on. This type of assessment relies on observations using checklists and parental interviews or questionnaires. One commonly used observation assessment instrument for newborn infants is the *Neonatal Behavioral Assessment Scale* (Brazelton, 1984), which includes both reflex items and behavioral observation items. Use of this scale to determine control states (e.g., sleeping, alert) underscores the importance of this aspect of infant behavior to more complex functions, such as attention (Mayes, 1991). This scale can be used with infants up to 1 month of age.

The *Uzgiris–Hunt Ordinal Scales of Psychological Development* (Uzgiris & Hunt, 1975) presents a Piagetian developmental perspective for assessment during the first 2 years of the infant's life. These six scales include assessment for such skills as visual pursuit, object permanence, manipulation of and interaction with factors in the environment, development of vocal and gestural imitation, and development of schemes for relating to the environment. This instrument requires the use of several objects and solicitation of reactions and responses from the infant. This system, a comprehensive assessment based on the Piagetian model, has been criticized for being developed using primarily infants from middle-class families (Mayes, 1991).

Another instrument used to assess young children and toddlers (ages 1–42 months) is the *Bayley Scales of Infant Development–II* (Bayley, 1993). This revised formal instrument now includes in the manual improved statistical research regarding reliability and validity. Like most infant/toddler instruments, the *Bayley* requires the examiner to manipulate objects and observe the reactions and behavior of the infant. The scale assesses mental functions such as memory, problem solving, and verbal ability, and motor functions such as coordination and control; it also includes a behavioral rating scale. In addition to the standardization sample, clinical samples

CHECK YOUR UNDERSTANDING

Check your knowledge of assessment instruments used in serving infants and toddlers by completing Activity 11.3.

were included in the development of this revision. The clinical samples included infants and young children who were premature, HIV positive, or exposed prenatally to drugs or asphyxiated at birth, and those who had Down syndrome, autism, developmental delays, or otitis media.

● ASSESSMENT OF TODDLERS AND YOUNG CHILDREN

Many of the instruments discussed in earlier chapters contain basal-level items for toddlers and young children, including the *K–ABC–II*, the *WJ IV Tests of Achievement*, the *Vineland Adaptive Behavior Scales*, Achenbach's *Child Behavior Checklist*, and the *Stanford–Binet V*. Following is a brief survey of some of the most commonly used and newest instruments that are specifically designed to assess the development and behavior of young children. Instruments that assess general developmental ability of toddlers and young children can also be used to collect additional data to determine the likelihood of disorders in language. For example, young children may appear to have global developmental delays; however, assessment of general development may indicate development is progressing as expected with the exception of expressive or receptive language disorders.

Mullen Scales of Early Learning: AGS Edition

This instrument assesses the cognitive functioning of children ages birth through 68 months (Mullen, 1995) and is to be used by assessment personnel with experience in the evaluation of infants and young children. The test's author estimates administration time to range from 15 minutes to 60 minutes, depending on the age of the child. The instrument uses many common manipulatives to assess the child's vision, gross- and fine-motor skills, and receptive and expressive language abilities.

The theoretical basis of the test's design is explained in the examiner's manual and is presented in developmental stages. The expectations of a given developmental stage are listed, followed by the tasks used to assess each of the expected developmental indicators. For example, at stage 2–4 months 0 days to 6 months 30 days, a child's vision is refined and visual reception is assessed using the following items: stares at hand, localizes on objects and people, looks for an object in response to a visual stimulus followed by an auditory stimulus.

Technical Data

Norming process. The manual provides information regarding the standardization process, which was completed over an 8-year time span and involved 1,849 children representing the southern, northeastern, western, northern, and south-central regions of the United States. The variables of gender, ethnicity, race, age, and community size were considered in construction of the sample.

Reliability. The reliability studies contained in the manual are split-half reliability for internal consistency, test–retest reliability, and interscorer reliability. Reliability coefficients range from adequate and low/adequate to high. This may in part reflect the instability of developmental scores at the very early ages. Several of the sample sizes used in the reliability studies for some ages were small (e.g., 38 for test–retest of the gross motor scale for ages 1 to 24 months).

Validity. Evidence of construct validity, concurrent validity, and exploratory factor analyses is presented in the examiner's manual. The research regarding developmental progression to support the constructs being measured suggests validity of the scales as developmental indicators.

The Wechsler Preschool and Primary Scale of Intelligence, Fourth Edition

The *Wechsler Preschool and Primary Scale of Intelligence, Third Edition (WPPSI–IV)* was developed for use with children ages 2–6 to 7– 7 (Wechsler, 2012). This test yields index scores of intellectual ability and a full scale IQ score. The index scores include: verbal comprehension index, visual-spatial index, fluid reasoning index, working memory index, and processing speed index. In addition, the examiner may also complete an ancillary analysis of the following abilities: vocabulary acquisition index, nonverbal index, general ability index, and a cognitive proficiency index.

Test developers note that the recent revision of this instrument updated the norms, added new subtests, made (OK) index scores available, and increased the age range to 7–7.

The *WPPSI–IV* has separate subtests for the major age divisions of 2–6 to 3–11 and 4–0 to 7–7. Children ages 2–6 to 3–11 are administered 7 of the 15 subtests. Children older than 3–11 are administered all subtests. An example of the kinds of abilities and skills that are assessed by the WPPSI–IV (Wechsler, 2012) is presented in the following subtest descriptions that are grouped according to the appropriate index for ages 4–0 to 7–7:

Verbal Comprehension Index

Information—The child is asked a question about a general topic and asked to select the best answer from the provided choices.

Similarities—The child is shown a picture and then asked to select another picture from a group of pictures that is within the same category as the first picture.

Visual-Spatial Index

Block design—The child works within specific time limits as he or she copies patterns of block designs.

Object assembly—This task requires the student to assemble puzzle pieces into a specific target object.

Fluid Reasoning Index

Matrix reasoning—The child is presented with an incomplete pattern or matrix and asked to select the stimulus that would complete the pattern.

Picture concepts—The child is shown rows of pictures and then asked to select one picture from each of the rows that has similar characteristics.

Working Memory Index

Picture memory—The child is first presented with a picture stimulus and then asked to find the same picture or pictures on the next page.

Zoo locations—On this timed subtest, the child is first presented with animal cards in specific zoo locations. Following the specified time period, the child is provided with the animal cards and asked to place each card in the previous zoo location.

Processing Speed Index

Bug search—The picture stimulus is one target bug in a row of bugs. The child is asked to select a bug from the row that matches the target bug.

Cancellation—On this timed subtest, the child is shown a page of pictures and must quickly scan and mark all of the target pictures included on the page.

Additional subtests include:

Vocabulary—The child is presented with a picture or the examiner says a word and the child must name the picture or tell the meaning of a word.

Animal Coding—The child is asked to indicate which animal shape corresponds with an animal picture.

Comprehension—The child is presented with a picture and must select an appropriate response or the child is asked a question and must provide an answer indicating understanding of a concept.

Receptive Vocabulary—When presented with a word read by the examiner, the child must select the correct name of the object

Picture Naming—When presented with a stimulus, the child names the object.

Technical Data

Norming process. During the development of this revision, children from the general population and special clinical groups were assessed. The standardization sample included 1,700 children in stratified age groups from age 2 years 6 months to 7 years 7 months. The variables considered in the norm group included age, sex, race/ethnicity (white, African American, Hispanic, Asian, other), parental education level, and geographic region. The standardization sample was selected to correspond with the 2010 U.S. Census.

The following special groups were included in validity studies during the development of this instrument: persons with intellectual disability, persons with autistic disorders and Asperger's disorder, persons with expressive language delay or mixed expressive–receptive language delay or preliteracy concerns, persons with attention deficit hyperactivity disorder, and individuals with disruptive behavior.

Reliability. The reliability for the full scale IQ across the age groups was in the mid-0.90s and for subtests and index scores it ranged from 0.71–0.95. Interrater reliability was in the mid-0.90s.

Validity. Evidence of validity is presented in the manual and includes measures of criterion-related validity, convergent validity studies, confirmatory factor analysis, and validity of use with special groups. The evidence presented indicates that the *WPPSI–IV* successfully discriminates between the special groups and the norm sample.

Scoring. The *WPPSI-IV* can be completed by hand or through using the publisher's web-based Q Global scoring platform. Available scores include subtest scale scores with a mean of 10 and a standard deviation of 3, standard scores for indexes and full scale IQ with a mean of 100, percentile ranks, and age equivalents.

AGS Early Screening Profiles

The *AGS Early Screening Profiles* (Harrison et al., 1990) present a comprehensive screening for children aged 2 to 6–11. The battery contains items that are administered directly to the child and surveys that are completed by parents, teachers, or both. The components, shown in Figure 11.2, are described in the following paragraphs.

Components

Cognitive/language profile. The child demonstrates verbal abilities by pointing to objects named or described by the examiner, discriminates pictures and selects those that are the same as the stimulus, solves visual analogies by pointing to the correct picture, and demonstrates basic school skills such as number and

FIGURE 11.2 Components of the *AGS Early Screening Profiles*

PROFILES

Cognitive/Language Profile	*Motor Profile*	*Self-Help/Social Profile*
Source: direct testing of child	Source: direct testing of child	Source: parent, teacher questionnaires
Time: 5 to 15 minutes	Time: 5 to 15 minutes	Time: 5 to 10 minutes
Cognitive Subscale	Gross-Motor Subtest (5 items)	Communication Domain (15 items)
Visual Discrimination Subtest (14 items)	Fine-Motor Subtest (3 items)	Daily Living Skills Domain (15 items)
Logical Relations Subtest (14 items)		Socialization Domain (15 items)
Language Subscale		Motor Skills Domain (15 items)
Verbal Concepts Subtest (25 items)		
Basic School Skills Subtest (25 items)		

SURVEYS

Articulation Survey	*Home Survey*	*Health History Survey*	*Behavior Survey*
Source: direct testing of child	Source: parent questionnaire	Source: parent questionnaire	Source: examiner questionnaire
Time: 2 to 3 minutes	Time: 5 minutes	Time: 5 minutes	Time: 2 to 3 minutes
Articulation of Single Words (20 items)	(12 items)	(12 items)	Cognitive/Language Observations (9 items)
Intelligibility During Continuous Speech (1 rating)			Motor Observations (13 items)

Source: Early Screening Profiles (ESP).

quantity concepts and the recognition of numbers, letters, and words. Items are presented in an easel format, and sample items are included to teach the tasks.

Motor profile. These items assess both gross-motor and fine-motor developmental skills. Gross-motor skills measured include imitating movements, walking on a line, standing on one foot, walking heel-to-toe, and performing a standing broad jump. Fine-motor tasks include stringing beads, drawing lines and shapes, and completing mazes.

Self-help/social profile. Questionnaires completed by teachers and parents measure the child's understanding of oral and written language, daily self-care skills such as dressing and eating, ability to do chores, and community skills such as telephone manners. Social skills that assess how well the child gets along with others and questions measuring the child's fine- and gross-motor skills are included in this section of the instrument.

Articulation survey. In this easel-format task, the examiner asks the child to say words that sample the child's ability to articulate sounds in the initial, medial, and final position.

Home survey and health history survey. These questionnaires completed by parents assess parent–child interactions; types of play; frequency of parent reading to the child; health problems of the mother's pregnancy, labor, and delivery; and health history of the child, such as immunization schedule.

Behavior survey. An observation form is used to rate the child's behavior in several categories such as attention, independence, activity level, and cooperativeness.

Technical Data

Norming process. The test manual provides detailed descriptions of the development of test items and questions included on parent and teacher questionnaires. The following variables, representative of the 1986 U.S. Census data, were considered in the national standardization sample: age, gender, geographic region, parental educational level, and race or ethnic group.

Reliability. Reliability research presented in the manual includes coefficient alpha for internal consistency and immediate test–retest and delayed test–retest research. Coefficients are adequate to moderately high for all measures.

Validity. Validity studies presented in the manual include content validity, construct validity, part–total correlations, and concurrent validity research with cognitive measures used with early childhood students. Many of the validity coefficients are low to adequate.

Kaufman Survey of Early Academic and Language Skills (K–SEALS)

The *K–SEALS* (Kaufman & Kaufman, 1993) was developed as an expanded version of the language measure of the *AGS Early Screening Profiles*. Normed for children aged 3-0 to 6–11, the instrument includes three subtests: Vocabulary; Numbers, Letters, and Words; and Articulation Survey. Scores for expressive and receptive language skills may be obtained from the administration of the Vocabulary and Numbers, Letters, and Words subtests. Scores for early academic skills, such as number skills and letter and word skills, may be computed for children aged 5–0 to 6–11. Items are presented in an easel format; visual and verbal stimuli are similar to the items on the *AGS Early Screening Profiles*. Half of the items from the Vocabulary and Numbers, Letters, and Words subtests are identical to those on the *AGS Early Screening Profiles*. The Articulation Survey from the *AGS* test is repeated in its entirety on the *K–SEALS*, but the error analysis is expanded on the *K–SEALS*.

Scoring. The manual includes norm tables for converting raw scores into percentile ranks and cutoff scores for the categories of "potential delay" or "OK."

Technical Data. The *K–SEALS* was standardized as part of the standardization of the *AGS Early Screening Profiles*. The same variables were considered to promote representativeness in the sample. Reliability and validity information for the *K–SEALS* includes split-half reliability, test–retest reliability, intercorrelations, construct validity, content validity, concurrent validity, and predictive validity. Individual subtest coefficients for reliability and validity studies ranged from low to adequate, but total test coefficients appear adequate for most studies cited.

BRIGANCE® Early Childhood Screen III

The *BRIGANCE® Early Childhood Screen III* (Brigance, 2013) is a system of assessment instruments designed to screen for both development risk and potential advanced development. The screens are designed for children ages 3 to 5 years and are arranged in easel format for administration. Parental and teacher ratings are included. The screening instrument is standardized and includes criterion-referenced items. The areas assessed include physical development, language development, and academic skills and cognitive development.

The domains assessed in the *BRIGANCE® Early Childhood Screen III* are visual/fine/and graphmotor, gross motor, quantitative concepts, personal information, receptive vocabulary, prereading/reading skills, expressive vocabulary, and articulation/verbal fluency/syntax. This assessment uses parent rating and information forms, professional data collection from doctors and others such as school nurses and speech therapists, teacher report forms, and criterion-referenced items.

Scoring. Norm tables provide age-equivalent scores for motor development, communication development, and cognitive development. Percentile ranks are presented for total scores.

Technical Data. The standardization sample for the 2013 restandardization was composed of 408 students. Demographic information is provided in the technical manual, which includes tables for the following characteristics: geographic sites, educational level of child, gender, racial and ethnic background, educational level of parents, family income (participation in free lunch program), parents' marital status, and ages. The technical manual also presents information regarding the performance of the sample by demographic characteristics (such as participation in free lunch program).

Reliability. The technical manual presents information for internal consistency, test–retest reliability, and interrater reliability. Total internal reliability ranged from 0.84 to 0.99. Interrater reliability coefficients were reported to range between 0.90 and 0.99. Test–retest reliability was reported to range from 0.84 to 0.99.

Validity. The technical manual reports information on content validity, construct validity, concurrent validity, predictive validity, and discriminant validity. Coefficients ranged widely from low to adequate.

BRIGANCE® Inventory of Early Development III Standardized (Brigance, 2013)

This version of the BRIGANCE® includes more items to assess developmental skills using a criterion-referenced format to evaluate children from birth through their

TABLE 11.1	
Possible Items Listed for the Social and Emotional Domain—BRIGANCE® **Inventory of Early Development III (2013)**	

By (date) _____, (child's name) _____ will
(list as appropriate)

1. help put things away;

2. show concern that playmates are not hurt;

3. perform simple errands;

4. take pleasure in doing simple favors for others;

5. be truthful when sharing information with others.

seventh year (7–11 months). The number of assessments varies by the age of the child so that children in the earliest age group, from birth to 11 months, have the fewest number of items, observations, and domains in which data are collected from parents.

The inventory includes assessments for physical development such as gross–motor skills, fine-motor skills, receptive and expressive language, cognitive development, adaptive behavior and daily living skills, and social and emotional development. This instrument includes a listing of possible objectives for individualized education programs (IEPs) at the end of each assessment area. Table 11.1 presents a partial list of objectives for the social-emotional domain.

Technical Data. More than 2,400 children were included in the standardization sample. The following variables were considered in the sample: typically developing children and children with special needs, geographic regions, urban and rural areas, and the demographic and socio-economic status were representative of the population of the United States.

Reliability. Reliability of the BRIGANCE® Inventory of Early Development Standardized was demonstrated using internal consistency, test–retest reliability, and inter-rater reliability.

Validity. Construct and content validity studies were included in the development of the inventory as well as criterion-related validity.

Developmental Indicators for the Assessment of Learning, Fourth Edition (DIAL–4)

This instrument was developed to screen for young children who might require additional assessment or interventions (Mardell & Goldenberg, 2011). The test may be used to assess children ages 3 years through 5 years 11 months. The test assesses the areas mandated by IDEA 1997, including motor skills, concepts, language, self-help, and social-emotional skills. Motor, concepts, and language skills are assessed through performance items presented to the child. Self-help or adaptive skills and social skills are assessed through parent and teacher questionnaires. Instructions are also presented for the examiner to assess social adjustment through observations obtained during the assessment session. A fairly detailed theoretical basis for the development of the test and research pertaining to specific areas assessed are presented in the manual.

The *DIAL–4* is available in both English and Spanish and the norm tables are for both the English and Spanish versions. Using item response theory (Rasch one-parameter model), the Spanish and English versions were equated so that the performance of Spanish-speaking examinees could be compared with the performance of

English-speaking examinees (Mardell-Czudnowski & Goldenberg, 1998, p. 75). The test includes several concrete manipulative items, including three dials to be used as stimuli for items in the concepts, motor, and language areas. Pictures, blocks, and a color chart are among the other items included.

Components

Motor. This component of the *DIAL–4* includes both fine- and gross-motor tasks. The child is asked to jump, throw a beanbag at a target, wiggle fingers, complete tasks with blocks, cut, and write his or her name (as appropriate).

Concepts. This component assesses the child's ability to identify colors and parts of the body as well as his or her understanding of concepts such as *biggest, cold,* and *longest.* The child's skills in counting, naming shapes, and sorting by shape are also assessed.

Language. This component assesses the child's ability to provide personal information such as name and age, to identify pictures of objects, and to name letters. In addition, the child's articulation is assessed for developmental risk.

Parent questionnaire. This questionnaire is used to assess self-help skills with 22 items, and social-emotional skills with a 28-item rating scale. In addition, there is a rating scale for parents to indicate their level of concern.

Teacher questionnaire. This questionnaire includes the same components as the parent questionnaire, including the rating scale for the teacher to indicate the level of concern about the child's developmental progress.

Examiner behavioral observations. During the evaluation, the examiner rates the child's behavior for each of the domains assessed. For example, separation from parent, attention, activity level, and other behaviors are rated during the motor tasks, concepts, and language items.

Scoring and Interpretation. The *DIAL-4* provides percentile ranks and standard scores with a mean of 100. The examiner's manual includes cutoff levels that the school district or agency determine in order to identify children who have potential developmental delay. The five cut-off levels from which to choose are based on the distance from the mean (Mardell & Golden, 2011). The levels are:

The 16% level would include about 16% of the norm sample and these scores are greater than 1 standard deviation below the mean.

The 10% level includes scores that are 1.3 standard deviations (SDs) from the mean.

The 7% level includes scores more than 1.5 SDs from the mean.

The 5% level includes scores more than 1.7 SDs from the mean.

The 2% level includes scores more than 2 SDs from the mean. (Mardell & Golden, 2011)

The lower the percent level, the fewer the number of children that would be captured in the category of potential delay. It is likely that these children in the lower percent levels would have the most significant risk for developmental challenges.

Technical Data. The tryout sample was composed of 1,574 children who ranged in age from 2 years 6 months to 5 years 11 months. The sample included African American, Hispanic, white, and other categories of children. The norm sample included 924 English-speaking children who completed the English assessment and 650 Spanish-speaking children who completed the Spanish version. The following variables were considered in selecting the sample: age, gender, geographic region, socio-economic condition, race/ethnicity, and parental educational level. Information is provided in the manual regarding children in the sample who received special services.

The norm sample for the standardization of the instrument included 1,400 children who were selected to be representative of the U.S. population based on the 2008 U.S. Census data. Race/ethnicity was represented by children from the following groups: African American, Asian, Hispanic, white, and other, which included American Indians, Alaska Natives, Native Hawaiians, Pacific Islanders, and others. Other variables considered in the selection were mother's educational level, mother's educational level within the race/ethnicity category, geographic region, child's educational setting, and children with clinical diagnoses (Mardell & Golden, 2011).

> *Reliability.* Internal reliability was researched using the split-half method. The coefficients for the total DIAL-4 across all age groups ranged from the low 0.90s to mid-0.90s. Parent and teacher questionnaire reliability ranged from 0.83 to 0.93. The adjusted total English *DIAL–4* test–retest reliability coefficients for the 2–6 to 3–11 age group was 0.83 and 0.88 for the 4–0 to 5–11 age group. The adjusted total Spanish *DIAL–4* test–retest reliability coefficients for the 2–6 to 3–11 age group was 0.91 and 0.92 for the 4–0 to 5–11 age group.

> *Validity.* Extensive information is provided in the manual about the development of the items in both the English and the Spanish versions. Information is presented concerning the reviews of items for content and potential bias as well as the rationale for selection of specific items.

Concurrent validity studies were conducted with the *DIAL–3,* the *Battelle Developmental Inventory, Early Screening Profiles,* and the *Vineland-II.* Corrected coefficients were scattered considerably, from extremely low to adequate.

An abbreviated scale, the Speed Dial, is also available with this revision. It is a very brief screener that consists of screening by using 10 tasks and requires about 20 minutes to administer.

● TECHNIQUES AND TRENDS IN INFANT AND EARLY CHILDHOOD ASSESSMENT

The assessment methods presented in this chapter are formal methods of assessment. Current literature suggests that alternative methods of assessment be used in conjunction with or in place of traditional assessment of infants and young children (Cohen & Spenciner, 1994; Fewell, 1991; Paget, 1990; Sinclair, Del'Homme, & Gonzalez, 1993). Among the alternative methods suggested by various studies are play evaluations, arena assessment, interactive strategies, observations, situational questionnaires, and ecobehavioral interviews.

Play evaluations can yield useful information about how the child interacts with people and objects and can be completed in a naturalistic environment. They can be useful in determining the child's activity level, reaction to novel stimuli, and affect. The characteristics of play are listed by Bailey and Wolery (1989) and include considerations such as: Is the child motivated to play and does the child independently select the type of play or play objects? Evaluators may also note the child's ease in changing from one play activity or object to another activity or object. These are some of the characteristics that can be included in a play evaluation. Using characteristics as guidelines, the examiner can assess many behaviors of the child in a naturalistic environment for developmental progress in social skills, activity level, motor skills, frustration tolerance, communication skills with the examiner or caretaker while playing, and so on.

CHECK YOUR UNDERSTANDING

Check your ability to answer questions about assessment instruments used with young children by completing Activity 11.4.

FIGURE 11.3 Team Members Conducting an Arena Assessment

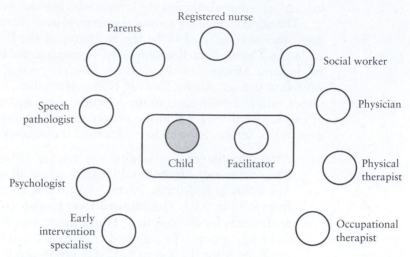

Source: Cohen/Spenciner, *Assessment of Young Children*, Figure 1.4, "Team members conducting an arena assessment," p. 31, 1994. Reproduced by permission of Pearson Education, Inc.

Arena assessment can be arranged for any method of assessment described in this chapter, except perhaps for formal cognitive assessment on standardized instruments. Arena assessment is a technique in which all members of the multidisciplinary team surround the child and examiner or facilitator and observe as they interact in multiple situations. Play evaluations, formal play or preacademic tasks, communication items, and so on may all be presented in this format. All members of the team record the child's responses throughout the evaluation session. This might be a more effective method of assessment of infants and young children because it may reduce the number of assessment sessions (Cohen & Spenciner, 1994). Figure 11.3 illustrates the arena assessment model.

Interactive strategies can be useful in the assessment of young children. These strategies assess the child's abilities to solve problems through interactions with the examiner (Paget, 1990). The examiner may alter the problems presented to observe the child's responses to frustration, humor, or different types or objects of play. Strategies are aimed at encouraging the child to communicate with the examiner to solve the problem.

Observations can be used in a variety of settings and across a variety of tasks. The child may be observed in the home or preschool classroom environment with peers, siblings, and caregivers. All areas of assessment in early childhood can be enhanced through observations. The child's behavior, social skills, communication skills, cognitive level, speech, motor skills, motor planning, adaptive behaviors, activity level, frustration tolerance level, attention span, and self-help skills can be assessed through multiple observations. When observations are combined with information from parental questionnaires and more formal assessment measures, the examiner can gain a holistic view of the child's developmental progress.

Situational questionnaires are useful when comparing the child's behavior in specific situations. Examples of these are the *Home Situations Questionnaire* and the *School Situations Questionnaire* (Barkley, 1990). The child's parents and teachers rate the child's behavior, activity level, and attention span in a variety of situations, such as when the parents talk on the telephone, when visitors are in the home, and when the child is interacting with peers. These questionnaires allow for more direct analysis of problematic behaviors so that appropriate interventions can occur.

In ecobehavioral interviews, parents and teachers describe a child's behaviors in everyday situations, such as during daily routines, bedtime, class activities, and transitions from one activity to the next (Barnett, Macmann, & Carey, 1992). These responses are analyzed to determine problem behaviors that occur across settings or situations. Behavioral interventions are then targeted to remediate the behaviors in the situations described.

● OTHER CONSIDERATIONS IN ASSESSING VERY YOUNG CHILDREN

The best practice of assessment across all ages of children involves multiple measures, multiple examiners, and multiple situations or environments. This is especially important for infants, toddlers, and young children because of the influence that temperament, physical health, and current physical state (alertness or sleepiness) may have during an evaluation period. A holistic view of the child's developmental level can be gained by observing the child in many different settings, using both formal and informal assessment, and analyzing the observed behaviors.

Because of the very rapid pace of development of young children, assessment and monitoring of progress should be ongoing, as stated in PL 99–457 (*Federal Register*, 1993). This rapid progress contributes to the instability of scores obtained at very young ages. The variability of the educational and home environments can also contribute to the instability of scores.

Analysis of formal early childhood assessment instruments indicates that the reliability and validity of the subtests are at moderately adequate to below-acceptable levels. The coefficients tend to be more acceptable for total test or total instrument scores. Barnett et al. (1992) cautioned against using profile analysis of individual subtests at young ages and suggested that only global scores be used. Katz (1989) warned of the dangers that could occur when very young children are falsely identified through assessment. That is, the child's scores might indicate developmental difficulties, but in reality, the child is not disabled. This false identification may result in changes in parent–child interactions and diminished expectations held for the child.

At the other end of the identification process are those children who need services but remain unidentified. In a study by Sinclair et al. (1993), children who were previously undiagnosed were referred for assessment of behavioral disorders. This study involved a three-stage, multiple-gating system that was used to screen preschool children for behavioral disorders. In this study, 5% of the sample who had not previously been identified as having behavioral difficulties were referred for a comprehensive evaluation.

Another concern raised by assessment of very young children is that the characteristics of specific types of disorders can be difficult to determine in that age group. For example, a child may manifest some of the behaviors typically associated with attention deficit disorder; however, the requirements for diagnosis of the disorder, such as persistence over time, may be difficult to determine using the instruments available for this age group of children (Smith & Corkum, 2007). This underscores the need for multiple types of assessments from multiple sources and in multiple settings for very young children.

Review of the literature on the assessment of infants and young children indicates that new trends are emerging. It is hoped that these trends will remedy some of the difficulties of assessing children at very young ages.

Table 11.2 summarizes the strengths and weaknesses of the instruments presented in this chapter.

TABLE 11.2

Summary of Instruments Used in Early Childhood Assessment

Instrument	Strengths	Weaknesses
Neonatal Behavioral Assessment Scale	Useful for infants through 1 month of age Assesses behavior and reflex actions	Not typically used in educational setting Requires specific training for use
Uzgiris–Hunt Ordinal Scales of Psychological Development	For children up to 2 years of age Good theoretical basis	Lengthy administration time Norm sample not representative
Bayley Scales of Infant Development–II	Manual has improved statistical data Standardization included clinical samples Assesses many areas of development	Lengthy administration time Specific training necessary
Mullen Scales of Early Learning: AGS Edition	Integration of developmental concepts and theoretical foundations included in manual Intended for ages birth through 68 months	Small sample sizes for reliability, validity data
Wechsler Preschool and Primary Scales of Intelligence, Fourth Edition	Subtests are like those in other Wechsler scales. Appropriate for ages 2–6 to 7–7 Reliability and validity for this edition ranges from high 0.80s to high 0.90s.	Clinical judgment must be used to determine when this test is appropriate for older age group and when WISC-V is appropriate.
AGS Early Screening Profiles	Include both direct and indirect assessment across multiple situations and skills	Low to adequate reliability and validity coefficients
Kaufman Survey of Early Academic and Language Skills	Expands the language sections of the *AGS Early Screening Profiles* Offers expanded analysis of articulation errors	Subtest coefficients low to adequate
BRIGANCE® Screens	Assesses across various ages; criterion-referenced; provides parent and teacher rating system	Norms could be expanded
Developmental Indicators for the Assessment of Learning, Fourth Edition	Spanish and English versions; parent questionnaire included; fairly comprehensive	More detailed information on technical quality could be provided with instrument

● PHONEMIC AWARENESS

Regulations require that the young child's level of functioning in the areas of physical development, cognitive development, communication development, social or emotional development, and adaptive development be addressed during the assessment process. Assessment in these areas provides information for educational personnel about how to implement interventions necessary for childhood development and future educational success. One skill area that may assist assessment personnel in understanding the preschool child's readiness for academic tasks is the area of phonemic awareness. A child with this skill is able to differentiate the separate sounds in spoken words. This awareness is a conscious awareness that words are made up of *phonemes,* or sounds (Snider, 1995).

The skills involved in being able to distinguish discrete sounds in words are important in learning to read (Turnbull et al., 2002). A comprehensive review of the literature regarding the effects of instruction in phonemic awareness on reading skills indicated that both word-reading skills and reading comprehension improved with phonemic awareness (Ehri et al., 2001). Research also suggests that early interventions that promote phonemic awareness may reduce the number of young students referred for special education services (Lennon & Slesinski, 1999).

Phonemic awareness is a composite of subskills and tasks that can be assessed by informal methods. For example, the skills of phonemic synthesis or blending of sounds, phonemic analysis or breaking words into sounds, rhyming, and substitution can all be evaluated informally by educators in the early childhood classroom setting (Snider, 1995). Assessment of subskills in preschool, such as rhyming, have been found to be significant predictors of later reading skills in first-grade readers (Missall et al., 2007). Specific tasks used to assess phonemic awareness listed by Ehri et al. (2001, p. 251) include the following:

1. Phonemic isolation, which requires recognizing individual sounds in words; for example, "Tell me the first sound in *paste*." (*/p/*)

2. Phoneme identity, which requires recognizing the common sound in different words; for example, "Tell me the sound that is the same in *bike, boy*, and *bell*." (*/b/*)

3. Phoneme categorization, which requires recognizing the word with the odd sound in a sequence of three or four words; for example, "Which word does not belong: *bus, bun, rug?*" (*rug*)

4. Phoneme blending, which requires listening to a sequence of separately spoken sounds and combining them to form a recognizable word; for example, "What word is */s//k//u//l/?*" (*school*)

5. Phoneme segmentation, which requires breaking the word into its sounds by tapping out or counting the sounds or by pronouncing and positioning a marker for each sound; for example, "How many phonemes in *sip?*" (3: */s//i//p/*)

6. Phoneme deletion, which requires recognizing what word remains when a specified phoneme is removed; for example, "What is *smile* without */s/?*" (*mile*).

An informal instrument for assessing phonemic awareness was constructed by Snider (1997). For example, on Snider's instrument, the child is asked to say the sounds in words, such as "say the sounds in cat," and then asked what word remains when a specific sound is omitted. The child might be asked what word remains if the /b/ sound is taken away from "bake." This instrument is but one example of instruments that assess emerging reading skills, and may be used to measure phonemic awareness in kindergarten students.

Preacademic reading skills, such as identifying the sounds of letters or rhyming, may be assessed using many of the instruments previously presented in this text, such as the *Woodcock Reading Mastery Test–Revised,* and instruments designed for use with preschool children, such as the *Developmental Indicators for the Assessment of Learning,* Third Edition (*DIAL–3*), and the *Kaufman Brief Survey of Early Academic and Language Skills.* The *Woodcock–Johnson III Tests of Achievement* include a subtest titled Sound Awareness that contains rhyming, deletion, and substitution sections. The *Wechsler Individual Achievement Test II* includes items that assess rhyming and ability to determine words with the same initial and ending sounds. These instruments may assist educators in determining how a student compares to a

CHECK YOUR UNDERSTANDING

Complete Activity 11.5 to determine your understanding of assessing early phonemic skills.

norm sample population as well as in determining which prereading skills the child has mastered.

● ASSESSMENT OF CHILDREN REFERRED FOR AUTISM SPECTRUM DISORDERS

The number of children with autism and autism spectrum disorders has been increasing in recent years. The Centers for Disease Control and Prevention (CDC) estimates that approximately 1 in every 110 children has an autism spectrum disorder (CDC, 2010). These disorders are categorized as *pervasive developmental disorders* and include three primary areas of potential impairment: (1) communication delays or abnormalities, (2) difficulties with social reciprocity or interactions with people, and (3) patterns of unusual or repetitive behaviors (American Psychiatric Association, 2000). Autism disorders are typically manifested by the age of 3 but may not be recognized or diagnosed until later ages because of a variety of complicating issues (Overton, Fielding, & Garcia de Alba, 2007).

One early indication that a child might have an autism spectrum disorder is that the child fails to have the social communication skills expected of a youngster (Filipek et al., 1999). These skills are expected to develop during the early toddler years, and therefore children who do not begin to develop these skills may be referred for assessments during this developmental period. Although children may be assessed prior to their 3rd birthday, generally speaking, the younger the child, the less reliable the assessment results. This lack of reliability at younger ages reflects the differences in development that occur during the early years.

The assessment of autism spectrum disorders, like other types of assessment for potential disabilities, involves observations and data collection from a variety of sources and environments. Moreover, the assessment of children referred for autism spectrum disorders should be developmentally appropriate, as suggested by the DEC (Sandall, Hemmeter, Smith, & McLean, 2005). Data should be collected from parents, early childhood caregivers, teachers, and, most important, from direct assessment of the child. These methods should include rating scales, interviews, observations in the natural environment (home or early childhood classroom or daycare setting), and age-appropriate assessment with specific diagnostic instruments for children referred for autism spectrum disorders. The following are selected screening and diagnostic instruments.

Gilliam Autism Rating Scale–3 (GARS–3)

The *GARS–3* (Gilliam, 2014) is a rating scale that can be used as a first-step screening assessment for children who are suspected of having characteristics of an autism spectrum disorder. Persons 3 years to 22 years of age can be screened with this instrument. The *GARS–3* may be completed by parents, teachers, or other professionals who know the child. This instrument has increased the number of items and now reflects the diagnostic revision criteria of the *Diagnostic and Statistical Manual*, Fifth Edition (American Psychiatric Association, 2013). It requires approximately 10 minutes to complete. Six subscales are provided in this latest revision for assessing the areas of autism spectrum disorders including Restrictive/Repetitive Behaviors, Social Interaction, Social Communication, Emotional Responses, Cognitive Style, and Maladaptive Speech. More than 1,859 children were included in the norming of the *GARS–3*, and the sample was modeled on U.S. 2011 Census data. The internal reliability information includes reliability coefficients for subscales and indexes that range from 0.85 to 0.93. Interrater reliability coefficients are within the low to mid-0.80s. The authors report high specificity and sensitivity coefficients.

PDD Behavior Inventory (PDD–BI)

The *PDD–BI* is a rating system that includes a form to be completed by the teacher and a form to be completed by the parent. Children as young as 18 months can be assessed using this indirect rating form. The rating system includes several subscales that measure both positive symptoms (those associated with autism spectrum disorders) and negative symptoms (those not associated with autism spectrum disorders). The rating forms are divided into two sections: Approach/Withdrawal Problems and Receptive/ Expressive Social Communication Abilities. Within each section are several subscales, including positive affect behaviors, gestural approach behaviors, social play behaviors, imaginative play, receptive language competence, and associative learning skills. Scores are yielded in the following domains: Sensory/ Perceptual Approach Behaviors, Ritualisms/Resistance to Change, Social Pragmatic Problems, Semantic/Pragmatic Problems, Arousal Regulation Problems, Specific Fears, Social Approach Behaviors, Expressive Language, and Learning, Memory, and Receptive Language. The information derived from assessment using this instrument can assist in educational planning for children with autism spectrum disorders.

Standardization was conducted with a sample of 277 teachers who rated children from 18 months to 12 years and 5 months of age and 369 parents of the same children rated by the teachers. Variables considered parental education and ethnicity, diagnosis of the child, and how the diagnosis was confirmed (e.g., through the use of the *ADOS* or the *ADI–R*).

The *PDD–BI* examiner's manual provides information about reliability and validity research on the rating scales. Evidence of reliability includes research on internal consistency, test–retest reliability, and interrater reliability. All reliability coefficients are adequate to high. Validity information includes research on the intercorrelations among the domains, factor analysis of the domains, developmental validity, and criterion-related validity. Factor analysis provides evidence of a two-factor structure with one factor measuring social avoidance, aggression, and asocial behaviors with the other factor measuring approach behaviors. The items assessing semantics and pragmatics were less clear on both factors. Criterion-related validity results were mixed depending on the instruments that were compared. For example, criterion-related validity was found to be stronger when like instruments were compared, such as other measures of parental interviews compared with the parentalrating form of the *PDD–BI*.

Childhood Autism Rating Scale, Second Edition (CARS2)

The *CARS2* (Schopler, Van Bourgondien, Wellman, & Love, 2010) features three versions for use in the assessment of children who display the characteristic behaviors of autism spectrum disorders. These are the Standard Version, the High-Functioning Version Rating Booklet, and the Parent/Caregiver Questionnaire, which may add information to assist in the use of the other forms. Each of the rating forms contains 15 items. The Standard Version is recommended for use with children who are 6 years of age or younger. The items provide a means of rating the child on indicators such as adaptation to change, relating to people, and imitation. On each item, the child's behavior is rated for severity and duration. This new edition of the *CARS* provides information to assist in making educational recommendations.

Autism Diagnostic Observation Schedule (ADOS-2)

The *ADOS* has been referred to as the "gold standard" in the assessment of autism spectrum disorders. The revision of the *ADOS*, the *ADOS-2*, now includes the following modules for administration:

Toddler Module—Designed to be used for children from ages 1 year to 30 months of age.

Module 1: This module can be used for children at ages 31 months and older who lack the consistent use of phrases in their communication with others.

Module 2: Designed for use with a child of any age who has phrase speech but whose speech lacks the typical fluency expected for his or her developmental level.

Module 3: For children who maintain consistent verbal fluency in their daily communications and who range in age from early childhood through adolescence.

Module 4: This module is administered to verbally fluent older adolescents and adults.

This instrument provides a method for direct assessment of children and adults who manifest the characteristics of autism. The *ADOS* assesses all behavioral areas of autism; however, cut-off scores are provided only for abnormalities in communication and in reciprocal social interactions (Lord, Rutter, DiLavore, & Risi, 2002). In order to assess repetitive stereotyped behaviors, additional assessments such as the *Autism Diagnostic Interview–Revised* (Rutter, LeCourteur, & Lord, 2002) should be administered. The *ADOS* has four levels, or modules, of administration.

This instrument sets up various interactions to observe how a child interacts with the examiner and the stimulus materials. Specific behaviors that are associated with the characteristic of autism disorders are noted during the administration. Because administration of the *ADOS* requires great skill and because the test requires complex scoring, it is recommended that a team of professionals administer the instrument and discuss the behavioral score for each item following administration. Although not required, it is also recommended that administration of the instrument be recorded on video so that the behaviors in question can be reviewed during the scoring process.

The *ADOS* was developed using the results obtained from earlier versions of the instrument, the *Pre-Linguistic Autism Diagnostic Observation Schedule (PL–ADOS)* (DiLavore, Lord, & Rutter, 1995), and the 1989 version of the *ADOS* (Lord et al., 1989). The current *ADOS* includes items from these earlier versions and additional items developed to assess older and more verbal individuals (Lord et al., 2002).

The *ADOS* was developed primarily by using results of samples of children who were referred for evaluations for potential developmental disorders (Lord et al., 2012). Results from clinical centers were combined, and the final sample upon which the *ADOS* was validated included all English-speaking children and adults. Ethnicity of the sample was 80% white, 11% African American, 4% Hispanic, 2% Asian American, and 2% other or mixed ethnic groups. Information provided in the manual includes summary statistics for all four modules for autistic, pervasive developmental disorder—not otherwise specified (PDD-NOS), and non-spectrum children and adults. Consistency was researched on the instrument by analysis of test–retest, interrater reliability, and internal consistency across all groups for the four modules. Additional reliability and validity information is provided for the Toddler Module.

The Autism Diagnostic Interview–Revised (ADI–R)

The *ADI–R* (Rutter et al., 2002), is an extensive clinical interview that should be completed by a professional trained in conducting interviews. In the school setting, the person most likely to conduct this type of interview is the school psychologist, counselor, or clinical social worker. The interview may take up to 2.5 hours. The results of the interview can assist the clinical team in (1) determining if the referred child has an autistic spectrum disorder and (2) knowing what additional data may need to be collected. The *ADI–R* includes questions about early behaviors that may be characteristic of an autistic spectrum disorder. For example, there are several questions about regression of language skills and repetitive behavior patterns. These items are not accounted for in the scoring of the *ADOS,* and therefore it is recommended that both the *ADOS* and the *ADI–R* be used in evaluation. These instruments, used in conjunction with other assessment techniques, are helpful in determining the specific disorder that may exist and can provide data to determine if more than one disorder is present (Overton et al., 2007). For example, children with autism may also exhibit symptoms of anxiety or depression. The team should employ a variety of methods to determine if the child has more than one area of concern.

● ASSISTIVE TECHNOLOGY AND ASSESSMENT

Assistive technology is a term that is used to designate any device that a student requires to function within the academic environment. Such devices range from a specially designed spoon for eating to computer software that can transfer spoken language to written language. Assistive technology may also include computer software programs that are necessary for instructional purposes because of the specific type of disability manifested by the child.

In order to determine if any assistive technology devices may be required for a student with special needs, an **assistive technology evaluation** is conducted. This evaluation should be conducted by professionals who are knowledgeable about such techniques and equipment and how to use them. Evaluation should include assessing the student's method of mobility, fine- and gross-motor needs, visual and auditory perceptual needs, accessibility needs to function within the environment, computer technology needs, communication needs, and any other area in which the child may require assistive devices.

Before any actual devices are selected, the student's general cognitive ability should be considered so that developmentally appropriate techniques and devices are employed. Once the student's assistive technology needs are determined, evaluation must consider how the actual devices will be used within the environment. The student also may need accommodations in order to use the devices. It is important that all devices be tested with the student so that it can be determined that selected devices fit the student's needs. All of these considerations will promote the student's access to the general educational curriculum. The techniques and equipment that are required for a successful education should be documented in the student's IEP. It is imperative that the team monitor the student's use of and success with any assistive technology deemed necessary for his or her academic success. As pointed out by Bryant (1998), part of follow-up should include assessing the teacher's understanding and skill in using the assistive technology in the school setting.

Read the following case.

CHECK YOUR UNDERSTANDING

Check your understanding of assessment for children who are referred for possible autism spectrum disorders by completing Activity 11.6.

Case Study

Javier is 4 years and 7 months of age. Realizing that their son would soon enter kindergarten, his parents were concerned that he was not developmentally ready to begin school. Javier had been at home during his infancy and preschool years and had not attended any preschool settings. He lives with both parents and his father's mother who cares for Javier when the parents are working. Javier was small for his age, seemed to be somewhat behind in motor skills and language development. Javier does not have any siblings but he does have seven cousins who live nearby. Javier enjoys activities that involve his cousins; however, he often plays beside his cousins rather than engaging in interactive play. Javier uses no sentences when he communicates and only recently began using phrases. His use of language is limited mostly to asking for things he wants or needs such as "me cookie" or "go outside?"

After meeting with school personnel, Javier's parents agreed to a comprehensive evaluation to determine if Javier would benefit from interventions. Here are the scores he obtained on the WPPSI:

> Verbal Comprehension Index 82
>
> Visual-Spatial Index 82
>
> Fluid Reasoning Index 80
>
> Working Memory Index 78
>
> Processing Speed 78
>
> Full Scale IQ 80

Following the cognitive assessment, the school psychologist also completed the DIAL-4 with input from Javier's parents.

> Motor 88
>
> Concepts 82
>
> Language 82
>
> Self-Help Skills 84
>
> Social-Emotional 82

CHECK YOUR UNDERSTANDING

Once you have completed reading about this young child, complete the questions for Activity 11.7 to demonstrate how the evaluation results can assist in educational planning.

CHAPTER SUMMARY

In this chapter you:

- Learned the legal history and regulations for early childhood special education
- Applied knowledge of early childhood evaluation techniques to interventions
- Analyzed evaluation results to determine the developmental strengths, weaknesses, and needs
- Synthesized evaluation results to plan effective interventions
- Evaluated case scenarios to select appropriate evaluation techniques

THINK AHEAD

Educators must be prepared to administer and interpret assessment instruments across grade levels. In the next chapter, you will learn the methods and instruments used in assessing secondary age students to determine transition needs for educational planning.

CHAPTER QUIZ

Complete the Chapter Quiz to assess your understanding of the considerations of assessing young children with developmental concerns.

12 Special Considerations of Transition

CHAPTER FOCUS

In this chapter you will:

- Learn transition assessment methods and techniques and the legal requirements for transition planning

- Apply case scenario assessment information to address transition planning

- Analyze transition assessment data to address legal requirements of transition assessment

- Synthesize the case scenario data for transition planning

- Evaluate assessment methods for transition planning

● TRANSITION AND POSTSECONDARY CONSIDERATIONS

In addition to the general legal requirements stated in the Individuals with Disabilities Education Act (IDEA) 2004 amendments for individualized education programs (IEPs) and assessment (see Chapter 2), there are requirements that focus on transition planning and transition assessment. Beginning in February 2011, school districts are required to report to the U.S. Department of Education the number of students who are in the transition process.

The important component for teachers of students of transition age is the requirement for age-appropriate transition assessment. The transition assessment must drive both planning and postsecondary goals. As stated in the law, transition planning must include courses of study, such as appropriate curriculum, and interventions that will increase the likelihood that the student will be able to meet carefully planned postsecondary goals. The mandate states that other persons, such as representatives from private companies or agencies, may participate in transition planning with the consent of the parent; students who have attained the age of majority (age 18 in many states) retain the right of consent to the presence of an outside agent at the planning meeting.

Transition assessment should include assessment of academic performance. It should also include functional assessment related to the skills needed to meet postsecondary goals, and, when appropriate, assessment of independent living skills and behavior. As can be expected, this comprehensive assessment will employ multiple methods, multiple informants, and multiple settings. It will likely include formal, standardized academic assessment, curriculum-based assessment, observations, authentic assessment, interviews, and questionnaires. Parents should be involved in the collection of data from interviews and surveys, and they should be included in all transition planning prior to the student's reaching the age of majority. When students reach their majority, they may opt to include their parents in the planning process.

Transition planning must be incorporated into the student's IEP and updated each year, with specific references to postsecondary goals and the measures that will need to be taken to meet those goals. By the time the student reaches age 16 (or sooner, if determined necessary for the transition goals set out by the IEP team), the IEP must include information regarding agencies that will need to be involved in the student's transition and the responsibilities of those agencies.

As indicated in the federal requirements, schools must provide evidence that students are invited to participate in their transition planning. To assist schools in documenting that this criterion has been complied with, the National Secondary Transition Technical Assistance Center has designed checklists that may be used during the development of the IEP. These checklists are presented in Figure 12.1 and Figure 12.2.

One year before the student reaches the age of majority expressed in state law, she or he must be informed of the rights that will be transferred to her or him upon attainment. This is to be acknowledged in a statement on the IEP.

Transition Assessment

Transition assessment should use methodologies that will identify and document the student's strengths and needs as stated in IDEA. Because the law requires that assessment also determine the student's preferences and interests, it is necessary to think about transition assessment as more comprehensive than that which is used to determine a specific academic weakness, such as poor reading comprehension. Assessment will drive the program the student will participate in; it will also determine in large measure the postsecondary goals and outcomes that will lead to the student's

FIGURE 12.1 IEP Checklist

NSTTAC Indicator 13 Checklist Form A
(Meets Minimum SPP/APR Requirements)

Percent of youth with IEPs aged 16 and above with an IEP that includes appropriate measurable postsecondary goals that are annually updated and based upon an age appropriate transition assessment, transition services, including courses of study, that will reasonably enable the student to meet those postsecondary goals, and annual IEP goals related to the student's transition services needs. There also must be evidence that the student was invited to the IEP Team meeting where transition services are to be discussed and evidence that, if appropriate, a representative of any participating agency was invited to the IEP Team meeting with the prior consent of the parent or student who has reached the age of majority. (20 U.S.C. I4I6(a)(3)(B))

1. Is there an appropriate measurable postsecondary goal or goals that covers education or training, employment, and, as needed, independent living?	Y N
Can the goal(s) be counted? Will the goal(s) occur *after* the student graduates from school? Based on the information available about this student, does (do) the postsecondary goal(s) seem appropriate for this student? • If *yes* to all three, then circle Y OR if a postsecondary goal(s) is (are) *not* stated, circle N	
2. Is (are) the postsecondary goal(s) updated annually?	Y N
Was (were) the postsecondary goal(s) addressed/updated in conjunction with the development of the current IEP? • If *yes.* then circle Y OR If the postsecondary goal(s) was (were) *not* updated with the current IEP. circle N	
3. Is there evidence that the measurable postsecondary goal(s) were based on age appropriate transition assessment?	Y N
Is the use of transition assessment(s) for the postsecondary goal(s) mentioned in the IEP or evident in the student's file? • If *yes.* then circle Y OR if *no.* then circle N	
4. Are there transition services in the IEP that will reasonably enable the student to meet his or her postsecondary goal(s)?	Y N
Is a type of *instruction, related service, community experience, or development of employment and other post-school adult living objectives, and if appropriate, acquisition of daily living skills, and provision of a functional vocational evaluation* listed in association with meeting the post-secondary goal(s)? • If *yes,* then circle Y OR if *no,* then circle N	
5. Do the transition services include courses of study that will reasonably enable the student to meet his or her postsecondary goal(s)?	Y N
Do the transition services include courses of study that align with the student's postsecondary goal(s)? • If *yes,* then circle Y OR if *no,* then circle N	
6. Is (are) there annual IEP goal(s) related to the student's transition services needs?	Y N
Is (are) an annual goal(s) included in the IEP that is/are related to the student's transition services needs? • If *yes.* then circle Y OR if *no,* then circle N	
7. Is there evidence that the student was invited to the IEP Team meeting where transition services were discussed?	Y N
For the current year, is there documented evidence in the IEP or cumulative folder that the student was invited to attend the IEP Team meeting? • If *yes.* then circle Y OR if *no.* then circle N	
8. If appropriate, is there evidence that a representative of any participating agency was invited to the IEP Team meeting with the prior consent of the parent or student who has reached the age of majority?	Y N NA
For the current year, is there evidence in the IEP that representatives of any of the following agencies/services were invited to participate in the IEP development including but not limited to: *postsecondary education, vocational education, integrated employment (including supported employment), continuing and adult education, adult services, independent living or community participation* for this post-secondary goal? Was consent obtained from the parent (or student, for a student the age of majority)? • If *yes* to both, then circle Y • If *no* invitation is evident and a participating agency is likely to be responsible for providing or paying for transition services and there was consent to invite them to the IEP meeting, then circle N • If it is too early to determine if the student will need outside agency involvement, or no agency is likely to provide or pay for transition services, circle NA • If parent or individual student consent (when appropriate) was *not* provided, circle NA	
Does the IEP meet the requirements of Indicator 13? (Circle one) **Yes** (all Ys or NAs for each item (1–8) on the Checklist or **No** (one or more Ns circled)	

Source: From National Secondary Transition Technical Assistance Center (2009). Used with permission.

FIGURE 12.2 IEP Checklist

NSTTAC Indicator 13 Checklist: Form B (Enhanced for Professional Development)

Percent of youth with IEPs aged 16 and above with an IEP that includes appropriate measurable postsecondary goals that are annually updated and based upon an age appropriate transition assessment, transition services, including courses of study, that will reasonably enable the student to meet those postsecondary goals, and annual IEP goals related to the student's transition services needs. There also must be evidence that the student was invited to the IEP Team meeting where transition services are to be discussed and evidence that, if appropriate, a representative of any participating agency was invited to the IEP Team meeting with the prior consent of the parent or student who has reached the age of majority. (20 U.S.C. 1416(a)(3)(B))

Questions	Postsecondary Goals		
	Education/ Training	Employment	Independent Living
1. Is there an appropriate measurable postsecondary goal or goals in this area?	Y N	Y N	Y N NA
Can the goal(s) be counted? Will the goal(s) occur *after* the student graduates from school? Based on the information available about this student, does (do) the postsecondary goal(s) seem appropriate for this student? • If *yes* to all three, then circle Y OR if a postsecondary goal(s) is (are) *not* stated. circle N			
2. Is (are) the postsecondary goal(s) updated annually?	Y N	Y N	Y N NA
Was (were) the postsecondary goal(s) addressed/updated in conjunction with the development of the current IEP? • If *yes*. then circle Y OR If the postsecondary goal(s) was (were) *not* updated with the current IEP. circle N			
3. Is there evidence that the measurable postsecondary goal(s) were based on age appropriate transition assessment?	Y N	Y N	Y N
Is the use of transition assessment(s) for the postsecondary goal(s) mentioned in the IEP or evident in the student's file? • If *yes*, then circle Y OR if *no*. then circle N			
4. Are there transition services in the IEP that will reasonably enable the student to meet his or her postsecondary goal(s)?	Y N	Y N	Y N
Is a type of *instruction, related service, community experience, or development of employment and other post-school adult living objectives, and if appropriate, acquisition of daily living skills, and provision of a functional vocational evaluation* listed in association with meeting the postsecondary goal(s)? • If *yes*, then circle Y OR if *no*. then circle N			
5. Do the transition services include courses of study that will reasonably enable the student to meet his or her postsecondary goal(s)?	Y N	Y N	Y N
Do the transition services include courses of study that align with the student's postsecondary goal(s)? • If *yes*, then circle Y OR if *no*. then circle N			
6. Is (are) there annual IEP goal(s) related to the student's transition services needs?	Y N	Y N	Y N
Is (are) an annual goal(s) included in the IEP that is/are related to the student's transition services needs? • If *yes*, then circle Y OR if *no*. then circle N			
7. Is there evidence that the student was invited to the IEP Team meeting where transition services were discussed?	Y N	Y N	Y N
For the current year, is there documented evidence in the IEP or cumulative folder that the student was invited to attend the IEP Team meeting? • If *yes*, then circle Y OR if *no*. then circle N			
8. If appropriate, is there evidence that a representative of any participating agency was invited to the IEP Team meeting with the prior consent of the parent or student who has reached the age of majority?	Y N NA	Y N NA	Y N NA
For the current year, is there evidence in the IEP that representatives of any of the following agencies/services were invited to participate in the IEP development including but not limited to: *postsecondary education, vocational education, integrated employment (including supported employment), continuing and adult education, adult services, independent living or community participation* for this post-secondary goal? Was consent obtained from the parent (or student, for a student the age of majority)? • If *yes* to both, then circle Y • If *no* invitation is evident and a participating agency is Likely to be responsible for providing or paying for transition services and there was consent to invite them to the IEP meeting, then circle N • If it is too early to determine if the student will need outside agency involvement, or no agency is likely to provide or pay for transition services, circle NA • If parent or individual student consent (when appropriate) was *not* provided, circle NA			

Does the IEP meet the requirements of Indicator 13? (Circle one)

Yes (all Ys or NAs for each item [1-8] on the checklist included in the IEP are circled)   or   **No** (one or more Ns circled)

Source: From National Secondary Transition Technical Assistance Center (2009). Used with permission.

autonomy and employment. In short, transition assessment data can inform the committee about the student's strengths and weaknesses, laying the foundation for specific, measurable goals as she or he moves into the wider world. Figures 12.1 and 12.2 provide guidance on this transition assessment process.

Transition assessment should address all areas of transition planning for specific programs. Kohler (1996) offers a taxonomy for transition planning that incorporates five criteria: (1) student-focused planning, (2) family involvement, (3) student development, (4) program structure, and (5) interagency collaboration. In order to write measureable goals for a transition program, students should be assessed in areas that relate to effective transition programs. For example, to determine if a student is able to participate in the planning process, it is important to determine that the student knows and understands self-advocacy, and the meaning and purpose of the IEP, the IEP process, the meaning of the term "age of majority," and other concepts that are inherent in the process. *Student development* refers to the student's ability to live as independently as possible, to practice functional academic and daily living skills, and to participate in postsecondary training in developing the skills needed for employment. The IEP team must ensure that other concerns, such as interagency collaboration, case management, family participation, program availability, and program planning and access, are also addressed.

The National Secondary Transition Technical Assistance Center (n.d.) suggests that the following types of assessment be administered for transition purposes when appropriate: work-related temperament scales, behavioral assessment, aptitude assessment, achievement assessment, intellectual assessment, career-readiness assessment, self-determination assessment, preferences tests, personality tests, and career inventories. Each of these types of instruments, in addition to informal observations, interviews, and informal curriculum-based assessments, can provide valuable information to assist in transition planning. Because the goal of transition assessment is to determine the student's strengths and interests and link those to postsecondary goals, the assessment process is quite different than assessment for special education eligibility.

The increased accountability set forth by federal regulations also requires that states report the outcome of students following their transition. In other words, districts must now account for the success of students or the results of their transition training. This includes students who are employed or who are in postsecondary schools or postsecondary training within 1 year after completing high school. This underscores the importance of well-planned programs that must be based on accurate transition assessment.

The reporting of postsecondary outcomes is one measure of effectiveness or accountability. This is an important concept that should drive program improvements. Figure 12.3 presents the percentage of students with disabilities who were employed when surveyed 1 to 4 years after completing high school.

Another indication of how successfully postsecondary outcomes for students with disabilities are being met is the duration of their employment. In Figure 12.4, the duration of employment of individuals with and without disabilities is presented. As can be seen, students with disabilities who participated in this study did not seem to remain employed as long as individuals without disabilities.

Linking Transition Assessment to Transition Services

Federal regulations expressed in IDEA 2004 require that transition services are results oriented, that is, focused on outcomes for the student after high school. They further require that transition services be based on the student's needs as related to assessed strengths, preferences, and interests. Transition planning must include objectives for employment, postsecondary education or training, and daily living, as appropriate. Statements regarding any necessary related services or special education support must also be included as needed.

FIGURE 12.3 Students with Disabilities Who Were Employed 1–4 Years after High School

Employment status	Learning disability	Speech/ language impairment	Mental retarda- tion	Emotio- nal distur- bance	Hearing impair- ment	Visual impair- ment	Ortho- pedic im- pairment	Other health im- pairment	Autism	Traumatic brain injury	Multiple disabilities	Deaf- blindness
					Percentage							
Percentage reported to have been:												
Employed at time of interview	63.6	57.5	31.0	42.3	53.9	42.7	27.3	67.8	46.9	43.4	48.8	‡
	(5.64)	(6.15)	(6.05)	(5.98)	(7.27)	(8.95)	(6.04)	(5.45)	(10.18)	(12.63)	(11.04)	
Employed since high school	77.2	72.8	51.8	63.4	65.5	59.9	39.5	79.9	66.4	62.5	50.4	50.5
	(4.40)	(5.03)	(5.99)	(5.20)	(6.33)	(8.50)	(5.98)	(4.29)	(8.83)	(10.90)	(9.48)	(11.40)

‡Responses for items with fewer than 30 respondents are reported.
NOTE: Standard errors are in parentheses. NLTS2 percentages are weighted population estimates based on samples ranging from approximately 2,130 to 2,620 youth.

Source: U.S. Department of Education, Institute of Education Sciences, National Center for Special Education Research, National Longitudinal Transition Study-2 (NLTS2), Waves 2 and 3 parent interview and youth interview/survey, 2003 and 2005.

FIGURE 12.4 Duration of Employment: Postsecondary Youth with and without Disabilities

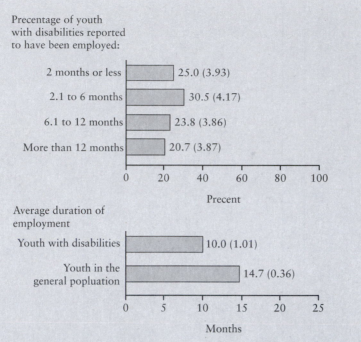

NOTE: Standard errors are in parentheses. Job characteristics are reported for youth out of high school from 1 to 4 years for youth's current or most recent job. NLTS2 percentages are weighted population estimates based on samples of approximately 1,420 youth for duration of employment.

---

2 Respondents were asked whether youth had had a paid job outside of the home within the past 2 years and, if so, whether they were currently employed. For those who were currently employed questions were asked about the current job; for those who were not currently employed, questions were asked about the youth's most recent job within the 2-year time frame. For reporting purposes, employment items were combined to reflect either the youth's current (at the time of the interview) or most recent job.

3 Respondents were asked, How long have you (has YOUTH) had this job?

Source: U.S. Department of Education, Institute of Education Sciences, National Center for Special Education Research, National Longitudinal Transition Study-2 (NLTS2), Waves 2 and 3 parent interview and youth interview/survey, 2003 and 2005. U.S. Department of Labor, Bureau of Labor Statistics, National Longitudinal Survey of Youth 1997 (NLSY97), round 5 youth questionnaire, 2001. Data are for 17- to 21-year-olds.

Research on effective practices in transition programs indicates that some aspects of special education programming and vocational/life skills instruction have positive predictive power on outcomes such as independent living and employment (National Secondary Transition Assistance Center, n.d.). For example, programs that include instruction in independent living skills were moderate predictors of success for independent living and had potential effects for employment. It is clear that transition planning requires careful assessment of academic and independent living skills. In their review of evidence-based practices, Test, Fowler, White, Richter, and Walker (2009) noted that evidence-based effective programs that engage students in meaningful learning that they can connect with their future ability to succeed as an adult had a positive impact on dropout prevention. It was also clear to these researchers that programs that actively involve students in transition planning and the IEP process and career programs that promote awareness and teach skill development, functional academics, specific coursework for vocational success, and functional behavior strategies are more likely to be effective.

The emphasis on transition services that assist students in their movement from school to adult life is a reflection of the data indicating negative outcomes for students with disabilities (Levinson, 1995; U.S. Department of Education, 1999; U.S. Department of Education Office of Special Education and Rehabilitative Services, 2009). The number of students with disabilities graduating from high school with a standard diploma has increased to 54.5% (U.S. Department of Education Office of Special Education and Rehabilitative Services, 2009). The remaining 45.5% of students with disabilities who leave high school receive a certificate of completion, reach the maximum age for services, or simply drop out of school. Students with disabilities who are least likely to receive a high school diploma are students with emotional disturbance, mental retardation, multiple disabilities, autism, and deaf/blindness. The high school completion rate varies by state and by reason. Table 12.1 provides information regarding students with disabilities and the reasons they exit the public school setting and the percentage of students with disabilities who transferred into general education. Examine the table to determine the rate of students with exceptional learning needs who graduated during the 2005–2006 year. Other reasons that students exited the public school system are also included.

One factor that may influence the number of students with disabilities who graduate from high school is the requirement by some states of exit examinations as criteria for graduation. Research indicates that students with disabilities are less likely to graduate if they are required to pass a high school exit examination. This finding was consistent regardless of the disability category; however, it proved to be most significant for students with intellectual disabilities and speech and language impairments (Thurlow, Ysseldyke, & Anderson, 1995). This situation may continue: Recall that the 1997 IDEA amendments mandate that the assessment of students with disabilities be consistent with the assessment of students without disabilities.

The disability category plays a role in the successful completion of high school. In Table 12.1, it can be seen that the dropout percentages vary by disability category. The information in this table indicates that the number of students with disabilities who complete high school has increased; however, for the categories of emotional disturbance, high school graduation continues to be a challenge.

● ASSESSMENT OF TRANSITION NEEDS

The focus of the assessment process for students nearing their teen years should change to reflect postsecondary school needs. The student's levels of functioning should be determined so that her or his needs in the areas of education, vocational training or employment, supported employment, community experiences, and adult daily living skills can be identified. IEP goals and objectives must include those that will allow the student to enter the adult world as independently as possible.

Research regarding best practice for transition assessment and planning has shown that the most successful transition plans result from involvement of both students and parents in the assessment and planning process (Brotherson, Berdine, 1993; Thoma, Rogan, & Baker, 2001). Student participation necessitates teaching students how to advocate for their needs or use the skills of self-determination (Lindsey, Wehmeyer, Guy, & Martin, 2001). *Self-determination* has been defined as "a combination of skills, knowledge, and beliefs that enable a person to engage in goal-directed, self-regulated, autonomous behavior" (Field, Martin, Miller, Ward, & Wehmeyer, 1998, p. 2). In order to assist students with their transition needs, educators must assess their self-advocacy skills.

Assessment of self-determination may include data collection from the student, the teacher, and the parent. Hoffman, Field, and Sawilowsky (2004) have constructed a series of instruments for this purpose, the *Self-Determination Battery* (available from http://www.ghaea.org/index.php?option=com_content&view=article&id=412%3 Atransition-planning-field-hoffman-self-determination-assessment-battery& catid=16&Itemid=105) that includes scales for students, parents, and teachers. A sample of the items from the battery is presented in Table 12.2. The items assess the student's

TABLE 12.1

Percentages of students ages 14 through 21 exiting IDEA, Part B, and school who graduated with a regular high school diploma or dropped out of school, by year and state: 2007–08 and 2010–11

State	2007–08		2010–11		Change Between 2007–08 and 2010–11[a]		Percent Change Between 2007–08 and 2010–11[b]	
	Graduated[c]	Dropped Out[d]	Graduated[c]	Dropped Out[d]	Graduated[c]	Dropped Out[d]	Graduated[c]	Dropped Out[d]
All states	59.0	24.6	63.6	20.1	4.5	-4.5	7.7	-18.2
Alabama	30.0	26.2	44.4	16.3	14.4	-9.9	48.1	-37.7
Alaska	47.1	37.9	48.5	34.7	1.4	-3.2	2.9	-8.4
Arizona	70.4	28.6	79.5	19.8	9.1	-8.8	12.9	-30.9
Arkansas	78.9	18.7	82.8	14.9	3.9	-3.8	5.0	-20.5
BIE schools	52.1	39.6	—	—	—	—	—	—
California	50.9	21.5	54.0	17.4	3.1	-4.1	6.1	-19.0
Colorado	62.9	31.6	66.4	29.9	3.5	-1.7	5.5	-5.5
Connecticut	77.8	18.4	80.2	16.5	2.4	-1.9	3.0	-10.2
Delaware	51.7	38.5	69.2	26.0	17.4	-12.5	33.7	-32.6
District of Columbia	—	—	52.4	38.9	—	—	—	—
Florida	45.2	26.5	53.3	20.0	8.1	-6.5	17.9	-24.7
Georgia	37.3	27.8	40.8	28.3	3.5	0.5	9.4	1.7
Hawaii	79.2	4.4	77.8	9.8	-1.4	5.4	-1.8	123.4
Idaho	48.9	26.2	34.6	15.9	-14.3	-10.4	-29.2	-39.6
Illinois	74.0	24.2	78.8	18.3	4.8	-5.9	6.5	-24.2
Indiana	55.3	29.8	75.0	11.5	19.7	-18.3	35.6	-61.5
Iowa	70.9	26.2	77.6	21.2	6.7	-5.0	9.5	-19.2
Kansas	70.2	27.9	78.8	18.5	8.7	-9.4	12.4	-33.6
Kentucky	67.4	23.3	74.1	14.5	6.7	-8.7	10.0	-37.5
Louisiana	26.6	45.9	28.8	37.2	2.2	-8.6	8.3	-18.8
Maine	69.8	25.3	75.7	20.6	5.9	-4.8	8.4	-18.9
Maryland	61.9	26.0	63.8	24.4	1.8	-1.5	3.0	-5.9

See notes at end of exhibit.

TABLE 12.1

Percentages of students ages 14 through 21 exiting IDEA, Part B, and school who graduated with a regular high school diploma or dropped out of school, by year and state: 2007–08 and 2010–11 (Continued)

State	Graduated with a Regular Diploma	Received a Certificate	Dropped Out	Reached Maximum Age	Died	Transferred to Regular Education	Moved, Known to Be Continuing[c]
Rhode Island	36.0	0.3	12.7	1.2	0.2	12.4	37.3
South Carolina	19.0	15.6	29.1	1.4	0.3	8.2	26.5
South Dakota	29.5	0.4	11.9	1.5	0.3	24.2	32.2
Tennessee	22.8	15.6	9.9	0.2	0.5	11.0	40.1
Texas	27.4	27.1	10.9	0.0	0.3	15.5	18.7
Utah	40.0	8.3	14.5	x	x	8.5	28.1
Vermont	37.1	0.8	17.0	0.9	0.5	16.3	27.4
Virginia	23.6	25.4	10.1	0.3	0.4	8.3	31.8
Washington	—	—	—	—	—	—	—
West Virginia	52.8	3.5	23.7	0.1	0.3	7.9	11.7
Wisconsin	57.7	1.9	15.7	1.5	0.4	15.4	7.4
Wyoming	34.0	1.3	18.6	x	x	27.6	17.4
All states	33.0	9.0	15.3	0.8	0.3	10.5	31.1

Source: U.S. Department of Education, Office of Special Education Programs, Data Analysis System (DANS), OMB #18200521: "Report of Children with Disabilities Exiting Special Education," 2005–06. Data were updated as of July 15, 2007. For actual data used, go to https://www.ideadata.org/Archive/ARCArchive.asp.

Notes: The U.S. Department of Education collects data on seven categories of exiters: five categories of exiters from both special education and school (i.e., *graduated with a regular high school diploma, received a certificate, dropped out, reached maximum age* for services and *died*) and two categories of exiters from special education, but not school (i.e., *transferred to regular education* and *moved, known to be continuing* in education). The seven categories are mutually exclusive.

[a]Percentage for each state was calculated by dividing the number of students ages 14 through 21 served under *IDEA*, Part B, in the exit reason category in the state by the total number of students ages 14 through 21 served under *IDEA*, Part B, in all the exiting categories in the state, then multiplying the result by 100. Percentage for "All states" was calculated by dividing the number of students ages 14 through 21 served under *IDEA*, Part B, in the exit reason category in all states with available data by the total number of students ages 14 through 21 served under *IDEA*, Part B, in all the exiting categories in all states with available data, then multiplying the result by 100. Percentage for "All states" includes suppressed data.

[b]Data are from the reporting period between July 1, 2005, and June 30, 2006.

[c]The *moved, known to be continuing* in education category includes exiters who moved out of the catchment area (e.g., state, school district) and are known to be continuing in an educational program. The catchment area is defined by the state education agency.

x Percentage cannot be calculated because data were suppressed to limit disclosure.

— Percentage cannot be calculated because data were not available.

Percentages of students ages 14 through 21 exiting IDEA, Part B, and school who graduated with a regular high school diploma or dropped out of school, by year and state: 2007–08 and 2010–11

State	2007–08		2010–11		Change between 2007–08 and 2010–11[a]		Percent change between 2007–08 and 2010–11[b]	
	Graduated[c]	Dropped Out[d]	Graduated[c]	Dropped Out[d]	Graduated[c]	Dropped Out[d]	Graduated[c]	Dropped Out[d]
West Virginia	65.0	27.4	68.2	21.4	3.2	-6.0	4.9	-21.9
Wisconsin	74.6	21.7	76.2	19.3	1.6	-2.4	2.2	-10.9
Wyoming	59.2	32.5	64.3	23.6	5.2	-8.9	8.7	-27.4

— Percentage cannot be calculated because data were not available.

Source: U.S. Department of Education, Office of Special Education Programs, Data Analysis System (DANS), OMB #1820-0521: "Report of Children with Disabilities Exiting Special Education," 2007–08 and 2010–11. Data for 2007–08 and 2010–11 were accessed spring 2012. Data for 2010–11 were accessed fall 2012. For actual data used, go to http://www.ed.gov/about/reports/annual/osep.

[a]Change between 2007–08 and 2010–11 was calculated for each state and "All states" by subtracting the percentage for 2007–08 from the percentage for 2010–11. Due to rounding, it may not be possible to reproduce the difference from the values presented in the exhibit.

[b]Percent change between 2007–08 and 2010–11 was calculated for each state and "All states" by subtracting the percentage for 2007–08 from the percentage for 2010–11, dividing the difference by the percentage for 2007–08, then multiplying the result by 100. Due to rounding, it may not be possible to reproduce the percent change from the values presented in the exhibit.

[c]*Graduated with a regular high school diploma* refers to students ages 14 through 21 served under *IDEA*, Part B, who exited an educational program through receipt of a high school diploma identical to that for which students without disabilities were eligible. These were students with disabilities who met the same standards for graduation as those for students without disabilities.

[d]*Dropped out* refers to students ages 14 through 21 served under *IDEA*, Part B, who were enrolled at the start of the reporting period, were not enrolled at the end of the reporting period, and did not exit special education through any other basis, such as *moved, known to be continuing*.

Note: The U.S. Department of Education collects data on seven categories of exiters from special education (i.e., the Part B program in which the student was enrolled at the start of the reporting period). The categories include five categories of exiters from both special education and school (i.e., *graduated with a regular high school diploma, received a certificate, dropped out, reached maximum age for services, and died*) and two categories of exiters from special education, but not school (i.e., *transferred to regular education and moved, known to be continuing in education*). The seven categories are mutually exclusive. This exhibit provides percentages for only two categories of exiters from both special education and school (i.e., *graduated with a regular high school diploma and dropped out*). For data on all seven categories of exiters, see exhibit 69. Percentage for each state was calculated by dividing the number of students ages 14 through 21 served under *IDEA*, Part B, by the state who were reported in the exit reason category for the year by the total number of students ages 14 through 21 served under *IDEA*, Part B, by the state who were reported in the five exit-from-both-special-education-and-school categories for that year, then multiplying the result by 100. Percentage for "All states" was calculated for all states with available data by dividing the number of students ages 14 through 21 served under *IDEA*, Part B, by all states who were reported in the exit reason category for the year by the total number of students ages 14 through 21 served under *IDEA*, Part B, by all states who were reported in the five exit-from-both-special-education-and-school categories for that year, then multiplying the result by 100. The percentages of students who exited special education and school by graduating and dropping out included in this report are not comparable to the graduation and dropout rates required under the *Elementary and Secondary Education Act of 1965*, as amended (*ESEA*). The factors used to calculate percentages of students who exited special education and school by graduating and dropping out are different from those used to calculate graduation and dropout rates. In particular, states often rely on factors such as the number of students who graduated in 4 years with a regular high school diploma and the number of students who entered high school 4 years earlier to determine their graduation and dropout rates under *ESEA*, as amended. For 2007–08, data are from the reporting period between July 1, 2007, and June 30, 2008. For 2010–11, data are from the reporting period between July 1, 2010, and June 30, 2011.

TABLE 12.2

Items from the *Self-Determination Battery* (Hoffman, Field, & Sawilowsky, 2004)

That's Me	That's Not Me
Doing well in school does *not* make me feel good.	
When I do not get something I want, I try a new approach.	
I do *not* know my weaknesses.	
Criticism makes me angry.	
I plan to explore many options before choosing a career.	
Goals give my life direction.	
I imagine myself being successful.	

Source: Hoffman, A., Field, S., & Sawilowsky, S. (1996; 2004). Self-Determination Student Scale (SDSS). Detroit, MI: Wayne State University. Used with permission.

beliefs about his or her ability to make his or her needs known, to make decisions, to establish his or her own goals, and to understand his or her feelings in different situations.

Other self-determination tools, including tools by level of severity of disability, and additional educational materials are available from the Zarrow Center for Learning Enrichment. These tools can assist teachers, parents, and students by providing rating scales and questionnaires that can help to identify students' weaknesses and contribute to discussions about goals and planning prior to writing the specific plans in the transition IEP. Specific resources are provided for writing goals, assisting students in writing their own IEP goals, and planning presentations for teachers and other professionals to review as they prepare for transition planning.

Assessment for transition planning incorporates standardized measures of performance to determine educational achievement and cognitive and behavioral functioning. The *Wechsler Intelligence Scales for Children, Fourth Edition*; the *Wechsler Intelligence Scales for Adults, Third Edition*; the *Stanford–Binet V*; the *Woodcock– Johnson III Tests of Achievement* and *Tests of Cognitive Abilities*; and the *Wechsler Individual Achievement Tests II* are often used throughout transitional periods to assess intelligence and achievement.

Assessment for transition also focuses on career and vocational interests and skills, life skills, and social and leisure skills. Clark offered several suggestions for assessment to plan for transition (Clark, 1996, pp. 89–90). For example, Clark suggests that the examiner assist the student by selecting evaluation methods that address the student's concerns about what the student wants to do in the future as well as what the student wants to learn about now. As with other considerations for assessment, transition planning and assessment should be free of bias and should use questions and strategies relevant for the student's culture.

The transitional needs of students can also be determined through a needs interview or use of a commercially published instrument. One such instrument is the *Transition Planning Inventory*, Second Edition (Patton & Clark, 2013).

Transition Planning Inventory, Second Edition (TPI)

This inventory contains four components: a student form, a home form, a school form, and a form for profiles and further assessments (Patton & Clark, 2013) for students ages 14 to 22 years. The forms are easy to complete and require informants to rate the student's current functioning in certain areas: employment, the need for further education and training, communication, self-determination, independent living, money management, community participation, leisure activities, health, and interpersonal relationships. Two additional questionnaire forms, one that is basic and one that is advanced, provide methods for assessing the student's preferences for planning. On these forms, students expand on the topics included on the rating forms by providing their personal preferences for working, learning, and living. The home form is available in English, Spanish, Chinese, and Korean. The student form also includes questions related to career awareness, future plans for living and working, community participation, and leisure and hobby interests. The authors recommend that if the reading level is beyond the student's reading level, the questions should be read to the student. An additional CD included in the second edition provides scripts for administration of the assessment and case scenarios to illustrate the use of the instrument as it is linked to planning. The revised TPI can be administered using the traditional paper-and-pencil format or through a computer assessment program.

This instrument allows for multiple informants to participate in assessing the transition needs of students receiving special education services and their families. The updated edition of the *TPI* includes resources in the publication titled Informal Assessments for Transition Planning, Second Edition (Erickson, Clark, & Patton, 2013). This book provides informal assessments to cover a wide variety of knowledge and skill areas such as a job preference checklist, steps to quitting a job, and living on my own. Additional independent-living informal assessments are included, such as what to do when you need to call 911, a health inventory, a health quiz, and a financial skills and abilities inventory. These specific informal assessments can provide detailed information to better assist the designing of successful transition plans and increase the likelihood of meaningful outcomes for students and their teachers and parents.

Technical Data

Instrument Construction. Because the *TPI* is not a norm-referenced instrument, the information included in the test manual focuses on test development and on the reliability and validity of the inventory. Based on the original development of the *TPI*, the authors indicate that the 57 transition-planning statements reflect the domains used across various states. The instrument may be administered in alternative ways for students with special needs. An explanation of expected student behaviors for each item is included in the manual. For example, for the education/training item "Knows how to gain entry to an appropriate postschool community employment training program," the explanation provided is: "Student knows how to find and get into an on-the-job training program of interest to the student" (Clark & Patton, 2006).

Reliability. The internal reliability was studied using coefficient alpha, and the reliability coefficients ranged between 0.70 and 0.95. Test–retest reliability coefficients ranged from 0.70 to 0.98.

Validity. Information for evidence of content and criterion-related validity is included in the manual. Evidence suggests that the *TPI* is viewed as including necessary content for transition planning.

An example of a case in which a student was assessed for transition planning is presented below. Use this information to complete Activity 12.1.

Case Study on Transition Planning

Eric's parents, Mr. and Mrs. Parks, met with his teacher, Mr. Keller, and the school counselor for a conference about Eric's future plans. His parents reported that Eric gets along very well with all family members and with the other children in the neighborhood. They stated that they are allowing Eric to participate in the driver's education course at school. They have not decided if Eric will be able to take his driver's test, and indicated that they are waiting to hear from Eric's instructor regarding his driving skills. Eric's father said that he has taken Eric out for some practice runs in a neighborhood parking lot on Sundays when there is no traffic in the area.

Mr. and Mrs. Parks expressed concern about Eric's independence and were especially eager to learn ways to assist Eric in learning independent living skills. Mrs. Parks reported that she has made attempts to engage Eric in learning how to cook simple dishes, but he does not appear to be interested. She said that he would live on pizza if the choice were left to him. Mr. and Mrs. Parks said that they envision Eric living in his own apartment someday and eventually marrying. They hope that he will be able to maintain employment and be able to support a family. They also stated that Eric currently has a crush on a neighborhood girl who lives on their block, but that she is not very interested in Eric. This has been a little difficult for Eric to understand, but his father reported that Eric seems to be feeling better about this issue. Mr. and Mrs. Parks expressed interest in Eric's continuing in a vocational training program for as long as possible. They also reported that they will assist Eric financially, if needed, to complete enough training so that he can maintain a job. They were interested in learning about community agencies where they could go for assistance after Eric leaves public school.

Mr. Keller shared with Eric's parents the results of the *Transition Planning Inventory*, which Eric had completed with his assistance. On this instrument, Eric had indicated the following areas of need:

Employment

How to get a job

General job skills and work attitude

Further education and training needed

How to gain entry into a community employment training program

Daily Living

How to locate a place to live

How to set up living arrangements

How to manage money

Community Participation

Understanding basic legal rights

How to make legal decisions

How to locate community resources

How to use community resources

How to obtain financial assistance

Parent Interview

Eric's parents agreed with the areas of need identified by Eric and added the following concerns:

Self-Determination

How to recognize and accept his own strengths and limitations

How to express his ideas and feelings appropriately

How to set personal goals

Interpersonal Relationships

How to get along with a supervisor

Interview with Eric

Eric was excited to come into the office for his interview. He said that his parents had told him about their interview the day before and now it was his turn to talk about getting a job and an apartment someday. Eric said that his favorite part of school is when he goes to the vocational training center in the afternoons. He likes learning about the mechanical aspects of cars. He also reported that the last activity of the day is his driver's education class. He hopes to be able to pass his driving test by the end of the school year but remarked that he may not be able to do that until next year.

Eric stated that he wants to get an apartment when he is older, "like when I am about 40." He said that he enjoys living with his parents and he enjoys living in his neighborhood. He stated that even if he moved into an apartment, he wanted to remain in the area where he currently lives. He said that he knows his way around and wants to live close to his friends. He recognizes that he will have to learn more about how to handle money so that he can live by himself.

Eric reported that he wants to learn more about how to get a job so that when his training is completed, he can start to work right away. He said he would like to save his money to buy a car. He said that he is not really anxious to live by himself and that he doesn't know much about buying groceries or doing laundry. He said his mother usually helps him with these chores.

With information derived from the *Transition Planning Inventory* and from interviews with Eric and his parents, Mr. Keller targeted skills Eric needed to develop in order to transition successfully into adult life. Then he, Mr. and Mrs. Parks, and other members of the transition team designed specific goals and strategies to assist Eric in developing those skills. To monitor Eric's progress, Mr. Keller used curriculum-based measurements. Now, as Eric approaches graduation from high school, both he and his parents feel more comfortable about his ability to live independently.

BRIGANCE® Transition Skills Inventory

This assessment system is a comprehensive criterion-referenced assessment that covers a range of skills needed for transition to work and independent living. The following areas are included in the inventory: career awareness, functional writing, listening and speaking, reading, math, independent living, postsecondary communication and technology skills, community participation, and self-rating instruments that cover skills and behavior. Within each of these areas, specific assessments are available for various skills. For example, in the postsecondary knowledge and skills area, the following assessments may be given: job interview questions, basic pre-employment vocabulary, words found on employment forms, phrases and questions on employment forms, directions found on employment forms, employment pay and benefit vocabulary, payroll statements and paychecks, direction words for performing manual skills, direction words for processing information, abbreviations, alphabetization, information on labels in the workplace, parts of a manual, and paragraphs in a workplace manual. (An example of the payroll statements and paychecks assessment page is presented in Figure 12.5.) The *BRIGANCE* provides additional information to assist in teaching these skills if the student requires this instruction. In addition, each assessment page provides a specific, measureable objective that can be included among or adapted for the student's transition IEP objectives. A new online data management tool is now provided by the publisher so that the examiner can input and generate reports. The system provides assistance with IEP goals and transition planning.

The *BRIGANCE® Comprehensive Inventory of Basic Skills* was presented in Chapter 6. Like the system presented in that chapter, the *BRIGANCE Transition Inventory* provides access to online support that will track and monitor students' progress as they work through transition skills. An additional transition activities kit, the Transition Skills Activities Kit (2012), is a resource that can assist with lesson and activity planning to teach needed transition skills determined through assessment. Using this resource, teachers can deliver targeted instruction to middle and high school students to meet transition needs.

CHECK YOUR UNDERSTANDING

Check your ability to determine the transition needs of a student by completing Activity 12.1.

FIGURE 12.5 Sample Assessment Page from the BRIGANCE® Transition Skills Inventory

NAME: _____

DATE: _____ EXAMINER: _____

DIRECTIONS: The payroll statements and paychecks below show information you may find on a paycheck. Use the information on the statements and checks to answer the questions. Write your answer on the line next to each question.

EMPLOYEE'S STATEMENT

Employee:	Howard Jones
Pay Period:	7/10-7/24/10
Hours Worked:	80
Salary/Rate:	$ 8.00
Gross Pay:	$
Deductions	
Fed. Inc. Tax	$96.00
FICA	$48.96
Health Ins.	$52.00
Union Dues	$ 6.00
Total Deductions:	$
Net Pay:	$

PAYROLL CHECK

FIRST CITY BANK
STAR, TEXAS 76880

No. 528

July 28, 2010

PAY TO THE ORDER OF __Howard Jones__

$ _____

_____ DOLLARS

DANDY COMPANY
784 BEACH AVENUE
STAR, TEXAS 76880

Thomas Anderson
COMPTROLLER

217 178:1177555

DATE 9/16/10	FED. INCOME TAX	DEDUCTIONS			CHECK 199
GROSS SALARY		STATE INCOME TAX	HEALTH INSURANCE	FICA	NET SALARY
$380.50	$57.08	$20.17	$32.64	$29.11	$

PAYROLL CHECK No. 199

FIRST STATE BANK
211 FIRST STREET
STAR, TEXAS 76880

July 26, 2010

PAY TO THE ORDER OF __Mary Salice__

$ _____

_____ Dollars

CITY MARKET
23 SECOND STREET
STAR, TEXAS 76880

Kristen Mortenson
MANAGER

---

1. How much money is deducted from Howard Jones's check for federal income tax? $ _____

2. What will Howard Jones's total deductions be? $ _____

3. Howard Jones's pay, before deductions, was how much? $ _____

4. How much is Howard Jones's deduction for health insurance? $ _____

5. What will be the amount of Howard Jones's check, or his take-home pay? $ _____

6. What is Mary Salice's pay before deductions? $ _____

7. Mary Salice's largest deduction is for _____

8. What is Mary Salice's deduction for Social Security? $ _____

9. How much money is deducted from Mary Salice's check for state income tax? $ _____

10. What will be the amount of Mary Salice's check, or her take-home pay? $ _____

Source: BRIGANCE Transition Skills Inventory, page 193-S. Copyright 2010. Brigance, A. H. (2010). *BRIGANCE Transition Skills Inventory.* N. Billerica, MA: Curriculum Associates.

● ASSESSING FUNCTIONAL ACADEMICS

As previously stated, standardized assessment instruments may be used to assess the current level of academic functioning of students with transition needs. The informal methods presented in Chapter 6 are appropriate for determining the level of academic functioning as it applies to everyday living situations.

In addition to previously mentioned methods and tests, the *Kaufman Functional Academic Skills Test (K–FAST)* may be used (Kaufman & Kaufman, 1994). It is presented in the following section.

Kaufman Functional Assessment Skills Test (K–Fast)

The *K–FAST* was designed to be administered individually to adolescent and adult students (Kaufman & Kaufman, 1994). This instrument assesses the examinee's skill in performing math- and reading-related tasks carried out in everyday life. The authors state that this test was not designed to replace other existing achievement batteries, but rather to add information regarding a student's competency for functioning outside the school environment. The instrument presents items in an easel format with oral directions by the examiner. Math items include such content as the value of money, telling time, reading graphs, and more difficult items covering percentages and calculating the area of a room. Reading items include reading signs, symbols, recipes, and want ads. The test may be administered to persons ranging from age 15 to age 75 and older. The scores provided include standard scores, percentile ranks, and descriptive categories.

Technical Data

Norming Process. The development of the *K–FAST* included developmental versions and tryout exams. The standardization sample was composed of 1,424 people from 27 states. Variables considered were age, gender, geographic region, socioeconomic status of parents or of examinees, and race/ethnic groups. The sample reflected the U.S. population in terms of characteristics and distribution of abilities when compared with the theoretical normal distribution.

Reliability. Two measures of reliability were obtained for the *K–FAST*: split-half reliability for internal consistency and test–retest reliability for consistency across time. Internal reliability coefficients ranged from 0.83 to 0.97. Test–retest coefficients ranged from 0.84 to 0.91.

Validity. Validity was studied using factor analytic studies for construct validity, developmental changes as support for construct validity, and concurrent criterion-related validity with general intellectual measures. The validity coefficients varied on the comparisons with tests of general intelligence; however, validity appears to range from adequate to high.

Planning Transition Assessment

Transition assessment must cover all areas that are relevant to the specific student's postsecondary outcomes. It is important to plan the assessment prior to the IEP process. For example, some students will require extensive assessment in independent living skills while other students will need to focus only on functional academics, job interviewing, and job retention skills. Once needs are determined, the program is planned in the IEP.

A guide for planning transition assessment is presented in Table 12.3.

Using the information in Table 12.3, complete Activity 12.2 by selecting the areas of needed assessment for this student.

CHECK YOUR UNDERSTANDING

Check your ability to determine the transition needs of students by completing Activity 12.2.

TABLE 12.3

Planning Transition Assessment

Potential Areas of Assessment	Possible Assessment Methods
Academics/Functional Academics Applied math for daily living Applied reading for daily living Applied writing for daily living	Norm-referenced academic achievement tests with criteria for planning and objectives
	Curriculum-based measurement of functional skills
	Criterion-referenced tests
	Work samples from classroom activities
Independent Living Skills	Criterion-referenced assessments
Clothing	Adaptive behavior assessments
Finances	Authentic assessments
Food	Work samples
Leisure skills	Transition skills assessments
Community/Citizenship	
Self-Determination	Informal interviews
Self-advocacy through IEP process	Observations
Self-advocacy in planning work goals	Parent/teacher checklists
Self-advocacy on the job	Student checklist/inventory
Problem-Solving Skills/Abilities	Cognitive ability assessments
Working memory	IQ assessments
Application of problem-solving skills	Authentic assessments
Resolving new problems	Work samples
Adaptation in problem solving	Interviews
	Observations
Job-Related Behavior/Attitudes	Behavior rating scales
	Behavior inventories
	Preference inventories
	Work style inventories
	Personality preference inventories
	Observations
	Interviews
	Checklists
Career Assessment	Career inventories
Awareness	Career checklists
Aptitudes	Aptitude tests

(Continued)

TABLE 13.3

Planning Transition Assessment (*continued*)

Potential Areas of Assessment	Possible Assessment Methods
Skills	Skill inventories
Preferences	Career interest inventories
	Authentic assessments
	Questionnaires
	Interviews
	Observations
Family Participation/Resources	Interviews
	Questionnaires
	Checklists
	Parent support group resources
Agency Participation	Review of community resources
	Review of local website resources
	Parent referral to agencies
	Review of state governmental work force agencies
	Review of local community college resources
	Review of local college resources
	Vocational training community resources

● RESEARCH AND ISSUES RELATED TO TRANSITION PLANNING AND ASSESSMENT

Despite the mandate for appropriate planning and the efforts of special educators and related personnel in establishing IEP goals and objectives that will assist students with disabilities in transitioning successfully into adult life, the outcomes for these students continue to be problematic.

1. Levine and Nourse (1998) found that young women with learning disabilities tend to be at risk for early-age pregnancy and for single motherhood.

2. Although self-determination has been cited as best practice for the development of effective transition planning, research indicates that students are not participating in a manner truly reflective of self-determination in the transition/IEP process (Thoma et al., 2001). These researchers found that students with cognitive disabilities attended meetings but were not active during the meetings. Moreover, teachers and parents tended to discuss issues about the students rather than engaging the students in the discussion.

3. Postsecondary research assessing the admission process and accommodations for students continuing their education in 2- and 4-year schools indicates that accommodations are applied inconsistently (Vogel, Leonard, Scales, Hayeslip,

Hermansen, & Donnells, 1998). Differences were found in where and how services were delivered to students with disabilities.

4. Even though students are to be told their rights in the educational process that will transfer to them upon reaching the age of majority, individuals with cognitive disabilities are often assumed to lack the competence to assert their opinions about their own education (Lindsey et al., 2001). This appears to be the case even though most students have not legally been declared as incompetent under state law.

5. Even when students are included in the formal planning process, there are a number of areas that should be evaluated to assist in determining the student's ability to transition well after the secondary school years. For example, students should be evaluated to determine their strengths and weaknesses in problem-solving, self-evaluation, self-monitoring, and communication skills (Hong, Ivy, Gonzalez, & Ehrensberger, 2007). These skills, along with self-determination, may increase the likelihood of postsecondary success.

6. In a study analyzing how parenting and family patterns influence postsecondary outcomes for students with disabilities, it was determined that students from families in which the parents exposed their children to employment and career activities fared better after high school (Lindstrom, Doren, Metheny, Johnson, & Zane, 2007). It was also noted that students whose parents acted as advocates tended to have better employment adjustments than students whose parents were protective and better than students whose parents were disengaged from the postsecondary process. This may suggest that these parents modeled more deterministic behavior and that their children were more engaged themselves in postsecondary planning and outcomes.

7. Carter, Trainor, Sun, and Owens (2009) found that educators consistently rated students with emotional challenges differently than students with learning disabilities on transition skills, indicating that students with behavioral challenges may present unique needs in developing transition skills and self-determination competence.

8. Newman, Wagner, Cameto, and Knokey (2009) reported on findings of the *National Longitudinal Transition Study–2* of 2006, which found that students with different types of disabilities vary in their self-determination skills. For example, students who had learning disabilities indicated more autonomy than students who had autism, speech impairments, visual impairments, emotional disturbances, and other impairments such as health or physical impairments. According to Newman and colleagues, this indicates the need for specialized interventions for various types of disabilities.

CHAPTER SUMMARY

In this chapter you:

- Learned transition assessment methods and techniques and the legal requirements for transition planning

- Applied case scenario assessment information to address transition planning

- Analyzed transition assessment data to address legal requirements of transition planning

- Synthesized the case scenario data for transition planning

- Evaluated assessment methods for transition planning

THINK AHEAD

Once the student with special needs has been administered a battery of tests, the teacher must be able to interpret assessment results and make educational recommendations. The next chapter discusses the steps to be taken in test interpretation.

CHAPTER QUIZ

Now complete the Chapter Quiz to measure your understanding of Chapter 12.

Once you have completed that exercise, assess your progress by completing the Course Progress Monitoring Activity. This activity will let you know if you are moving toward target for course objectives.

Part 4

Interpretation of Assessment Results

Chapter 13
Interpreting Assessment for
Educational Intervention

13 Interpreting Assessment for Educational Intervention

● INTRODUCTION TO TEST INTERPRETATION

Test results are most useful when interpreted and presented in a clear format with specific information relating to educational and behavioral strategies. IDEA regulations require that assessment data be interpreted and used to develop educational and behavioral interventions that will be of benefit to the student. Hoy and Retish (1984) determined that test reports generally lacked the characteristics necessary for ease of educational planning. In this chapter, a model of interpreting test results to assist with eligibility decisions and plan program interventions is presented. The second part of the chapter illustrates how to use test results to write effective behaviorally stated short-term objectives, benchmarks, and long-term goals and how to continue to monitor student progress through direct assessment. Behaviorally stated short-term goals include specific observable expectations of the student. For example, rather than "the student will improve in reading ability," the behaviorally stated short-term objective is "When provided with fifth-grade-level reading passages, the student will be able to read the passages and correctly answer 90% of the comprehension questions by October 15th." Benchmarks are set levels of performance that students are expected to reach before moving to the next level. For example, students in the third grade may be expected to reach the math benchmark of proficiency above 80% in multiplication facts before moving to the next level in math. Long-term goals are the general expectation for the student over a longer period of time. A long-term goal may be to reach and demonstrate proficiency in math and reading benchmarks or to be able to read and comprehend sixth-grade-level passages by the end of the school year.

When interpreting the results of standardized tests, classroom observations, student interviews, parental interviews, questionnaires, surveys, and other forms of assessment, it is important to view the child or adolescent and her or his environment holistically. Tharinger and Lambert (1990) offered insights educators should bear in mind during the assessment and interpretive processes, such as remembering the level of influence the environment and parents have on a child's education and behavior and how the child responds to conflicts that happen within the environment. For these reasons, these authors stress the need to assess the child and the child's whole environment and to consider these in test interpretation.

● INTERPRETING TEST RESULTS FOR EDUCATIONAL DECISIONS

One purpose of the assessment process is to consider test results to determine if a student requires interventions provided through special education services. Eligibility is determined by using set criteria stated in the Individuals with Disabilities Education Act (IDEA). These criteria may vary from state to state for the different types of disabilities, but they must remain within the IDEA guidelines. This means that definitions and criteria may be written by the state; however, students who would be found eligible according to the federal law must not be excluded by state criteria. The scope of this text focuses primarily on mild to moderate disabilities. The most common types of mild to moderate disabilities are learning disabilities, mental retardation, speech/language impairment, and emotional or behavioral disturbances. Students with attention disorders are also often served by educators who teach students with mild to moderate disabilities. These students may be served in the general education environment under the provisions of Section 504 of the Rehabilitation Act of 1973 (refer to Chapter 2) or under the IDEA category of Other Health Impaired if the attention problem does not coexist with another disability, such as a learning disability.

The criteria for the qualification of a specific category and eligibility for special education services as stated in IDEA are used as a basis for interpreting test results. Table 13.1 lists the criteria for mild to moderate disabilities as well as the common characteristics of students with attention deficit disorders.

TABLE 13.1

Key Diagnostic Criteria of IDEA for Attention Disorders and Mild/Moderate Disabilities

Disability	Key Criteria	Assessment Techniques
Intellectual disability	Subaverage intellectual, academic, and adaptive behavior (two or more standard deviations below expectancy for age and according to generally accepted guidelines)	Standardized IQ tests, academic achievement and diagnostic tests, adaptive behavior scales, parent interviews, classroom observations
Learning disability	Average or above in intelligence; specific deficits in academics, cognitive language, or perceptual processing weaknesses may be used. Discrepancy between cognitive ability and achievement *not* required. Response to evidence-based or research-based interventions and performance on academic work should be considered in the decision-making process.	Standardized IQ tests, academic achievement and diagnostic tests, classroom observations, permanent products, informal measures, parental interviews, perceptual–motor tests, curriculum-based measurement
Emotional disturbance	Behavioral or emotional difficulties that interfere with academic or developmental progress; unexplained physical problems, pervasive unhappiness, withdrawal, etc.	Standardized IQ tests, academic achievement and diagnostic tests, clinical interviews, parent interviews, classroom observations, projective tests, personality or behavioral inventories, *Diagnostic and Statistical Manual of Mental Disorders–Fourth Edition* (*DSM–IV*) criteria
Speech/language impairment	Communication difficulty that interferes with academic achievement, ability to speak, or normal developmental progress	Speech or language diagnostic tests, classroom observations, parent interviews, academic achievement tests
Attention deficit disorders		
1. Predominantly hyperactivity/ impulsive presentation	Externalizing behaviors, talking out, talking too much, impulsive actions, activity level beyond developmental expectations, poor schoolwork, incomplete or missing assignments	*DSM–V* evaluation, behavioral ratings by different persons and in different environments, continuous performance tests, cognitive and achievement tests, multiple direct classroom observations
2. Predominantly inattentive presentation	Poor schoolwork, incomplete or missing assignments, confusion, excessive daydreaming, self-distracting behavior, difficulty following directions and following through	Same as for hyperactive type
3. Combined presentation	Combination of characteristics found in hyperactive and inattentive attention deficit disorder	Same as for hyperactive type
4. Autism spectrum disorders	Significant deficits in the capacity for social reciprocity; abnormalities in communication; repetitive, restrictive, stereotyped patterns of behavior	Indirect assessment using rating scales, observations in natural environment, direct assessment of child (e.g., *ADOS-2*), developmental clinical interview with caregivers, cognitive assessment for intellectual ability, other assessments to determine possible emotional disorders or medical conditions

● THE ART OF INTERPRETING TEST RESULTS

Most of this text has focused on quantitative measurement, informal data collection, and information from multiple informants about student abilities. A teacher or diagnostician may know how to effectively administer test items, score tests, and collect data; however, she or he must also master the art of interpreting—deriving meaning from—that data. Accurate interpretation involves both interindividual and intraindividual interpretation of test results. Interindividual interpretation involves comparing the student with other students in the norm group to determine how different the student is from that group. Intraindividual interpretation may be even more important than interindividual interpretation. For intraindividual interpretation, the teacher uses test results and other data collected to compare the student's relative strengths and weaknesses. These strengths and weaknesses are then used in effective educational and behavioral planning.

Generally, all possible areas of suspected disability are assessed according to the recommended tests and evaluation measures given in Table 13.1. The following procedures are suggested for evaluating the student and interpreting test results:

1. *Parental permission.* The professional must secure parental permission before conducting an individual assessment or making a referral.

2. *Screening for sensory impairments or physical problems.* Before a psychoeducational evaluation is recommended, the student's vision, hearing, and general physical health should be screened. When these areas are found to be normal or corrections for vision/hearing impairments are made, the evaluation procedure can continue.

3. *Parent interview.* The professional should question the parent regarding the student's progress, development, developmental history, family structure, relationships with family and peers, and independent adaptive behavior functioning.

4. *Intellectual and academic assessment.* Team members should administer an intelligence measure and academic achievement or diagnostic instrument, conduct classroom observations, and complete an informal evaluation.

5. *Behavioral assessment.* If the assessment and the information from the parents and teacher indicate behavioral, emotional, or attention problems, the student should also be assessed by a school or clinical psychologist to obtain behavioral, emotional, and personality information.

6. *Test interpretation.* Several members of the evaluation team may interpret test results. Team members may write separate or combined reports. In interpreting results, the assessment team should do the following:

   a. Rule out any sensory acuity problems and refer to or consult with medical personnel if physical problems are suspected.
   b. Determine whether any home conflicts are present and enlist the services of the school psychologist or school counselor if such conflicts are suspected or indicated.
   c. If appropriate, consider the student's previous educational experiences and how these experiences might have influenced the student's achievement. Frequent moves, migrant experiences, the amount of time the student has lived in the United States, parental educational experiences and views on the educational process, and frequent absences from school all have a bearing on academic achievement.
   d. If appropriate, consider and assess any language factors that impact achievement. Assessment to determine the student's primary language should be completed during the referral/assessment process, and interviews with parents or caregivers should be conducted to determine the language spoken in

CHECK YOUR UNDERSTANDING

To check your understanding of the mild/moderate criteria, complete Activity 13.1.

the home. For bilingual students, assessment should determine proficiency levels in both languages.

e. Determine whether learning or school problems are exhibited in a particular school environment (e.g., unstructured play or lunchroom) or are associated with one subject area or a particular teacher, peer, or adult.

f. Compare ability on intellectual, academic, or adaptive behavior measures. Are there apparent discrepancies in functioning? Do perceptual or motor deficits appear to influence ability in specific academic areas? Is the student functioning at a higher level in one area than in others? Is the student functioning significantly below expectancy in one or more areas? How do formal test results compare with informal classroom assessments and classroom performance?

g. Determine whether emotional/behavioral problems exist. Does the student appear to be progressing slowly because of behavioral or emotional difficulties? Does the student adapt well in various situations? Does the student have good relationships with peers and adults? Is the student's attention or activity level interfering with her or his academic and social progress? Does a functional behavioral assessment need to be completed?

g. Determine whether speech/language problems are present. Is the student having difficulty understanding language or following oral lectures or directions? Does the student make articulation errors that are not age appropriate?

As these questions are answered, the diagnostician or special education teacher begins to form a picture of how the student processes information and how the strengths and weaknesses noted during test performance and observations may affect learning and behavior. From these interpretations, the teacher can make recommendations that will provide educational intervention and support to benefit the student and promote academic progress. The psychoeducational report or reports are then written to facilitate appropriate intervention strategies.

Intelligence and Adaptive Behavior Test Results

Cognitive or intellectual measures are generally administered by school psychologists, clinical psychologists, or educational diagnosticians. The results from these tests should be interpreted and used to plan educational interventions. Interindividual interpretations may indicate that the student is within the range of mental retardation or has a specific learning disability, emotional disturbance, developmental immaturity, or average or above-average intellectual functioning. Intraindividual interpretations should be provided by the person who administered the tests. These interpretations may pinpoint specific demonstrated strengths as well as problems with distractibility, attention deficits, auditory short-term memory, visual retention, verbal comprehension, abstract visual reasoning, visual memory difficulties, and so on. Interpretation of the cognitive measures may refer to patterns of functioning noticed. *Patterns of functioning* may be understood as significant differences between verbal areas of functioning and visual–motor abilities, spatial reasoning or functioning, or perceptual–organization abilities. These patterns may be indicated by significant weaknesses in particular areas or by marked differences between verbal and performance index scores on a test of intellectual ability (e.g., a verbal index of 108 and a performance index of 71). These weaknesses or discrepancies may be linked to particular learning difficulties and academic differences. The examiner's descriptions of the student's performance may help the team plan effective educational strategies.

A more in-depth analysis of cognitive-processing scores across several instruments may be included in the interpretation of results by the school psychologist, school neuropsychologist, or a clinical psychologist. This type of analysis, in which a student's skills and abilities are analyzed across several instruments, is known as **cross-battery assessment** (Flanagan & Harrison, 2005; Flanagan & Ortiz, 2001). Specifically, this type of interpretation has a theoretical basis in the

CHECK YOUR UNDERSTANDING

To check your understanding of the procedures for evaluation, complete Activity 13.2.

Cattell-Horn-Carroll (CHC) theory of cognitive ability. This type of analysis is often used to evaluate the abilities of students who are referred for learning disabilities, traumatic brain injury, neuro-developmental disorders, or other types of disabilities that originate from frank organic brain abnormalities (Miller, 2007).

Educational Achievement and Diagnostic Test Results

The educator may be responsible for administering norm-referenced educational achievement and other diagnostic tests. Although administering and scoring these instruments may seem somewhat mechanical, the teacher should take great care in doing so and in interpreting test results. Many cognitive and academic assessments have computer-scoring programs in which the examiner enters raw scores and derived scores are provided in report format. The first method of interpretation involves interindividual interpretation, comparing the student with age/grade expectations. Data provided on norm tables enable the examiner to determine how a student compares with age/grade peers. Is the student significantly above expectations (e.g., in the 90th percentile)? Is the student average (in the 50th percentile range) on some measures, but significantly below peers (below the 10th percentile) on other measures? The examiner should plot a profile of how the student performs when compared to these expectations.

In conducting intraindividual interpretation, the examiner identifies specific strengths and weaknesses in academic achievement, other abilities, and behavioral areas. Because the areas of strength and needs should be defined as specifically as possible, tests that provide error analysis are most helpful. This analysis can be broken down further by task and used to develop teacher-made tests or informal probes if more information is needed.

● WRITING TEST RESULTS

Interpreting and writing test results so that meaningful information is available for the persons responsible for the delivery of educational services is the most important concern when preparing reports. Bagnato (1980) suggested organizing test results by domains or by developmental levels rather than by instruments, with an emphasis on processing skills for developing learning strategies. Bagnato reminds evaluators that the purpose of the assessment process is to develop effective interventions for learning and behavior to improve academic achievement.

Although psychoeducational reports may differ in format, they include the same general content. Typically, the identifying information is presented first: student name, date of birth, parents' names, address, grade placement, date(s) of evaluation, methods of evaluation, and the name of the examiner. Presented next is the background and referral information, which may include sociological information such as the size of family, the student's relationship with family members, other schools attended, and any previous academic, behavioral, developmental, or health problems.

Test results follow this preliminary information. An interpretation is presented, and recommendations for interventions, further evaluations, or changes in placement are then suggested. The following is an outline of a psychoeducational report:

I. Identifying Data

II. Background and Referral Information

    A. Background

    B. Referral

    C. Classroom Observation

    D. Parent Information

III. Test Results

IV. Test Interpretations

V. Summary and Conclusions

   A. Summary

   B. Recommendations for Educational Interventions

   C. Recommendations for Further Assessment

Writing style is critically important in communicating test results. Words should be selected carefully to convey an objective assessment. Goff (2002) suggested specific guidelines for educators to follow in report preparation when normative tests are used. These guidelines, presented in Table 13.2, include samples of educators' reports and suggested improvements.

TABLE 13.2

Guidelines for Writing Objective Reports

Background Information

- Make sure that all statements are attributed. The statement *Jack's mother is very supportive, which contributes to his academic success* is not attributed. Jack's father may strongly disagree if there is a custody battle. This statement could easily be rewritten to attribute the comment to its source: *Ms. Jones, Jack's teacher, reported that Jack's mother has been very supportive and that this support has contributed to Jack's academic success.*
- Do not ask the reader to make assumptions. The statement *Her teacher reports a noticeable difference in Jill's attention span when she does not take her medication* requires the reader to make an assumption. Some students will perform better when not on medication because they become more diligent in monitoring their own behavior to prove they do not need it.

Classroom Observations and Test Observations

- Make sure that you provide observations, not interpretations of behavior. The statement *James really liked the lesson* is an interpretation. This could be rewritten as *James stated, "I really like this work."* Note: This is not an interpretation because you are directly quoting Jack. The statement *The work he was given was too hard for James* is also an interpretation and could be rewritten as *James did not complete the more difficult items successfully.*

Test Results

- Make a standard comment about the mean and standard deviation of the test used. For example: *The standard scores for the WJ IV have a mean of 100 and a standard deviation of 15.*
- Report standard scores, percentile ranks, and standard errors of measure. Report both subtest scores and composite or broad area scores. A table in the body of the report or at the end is usually the clearest way to communicate this information.

Test Interpretation

- Discuss clear strengths and weaknesses in performance only if variation in scores reaches statistical significance (usually to the 0.05 level). Otherwise, the variation should be considered to be normal variability.

Summary and Conclusions

- Tie a review of the background information, observations, test results, and test interpretation together in summary form. Your summary should pull everything together.
- Your strongest conclusions will be based on concerns supported by background information, observations, and test interpretation. *Observations and evaluation data support the parents' and teacher's concern that Billy has a reading deficit. In addition, he scored well below average on assessments of written language.* This supports a recommendation of remediation services in language arts.
- If a student does better in one part of a domain than another, note this difference. *Tonya performed at an average level on a subtest that assesses reading comprehension, but scored well below average on a subtest that assesses word identification skills.* This supports a recommendation that, while remediating word-attack skills, the student could continue to be presented with age-appropriate content.

TABLE 13.2

Guidelines for Writing Objective Reports (*Continued*)

- If the testing data do not support a claim of weakness, look first to differences in task demands of the testing situation and the classroom when hypothesizing a reason for the difference. *Although weaknesses in mathematics were noted as a concern by his teacher, Billy scored in the average range on assessments of mathematics skills. These tests required Billy to perform calculations and to solve word problems that were read aloud to him. It was noted that he often paused for 10 seconds or more before starting pencil-and-paper tasks in mathematics.* This supports a recommendation that the teacher attempt to redirect him to task frequently and to avoid the assumption that a long pause means that Billy is unable to solve a problem.

- If testing data indicate a weakness that was not identified as a concern, give first priority to explaining the discrepancy and the limitations with the testing. *Billy stated that he does well in spelling. However, he scored well below average on a subtest of spelling skills. Billy appeared to be bored while taking the spelling test, so a lack of vigilance in his effort may have depressed his score. Also, the spelling tests he takes in school use words he has been practicing for a week. The lower score on the spelling subtest of this assessment might indicate that he is maintaining the correct spelling of words in long-term memory.*

- Do not use definitive statements of the "real" child when reporting assessment results. A 45-minute test does not give you definitive knowledge of the student. The statement *The results of this screening show that Jack has strength in language arts and is weak in mathematics* could be rewritten as *Based on the results of this screening, Jack's language arts skills were assessed to be an area of strength while his mathematics skills were assessed to be an area of weakness.*

Recommendations

- Be careful of using the word *should* in your recommendations. Doing so means that you are directing the activities of another professional even though that professional may have a much more comprehensive knowledge of the child than you.

- Do not make placement recommendations based solely on the results of an achievement test. Make academic recommendations only if your full assessment provides adequate information to make these recommendations with confidence. Remember: Specific recommendations can be made only by someone with thorough knowledge of the curriculum and the domain being assessed.

Source: Guideline for Writing Reports. Reprinted with permission of author: W. H. Goff (2002).

Case Study: Rosalinda

Name: Rosalinda Merrick

Date of Birth: April 7, 2006

Date of RTI Meeting: May 7, 2014

Age: 8–1

Current Grade Placement: 2. 8

Rosalinda, a second-grade student, was not making the progress in reading expected of a typically developing child at the beginning of second grade. In October, through a universal screening test administered to all second-grade students, Rosalinda's teacher, Mr. Silver, determined that Rosalinda and three other students were significantly behind their classmates in their ability to read words and sentences fluently. Rosalinda also had difficulty with decoding. Mr. Silver met with the RTI committee members and discussed interventions that would be implemented in small-group format with the four low-achieving students. Interventions included using a program called Earobics© to address reading fluency and decoding skills. The program was selected because it addresses the specific skill area of reading

CHECK YOUR UNDERSTANDING

To check your understanding of decisions made in the RTI process, complete Activity 13.3.

fluency that Rosalinda needs and because it has been rated as having positive effects for her grade level. For example, the program includes sound blending, rhyming, auditory processing, and discriminating phonemes within words. The program includes adaptations for the teacher to use with English Language Learners. Because Rosalinda's mother's primary language is Spanish, which Rosalinda often speaks at home, the response-to-intervention (RTI) committee believed the program was appropriate. Interventions were presented to the group of four students two times each week for 20 minutes. After 4 weeks of instruction, Mr. Silver found that Rosalinda continued to struggle and that her progress was slow.

The RTI committee met at the end of November to review Rosalinda's progress. They determined that she required additional time each week for the interventions and recommended that instruction in the currently used curriculum occur for 45 minutes two times each week. Figure 13.1 presents Rosalinda's progress in decoding and fluency.

The following case study presents test results and interpretations. Read the results and interpretations and how they are implemented in the educational recommendations. For instructional purposes, the reasons for the recommendations are given with each recommendation. Reasons for recommendations are not typically included in reports.

Case Study: Susie

Name: Susie Smith

Date of Birth: June 8, 2004

Dates of Evaluation: November 20, 2014, and November 28, 2014

Age: 10–6

Current Grade Placement: 3.3

Examiner: Hazel Compton

Assessment Instruments/Methods:

Wechsler Intelligence Scale for Children–Fifth Edition

Woodcock–Johnson IV Tests of Achievement: Standard and Extended Battery

Test of Auditory Perceptual Skills

Teacher Report Form (Achenbach/CBCL)

Work sample analysis

Classroom observations

Conference with parents

BACKGROUND INFORMATION AND REFERRAL

Susie was referred for testing by her parents for the possible consideration of special education services. Although Susie had been receiving targeted interventions for reading, she did not make the progress expected. Susie's RTI committee tried alternative interventions; however, her progress continued to be slow. Susie's parents expressed their concerns and decided to refer Susie rather than wait for another change in the interventions at the Tier III level.

Sociological information reported normal developmental progress and a warm, caring home environment. Susie's parents reported that they felt education was

FIGURE 13.1 Rosalinda's Reading Fluency

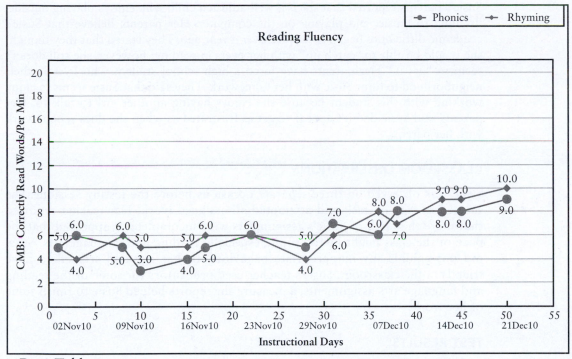

Data Table

Obsv#	Date	Phonics	Rhyming		Obsv#	Date	Phonics	Rhyming
					9	2 December 2010	7	5
Phase Change					10	7 December 2010	6	8
1	2 November 2010	5	5		11	9 December 2010	8	7
2	4 November 2010	6	4		12	14 December 2010	8	9
3	9 November 2010	5	6		13	16 December 2010	8	9
4	11 November 2010	3	5		14	21 December 2010	9	10
5	16 November 2010	4	5					
6	18 November 2010	5	6					

important and wanted Susie's progress to improve. Susie appears to have good relationships with both parents and her two older brothers.

Susie repeated kindergarten and received low grades during her first- and second-grade years. She is currently enrolled in third grade, and the teacher reported that Susie has difficulty with phonics and reading words that "she should know." Susie attended a special summer program in an attempt to improve her reading skills. As mentioned, she has not responded to instructional interventions that focus on reading.

Susie has normal vision and hearing and no apparent physical problems. Peer relationships are as expected for her age.

PARENT CONFERENCE

Susie's parents reported that she is a well-adjusted child who enjoys playing outside, listening to music, and playing on the computer. Her parents believe that Susie's academic difficulties began to surface over a year ago. They stated that they thought she would be able to "catch up" with her peers in reading; however, she still doesn't seem to "get it." Her parents have hired a high school student who lives in their neighborhood to tutor Susie with her homework. They said that Susie seems to enjoy working with this student because she enjoys having another girl to talk to. Her parents said Susie doesn't appear to get as frustrated as when she does school work with her parents.

CLASSROOM OBSERVATIONS

Susie was observed on three separate occasions before the testing sessions. She seemed to stay on task and attempted all assigned work. Her teacher reported that more than half of Susie's assignments were incomplete. It appeared that the pace of the class might be too rapid, especially reading and language arts. Susie did not exhibit any inappropriate behaviors for her age and seemed to have friends in the classroom. Susie's teacher used peer tutors for some of the reading and language arts assignments, a measure she reports helped Susie to finish some of her work.

TEST RESULTS

WECHSLER INTELLIGENCE SCALE FOR CHILDREN–V

Block Design	10
Similarities	9
Digit Span	4
Information	9
Visual Puzzles	10
Coding	5
Vocabulary	7
Letter–Number Sequencing	5
Matrix Reasoning	7
Arithmetic	7
Comprehension	9
Symbol Search	5
Picture Span	6
Cancellation	5

	Standard Score	95% Confidence Interval	Percentile Rank
Verbal Comprehension	85	(77–91)	17
Visual Spatial	88	(81–97)	21
Working Memory	68	(63–78)	2
Processing Speed	73	(67–85)	4
Full Scale	74	(69–79)	4

WOODCOCK–JOHNSON IV TESTS OF ACHIEVEMENT: STANDARD AND EXTENDED BATTERIES

Cluster/Test	PR	SS	(90% BAND)	GE
Reading	0.3	59	(56–62)	1.9
Broad Reading	0.2	57	(54–60)	1.5
Broad Math	23	89	(85–93)	3.5
Broad Written Language	0.4	60	(54–66)	1.6
Basic Reading Skills	0.3	59	(55–63)	1.3
Reading Rate	0.5	62	(56-68)	1.5
Reading Fluency	0.3	57	(54–62)	1.2
Reading Comprehension	1	67	(62–72)	1.7
Math Calculation Skills	39	96	(90–101)	4.4
Math Problem Solving	30	92	(87–97)	3.8
Basic Writing Skills	2	68	(63–73)	1.7
Written Expression	4	74	(66–81)	2.3
Academic Skills	1	66	(63–69)	1.7
Academic Fluency	3	72	(69–76)	2.2
Academic Applications	4	75	(70–79)	1.9
Academic Knowledge	35	94	(87–101)	4.3
Phoneme/Grapheme Knowledge	0.2	56	(49–63)	1.0
Form A				
Letter–Word Identification	<0.1	48	(43–52)	1.1
Sentence-Reading Fluency	5	76	(72–79)	2.2
Reading Recall	2	68	(50–86)	K.3
Number Matrices	30	88	(80-96)	2.2
Calculation	76	110	(101–120)	6.2
Math Facts Fluency	1	62	(56–67)	1.5
Spelling	<0.1	52	(45–60)	K.9
Sentence-Writing Fluency	5	75	(66–83)	2.5
Passage Comprehension	2	68	(61–74)	1.5
Applied Problems	12	82	(76–89)	2.6
Writing Samples	8	79	(68–90)	1.9
Word Attack	5	75	(68–82)	1.6
Oral Reading	17	65	(57-73)	2.5
Editing	14	84	(77–91)	2.9
Reading Vocabulary	7	78	(73–83)	1.9
Academic Knowledge	35	94	(87–101)	4.3
Spelling of Sounds	<0.1	26	(11–41)	<K.0

TEST OF AUDITORY–PERCEPTUAL SKILLS

	Scaled Score	Percentile Rank
Auditory Number Memory		
Forward	6	9
Reversed	5	5
Auditory Sentence Memory	8	25
Auditory Word Memory	5	5
Auditory Interpretation of Directions		
Total Correct Sentences	7	16
Auditory Word Discrimination	3	1
Auditory Processing (thinking and reasoning)	7	16
Auditory Quotient	70	

TEST INTERPRETATION

On measures of intellectual ability, Susie performed in the low-average/borderline range. This indicates that, on this assessment, Susie is considered to have a range of abilities consistent with the low end of average and bordering in the below-average range. Discrepancies exist between her higher-end scores of verbal comprehension and perceptual reasoning skills and her lower scores of working memory and processing speed. Susie performed with relative strength on tasks requiring verbal skills and concepts and on tasks requiring abstract visual–perceptual reasoning skills. Susie seems to have more difficulty with tasks requiring her to sustain attention to encode and sequence information using auditory memory skills. She worked at a somewhat slow and deliberate pace on some tasks, which may have influenced her processing speed score.

On overall achievement measures of the *Woodcock–Johnson IV Tests of Achievement (WJ IV)*, Susie performed as expected for her age on items requiring math calculation and math reasoning. Susie's general academic knowledge was in the range expected for her age when she completed tasks of science, social studies, and humanities. Susie also demonstrated age-appropriate skills in the ability to comprehend orally and in handwriting ability.

Susie's difficulties in academics were demonstrated through formal assessment in the areas of written language, including reading, spelling, and phoneme/grapheme knowledge. These weaknesses result in the inability to decode new words, spell sounds, and comprehend content that is read. An error analysis of word-attack skills revealed weaknesses in decoding single consonants, digraphs, consonant blends, vowels, and multisyllabic words.

Susie demonstrated weakness in most areas assessed by the *Test of Auditory–Perceptual Skills*. She seems to have relative weaknesses on subtests that measure memory for isolated words and numbers. She appears to have slightly higher ability to remember meaningful auditory stimuli, such as sentences or directions. However, she had difficulty on similar items of the WJ IV, indicating inconsistent skill mastery or inconsistent abilities.

On items requiring oral language responses, Susie was somewhat shy and tended to limit her responses to one-word answers. This may have affected some of her scores on tests assessing the language areas. These scores may underestimate her true ability.

Responses provided by Susie's teacher on the Teacher Report Form of the *Child Behavior Checklist* indicated that Susie is unable to complete most of her schoolwork as expected of students her age. The teacher endorsed items that indicate Susie may be having some emerging problems with anxiety. Items were also endorsed that are consistent with difficulties with concentration and attention. These may be related to her current performance in school. None of Susie's scores was within a clinical range for behavior problems.

Work sample analysis indicated that Susie has a relative strength in the ability to compute simple math operations and to understand math concepts and math reasoning. Her samples for spelling, writing, and reading comprehension were in the failure range. Work samples indicated weakness in her ability to associate written letters with sounds, which is consistent with her performance on standardized achievement measures.

Three separate classroom observations were conducted. Susie was cooperative and remained quiet during all of the observation periods. She attempted to begin her work when directed to do so, but was unable to complete language arts assignments. She was off task during language arts classes more often than during math classes.

SUMMARY AND CONCLUSIONS

Susie is currently functioning in the low-average range of intellectual ability, with significant weaknesses in phoneme/grapheme awareness and short-term auditory memory. These weaknesses influence her ability to decode words, spell, and comprehend new material. They may also decrease the efficiency with which Susie can obtain new information through a standard teaching (lecture) format. Susie's performance on standardized and informal assessment instruments resulted in a profile consistent with that of a student with specific learning disabilities in the areas of reading and written language skills. This may be the result of her difficulties with processing information presented auditorily and an inability to form sound–symbol relationships.

RECOMMENDATIONS

1. Susie might benefit from additional educational support in the areas of reading and language arts. (Reason: Susie has difficulty with sound awareness, phoneme/grapheme awareness, auditory memory, verbal skills, and attention.)

2. New material should be presented in both visual and auditory formats. (Reason: Susie's weakness appears to be auditory memory; pairing all auditory material with visual cues may help her maintain focus.)

3. Susie will benefit from direct instruction techniques that require her to actively respond to new material. (Reason: Increased academic engaged time and active responding will help Susie focus on the tasks she is given, resulting in attention and positive reinforcement from her teacher.)

4. Susie might benefit from phonemic awareness training activities. (Reason: Assessment results are consistently low in this area; additional instruction may decrease Susie's difficulty with sound–symbol relationships.)

5. Susie might benefit from advance organizers in content-area reading assignments, the introduction of new vocabulary prior to reading passages in which that vocabulary is used, outlines of class lectures or presentations, and instruction in notetaking. (Reason: Susie might improve her ability to focus on relevant material and increase her attention to task.)

Hazel Compton, M.Ed.

Educational Diagnostician

CHECK YOUR UNDERSTANDING

To check your understanding of this case, complete Activity 13.4.

● WRITING EDUCATIONAL OBJECTIVES

At the eligibility meeting, team members discuss the results and recommendations of the psychoeducational reports with the parents. If the student is eligible for special education services, the team writes the specific educational objectives that comprise the student's individualized education program (IEP). If the student does not meet eligibility criteria, then she or he may be found eligible for accommodations under Section 504. The team may also decide that the student does not need additional services under 504 or IDEA, but additional referrals, programs, or interventions may be suggested within the general curriculum. Let's continue with the example of Susie Smith to see how the team would use its results to write Susie's educational objectives.

IEP Team Meeting Results

Results of Susie's assessment were presented in the IEP team meeting along with additional information from Susie's parents, the school psychologist, and Susie's classroom teacher. The team agreed that Susie would receive reading and language arts instruction in a resource room setting. This decision was made so that Susie could receive intensive training in phonemic awareness, decoding, reading comprehension, reading fluency, and spelling in one-on-one and small-group settings. The team decided to complete additional testing to further pinpoint Susie's weaknesses in phoneme/grapheme awareness and other areas of language arts. The resource room teacher expressed her intention to use curriculum-based measurement to monitor Susie's progress.

Susie's IEP

During the IEP meeting, long-range goals and short-term objectives were developed for Susie. Portions of her IEP are presented here.

Student's Present Level of Educational Performance

Cognitive Abilities. Current assessment data indicate that Susie is functioning in the low-average range of intelligence. Her strengths are in the areas of performance or nonverbal skills.

Reading.

- *Basic Reading Skills.* Formal assessment, curriculum-based assessments, and informal measures indicate that Susie is performing below the range expected for her age on tasks of decoding—specifically, word attack and phoneme/grapheme awareness. Her performance in curriculum-based measures is at the first- to second-grade level.
- *Comprehension.* Susie's reading comprehension skills are at the first- to second-grade level as indicated on all measures.
- *Fluency.* Susie's reading fluency is at the first- to second-grade level according to all measures.

Spelling. Susie's spelling skills are at the first-grade level. She has particular difficulty with the spelling of basic consonant–vowel–consonant (CVC) words.

Written Language. Susie's written language skills are at the first- to second-grade level on both formal and informal classroom measures.

Mathematics. Susie is performing at the level expected for her age in the areas of math calculation and math reasoning.

Science. Susie's standardized achievement scores and classroom measures indicate that she is comprehending science concepts at the level expected for her age.

Social Studies. Susie's standardized achievement scores and classroom measures indicate that she is performing at the level expected for her age.

To write these present levels of performance into IEP objectives, the conditions under which the student will be expected to complete an objective must be stated—for example, "when Susie is presented with addition math calculation problems." Following the condition, the expected behavior is stated; for example, "she will correctly solve the problems within 2 minutes"; and this is followed by how it will be known that she met the objective or expectation; for example, "with 85% accuracy." Objectives that are written and include these factors are measureable and will alert the teacher that new objectives should be written once these target expectations have been met.

Additional classroom assessment indicates that Susie has difficulty with several letter/sound associations when asked to decode words. She also has difficulty with the spelling of first-grade-level words.

Sample IEP Annual Goal for Basic Reading Skills

Susie will master the decoding skills required in the reading series Spinners at the mid-second-grade level by the end of the school year.

Sample IEP Short-Term Objective

When given a list of 20 random words from the highest-level first-grade reader (1.E Level) from the series Spinners, Susie will be able to decode the list with 85% accuracy at the end of the 6-week reporting period.

Methods and Evaluation

Methods/Material Used	Method of Monitoring/Assessment
Spinners Reader Level 1.E	Curriculum-based measurement

● REEVALUATIONS

The 1997 IDEA amendments changed the focus of the reevaluation process. In the past, students were assessed in the same areas they were assessed for their initial evaluations (cognitive, academic, speech/language, adaptive functioning, etc.). The regulations now state that data should be collected only in those areas in which team members believe they need additional information in order to make a decision regarding continued eligibility and interventions. For example, a student with a specific learning disability in math may need additional data and/or assessment only in the area of math. Rather than requiring total comprehensive evaluations every 3 years, reevaluations now consist of only the additional assessment determined to be needed in order to thoroughly review the case.

CHECK YOUR UNDERSTANDING

To check your understanding of writing IEP objectives, complete Activity 13.5.

Case Study: Travis

Name: Travis Shores

Date of Birth: August 9, 1996

Date of Evaluation: October 28, 2014

Age: 18–3

Examiner: Mark House

Assessment Instruments/Methods:

 Wechsler Adult Intelligence Scale–Fourth Edition

 Conners Continuous Performance Test

 Clinical interview

BACKGROUND AND REFERRAL INFORMATION

Travis is currently enrolled as a first-year student at Burlington Community College. He reports having difficulty with study habits, time management, spelling skills, writing skills, reading comprehension, and grammar. He also expressed concern about his ability to pay attention and work at the college level. Travis said that he has difficulty with maintaining attention, finishing tasks, taking tests, and listening in class. He reported that he is distracted easily in lecture classes.

Travis reported that he has no history of testing for learning or attention difficulties. He stated that he had a difficult time in high school during his sophomore year, but then felt that things were better for him during his junior and senior years. He is taking an economics course and believes he is doing well in that class.

TEST RESULTS

WECHSLER ADULT INTELLIGENCE SCALE–FOURTH EDITION

Vocabulary	9	Block Design	14
Similarities	11	Matrix Reasoning	13
Information	8	Visual Puzzles	14
Verbal Comprehension Index	98	**Perceptual Reasoning Index**	118
Digit Span	8	Symbol Search	12
Arithmetic	8	Coding	13
Working Memory Index	82	**Processing Speed Index**	128

Full-Scale IQ 105

CONNERS CONTINUOUS PERFORMANCE TEST

Measure	Percentile	Range of Performance
Number of Hits	99.59	Markedly atypical
Number of Omissions	94.86	Markedly atypical
Number of Commissions	50.90	Within average range
Hit Rate	21.46	Within average range
Hit Rate Standard Error	93.44	Markedly atypical
Variability of SES	77.87	Within average range
Attentiveness	84.42	Mildly atypical
Risk Taking	99.00	Markedly atypical
Hit RT Block Change	95.96	Markedly atypical
Hit SE Block Change	82.60	Within average range
Hit RT ISI Change	80.90	Within average range
Hit SE ISI Change	76.78	Within average range

Travis performed with some inconsistency on the *Conners Continuous Performance Test*. He performed like students his age with attention problems on several indices. He was within the average range on other indices. His performance indicates that he may have difficulty sustaining attention on some tasks but not others. His performance showed some evidence of an impulsive responding pattern. Travis is currently functioning in the average range of intellectual ability. Differences exist between his index scores, with lower scores in verbal comprehension and working memory and higher scores in perceptual reasoning and processing speed. This indicates that Travis is able to use nonverbal strategies better than verbal strategies for most problem solving. This discrepancy also indicates that Travis's full scale IQ score may not be representative of his true ability. Analysis of individual subtests and index scores also indicates strengths and weaknesses in processing. Travis demonstrated significant strength in visual–perceptual organization of nonverbal stimuli and processing speed. His performance on this instrument indicates relative weakness in short-term auditory memory and in the ability to remain free from distraction. Travis appears to have relative weakness in long-term retention of factual information, although his scores are in the average range.

Travis was administered the *Conners Continuous Performance Test* to determine whether he has significant difficulty maintaining sustained, focused attention. On this instrument, the more measures that are found to be in the atypical range, the greater the likelihood is that attention problems exist. On this test, Travis gave slower responses at the end than at the beginning of the test, indicating an ability to sustain attention. He made a greater number of omission errors, indicating poor attention to the task. He was highly inconsistent in responding, indicating inattentiveness as measured by standard error. Numerous indices strongly suggest that Travis has attention problems according to his performance on this test.

RECOMMENDATIONS

Review the information in the preceding case study. Discuss appropriate instructional interventions that might be helpful for Travis during class; offer additional interventions related to Travis's studying outside of class. Also suggest accommodations for Travis that are appropriate at the college level. Should Travis be referred for additional services from any other agencies or other professionals? What considerations should be discussed with Travis regarding his future plans and course of study at the college level? What issues regarding his functioning as an adult should be considered?

CHECK YOUR UNDERSTANDING

To check your understanding of the test interpretation for Travis, complete Activity 13.6.

CHECK YOUR UNDERSTANDING

To check your understanding of determining recommendations for Travis, complete Activity 13.7.

Case Study: Burt

Name: Burt Down

Date of Birth: May 8, 1998

Date of Evaluation: November 20, 2014

Age: 16–6

Current Grade Placement: 10.3

Examiner: Phil Clemens

Assessment Instruments/Methods:

Selected subtests of the *Woodcock–Johnson IV*

Math work samples

Behavior Assessment System for Children: Self-Report (ages 12–18; BASC)

Behavioral observation data

Functional behavior assessment

BACKGROUND AND REFERRAL INFORMATION

Burt was referred for reevaluation because of recent behavioral difficulties. Burt has been receiving special education support for specific learning disabilities since he was in the fourth grade. He receives his English instruction in the resource room setting. He has previously been found to have attention deficit hyperactivity disorder and has been prescribed medication as part of his treatment for this disorder. His parents and teachers have agreed that his behavior improves when he complies with his medication regimen. His parents have also acknowledged that things have been rough at home lately. They told the team that they have not been able to manage Burt's behavior in the home and attribute this to "just his age." They reported that Burt has been staying out later than he is supposed to and that he argues with them about school and homework. They said that Burt tells them he is old enough to make up his own mind about curfews and selecting his friends. Mr. and Mrs. Down said they do not approve of Burt's friends.

Burt was assessed last year for his regular triennial evaluation. His cognitive ability has been assessed to be within the average range (full scale IQ 108). As a result of recent difficulties in mathematics and his behavioral difficulties, another evaluation was requested. The team members, including Burt's parents, met to discuss possible data needed to analyze current areas of difficulty. All members agreed that a behavioral analysis and other measures of behavior would be collected. In addition, selected subtests of the WJ IV and math work samples would be analyzed.

TEST RESULTS
WOODCOCK–JOHNSON IV TESTS OF ACHIEVEMENT

Clusters	PR	SS (90% BAND)	GE
Broad Math	6	77 (73–81)	4.7
Math Calculation Skills	7	78 (72–84)	5.2
Mathematics	16	85 (80–90)	5.3
Number Matrices	15	84 (76–93)	5.7
Math Facts Fluency	3	71 (67–75)	4.2
Applied Problems	8	79 (74–84)	4.1
Math Problem Solving	40	96 (89–104)	7.5

MATH WORK SAMPLES

An analysis of Burt's math class work indicates that he attempted to answer 80% of the problems he was assigned in class; however, he successfully completed only 35% of those problems. His errors included miscalculations, errors of alignment, incorrect applications in story problems (adding when he should subtract), and skipping steps needed in multiple-step problems. Burt was not able to complete an entire math assignment, working only about 75 to 85% of the problems before he either quit or ran out of time.

Burt's math homework assignments have not shown much evidence that he understands the tasks presented. He has turned in only 6 of 15 assignments since the beginning of the school year, and he successfully completed only 38% of the problems assigned. His errors on homework assignments have been consistent with the errors he has made on his seatwork assignments.

BEHAVIORAL ASSESSMENTS
BEHAVIORAL ASSESSMENT SYSTEM FOR CHILDREN: SELF-REPORT (AGES 12–18; BASC)

Rank[*]	T-Score[*]	Percentile
Clinical Profile		
Attitude toward School	68	95
Attitude toward Teachers	68	94
Sensation Seeking	67	95
School Maladjustment Composite	72	99
Atypicality	52	65
Locus of Control	74	98
Somatization	50	62
Social Stress	64	94
Anxiety	49	51
Clinical Maladjustment Composite	60	81

BEHAVIORAL ASSESSMENT SYSTEM FOR CHILDREN:
SELF-REPORT (AGES 12–18; BASC)

Rank[*]	T-Score[*]	Percentile
Clinical Profile		
Depression	85	99
Sense of Inadequacy	83	99

*On the clinical scales, a *T*-score of greater than 70 is considered to be the area of caution for the student's current behaviors. For percentile ranks on clinical scales, the higher the score, the more significant. A percentile rank of 50 is average.

Rank*	T-Score*	Percentile
Adaptive Profile		
Relations with Parents	12	1
Interpersonal Relations	43	18
Self-Esteem	26	4
Self-Reliance	39	15
Personal Adjustment Composite	23	2

*High scores on the adaptive scales indicate high levels of adaptive skills.

On the BASC, Burt endorsed critical items indicating that he feels he has trouble controlling his behavior, he feels he does not do anything right, he thinks no one understands him, he doesn't care anymore, and he feels that nothing goes his way and that no one listens to him.

Figure 13.2 illustrates the results of behavioral observations of Burt during math class for "off-task" behavior across three observation periods. To compare Burt's

FIGURE 13.2 Frequency of Off-Task Behavior in Math Class

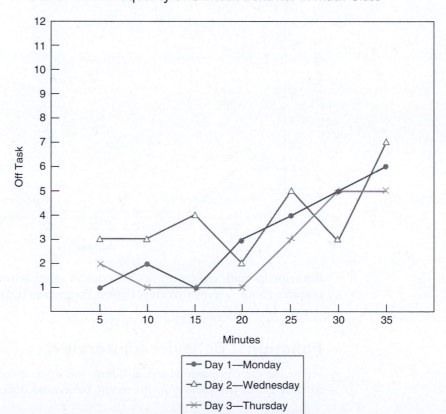

FIGURE 13.3 Frequency of Off-Task Behavior in English Class

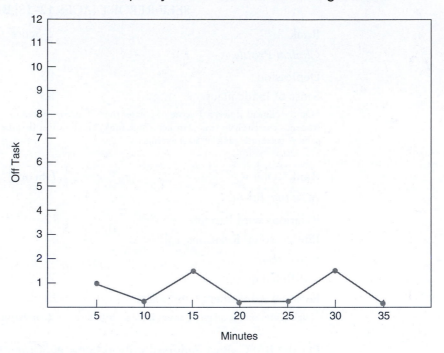

FIGURE 13.4 Frequency of Off-Task Behavior in Art Class

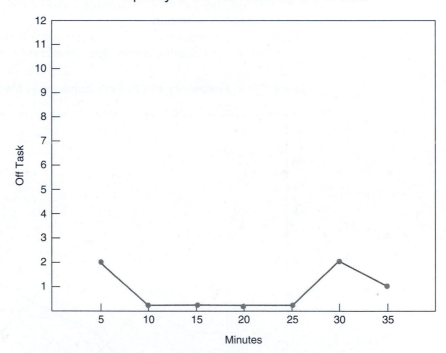

behavior in math class with his behavior in other settings, he was observed in the resource room, where he receives English instruction (Figure 13.3), and in his art class (Figure 13.4).

Functional Behavioral Interview

Following the observations sessions, Burt was interviewed by the school psychologist to elicit Burt's perspective on his recent behavioral difficulties and to determine the

CHECK YOUR UNDERSTANDING

To check your understanding of the test interpretation for Burt, complete Activity 13.8.

CHECK YOUR UNDERSTANDING

To check your understanding of determining recommendations for Burt, complete Activity 13.9.

function of these behaviors. Burt told the psychologist he knows that he is not doing well in math and that he just can't seem to keep up. He stated that he was able to do math last year and felt his teacher was "nicer to me." He stated that his teacher last year offered to stay after school and help him so he could complete his homework assignments. Burt reported that he feels lost in math so he gets bored and wants to do something else. He figures there is no use in trying to do the work, because "I just get Fs anyway."

When Burt is in his other classes, he says he can get along just fine. He says he has lots of friends in his other classes who help him with things he doesn't understand.

Burt reported that his parents have been yelling at him about his grades in math. He said his parents try to help him, but he still doesn't get it and so they get even more upset. He stated that he has been avoiding going home, because "I know they will yell at me some more."

When asked about his medication, Burt said that he hasn't been taking it as prescribed. He said he doesn't like the way he feels when he takes it, even though he agreed that he can pay attention better in school when he takes his medicine. He reported that some of his friends found out that he has to take medicine and that they began calling him names like "hyper" and "dummy." He said that he doesn't feel as good about himself or his relationships with his peers as he did last year.

Case Study: Alicia

> *Name*: Alicia Flores
>
> *Date of Birth*: February 2, 2011
>
> *Date of Evaluation*: April 13, 2014
>
> *Age*: 3–2
>
> *Current Grade Placement*: None
>
> *Examiner*: Beth Hohman
>
> *Assessment Instruments/Methods*:
>
>> Stanford–Binet V
>>
>> Vineland Adaptive Behavior Scales
>>
>> AGS Early Screening Profiles
>>
>> Play evaluation
>>
>> Home visit
>>
>> Parent interview

BACKGROUND AND REFERRAL INFORMATION

Alicia was referred by her maternal grandmother, Mrs. Flores, who is her legal guardian. Information provided by the family's social worker indicates that Mrs. Flores does not know Alicia's mother's residence at this time. Health information provided by Mrs. Flores on the Health History Survey indicates that Alicia was born prematurely and that Alicia's mother has a long history of substance abuse. At the time of Alicia's birth, Alicia's mother was 17 years of age. Alicia has one older sibling, a 6-year-old brother who is currently receiving special education support services. Alicia's grandmother believes that Alicia is not developing at the expected pace and requested a screening evaluation to determine whether Alicia might be considered for the early childhood at-risk program.

TEST RESULTS

K–ABC–II

Age 3: Global Scale Index
Mental Processing Composite

	Scaled Scores
Atlantis	6
Conceptual Thinking	7
Face Recognition	6
Triangles	6
Word Order	6
Mental Processing Composite Standard Score	66
95% Confidence Interval	59–77

VINELAND ADAPTIVE BEHAVIOR SCALES: INTERVIEW EDITION (EXPANDED FORM)

Communication

Receptive	Moderately low
Expressive	Low
Written	Low

Daily Living Skills

Personal	Moderately low
Domestic	Low
Community	Low

Socialization

Interpersonal Relationships	Low
Play and Leisure Time	Moderately low
Coping Skills	Low

AGS EARLY SCREENING PROFILES

	Standard Score	Percentile Rank	Age Equivalent
Cognitive/Language	60	1	2–0
Motor	75	5	2–1
Self-Help/Parent	68	2	2–0

SURVEY SCORES

Articulation	Below average/poor
Home Behavior	Average
Cognitive/Language	Below average
Motor	Below average

Play Evaluation and Home Visit

Alicia sat quietly on the carpet during the play evaluation. Alicia's grandmother was present during the first part of the evaluation. When her grandmother left the room to complete a survey, Alicia sat motionless and did not exhibit any change in behavior following the separation. Alicia did not initiate any spontaneous use of language or communication, such as gesturing. She did not interact with the examiner when encouraged to do so and played with only one object, a stuffed toy. Her play can be best described as mechanistic and without any noticeable motive or affect exhibited. Alicia did not react to her grandmother when she returned, but joined her grandmother on the sofa when requested.

A home visit was made 2 days following the evaluation. The home environment was clean, and several educational toys and materials were available. All interactions between Mrs. Flores and Alicia were initiated by Mrs. Flores. Alicia displayed very flat affect during both the home visit and the evaluation. Mrs. Flores stated that the only reaction she sees from Alicia occurs when it is time to eat. She described Alicia's appetite as "fair" because Alicia likes only a few types of food. When she is given something new to taste, she usually spits it out after she tries it.

Parental Interview

When Mrs. Flores was asked to list her priorities and concerns for Alicia, she expressed the need for some support to help her toilet train Alicia, improve Alicia's speech development, and improve Alicia's self-help skills, such as dressing and washing her face. Alicia's grandmother believes that Alicia's motor skills are different from her grandson's. She believes that Alicia is somewhat clumsy and too dependent on her for routine activities that other 3-year-olds are learning to do, such as self-feed with a spoon.

Mrs. Flores reported that she has been able to access monetary assistance using public resources including Medicaid for Alicia's medical needs and transportation to and from community agencies for Alicia's care. She reported that Alicia's needs are primarily being met in the home, but expressed desire for additional assistance in training Alicia in the home and in managing her behavior.

CHECK YOUR UNDERSTANDING

To check your understanding of test interpretation for Alicia, complete Activity 13.10.

CHECK YOUR UNDERSTANDING

To check your understanding of determining recommendations for Alicia, complete Activity 13.11.

CHAPTER SUMMARY

In this chapter you:

- Learned the basic principles of test interpretation
- Applied case assessment information to report writing
- Analyzed assessment data to write recommendations for interventions
- Synthesized case scenario data using multiple assessments to write interpretations
- Evaluated formal and informal assessment data to write meaningful recommendations

CHAPTER QUIZ

Now complete the Chapter Quiz to measure your understanding of the content in this chapter.

See how you are doing in the course after the conclusion of Part IV by completing the Course Progress Monitoring Activity.

absolute change The amount of difference between a baseline point and the final intervention point.

accommodations Necessary changes in format, response mode, setting, or scheduling that will enable a student with one or more disabilities to complete the general curriculum or test.

acculturation The influence of one culture on another culture.

achievement tests Tests used to measure academic progress—what the student has retained from instruction.

adaptive behavior One's ability to function in various environments.

adaptive behavior scales Instruments that assess a student's ability to adapt to different situations.

adequate yearly progress The criterion set for schools based on high-stakes testing results.

age equivalent scores Age score assigned to a mean raw score of a group during the norming process or an age score provided in statewide assessments.

age of majority Age that the state considers to be adult or when the student can be legally independent of parents.

aimline The goal line against which progress is measured in curriculum-based measurement.

alternate forms reliability Synonymous term for equivalent forms reliability.

alternative assessments Assessments that are appropriate for students with disabilities and that are designed to measure their progress in the general curriculum.

alternative plan A plan designed for educational intervention when a student has been found not eligible for special education services.

anecdotal recording Observations of behavior in which the teacher notes all behaviors and interactions that occur during a given period of time.

annual goals Long-term goals for educational intervention.

antecedent An event that occurs prior to the target behavior and increases or decreases the probability of the target behavior.

apperception tests A student's feelings about what she or he perceives to be happening in a picture or other stimulus; influenced by personal experiences.

aptitude tests Tests designed to measure strength, talent, or ability in a particular area or domain.

arena assessment Technique that places the child and facilitator in the center of multidisciplinary team members during evaluation.

assessment The process of gathering information to monitor progress and make educational decisions if necessary.

assistive technology Any assistive device that enables persons with disabilities to function better in their environments; necessary technology that enables the student to participate in a free, appropriate public education.

assistive technology evaluation An assessment to determine what devices are needed to promote successful functioning within the school environment.

at risk for developmental delay When a child is believed to be at risk for delay in one or more areas if interventions are not provided.

authentic assessment Assessment that requires the student to apply knowledge in the world beyond the classroom.

autism spectrum disorders A group of pervasive disorders that are characterized by significant difficulties in capacity for social reciprocity, communication delays, and repetitive behavior patterns.

basal Thought to represent the level of skills below which the student would correctly answer all test items.

baseline The frequency, duration, or latency of a behavior determined before behavioral intervention.

baseline score The beginning score against which student progress is measured.

behavioral intervention plan A plan designed to increase positive behaviors and decrease negative behaviors before these become problematic.

behaviorally stated short-term objectives Observable and measurable objectives that provide evidence of a student's progress toward annual goals.

benchmarks The major markers that provide evidence of a student's progress toward annual goals.

bimodal distribution A distribution that has two most frequently occurring scores.

biological risk factors Health factors such as birth trauma that place a child at risk for developmental disabilities.

ceiling Thought to represent the level of skills above which all test items would be answered incorrectly; the examiner discontinues testing at this level.

checklists Lists of academic, developmental, or behavioral skills that must be mastered by the student and are used to monitor progress.

chronological age The numerical representation of a student's age expressed in years, months, and days.

coefficient alpha A formula used to check consistency across terms of an instrument with responses with varying credit.

compliance Operating within the federal regulations.

comprehensive educational evaluation A complete assessment in all areas of suspected disability.

concurrent validity A comparison of one instrument with another within a short period of time.

confidence interval The range of scores for an obtained score determined by adding and subtracting standard error of measurement units.

consent form Written permission form that grants permission for evaluation or placement.

construct validity The ability of an instrument to measure psychological constructs.

content validity Occurs when the items contained within the test are representative of the content purported to be measured.

correct letter sequence The sequence of letters in a specific word.

correlation coefficient The expression of a relationship between two variables.

correlation A statistical method of observing the degree of relationship between two sets of data on two variables.

criterion-referenced tests Tests designed to accompany and measure a set of criteria or skill-mastery criteria.

criterion-related assessment Use of an assessment instrument in which items are related to meeting objectives or passing skill mastery objectives.

criterion-related validity Statistical method of comparing an instrument's ability to measure a skill, trait, or domain with an existing instrument or other criterion.

cross-battery assessment Administering subtests from two or more tests to determine if a weakness exists in a particular skill or ability.

curriculum-based assessment Use of content from the currently used curriculum to assess student progress.

curriculum-based evaluation Evaluation of curriculum materials, records, and assessments to make instructional decisions

curriculum-based measurement Frequent measurement comparing student's actual progress with an expected rate of progress.

cut-off point An arbitrary score that must be met to indicate change or response to intervention.

deciles A method of reporting scores that divides data into 10 groups with each group representing 10% of the obtained scores.

derived scores Scores obtained by using a raw score and expectancy tables.

descriptive statistics Statistics used to organize and describe data.

developmental delay When an infant or child experiences delay in physical, cognitive, communicative, social, emotional, or adaptive development.

developmental version The experimental edition of a test that is field-tested and revised before publication.

diagnostic tests Individually administered tests designed to determine specific academic skills and are used to obtain further information about student performance.

direct measurement Measuring progress by using the same instructional materials or tasks that are used in the classroom.

direct observation Observations of student behaviors in the environment in which the behaviors occur.

discrepancy analysis Comparison of a student's intellectual ability and academic achievement.

disproportionality Condition that exists when students of a specific ethnic group are at risk for overidentification or are at risk for underrepresentation in special education.

domain Area of cognitive development or ability thought to be evidenced by certain behaviors or skills.

drawing tests Tests in which student draws figures, houses, trees, or families; scored developmentally and projectively.

due process The right to a hearing to settle disputes; a protection for children with disabilities and their families.

duration recording Observations that involve the length of time a behavior occurs.

dynamic assessment Assessment in which the examiner prompts or interacts with the student to determine the student's potential to learn a skill.

early intervening services Evidence-based methods for addressing the needs of students at risk for learning or behavioral disabilities or students who have exited from such services.

ecobehavioral interviews Interviews of parents and teachers that assess behavior in different settings and routines.

ecological assessment Method of assessing a student's total environment to determine factors that might be contributing to learning or behavioral problems.

educational planning Interventions and strategies used to promote educational success.

Elementary and Secondary Education Act (ESEA) Law of 2001 that holds general education accountable for all students' academic achievement.

eligibility decisions The determination of whether a student will receive special education services.

eligibility meeting A conference held after a preplacement evaluation to determine if a student is eligible for services.

environmental assessment Method of assessing the student's classroom environment.

environmental influence The impact of the environment on the student's learning ability.

environmental risk factors Environmental influences such as the mother's young age that place a child at risk for developmental disabilities.

equivalent forms reliability Consistency of a test to measure some domain, traits, or skill using like forms of the same instrument.

error analysis Analyzing a student's learning problems by determining error patterns.

establishing operation Events occurring before the target behavior that alter the receptivity of the consequence and increase or decrease the probability of occurrence of the target behavior.

estimated true score A method of calculating the amount of error correlated with the distance of the score from the mean of the group.

event recording Recording the frequency of a target behavior; also called *frequency counting.*

expressive language Language skills used in speaking or writing.

expressive language disorders Significant difficulty with oral expression.

family-centered program Program in which assessment and goals are driven by the family's needs and priorities.

family-focused program Program in which the family's needs are considered, but goals and plans are reached through mutual agreement between the family and education professionals.

field test The procedure of trying out a test by administering it to a sample population.

formative assessment Ongoing assessment that is completed during the acquisition of a skill.

frequency counting Counting the occurrence of a specific behavior; also known as *event recording.*

frequency distribution Method of determining how many times each score occurs in a set of data.

frequency polygon A graphic representation of how often each score occurs in a set of data.

functional assessment Assessment of the skills, academic and otherwise, applied in everyday living.

functional assessment interviews The interview component of the functional behavioral assessment (FBA) that provides information about possible purposes of target behaviors.

functional behavioral analysis An analysis of the exploration of behaviors that occur when variables such as antecedents or consequences are manipulated.

functional behavioral assessment A multicomponent assessment to determine the purpose of target behaviors.

grade-level scores Grade scores assigned to a mean raw score of a group during the norming process or a grade score provided in statewide assessments.

high-stakes testing Accountability assessment of state or district standards, which may be used for funding or accreditation decisions.

IDEA Individuals with Disabilities Education Act, passed in 1990 (also known as PL 94–142); federal law mandating education of all students with disabilities.

IDEA 2004 Law that reauthorized and improved the 1997 Individuals with Disabilities Education Act (IDEA).

IDEA regulations Governing document that explains IDEA in operational terms.

impartial due process hearing A hearing by an impartial officer that is held to resolve differences between a school and parents of a student with disabilities.

impartial hearing officer Person qualified to hear disputes between schools and parents; this person is not an employee of the local education agency (LEA).

independent educational evaluation Comprehensive evaluation provided by a qualified independent evaluator.

individual assessment plan A plan that lists the specific tests and procedures to be used for a student who has been screened and needs further assessment.

Individual family service plan (IFSP) Plan required by PL 99–457 that includes the related needs of the family of the child with disabilities; plan designed for children ages 3 and younger that addresses the child's strengths and weaknesses as well as the family's needs.

individualized education program (IEP) A written plan of educational interventions designed for each student who receives special education.

individualized education program (IEP) team The team specified in IDEA amendments that makes decisions about special education eligibility and interventions.

Individuals with Disabilities Education Act See *IDEA*.

informal assessment Nonstandardized methods of evaluating progress, such as interviews, observations, and teacher-made tests.

informed consent Parents are informed of rights in their native language and agree in writing to procedures for the child; consent may be revoked at any time.

initial evaluation A comprehensive evaluation that must be conducted before a student receives special education services.

innate potential Thought to be one's ability from birth.

intelligence A general concept of an individual's ability to function effectively within various settings; usually assessed by intelligence tests.

interactive strategies Strategies used by the examiner that encourage the child to use communication to solve problems.

interindividual interpretation Comparing a student to a peer norm group.

internal consistency The consistency of the items on an instrument to measure a skill, trait, or domain.

interpolation The process of dividing existing data into smaller units for establishing tables of developmental scores.

interrater reliability The consistency of a test to measure a skill, trait, or domain across examiners.

interresponse time The amount of time between target behaviors.

interval recording Sampling a behavior intermittently for very brief periods of time; used to observe frequently occurring behaviors.

interval scale A scale that uses numbers for ranking in which numerical units are equidistant.

interviews Formal or informal questions asked orally by the examiner.

intraindividual interpretation Comparing a student with his or her own performance.

IQ Intelligence quotient; expressed as a standard score, usually with a mean of 100.

item pool A large collection of test items thought to effectively represent a particular domain or content area.

Kuder–Richardson (K–R) 20 A formula used to check consistency across items of an instrument with right/wrong responses.

language assessment Measuring verbal concepts and verbal understanding.

latency recording Observations involving the amount of time that elapses from the presentation of a stimulus until the response occurs.

least restrictive environment The educational environment determined to be most like that of typically developing students.

long-term goals Statements of anticipated progress that a student will make in 1 year upon which short-term objectives and benchmarks are based.

manifestation determination A hearing to determine if a student's behavior is the result of the student's disability.

maze A measure of reading comprehension that requires the student to supply a missing word in a passage.

mean Arithmetic average of a set of data.

measures of central tendency Statistical methods for observing how data cluster around the mean.

measures of dispersion Statistical methods for observing how data spread from the mean.

median The middlemost score in a set of data.

mediation Process of settling a dispute between parents and schools without a full third-party hearing.

minority overrepresentation When the percentage of a culturally different group is greater in special education classes than in the local education agency (LEA).

mode The most frequently occurring score in a set of scores.

multimodal distribution A distribution with three or more modes.

negatively skewed Describes a distribution in which more of the scores fall above the mean.

nominal scale Numerical scale that uses numbers for the purpose of identification.

nondiscriminatory assessment Fair and objective testing practices for students from all cultural and linguistic backgrounds.

norm group A large number of people who are administered a test to establish comparative data of average performances.

norm-referenced tests Tests designed to compare individual students with national averages or norms of expectancy.

normal distribution A symmetrical distribution with a single numerical representation for the mean, median, and mode.

observation An informal assessment method of activities, language, and interactions in various settings.

obtained score The observed score of a student on a particular test on a given day.

oral-reading fluency The number of words the student is able to read aloud in a specified period of time.

ordinal scale Numerical scale in which numbers are used for ranking.

overidentification Identification of students who seem to be eligible for special education services but who actually are not disabled.

overrepresentation The percentage of students of a culturally different group is greater than the percentage of individuals of that group in the local education agency (LEA).

parents' rights booklet Used to convey rights and procedural safeguards to parents.

Pearson's *r* A statistical formula for determining strength and direction of correlations.

percent change A measure of change that subtracts the mean intervention score from the mean baseline score and divides this by the mean baseline score.

percent of nonoverlapping data points A measure of change that uses only the data points above the highest baseline point.

percentile ranks Scores that express the percentage of students who scored as well as or lower than a given student's score.

performance assessment Assessment that utilizes a student-created product as a demonstration of knowledge.

permanent products Products made by the student that may be analyzed for academic or behavioral interventions.

phonemic analysis The breaking up of a word into isolated sounds.

phonemic awareness Perception of the individual sounds that make up words.

phonemic synthesis The blending of isolated sounds into a whole word.

play evaluations Observational informal assessment in a natural play environment.

portfolio assessment Evaluating student progress, strengths, and weaknesses using a collection of different measurements and work samples.

positively skewed Describes a distribution in which more of the scores fall below the mean.

postsecondary goals Carefully designed goals driven by assessment and linked to positive postsecondary outcomes.

predictive validity A measure of how well an instrument can predict performance on some other variable.

prereferral intervention strategies Methods used by teachers and other team members to observe and modify student behaviors, the learning environment, and/or teaching methods before making a formal referral.

presentation format The method by which items of an instrument are presented to a student.

probes Tests used for in-depth assessment of the mastery of a specific skill or subskill.

problem-solving model Strategies for intervention that (1) identify the problem, (2) propose a hypothesis for intervention, and (3) measure the effectiveness of interventions in meeting students' needs.

procedural safeguards Provisions of IDEA designed to protect students and parents in the special education process.

progress monitoring Monitoring all students to determine that they are making progress through the curriculum as expected.

projective techniques Techniques used to analyze a student's feelings by what the student projects into the story card or other stimulus.

protocol The response sheet or record form used by the examiner to record the student's answers.

Public Law 94–142 Education for All Handicapped Children Act of 1975; guarantees the right to a free and appropriate education in the least restrictive environment; renamed IDEA in 1990.

Public Law 99–457 IDEA amendments that extend services for special needs children through infancy and preschool years; this law mandates services for children ages 3–5 with disabilities.

questionnaires Questions about a student's behavior or academic concerns that may be answered by the student or by the parent or teacher; also called *interviews*.

range The distance between the highest and lowest scores in a data set.

ratio scale Numerical scale with the quality of equidistant units and absolute zero.

raw score The first score obtained in testing; usually represents the number of items correct.

receptive language Inner language concepts applied to what is heard.

receptive language disorders Significant difficulty understanding spoken language.

related services Services related to special education but not part of the educational setting, such as transportation and therapies.

reliability The dependability or consistency of an instrument across time or items.

reliable change index A measure of change that divides the difference between the baseline score and post-intervention score by the standard error of the difference.

replacement behaviors Appropriate behaviors that are incompatible with the negative behaviors they replace.

response mode The method required for the examinee to answer items of an instrument.

response to intervention (RTI) The application of learning or behavioral interventions and measurement of students' responses to such interventions.

sample A small group of people thought to represent the population for whom the test was designed.

scattergram Graphic representation of a correlation.

schoolwide positive behavioral support Proactive strategies defined by school staff and based on behavioral principles.

screening A review of records of a student's school achievement to determine what interventions or additional assessments are needed.

screening tests Brief tests that sample a few items across skills or domains.

Section 504 of the Rehabilitation Act of 1973 A civil rights law that includes protection from discrimination and that provides for reasonable accommodations.

self-determination Ability to make one's needs known and to advocate for oneself.

sentence completion tests Stems of sentences that the student completes; analyzed for themes.

sequential processing Presenting one stimulus at a time so that it is processed in sequence and linked to a previous stimulus.

setting event A specific event that occurs before the target behavior but is removed from the actual environment in which the behavior occurs.

simultaneous processing Presenting stimuli at the same time to be processed and integrated.

situational questionnaires Questionnaires that assess the child's behavior in various situations.

skewed Describes a distribution that has either more positively distributed scores or more negatively distributed scores.

sociograms Graphic representation of the social dynamics within a group.

special education services Services not provided by regular education but necessary to enable an individual with disabilities to achieve in school.

split-half reliability A method of checking the consistency across items by halving a test and administering two half-forms of the same test.

standard deviation A unit of measurement that represents the typical amount that a score can be expected to vary from the mean in a given set of data.

standard error of measurement The amount of error determined to exist using a specific instrument, calculated using the instrument's standard deviation and reliability.

standard scores Scores calculated during the norming process of a test that follow normal distribution theory.

standardized tests Tests developed with specific standard administration, scoring, and interpretation procedures that must be followed precisely to obtain optimum results.

Standards for Educational and Psychological Testing Professional and ethical standards that suggest minimum criteria for assessing students.

stanines A method of reporting scores that divides data into nine groups, with scores reported as 1 through 9 with a mean of 5.

subskill A component of a more complex skill; used in task analysis.

subtask Small units of a task used to complete a task analysis.

summative assessment Assessment that is completed at the conclusion of an instructional period to determine the level of skill acquisition or mastery.

supported employment Employing a person with a disability with persons without disabilities; the arrangement is for at least minimum wage and may include a job coach or other supports.

surrogate parent Person appointed by the court system to be legally responsible for a child's education.

target behaviors Specific behaviors that require intervention by the teacher to promote optimal academic or social learning.

task analysis Breaking a task down into parts to determine which part is causing difficulty for the student.

teacher assistance team A team of various professionals who assist the teacher in designing interventions for students who are not making academic progress.

test manual A manual accompanying a test instrument that contains directions for administration and norm tables.

test–retest reliability Study that employs the readministration of a single instrument to check for consistency across time.

testing A method to determine a student's ability to complete certain tasks or demonstrate mastery of a skill or knowledge of content.

time sampling When the behavioral observation samples behavior throughout the day or class period.

transition assessment Age-appropriate assessment of academics, functional skills, and independent living.

transition planning Planning for meeting the student's needs following high school.

transition services Services designed to help students make the transition from high school to the postsecondary education or work environment.

true score The student's actual score.

universal screening Assessment of all students in the general education classroom to determine if any are at risk or are below the level of expected performance for their grade.

validity The quality of a test; the degree to which an instrument measures what it was designed to measure.

validity of test use The appropriate use of a specific instrument.

variability Describes how scores vary.

variance Describes the total amount by which a group of scores varies in a set of data.

visual inspection An examination of data graphs or other data that indicates consistent change.

work samples Samples of a student's work; one type of permanent product.

written language Understanding language concepts and using them in writing.

z scores Derived scores that are expressed in standard deviation units.

References

Achenbach, T. M. (1986). *Child behavior checklist: Direct observation form, revised edition*. Burlington: University of Vermont Center for Children, Youth, and Families.

Achenbach, T. M. (1991a). *Child behavior checklist/4–18 and 1991 profile: Manual*. Burlington: University of Vermont Department of Psychiatry.

Achenbach, T. M. (1991b). *Child behavior checklist and 1991 profile: Manual for the teacher report form*. Burlington: University of Vermont Department of Psychiatry.

Achenbach, T. M. (1991c). *Child behavior checklist and 1991 profile: Manual for the youth self-report form*. Burlington: University of Vermont Department of Psychiatry.

Achenbach, T. M., & McConaughy, S. H. (1989, 1990). *Semistructured clinical interview: Observation form*. Burlington: University of Vermont Center for Children, Youth, and Families.

Achenbach, T. M., & Rescorla, L. A. (2000). *Manual for the ASEBA preschool forms & profiles: An integrated system of multi-informant assessment*. Burlington, VT: Authors.

Achenbach, T. M., & Rescorla, L. A. (2001). *Manual for the ASEBA school-age forms & profiles*. Burlington, VT: University of Vermont, Research Center for Children, Youth, & Families.

AIMSweb (n.d.). *AIMSweb progress monitoting and RTI system*. Retrieved from http://www.aimsweb.com/

Algozzine, B., & Ysseldyke, J. E. (1981). Special education services for normal children: Better safe than sorry. *Exceptional Children, 48*, 238–243.

Algozzine, B., Wang, C., White, R., Cooke, N., Marr, M. B., Algozzine, K., Helf, S., & Duran, G. Z. (2012). Effects of multitier academic and behavior instruction on difficult-to-teach students. *Exceptional Children, 79*(1), 45–64.

Allinder, R. N. (1995). An examination of the relationship between teacher efficacy and curriculum-based measurement and student achievement. *Remedial and Special Education, 16*, 247–254.

Allinder, R. N., & Fuchs, L. S. (1992). Screening academic achievement: Review of the *Peabody Individual Achievement Test–Revised. Learning Disabilities Research & Practice, 7*(1), 45–47.

Alt, M., Arizmendi, G. D., Beal, C. R., & Hurtado, J. S. (2013). The effect of test translation on the performance of second grade English learners and the KeyMath-3. *Psychology in the Schools, 50*(1), 27–36. DOI: 10.1002/pits.21656

American Association on Intellectual and Developmental Disabilities (2004). *Supports Intensity Scale*. Washington, DC: Author

American Association on Intellectual and Developmental Disabilities. (2010). *Intellectual disability: Definition, classification, and systems of supports* (11th ed). Washington, DC: Author.

American Educational Research Association (AERA), American Psychological Association (APA) & National Council on Measurement in Education (NCME). (1999). *Standards for educational and psychological testing*. Washington, DC: AERA.

American Psychiatric Association (2013). *Diagnostic and Statistical Manual of Mental Disorders*, 5th ed. Arlington, VA: Author.

American Psychiatric Association. (2000). *Diagnostic and statistical manual of mental disorders*, (4th ed. rev.). Arlington, VA: Author.

American Psychological Association. (1999). *Standards for educational and psychological testing*. Washington, DC: Author.

Anastasi, A. (1988). *Psychological testing* (6th ed.). New York: Macmillan.

Anastasi, A., & Urbina, S. (1998). *Psychological testing* (7th ed.). Upper Saddle River, NJ: Prentice Hall.

Archbald, D. A. (1991). Authentic assessment: Principles, practices, and issues. *School Psychology Quarterly, 6*, 279–293.

Arciuli, J., Stevens, K., Trembath, D., & Simpson, I. C. (2013). The relationship between adaptive behavior and direct assessment of reading ability in children with autism spectrum disorder. *Journal of Speech, Language, and Hearing Research, 56*(6), 1837–1844.

Ardoin, S. P., Witt, J. C., Suldo, S. M., Connell, J. M., Koenig, J. L., Resetar, . . . Williams, K. L. (2004). Examining the incremental benefits of administering maze and three versus one curriculum-based measurement reading probes when conducting universal screening. *School Psychology Review, 33*(2), 218–233.

Ardoin, S. P., & Christ, T. J. (2009). Curriculum-based measurement of oral reading: Standard errors associated with progress monitoring outcomes from DIBELS, AIMSweb, and an experimental passage set. *School Psychology Review, 38*(2), 266–283.

Armistead, L., & Provenzano, F. (2014). *Ethical and professional practices in the digital age*. Presentation at the National Association of School Psychologists Annual Conference, Washington, DC: February 18.

Bagnato, S. (1980). The efficacy of diagnostic reports as individualized guides to prescriptive goal planning. *Exceptional Children, 46*, 554–557.

Bailey, D. B., & Wolery, M. (1989). *Assessing infants and preschoolers with handicaps*. Upper Saddle River, NJ: Merrill/Prentice Hall.

Baker, S. K., & Good, R. (1995). Curriculum-based measurement of English reading with bilingual Hispanic students: A validation study with second grade students. *School Psychology Review, 24*(4), 561–578.

Ball, C. R., & Christ, T. J. (2012). Supporting valid decision making: Uses and misuses of assessment data within the context of RTI. *Psychology in the Schools, 49*(3), 231–244. DOI10.1002/pits.21592

Barkley, R. A. (1990). *Attention deficit hyperactivity disorder: A handbook for diagnosis and treatment*. New York: Guilford.

Barkley, R. A., DuPaul, G. J., & McMurray, M. B. (1990). Comprehensive evaluation of attention deficit disorder with and without hyperactivity as defined by research criteria. *Journal of Consulting and Clinical Psychology, 58*, 775–789.

Barnes, W. (1986). Informal assessment of reading. *Pointer, 30*, 42–46.

Barnett, D. W., Macmann, G. M., & Carey, K. T. (1992). Early intervention and the assessment of developmental skills: Challenges and directions. *Topics in Early Childhood Special Education, 12*(1), 21–43.

Barnett, D., Zins, J., & Wise, L. (1984). An analysis of parental participation as a means of reducing bias in the education of handicapped children. *Special Services in the Schools, 1*, 71–84.

Barnett, D. W., Daly, E. J. D., Jones, K. M., & Lentz, F. E. (2004). Response to intervention: Empirically based special service decisions from single-case designs of increasing and decreasing intensity. *The Journal of Special Education, 38*(2), 66–70.

Bayley, N. (1993). *Bayley scales of infant development-II*. San Antonio: Psychological Corporation.

Bellak, L., & Bellak, S. S. (1949). *Children's apperception test (animal figures)*. Larchmont, NY: C.P.S.

Bellak, L., & Bellak, S. S. (1952). *Manual for the supplement for the* Children's Apperception Test. Larchmont, NY: C.P.S.

Bellak, L., & Hurvich, M. S. (1965). *Children's apperception test (human figures): Manual.* Larchmont, NY: C.P.S.

Bender, W., & Golden, L. (1988). Adaptive behavior of learning disabled and non-learning disabled children. *Learning Disability Quarterly, 11,* 55–61.

Benedict, A. E., Thomas, R. A., Kimberling, J., & Leko, C. (May/June 2013). Trends in teacher education: What every special education teacher should know. *Teaching Exceptional Children, 45(5),* 60–68.

Benedict, E. A., Horner, R. H., & Squires, J. K. (2007). Assessment and implementation of positive behavior support in preschools. *Topics in Early Childhood Special Education, 27(3),* 174–192.

Bennett, T., Lee, H., & Lueke, B. (1998). Expectations and concerns: What mothers and fathers say about inclusion. *Education and Training in Mental Retardation and Developmental Disabilities, 33(2),* 108–122.

Berninger, V. L. (2006). Research-supported ideas for implementing reauthorized IDEA with intelligent professional psychological services. *Psychology in the Schools, 43(7),* 781–796.

Bersoff, D. N. (1981). Testing and the law. *American Psychologist, 36,* 1047–1056.

Bocian, K. M., Beebe, M. E., MacMillan, D., & Gresham, F. M. (1999). Competing paradigms in learning disabilities classification by schools and the variations in the meaning of discrepant achievement. *Learning Disabilities Research, 14(1),* 1–14.

Bolt, S. E., & Ysseldyke, J. (2008). Accommodating students with disabilities in large-scale testing: A comparison of differential item functioning (DIF) identified across disability groups. *Journal of Psychoeducational Assessment, 26(2),* 121–138. doi:10.1177/0734282907307703

Bracken, B. A., & McCallum, R. S. (1998). *Universal test of nonverbal intelligence: Examiner's manual.* Itasca, IL: Riverside Publishing Company.

Brantlinger, E. (1987). Making decisions about special education placement: Do low-income parents have the information they need? *Journal of Learning Disabilities, 20,* 94–101.

Brazelton, T. (1984). *Neonatal behavioral assessment scale–second edition.* Philadelphia: Lippincott.

Brigance, A. H. (2010). *Brigance diagnostic comprehensive inventory of basic skills–II.* N. Billerica, MA: Curriculum Associates.

Brigance, A. H. (2012). *Brigance Transition Skills Inventory.* North Billerica, MA: Curriculum Associates.

Brigance, A. H. (2013). *Brigance Early Childhood Screen, III.* North Billerica, MA: Curriculum Associates.

Broekkamp, H., Van Hout-Wolters, B. H. A. M., Van den Bergh, H., & Rijlaarsdam, G. (2004). Teachers' task demands, students' test expectations, and actual test content. *British Journal of Educational Psychology, 74,* 205–220.

Brotherson, M. J., & Berdine, W. H. (1993). Transition to adult services: Support for ongoing parent participation. *Remedial & Special Education, 14(4),* 44–52.

Brown, L., & Hammill, D. (1990). *Behavior rating profile* (2nd ed.). Austin, TX: Pro-Ed.

Brown, L., Sherbenou, R. J., & Johnsen, S. K. (1997). *Test of nonverbal intelligence* (3rd ed.). Austin, TX: Pro-Ed.

Brown, T., Reynolds, C. R., & Whitaker, J. S. (1999). Bias in mental testing since Bias in Mental Testing. *School Psychology Quarterly, 14(3),* 208–238.

Brown, V. L., Cronin, M. E., & McEntire, E. (1994). *Test of mathematical abilities* (2nd ed.). Austin, TX: Pro-Ed.

Brown, V. L., Wiederholt, J. L., & Hammill, D. D. (2009). *Test of reading comprehension* (4th ed.). Austin, TX: Pro-Ed.

Bruininks, R., Thurlow, M., & Gilman, C. (1987). Adaptive behavior and mental retardation. *Journal of Special Education, 21,* 69–88.

Bryant, B. R. (1998). Assistive technology: An introduction. *Journal of Learning Disabilities, 31(1),* 2–3.

Burnette, J. (1998, March). Reducing the disproportionate representation of minority students in special education. ERIC/OSEP Digest E566.

Burns, M. K, & Scholin, S. (2013). Response to intervention: School-wide prevention of academic difficulties, pp. 8–17 in J. W. Lloyd, T. J. Landrum, B. G. Cook, and M. Tankersley, Eds. *Research-Based Approaches for Assessment.* Upper Saddle, NJ: Pearson Education Inc.

Campbell, E., Schellinger, T., & Beer, J. (1991). Relationship among the ready or not parental checklist for school readiness, the Brigance kindergarten and first grade screen, and SRA scores. *Perceptual and Motor Skills, 73,* 859–862.

Canivez, G. L. (1995). Validity of the *Kaufman Brief Intelligence Test:* Comparisons with the *Wechsler Intelligence Scale for Children* (3rd ed.). *Psychological Assessment Resources, Inc. 2(2),* 101–111.

Canivez, G. L. (1996). Validity and diagnostic efficiency of the *Kaufman Brief Intelligence Test* in reevaluating students with learning disability. *Journal of Psychoeducational Assessment, 14,* 4–19.

Canivez, G. L. (2013). Incremental criterion validity of WAIS-IV factor index scores: Relationship with WIAT-II and WIAT III subtest and composite scores. *Psychological Assessment, 25(2),* 484–495. DOI: 10.1037/a0032029.

Canter, A. (1991). Effective psychological services for all students: A data-based model of service delivery. In G. Stoner, M. R. Shinn, & H. M. Walker (Eds.), *Interventions for achievement and behavioral problems* (pp. 49–78). Silver Spring, MD: National Association of School Psychologists.

Canter, A. S. (1997). The future of intelligence testing in the schools. *School Psychology Review, 26(2),* 255–261.

Carroll, J. B. (2005). The three stratum theory of cognitive abilities. In D. P. Flanagan & P. L. Harrison (Eds.), *Contemporary intellectual assessment: Theories, tests, and issues* (pp. 69–76). New York: The Guilford Press.

Carter, E. W., Trainor, A. A., Sun, Y., & Owens, L. (2009). Assessing the transition- related strengths and needs of adolescents with high-incidence disabilities. *Exceptional Children, 76(1),* 74–94.

Cascella, P. W. (2006). Standardized speech-language tests and students with intellectual disability: A review of normative data. *Journal of Intellectual & Developmental Disability, 3(2),* 120–124.

Cheng, S., & Rose, S. (2005). Assessing written expression for students who are deaf or hard of hearing: Curriculum-based measurement. *Technical Report 11: Research Institute on Progress Monitoring.*

Clarizio, H. F., & Higgins, M. M. (1989). Assessment of severe emotional impairment: Practices and problems. *Psychology in the Schools, 26,* 154–162.

Clark, G. M. (1996). Transition planning assessment for secondary-level students with learning disabilities. *Journal of Learning Disabilities, 29(1),* 79–93.

Clark, G. M., & Patton, J. R. (2006). *Transition planning inventory: Update version.* Austin, TX: Pro-Ed.

Clark, G. M., & Patton, J. R. (2014). *Transition Planning Inventory,* 2nd ed. Austin, TX: ProEd.

Clarke, B., & Shinn, M. R. (2004). A preliminary investigation into the identification and development of early mathematics curriculum-based measurement. *School Psychology Review, 33(2),* 234–248.

Cohen, L. G., & Spenciner, L. J. (1994). *Assessment of young children.* New York: Longman.

Cole, J. C., Muenz, T. A., Ouchi, B. Y., Kaufman, N. L., & Kaufman, A. S. (1997). The impact of pictorial stimulis on written expression output of adolescents and adults. *Pyschology in the Schools, 34,* 1–9.

Cole, J., D'Alonzo, B., Gallegos, A., Giordano, G., & Stile, S. (1992). Test biases that hamper learners with disabilities. *Diagnostique, 17,* 209–225.

Cole, N. (1981). Bias in testing. *American Psychologist, 36,* 1067–1075.

Connelly, J. (1985). Published tests: Which ones do special education teachers perceive as useful? *Journal of Special Education, 19,* 149–155.

Conners, C. K. (1993). *Conners' continuous performance test.* North Tonawanda, NY: Multi-Health Systems.

Conners, C. K. (1997). *Conners' rating scales–revised: Technical manual.* North Tonawanda, NY: Multi-Health Systems.

Conners, C. K. (2014). *Conners Continuous Performance Test,* 3rd ed. North Tonawanda, NY: Multi-Health Systems, Inc.

Connolly, A. J. (1988). *KeyMath–revised: A diagnostic inventory of essential mathematics. Manual for forms A and B.* Circle Pines, MN: American Guidance Service.

Connolly, A. J. (2007). *KeyMath 3: Diagnostic battery.* Minneapolis, MN: NCS Pearson, Inc.

Conroy, M. A., Clark, D., Gable, R. A., & Fox, J. (1999). Building competence in the use of functional behavioral assessment. *Preventing School Failure, 43*(4), 140–144.

Council of Administrators of Special Education. (2006). *Response to intervention: NASDSE and CASE white paper on RTI.* Retrieved from http://www.casecec.org/pdf/rti/RtI%20An%20Administrator's%20Perspective%201-061.pdf

Daves, D. P., & Walker, D. W. (2012). RTI: Court and case law–confusion by design. *Learning Disabilities Quarterly, 35*(2), 68–71.

Davis, L. B., Fuchs, L. S., Fuchs, D., & Whinnery, K. (1995). "Will CBM help me learn?" Students' perception of the benefits of curriculum-based measurement. *Education and Treatment of Children, 18,* 19–32.

Davis, W., & Shepard, L. (1983). Specialists' use of tests and clinical judgments in the diagnosis of learning disabilities. *Learning Disabilities Quarterly, 6,* 128–137.

Decker, S. L., Englund, J., & Albritton, K. (2012). Integrating multitiered measurement outcomes for special education eligibility with sequential decision-making methodology. *Psychology in the Schools, 49*(4), 368–384. DOI: 10.1002/pits.21601

Decker, S. L., Hale, J. B., Flanagan, D. P. (2013). Professional practice issues in the assessment of cognitive functioning for educational applications. *Psychology in the Schools, 50*(3), 300–313. DOI: 10.1002/pits.21675

deGruijter, D. N. M. (1997). On information of percentile ranks. *Journal of Educational Measurement, 34,* 177–178.

Deno, S. L. (1985). Curriculum-based measurement: The emerging alternative. *Exceptional Children, 52*(3), 219–232.

Deno, S. L., Fuchs, L. S., Marston, D., & Shin, J. (2001). Using curriculum-based measurement to establish growth standards for students with learning disabilities. *School Psychology Review, 30*(4), 507–524.

Deno, S. L., Marston, D., & Mirkin, P. (1982). Valid measurement procedures for continuous evaluation of written expression. *Exceptional Children, 48*(4), 368–371.

Deno, S. L., Marston, D., Shinn, M., & Tindal, G. (1983). Oral reading fluency: A simple datum for scaling reading disability. *Topics in Learning and Learning Disabilities, 2*(4), 53–59.

Diana v. State Board of Education, Civil Act. No. C-70-37 (N.D. Cal, 1970, further order, 1973).

DiLavore, P., Loard, C., & Rutter, M. (1995). Pre-linguistic autism diagnostic observation schedule (PL–ADOS). *Journal of Autism and Pervasive Developmental Disorders, 25,* 355–379.

Doll, E. A. (1935). A genetic scale of social maturity. *American Journal of Orthopsychiatry, 5,* 180–188.

Downs, A., & Strand, P. S. (2006). Using assessment to improve the effectiveness of early childhood education. *Journal of Child & Family Studies, 15*(6), 671–680.

Drasgow, E., & Yell, M. (2001). Functional behavioral assessments: Legal requirements and challenges. *School Psychology Review, 30*(2), 239–251.

Drasgow, E., Yell, M. L., Bradley, R., Shriner, J. G. (1999). The IDEA Amendments of 1997: A school-wide model for conducting functional behavioral assessments and developing behavioral intervention plans. *Education and Treatment of Children, 22*(3), 244–266.

Dunn, L. M., & Dunn, D. M. (2007). *Peabody picture vocabulary test–4.* Wascana Limited Partnership. Minneapolis: NCS Pearson, Inc.

Dunst, C. J., Johanson, C., Trivette, C. M., & Hamby, D. (1991). Family-oriented early intervention policies and practices: Family-centered or not? *Exceptional Children, 58,* 115–126.

Eaves, R. (1985). Educational assessment in the United States [Monograph]. *Diagnostique, 10,* 5–39.

Eckert, T. L., Shapiro, E. S., & Lutz, J. G. (1995). Teachers' ratings of the acceptability of curriculum-based assessment methods. *School Psychology Review, 24,* 497–511.

Education of the Handicapped Act (1975, 1977). PL 94–142, 20 U.S.C. §§ 1400–1485, 34 CFR-300.

Ehri, L. C., Nunes, S. R., Willows, D. M., Schuster, B. V., Yaghoub-Zadeh, Z., & Shanahan, T. (2001). Phonemic awareness instruction helps children learn to read: Evidence from the national reading panel's meta-analysis. *Reading Research Quarterly, 36*(3), 250–287.

Elliot, C. D. (2007). *Differential ability scale: Administration and scoring manual* (2nd ed.). San Antonio, TX: Pearson.

Elliot, S. N., Busse, R. T., & Gresham, F. M. (1993). Behavior rating scales: Issues of use and development. *School Psychology Review, 22,* 313–321.

Elliott, S. N., & Fuchs, L. S. (1997). The utility of curriculum-based measurement and performance assessment as alternatives to traditional intelligence and achievement tests. *School Psychology Review, 26*(3) 224–233.

Elliott, S. N., Kratochwill, T. R., & Schulte, A. G. (1998). The assessment accommodation checklist. *Teaching Exceptional Children,* Nov./Dec., 10–14.

Engiles, A., Fromme, C., LeResche, D., & Moses, P. (1999). *Keys to access: Encouraging the use of mediation by families from diverse backgrounds.* (Document No. EC 307 554). Consortium for Appropriate Dispute Resolution in Special Education. (ERIC Document Reproduction Service No. ED 436 881)

Epstein, M. H., & Cullinan, D. (1998). *Scale for assessing emotional disturbance.* Austin, TX: Pro-Ed.

Erickson, A. S. G., Clark, G. M., & Patton, J. R. (2013). Informal assessment for transition planning, 2nd ed. Austin, TX: ProEd.

Ervin, R. A., Radford, P. M., Bertsch, K., Piper, A. L., Ehrhardt, K. E., & Poling, A. (2001). A descriptive analysis and critique of the empirical literature on school-based functional assessment. 193–210.

Evans, L., & Bradley-Johnson, S. (1988). A review of recently developed measures of adaptive behavior. *Psychology in the Schools, 25,* 276–287.

Evans, S., & Evans, W. (1986). A perspective on assessment for instruction. *Pointer, 30,* 9–12.

Evans, W. H., Evans, S. S., & Schmid, R. E. (1989). *Behavioral and instructional management: An ecological approach.* Boston: Allyn & Bacon.

Federal Register (1977, August 23). Washington, DC: U.S. Government Printing Office.

Federal Register (1993, July 30). Washington, DC: U.S. Government Printing Office.

Federal Register. (1992, September 29). Washington, DC: U.S. Government Printing Office.

Fewell, R. R. (1991). Trends in the assessment of infants and toddlers with disabilities. *Exceptional Children, 58,* 166–173.

Field, S., Martin, J., Miller, R., Ward, M., & Wehmeyer, M. (1998). *A practical guide to teaching self-determination.* Reston, VA: Council for Exceptional Children.

Filipek, P. A., Accardo, P. J., Baranek, G. T., Cook, E. H., Jr., Dawson, G., Gordon, B., et al. (1999). The screening and diagnosis of autism spectrum disorders. *Journal of Autism and Developmental Disabilities, 29*(6), 439–484.

Finch, M. E. H. (2012). Special considerations with response to intervention and instruction for students with diverse backgrounds. *Psychology in the Schools, 49*(3), 285–296. DOI: 10.1002/pits.21597

Flanagan, D. P., & Harrison, P. L. (Eds.) (2005). *Contemporary intellectual assessment: Theories, tests, and issues.* New York: The Guilford Press.

Flanagan, D. P., & Ortiz, S. (2001). *Essentials of cross-battery assessment.* New York: John Wiley & Sons, Inc.

Flanagan, D. P., & Harrison, P. L. (2012). *Contemporary Intellectual Assessment,* NY: Guilford Press.

Flaugher, R. (1978). The many definitions of test bias. *American Psychologist, 33,* 671–679.

Fletcher, T. V., & Navarrete, L. A. (2010). Learning disabilities or difference: A critical look at issues associated with the misidentification and placement of Hispanic students in special education programs. Classic *RSEQ* article reprinted from *Rural Special Education Quarterly, 30*(1), 30–38.

Flippo, R. F., Holland, D. D., McCarthy, M. T., & Swinning, E. A. (2009). Asking the right questions: How to select an informal reading inventory. *The Reading Teacher, 63*(1), 79–83. DOI:10.1598/RT.63.1.8

Foegen, A., Jiban, C., & Deno, S. (2007). Progress monitoring measures in mathematics: A review of the literature. *The Journal of Special Education, 4*(2), 121–139.

Foster-Gaitskell, D., & Pratt, C. (1989). Comparison of parent and teacher ratings of adaptive behavior of children with mental retardation. *American Journal of Mental Retardation, 94,* 177–181.

Fradd, S., & Hallman, C. (1983). Implications of psychological and educational research for assessment and instruction of culturally and linguistically different students. *Learning Disabilities Quarterly, 6,* 468–477.

Freberg, M. E., Vandiver, B. J., Watkins, M. W., Canivez, G. L. (2008). Significant factor score variability and the validity of the WISC-III full scale IQ in predicting later academic achievement. *Applied Neuropsychology, 15,* 131–139. DOI 10.1080/09084280802084010

Fuchs, D. (1991). Mainstream assistance teams: A prereferral intervention system for difficult to teach students. In G. Stoner, M. R. Shinn, & H. M. Walker(Eds.), *Interventions for achievement and behavior problems* (pp. 241–267). Silver Spring, MD: National Association of School Psychologists.

Fuchs, D., & Fuchs, L. (1989). Effects of examiner familiarity on Black, Caucasian, and Hispanic children: A meta-analysis. *Exceptional Children, 55,* 303–308.

Fuchs, D., Fuchs, L., Benowitz, S., & Barringer, K. (1987). Norm-referenced tests: Are they valid for uses with handicapped students? *Exceptional Children, 54,* 263–271.

Fuchs, D., Fuchs, L. S., & Compton, D. L. (2012). Smart RTI: A next-generation approach to multilevel prevention. *Exceptional Children, 78*(3), 263–279.

Fuchs, D., Zern, D., & Fuchs, L. (1983). A microanalysis of participant behavior in familiar and unfamiliar test conditions. *Exceptional Children, 50,* 75–77.

Fuchs, L. Fuchs, D., & Hamlett, C. (1989). Effects of instrumental use of curriculum-based measurement to enhance instructional programs. *Remedial and Special Education, 10,* 43–52.

Fuchs, L. Fuchs, D., Hamlett, C. L., Phillips, N. B., & Bentz, J. (1994). Classwide curriculum-based measurement: Helping general educators meet the challenge of student diversity. *Exceptional Children, 60,* 518–537.

Fuchs, L. S. (2004). The past, present, and future of curriculum-based measurement research. *School Psychology Review, 33*(2), 188–192.

Fuchs, L. S., & Fuchs, D. (1986). Effects of a systematic formative evaluation: A meta-analysis. *Exceptional Children, 53,* 199–208.

Fuchs, L. S., & Fuchs, D. (1996). Combining performance assessment and curriculum-based measurement to strengthen instructional planning. *Learning Disabilities Research & Practice, 11,* 183–192.

Fuchs, L. S., Deno, S. L., & Mirkin, P. (1984). Effects of frequent curriculum-based measurement and evaluation on pedagogy, student achievement, and student awareness of learning. *American Educational Research Journal, 21,* 449–460.

Fuchs, L. S., Fuchs, D., Hamlett, C. L., & Stecker, P. M. (1991). Effects of curriculum-based measurement and consultation on teacher planning and student achievement in mathematics operations. *American Educational Research Journal, 28,* 617–641.

Fuchs, L. S., Fuchs, D., Hamlett, C. L., Walz, C. L., & Germann, G. (1993). Formative evaluation of academic progress: How much growth can we expect? *School Psychology Review, 22*(1), 27–48.

Fuchs, L., & Fuchs, D. (1992). Identifying a measure for monitoring student reading progress. *School Psychology Review, 21,* 45–58.

Fuchs, L., Butterworth, J., & Fuchs, D. (1989). Effects of ongoing curriculum-based measurement on student awareness of goals and progress. *Education and Treatment of Children, 12,* 41–47.

Fuchs, L., Fuchs, D., Eaton, S., & Hamlett, C. (2003). *Dynamic Assessment of Test Accommodations.* San Antonio, TX: The Psychological Corporation.

Fuchs, L., Tindal, G., & Deno, S. (1984). Methodological issues in curriculum-based assessment. *Diagnostique, 9,* 191–207.

Fuchs, L. S., Fuchs, D., Capizzi, A. M. (2005). Identifying appropriate test accommodations for students with learning disabilities. *Focus on Exceptional Children, 37*(6), 1–8.

Gable, R. A., Hendrickson, J. M., & Smith, C. (1999). Changing discipline policies and practices: Finding a place for functional behavioral assessments in schools. *Preventing School Failure, 43*(4), 167–170.

Gable, R. A., Park, K. L., Scott, T. M. (2014). Functional behavioral assessment and students at risk for or with emotional disabilities: Current issues and considerations. *Education and Treatment of Children, 37*(1), 111–135.

Gage, N., Gersten, R., Sugai, G., & Newman-Gonchar, R. (2013). Disproportionality of English learners with emotional and/or behavioral disorders: A comparative meta-analysis with English learners with learning disabilities. *Behavioral Disorders, 38*(3), 123–136.

Gardner, H. (1993). *Multiple intelligences: The theory in practice.* New York: Basic Books.

German, D., Johnson, B., & Schneider, M. (1985). Learning disability vs. reading disability: A survey of practitioners' diagnostic populations and test instruments. *Learning Disability Quarterly, 8,* 141–156.

Gilliam, J. E. (2014). *Gilliam Autism Rating Scale,* 3rd ed. Austin, TX: PRO-ED.

Glaser, R. (1963). Instructional technology and the measurement of learning outcomes: Some questions. *American Psychologist, 18*(2), 519–521.

Glatthorn, A. A. (1998). *Performance assessment and standards-based curricula: The achievement cycle.* Larchmont, NY: Eye on Education.

Goff, W. H. (2002). *Guidelines for writing objective reports.* Unpublished manuscript.

Goldstein, S., & Turnbull, A. (1982). Strategies to increase parent participation in IEP conferences. *Exceptional Children, 48,* 360–361.

Goldstein, S., Strickland, B., Turnbull, A., & Curry, L. (1980). An observational analysis of the IEP conference. *Exceptional Children, 46,* 278–286.

Good, R. H., & Kaminski, R. A. (Eds.). (2002). *Dynamic indicators of basic early literacy skills* (6th ed.). Eugene, OR: Institute for the

Development of Education Achievement. Retrieved from http://dibels.uoregon.edu

Goodman, J. F., & Hover, S. A. (1992). The Individual Family Service Plan: Unresolved problems. *Psychology in the Schools, 29,* 140–151.

Gordon, M. (1983). *Gordon diagnostic system.* DeWitt, NY: Gordon Diagnostic Systems.

Government Accountability Office (2013). *Individuals with Disabilities Education Act: Standards needed to improve identification of racial and ethnic overrepresentation in special education.* Washington, DC: Author.

Graden, J., Casey, A., & Christenson, S. (1985). Implementing a pre-referral intervention system: Part I. The model. *Exceptional Children, 51,* 377–384.

Graham, M., & Scott, K. (1988). The impact of definitions of high risk on services of infants and toddlers. *Topics in Early Childhood Special Education, 8*(3), 23–28.

Greenspan, S. I. (1992). *Infancy and early childhood: The practice of clinical assessment and intervention with emotional and developmental challenges.* Madison, CT: International University Press.

Greenwood, C. R., Tapia, Y., Abott, M., & Walton, C. (2003). A building-based case study of evidence-based literacy practices: Implementation, reading behavior, and growth in reading fluency, K–4. *Journal of Special Education, 37*(2), 95–111.

Gresham, F. M., Watson, T. S., & Skinner, C. H. (2001). Functional behavioral assessment: Principles, procedures, and future directions. *School Psychology Review, 30*(2), 156–172.

Gresham, F. M. (2005). Response to intervention: An alternative means of identifying students as emotionally disturbed. *Education and Treatment of Children, 28*(4), 328–344.

Grisham-Brown, J., Hallam, R., & Brookshire, R. (2006). Using authentic assessment to evidence children's progress toward early learning standards. *Early Childhood Education Journal, 34*(1), 45–51.

Guerin, G. R., & Maier, A. S. (1983). *Informal assessment in education.* Palo Alto, CA: Mayfield.

Haager, D. (2007). Promises and cautions regarding using response to intervention with English language learners. *Learning Disabilities Quarterly, 30*(3), 213–218.

Hale, J. B., Kaufman, A., Naglieri, J. A., & Kavale, K. A. (2006). Implementation of IDEA 2004: Integrating response to intervention and cognitive assessment methods. *Psychology in the Schools, 43*(7), 753–770.

Hammill, D. D., & Larsen, S. C. (1999). *Test of written language* (4th ed.). Austin, TX: Pro-Ed.

Hammill, D. D., & Newcomer, P. L. (2008). *Test of language development–intermediate* (4th ed.). Austin, TX: Pro-Ed.

Haraway, D. L. (2012). Monitoring students with ADHD within the RTI framework. *The Behavior Analyst Today, 13*(2), 17–21.

Harris, D. B. (1963). *Goodenough–Harris drawing test.* New York: Harcourt Brace.

Harris, K., & Graham, S. (1994). Constructivism: Principles, paradigms, and integration. *Journal of Special Education, 28,* 233–247.

Harrison, P. (1987). Research with adaptive behavior scales. *Journal of Special Education, 21,* 37–61.

Harrison, P. L., & Oakland, T. (2003). *Adaptive behavior assessment system* (2nd ed.). San Antonio, TX: The Psychological Corporation.

Harrison, P. L., Kaufman, A. S., Kaufman, N. L., Bruininks, R. H., Rynders, J., Ilmer, S., et al. Cicchetti, D. V. (1990). *AGS early screening profiles.* Circle Pines, MN: American Guidance Service.

Harry, B., & Anderson, M. G. (1995). The disproportionate placement of African American males in special education programs: A critique of the process. *Journal of Negro Education, 63*(4), 602–619.

Hart, J. E. (2009) Strategies for culturally and linguistically diverse students with special needs. *Preventing School Failure, 53*(3), 197–206.

Hart, K. E., & Scuitto, M. J. (1996). Criterion-referenced measurement of instructional impact on cognitive outcomes. *Journal of Instructional Psychology, 23,* 26–34.

Hebbeler, K., Barton, L. R., & Mallik, S. (2008). Assessment and accountability for programs serving young children with disabilities. *Exceptionality, 16*(1), 48–63.

Heilig, J. V., & Darling-Hammond, L. (2008). Accountability Texas-style: The progress and learning of urban minority students in a high-stakes testing context. *Educational Evaluation and Policy Analysis, 30*(2), 75–110. doi:10.3102/0162373708317689

Heller, K., Holtzman, W., & Messick, S. (Eds.). (1982). *Placing children in special education: A strategy for equity.* Washington, DC: National Academy Press.

Herrnstein, R. J., & Murray, C. (1994). *The bell curve: Intelligence and class structure in American life.* New York: The Free Press.

Heshusius, L. (1991). Curriculum-based assessment and direct instruction: Critical reflections on fundamental assumptions. *Exceptional Children, 57,* 315–328.

Hintze, J. M., & Christ, T. J. (2004). An examination of variability as a function of passage variance in CBM monitoring. *School Psychology Review, 33*(2), 204–217.

Hintze, J. M., Shapiro, E. S., & Lutz, J. G. (1994). The effects of curriculum on the sensitivity of curriculum-based measurement in reading. *Journal of Special Education, 28,* 188–202.

Hobbs, R. (1993). Portfolio use in a learning disabilities resource room. *Reading & Writing Quarterly: Overcoming Learning Difficulties, 9,* 249–261.

Hong, B. S. S., Ivy, W. F., Gonzalez, H. R., & Ehrensberger, W. (2007). Preparing students for post-secondary education. *Teaching Exceptional Children, 40*(1), 32–38.

Hoover, J. J. (2010). Special education eligibility decision making in response to intervention models. *Theory to Practice, 49:* 289–296.

Hopkins, K. D., Stanley, J. C., & Hopkins, B. R. (1990). *Educational and psychological measurement and evaluation* (7th ed.). Upper Saddle River, NJ: Prentice Hall.

Horn, E., & Fuchs, D. (1987). Using adaptive behavior in assessment and intervention. *Journal of Special Education, 21,* 11–26.

Hosp, J. L., Hosp, M. A., & Dole, J. K. (2011). Potential bias in predictive validity of universal screening measures across disaggregation subgroups. *School Psychology Review, 40*(1), 108–131.

Hosp, J. L., Hosp, M. K., Howell, K. W., & Allison, R. (2014). *The ABCs of Curriculum-Based Evaluation: A Practical Guide to Effective Decision Making.* New York: The Guilford Press.

Howell, K. W., & Morehead, M. K. (1987). *Curriculum-based evaluation for special and remedial education.* Columbus, OH: Merrill.

Hoy, M., & Retish, P. (1984). A comparison of two types of assessment reports. *Exceptional Children, 51,* 225–229.

Huebner, E. (1988). Bias in teachers' special education decisions as a further function of test score reporting format. *Journal of Educational Researcher, 21,* 217–220.

Huebner, E. (1989). Errors in decision making: A comparison of school psychologists' interpretations of grade equivalents, percentiles, and deviation IQs. *School Psychology Review, 18,* 51–55.

Hultquist, A. M., & Metzke, L. K. (1993). Potential effects of curriculum bias in individual norm-referenced reading and spelling achievement tests. *Journal of Psychoeducational Assessment, 11,* 337–344.

Individuals with Disabilities Education Act Amendments of 1997, PL. 105–17, 105th Congress.

Individuals with Disabilities Education Improvement Act of 2004, P. L. 108–446, 20 U.S.C. § 1400 et seq.

Jackson, G. D. (1975). Another psychological view from the Association of Black Psychologists. *American Psychologist, 30,* 88–93.

Jackson, S., Pretti-Frontczak, K., Harjusola-Webb, S., Grisham-Brown, J., & Romani, J. M. (2009). Response to intervention: Implications for early childhood professionals. *Language, Speech, and Hearing Services in Schools, 40*(4), 424–434.

Jacobson, N. S., & Truax, P. (1991). Clinical significance: A statistical change approach to defining meaningful change in psychotherapy research. *Journal of Clinical and Counseling Psychology, 59*(1), 12–19.

Johnson, S. B. (1999). Test reviews: Normative update for *Kaufman Educational Achievement, Peabody Individual Achievement Test–Revised, KeyMath–Revised,* and *Woodcock Reading Mastery Test–Revised. Psychology in the Schools, 36*(2), 175–176.

Kamphaus, R. (1987). Conceptual and psychometric issues in the assessment of adaptive behavior. *Journal of Special Education, 21,* 27–35.

Kamphaus, R. W., Winsor, A. P., Rowe, E. W., & Kim, S. (2005). A history of intelligence test interpretation. In D. P. Flanagan & P. L. Harrison (Eds.), *Contemporary intellectual assessment: Theories, tests, and issues* (pp. 23–37). New York: The Guilford Press.

Kamps, D., Abbott, M., Greenwood, C., Arregaga-Mayer, C., Wills, H., et al. (2007). Use of evidence-based, small group reading instruction for English language learners in elementary grades: Secondary-tier intervention. *Learning Disability Quarterly, 30*(3), 153–168.

Katsiyannis, A. (1994). Prereferral practices: Under Office of Civil Rights scrutiny. *Journal of Developmental and Physical Disabilities, 6,* 73–76.

Katsiyannis, A. (1994). Prereferral practices: Under Office of Civil Rights scrutiny. *Journal of Developmental and Physical Disabilities, 6,* 73–76.

Katz, K. S. (1989). Strategies for infant assessment: Implications of P.L. 99–457. *Topics in Early Childhood Special Education, 9*(3), 99–109.

Kaufman, A. S. (1979). *Intelligent testing with the* WISC–R. New York: Wiley.

Kaufman, A. S. (1994). *Intelligent testing with the* WISC–III. New York: Wiley.

Kaufman, A. S., & Kaufman, N. L. (1990). *Kaufman brief intelligence test.* Circle Pines, MN: American Guidance Service.

Kaufman, A. S., & Kaufman, N. L. (1993). *K–SEALS: Kaufman survey of early academic and language skills.* Circle Pines, MN: American Guidance Service.

Kaufman, A. S., & Kaufman, N. L. (1994). *Kaufman functional academic skills test.* Circle Pines, MN: American Guidance Service, Inc.

Kaufman, A. S., & Kaufman, N. L. (2004). *Kaufman test of educational achievement* (2nd ed.). Circle Pines, MN: AGS Publishing.

Kaufman, A. S., & Wang, J. (1992). Gender, race, and education differences on the *K–BIT* at ages 4 to 90 years. *Journal of Psychoeducational Assessment, 10,* 219–229.

Kaufman, A. S., & Kaufman, N. L. (2014). *Kaufman Test of Educational Achievement,* 3rd ed. San Antonio, TX: The Psychological Corporation.

Keogh, B. K., Forness, S. R., & MacMillan, D. L. (1998). The real world of special education. *American Psychologist, 53*(10), 1161–1162.

Kerr, M. M., & Nelson, C. M. (2002). *Strategies for addressing behavioral problems in the classroom* (4th ed.). Upper Saddle River, NJ: Merrill/Prentice Hall.

Klinger, J. K., Vaughn, S., Schumm, J. S., Cohen, P., & Forgan, J. W. (1998). Inclusion or pull-out: Which do students prefer? *Journal of Learning Disabilities, 31,* 148–158.

Knoff, H. M., & Prout, H. T. (1985). *Kinetic family drawing system for family and school: A handbook.* Los Angeles: Western Psychological Services.

Kohler, P. D. (1996). *Taxonomy for transition programming: Linking research to practice.* Champaign: University of Illinois at Urbana–Champaign, Transition Research Institute.

Koppitz, E. (1968). *Human figure drawing test.* New York: Grune & Stratton.

Kubicek, F. C. (1994). Special education reform in light of select state and federal court decisions. *Journal of Special Education, 28,* 27–42.

Kubick, R. J., Bard, E. M., & Perry, J. D. (2000). Manifestation determinations: Discipline guidelines for children with disabilities. In C. F. Telzrow & M. Tankersley (Eds.), *IDEA: Amendments of 1997: Practice guidelines for school-based teams* (pp. 1–28). Bethesda, MD: National Association of School Psychologists.

LaGrow, S., & Prochnow-LaGrow, J. (1982). Technical adequacy of the most popular tests selected by responding school psychologists in Illinois. *Psychology in the Schools, 19,* 186–189.

Lambert, N., Nihira, K., & Leland, H. (1993). *AAMR adaptive behavior scale–school, second edition.* Austin, TX: Pro-Ed.

Larry P. v. Riles, 343 F. Supp. 1306, aff'd., 502 F.2d 963, further proceedings, 495 F. Supp. 926, aff'd., 502 F.2d 693 (9th Cir. 1984).

Larsen, S. C., Hammill, D. D., Moats, L. C. (2013). *Test of Written Spelling,* 5th ed. Austin, TX: Pro-Ed.

Lennon, J. E., & Slesinski, C. (1999). Early intervention in reading: Results of a screening and intervention program for kindergarten students. *School Psychology Review, 28,* 353–365.

Levine, P., & Nourse, S. W. (1998). What follow-up studies say about postschool life for young men and women with learning disabilities: A critical look at the literature. *Journal of Learning Disabilities, 31*(3), 212–233.

Levinson, E. M. (1995). Best practices in transition services. In A. Thomas & J. Grimes (Eds.), *Best practices in school psychology–III* (pp. 909–915). Washington, DC: The National Association of School Psychologists.

Lidz, C. S. (1997). Dynamic assessment approaches. In D. P. Flanagan, J. L. Genshaft, & P. L. Harrison (Eds.), *Contemporary intellectual assessment: Theories, tests, and issues* (pp. 281–296). New York: Guilford Press.

Linan-Thompson, S., Vaughn, S., Prater, K., & Cirino, P. T. (2006). The response to intervention of English language learners at risk for reading problems. *Journal of Learning Disabilities, 39*(5), 390–398.

Lindsey, P., Wehmeyer, M. L., Guy, B., & Martin, J. (2001). Age of majority and mental retardation: A position statement of the division on mental retardation and developmental disabilities. *Education and Training in Mental Retardation and Developmental Disabilities, 36*(1), 3–15.

Lindstrom, L., Doren, B., Metheny, J., Johnson, P., & Zane, C. (2007). Transition to employment: Role of the family in career development. *Exceptional Children, 73*(3), 348–366.

Lipsky, D. K., & Gartner, A. (1997). *Inclusion and school reform: Transforming America's classrooms.* Baltimore, MD: Brookes Publishing.

Lopez, E. C. (1995). Best practices in working with bilingual children. In A. Thomas and J. Grimes (Eds.), *Best practices in school psychology* (3rd ed., p. 1113). Bethesda, MD: National Association of School Psychologists.

Lora v. New York City Board of Education, 1984: Final order, August 2, 1984, 587F. Supp. 1572 (E.D.N.Y. 1984).

Lord, C., Luyster, R. J., Gotham, K., & Guthrie. (2012). *Autism Diagnostic Observation Schedule, 2nd ed. (ADOS-2) Manual (Part II): Toddler Module.* Torrence, CA: Western Psychological Services.

Lord, C., Rutter, M., DiLavore, P. C., & Risi, S. (2002). *Autism diagnostic observation schedule.* Los Angeles, CA: Western Psychological Services.

Lord, C., Rutter, M., DiLavore, P. C., Risi, S., Gotham, K., & Bishop, S. (2012). *Autism Diagnostic Observation Schedule, 2nd ed. (ADOS-2) Manual (Part I): Modules 1–4.* Torrence, CA: Western Psychological Services.

Lord, C., Rutter, M., Goode, S., Heemsbergen, J., Jordan, H., Mawhood, L., & Schopler, E. (1989). *Autism Diagnostic Observation Schedule: A standardized observation of communicative* and social behavior. *Journal of Autism Spectrum Disorders, 19*, 185–212.

Lusting, D. D., & Saura, K. M. (1996, Spring). Use of criterion-based comparisons in determining the appropriateness of vocational evaluation test modifications for criterion-referenced tests. *Vocational Evaluation and Work Adjustment Bulletin*.

Lyon, G. R., Fletcher, J. M., Shaywitz, S. E., Shaywitz, B. A., Torgesen, J. K., Wood, F. B., et al. (2001). Rethinking learning disabilities. In C. E. Finn, A. J. Rotherham, & C. R. Hokanson (Eds.), *Rethinking special education for a new century*, pp. 259–287. Retrieved from http://www.ppionline.org/ppi_ci.cfm?knlgAreaID5110&subsecID5181&contentID53344

MacMillan, D. L., & Forness, S. R. (1998). The role of IQ in special education placement decisions: Primary and determinative or peripheral and inconsequential. *Remedial and Special Education, 19*, 239–253.

MacMillan, D. L., Gresham, F. M., & Bocian, K. (1998). Discrepancy between definitions of learning disabilities and school practices: An empirical investigation. *Journal of Learning Disabilities, 32*(4), 314–326.

Marchand-Martella, N. E., Ruby, S. F., & Martella, R. C. (2007). Intensifying reading instruction for students within a three-tier model: Standard protocol and problem solving approaches within a response-to-intervention (RTI) system. *Teaching Exceptional Children Plus: 3, 5*, Article 2. Retrieved from http://escholarship.bc.edu/education/tecplus/vol13/iss5/art2

Marcotte, A. M., & Hintze, J. M. (2009). Incremental and predictive utility of formative assessment methods for reading comprehension. *Journal of School Psychology, 47*, 315–335.

Mardell, C., & Goldenberg, D. S. (2011). *Developmental Indicators for the Assessment of Learning*, 4th ed. Bloomingdale, MN: Pearson.

Mardell-Czudnowski, C. (1995). Performance of Asian and White children on the *K–ABC*: Understanding information processing differences. *Psychological Assessment Resources, Inc., 2*(1), 19–29.

Mardell-Czudnowski, C., & Goldenberg, D. (1998). *Developmental indicators for the assessment of learning* (3rd ed.). Circle Pines, MN: American Guidance Service.

Markwardt, F. C. (1989). *Peabody individual achievement test–revised*. Circle Pines, MN: American Guidance Service.

Marso, R. N., & Pigge, F. L. (1991). An analysis of teacher-made tests: Item types, cognitive demands, and item construction errors. *Contemporary Educational Psychology, 16*, 279–286.

Marston, D. (2005). Tiers of intervention in responsiveness to intervention: Prevention outcomes and learning disabilities identification patterns. *Journal of Learning Disabilities, 38*(6), 539–544.

Marston, D., Fuchs, L., & Deno, S. (1986). Measuring pupil progress: A comparison of standardized achievement tests and curriculum related measures. *Diagnostique, 11*, 77–90.

Marston, D., Mirkin, P. K., & Deno, S. L. (1984). Curriculum-based measurement: An alternative to traditional screening, referral, and identification. *Journal of Special Education, 18*, 109–118.

Marston, D., Muyskens, P., Lau, M., & Canter, A. (2003). Problem-solving model for decision making with high incidence disabilities: The Minneapolis experience. *Learning Disabilities Research & Practice, 18*(3), 187–201.

Mather, N. (2014). *The WJ IV and SLD: Use of discrepancy and variation procedures*. Presentation at the National Association of School Psychologists, February 19, 2014.

Maxam, S., Boyer-Stephens, A., & Alff, M. (1986). *Assessment: A key to appropriate program placement*. (Report No. CE 045 407, pp. 11–13). Columbia: University of Missouri Columbia, Department of Special Education and Department of Practical Arts and Vocational-Technical Education. (ERIC Document Reproduction Service No. ED 275 835).

May, K. O., & Nicewander, W. A. (1997). Information and reliability for percentile ranks and other monotonic transformations of the number-correct score: Reply to De Gruijter. *Journal of Educational Measurement, 34*, 179–183.

May, K., & Nicewander, W. A. (1994). Reliability and information functions for percentile ranks. *Journal of Educational Measurement, 31*, 313–325.

Mayes, L. C. (1991). Infant assessment. In M. Lewis (Ed.), *Child and adolescent psychiatry: A comprehensive textbook* (pp. 437–447). Baltimore: Williams & Wilkins.

McArthur, D. S., & Roberts, G. E. (1982). *Roberts apperception test for children: Manual*. Los Angeles: Western Psychological Services.

McCarney, S. B., & Arthaud, T. J. (2005). *Behavior Evaluation Scale*, 3rd ed. Columbia, MO: Hawthorne Educational Services.

McConaughy, S. H., & Achenbach, T. M. (1993). Advances in empirically based assessment of children's behavioral and emotional problems. *School Psychology Review, 22*, 285–307.

McCook, J. E. (2006). *The RTI guide:Developing and implementing a model in your schools*. Horsham, PA: LRP Publications.

McDermott, P. A., Watkins, M. W., & Rhoad, A. M. (2014). Whose IQ is it? Assessor bias variance in high-stakes psychological assessment. *Psychological Assessment, 26*(1), 207–214.

McGlinchey, M. T., & Hixson, M. D. (2004). Using curriculum-based measurement to predict performance on state assessments in reading. *School Psychology Review, 33*(2), 193–203.

McGrew, K. (2014). *WJ IV Tests of Cognitive Ability: Overview of GIA and CHC clusters, new and revised tests, and selected data analysis*. Presented at the National Association of School Psychologists, February 19, 2014.

McGrew, K. S., & Flanagan, D. P. (1998). *The intelligence test desk reference (ITDR): Gf-Gc cross-battery assessment*. Boston: Allyn & Bacon.

McIntyre, L. (1988). Teacher gender: A predictor of special education referral? *Journal of Learning Disabilities, 21*, 382–384.

McLoughlin, J. A., & Lewis, R. B. (1990). *Assessing special students* (4th ed.). Upper Saddle River, NJ: Merrill/Prentice Hall.

McLoughlin, J., & Lewis, R. (2001). *Assessing special students* (5th ed.). Upper Saddle River, NJ: Merrill/Prentice Hall.

McNamara, K., & Hollinger, C. (2003). Intervention-based assessment: Evaluation rates and eligibility findings. *Exceptional Children, 69*(2), 181–193.

Mehrens, W. A., & Clarizio, H. F. (1993). Curriculum-based measurement: Conceptual and psychometric considerations. *Psychology in the Schools, 30*, 241–254.

Mehrens, W., & Lehmann, I. (1978). *Standardized tests in education*. New York: Holt, Rinehart & Winston.

Mercer, J. *System of multicultural assessment*. NY: The psychological corporation.

Messick, S. (1980). Test validity and the ethics of assessment. *American Psychologist, 35*, 1012–1027.

Messick, S. (1984). Assessment in context: Appraising student performance in relation to instructional quality. *Educational Researcher, 13*, 3–8.

Michael, J. (2000). Implications and refinements of the establishing operation concept. *Journal of Applied Behavior Analysis, 33*, 401–410.

Mick, L. (1985). Assessment procedures as related to enrollment patterns of Hispanic students in special education. *Educational Research Quarterly, 9*, 27–35.

Miller, D. C. (2007). *Essentials of school neuropsychological assessment*. New York: John Wiley & Sons, Inc.

Millman, J. (1994). Criterion-referenced testing 30 years later: Promise broken, promise kept. *Educational Measurement: Issues and Practices, 13*, 19–20, 39.

Minke, K. M., & Scott, M. M. (1993). The development of Individualized Family Service Plans: Roles for parents and staff. *Journal of Special Education, 27*, 82–106.

Missall, K., Reschly, A., Betts, J., McConnell, Heistad, et al. (2007). Examination of the predictive validity of preschool early literacy skills. *School Psychology Review, 36*(3), 433–452.

Mitchell, B. B., Deshler, D. D., & Lenz, B. Keith Ben-Hanania Lenz. (2012). Examining the role of the special educator in a response to intervention model. *Learning Disabilities: A Contemporary Journal, 10*(2), 53–74.

Mullen, E. M. (1995). *Mullen scales of early learning: AGS edition*. Circle Pines, MN: American Guidance Service, Inc.

Naglieri, J. A. (1988). *Draw-a-person: A quantitative scoring system*. New York: Psychological Corporation.

Naglieri, J. A., McNeish, T. J., & Bardos, A. N. (1991). *Draw-a-person: Screening procedure for emotional disturbance*. Austin, TX: Pro-Ed.

National Council of Teachers of Mathematics. (2000). *Principles and standards for mathematics*. Retrieved from http://standards.nctm.org

National Dropout Prevention Center (2013). *An analysis of states' FFY 2011 annual performance data for Indicator B1 (Graduation): A report prepared for the U.S. Department of Education Office of Special Programs*. Clemson, SC: Author.

National Secondary Transition Technical Assistance Center (n.d.). *In-school predictors of post-school success in secondary transition*. Retrieved from http://www.nsttac.org/ebp/PredictorFiles/InschoolPredictorsofPostSchoolSuccess.pdf

National Secondary Transition Technical Assistance Center. (2009). *Checklist form A indicator 13*. Retrieved from http://www.nsttac.org/indicator13/indicator13_checklist.aspx

National Secondary Transition Technical Assistance Center. (2009). *Checklist form B indicator 13*. Retrieved from http://www.nsttac.org/indicator13/indicator13_checklist.aspx

Newcomer, P. L., & Hammill, D. D. (2008). *Test of language development—primary* (4th ed.). Austin, TX: Pro-Ed.

Newman, L., Wagner, M., Cameto, R., & Knokey, A. M. (2009). *The post-high school outcomes of youth with disabilities up to 4 years after high school: A report of findings from the National Longitudinal Transition Study-2 (NLTS2) (NCSER 2009–3017)*. Menlo Park, CA: SRI International. Retrieved from www.nlts2.org/reports/2009_04/nlts2_report_2009_04_complete.pdf.

Nichols, S. L., & Berliner, D. C. (2007) *Collateral damage: How high stakes testing corrupts America's schools*. Cambridge, MA: Harvard Educational Press.

Nilsson, N. L. (2008). A critical analysis of eight informal reading inventories. *The Reading Teacher, 61*(7), 526–536. DOI:10.1598/RT.61.7.2

Northup, J., & Gulley, V. (2001). Some contributions of functional analysis to the assessment of behaviors associated with attention deficit hyperactivity disorder and the effects of stimulant medication. *School Psychology Review, 30*(2), 227–238.

O'Connor, R. E., & Klingner, J. (2010). Poor responders in RTI. *Theory into Practice, 49*: 297–304.

O'Neill, R. E., Horner, R. H., Albin, R. W., Sprague, J. R., Storey, K., & Newton, J. S. (1997). *Functional assessment and program development for problem behavior*. Pacific Grove, CA: Brooks/Cole Publishing.

Oaksford, L., & Jones, L. (2001). *Differentiated instruction abstract*. Tallahassee, FL: Leon County Schools.

Office of Special Education and Rehabilitative Services. (2000). *Questions and answers about provisions in the Individuals with Disabilities Education Act Amendments of 1997 related to students with disabilities and state and district wide assessments*. Washington, DC: Author.

Overton, T. (1987). Analyzing instructional material as a prerequisite for teacher effectiveness. *Techniques: A Journal for Remedial Education and Counseling, 3*, 111–115.

Overton, T. (2003). Promoting academic success through assessment of the academic environment. *Intervention in School and Clinic, 39*(3), 147–153.

Overton, T., Fielding, C., & Garcia de Alba, R. (2007). Differential diagnosis of Hispanic children referred for autism spectrum disorders. *Journal of Autism and Developmental Disorders, 37*(2), 1996–2007.

Paget, K. D. (1990). Best practices in the assessment of competence in preschool-age children. In A. Thomas & J. Grimes (Eds.), *Best practices in school psychology–II* (pp. 107–119). Washington, DC: National Association of School Psychologists.

Paratore, J. R. (1995). Assessing literacy: Establishing common standards in portfolio assessment. *Topics in Language Disorders, 16*, 67–82.

Parette, H. P., Peterson-Karlan, G. R., Wojcok, B. W., & Bardi, N. (2007). Monitor that progress: Interpreting data trends for assistive technology decision making. *Teaching Exceptional Children, 40*(1), 22–29.

Parker, L. D. (1993). The *Kaufman Brief Intelligence Test*: An introduction and review. *Measurement and Evaluation in Counseling and Development, 26*, 152–156.

PASE (Parents in Action in Special Education) *v. Hannon*, 506 F. Supp. 831 (N.D. Ill. 1980).

Peterson, L. S., Martinez, A., Turner, T. L. (2010). Test review: Process Assessment of the Learner–2nd ed. *Journal of Psychoeducational Assessment, 28*(1), 80–86.

Phillips, N. B., Hamlett, C. L., Fuchs, L. S., & Fuchs, D. (1993). Combining classwide curriculum-based measurement and peer tutoring to help general educators provide adaptive education. *Learning Disabilities Research & Practice, 8*, 148–156.

Poon-McBrayer, F., & Garcia, S. B. (2000). Profiles of Asian American students with learning disabilities at initial referral, assessment, and placement in special education. *Journal of Learning Disabilities, 33*(1), 61–71.

Portes, P. R. (1996). Ethnicity and culture in educational psychology. In D. C. Berliner & R. C. Calfee (Eds.), *Handbook of Educational Psychology* (pp. 331–357). New York: Simon Schuster McMillan.

Prewett, P. N. (1992). The relationship between the *Kaufman Brief Intelligence Test (K–BIT)* and the WISC–R with referred students. *Psychology in the Schools, 29*, 25–27.

Prewett, P. N., & McCaffery, L. K. (1993). A comparison of the *Kaufman Brief Intelligence Test (K–BIT)* with the *Stanford–Binet*, a two-subtest short form, and the *Kaufman Test of Educational Achievement (K–TEA)* brief form. *Psychology in the Schools, 30*, 299–304.

Prifitera, A., Saklofske, D. H., & Weiss, L. G., & Rolfus, E. (2005). *WISC–IV: Clinical use and interpretation*. Burlington, MA: Elsevier Academic Press.

PsychCorp (2008). *Wechsler fundamentals: Academic skills*. Bloomington, MN: Author.

Pyle, N. & Vaughn, S. (2012). Remediating reading difficulties in a response to intervention model with secondary students. *Psychology in the Schools, 49*(3), 273–284. DOI10.1002pits

Reschly, D. (1981). Psychological testing in educational classification and placement. *American Psychologist, 36*, 1094–1102.

Reschly, D. (1982). Assessing mild mental retardation: The influence of adaptive behavior, sociocultural status, and prospects for non-biased assessment. In C. R. Reynolds & T. B. Gutkin (Eds.), *The handbook of school psychology* (pp. 209–242). New York: Wiley.

Reschly, D. (1986). Functional psychoeducational assessment: Trends and issues. *Special Services in the Schools, 2*, 57–69.

Reschly, D. (1988). Assessment issues, placement litigation, and the future of mild mental retardation classification and programming. *Education and Training in Mental Retardation, 23*, 285–301.

Reschly, D. (1988). Special education reform. *School Psychology Review, 17*, 459–475.

Reschly, D. J., & Grimes, J. P. (1995). Best practices in intellectual assessment. In A. Thomas & J. Grimes (Eds.), *Best practices in school psychology–II*. Washington, DC: National Association of School Psychologists.

Reynolds, C. R. (1982). The problem of bias in psychological assessment. In C. R. Reynolds & T. B. Gutkin (Eds.), *The handbook of school psychology*, (pp. 178–208). New York: Wiley.

Reynolds, C. R., & Lowe, P. A. (2009). The problem of bias in psychological assessment. In T. Gutkin & C. R. Reynolds (Eds.), *The Handbook of School Psychology*, 4th ed., 332–374. Hoboken, NJ: Wiley.

Roberts, G. E. (1982). *Roberts apperception test for children: Test pictures*. Los Angeles: Western Psychological Services.

Roberts, G. E., & Gruber, C. (2005). *Roberts–2*. Los Angeles: Western Psychological Services.

Roberts, M. L., Marshall, J., Nelson, J. R., & Albers, C. A. (2001). Curriculum-based assessment procedures embedded within functional behavioral assessments: Identifying escape-motivated behaviors in a general education classroom. *School Psychology Review*, 30(2), 264–277.

Rodriguez, Michael, C. (2009). Considerations for alternative assessment based on modified academic achievement. *Peabody Journal of Education*, 84(4), 595--602 DOI: 10.1080/01619560903241143

Roid, G. H. (2003a). *Stanford–Binet intelligence scales* (5th ed.). Itasca, IL: Riverside Publishing.

Roid, G. H. (2003b). *Stanford–Binet intelligence scales* (5th ed.). *Examiner's manual*. Itasca, IL: Riverside Publishing.

Roid, G. H. (2003c). *Stanford–Binet intelligence scales* (5th ed.). *Technical manual*. Itasca, IL: Riverside Publishing.

Roid, G. H., & Pomplin, M. (2005). Interpreting the *Stanford–Binet Intelligence Scales* (5th ed.). In D. P. Flanagan & P. L. Harrison (Eds.), *Contemporary intellectual assessment: Theories, tests, and issues* (pp. 325–343). New York: The Guilford Press.

Rorschach, H. (1921, 1942). *Psycho-diagnostics: A diagnostic test based on perception* (P. Lemkau & B. Kroenburg, Trans.). Berne: Heber. (First German Edition, 1921. Distributed in the United States by Grune & Stratton.)

Rotter, J., & Rafferty, J. (1950). *The Rotter incomplete sentence test*. New York: Psychological Corporation.

Rubin, J. (2011). Organizing and evaluating results from multiple reading assessments. *The Reading Teacher*, 64(8), 606–611. DOI: 10.1598/RT.64.8.6

Ruddell, M. R. (1995). Literacy assessment in middle level grades: Alternatives to traditional practices. *Reading & Writing Quarterly: Overcoming Learning Difficulties*, 11, 187–200.

Rueda, R., & Garcia, E. (1997). Do portfolios make a difference for diverse students? The influence of type of data on making instructional decisions. *Learning Disabilities Research & Practice*, 12(2), 114–122.

Rutter, M., LeCouteur, A., & Lord, C. (2003). *Autism diagnostic interview–revised*. Los Angeles, CA: Western Psychological Services.

Sabers, D., Feldt, L., & Reschly, D. (1988). Appropriate and inappropriate use of estimated true scores for normative comparisons. *Journal of Special Education*, 22, 358–366.

Salend, S. J., & Taylor, L. (1993). Working with families: A cross-cultural perspective. *Remedial and Special Education*, 14(5), 25–32, 39.

Salvia, J., & Hughes, C. (1990). *Curriculum-based assessment: Testing what is taught*. New York: Macmillan.

Salvia, J., & Ysseldyke, J. (1988a). *Assessment in remedial and special education* (4th ed.). Dallas: Houghton Mifflin.

Salvia, J., & Ysseldyke, J. (1988b). Using estimated true scores for normative comparisons. *Journal of Special Education*, 22, 367–373.

Salvia, J., & Ysseldyke, J. E. (1988). *Assessment in special and remedial education* (4th ed.). Boston: Houghton Mifflin.

Sandall, S., Hemmeter, M. L., Smith, B. J., & McLean, M. E. (2005). DEC recommended practices: A comprehensive guide for practical approaches in early intervention/early childhood. Longmont, CO: Sopris West.

Sapp, G., Chissom, B., & Horton, W. (1984). An investigation of the ability of selected instruments to discriminate areas of exceptional class designation. *Psychology in the Schools*, 5, 258–262.

Schaughency, E. A., & Rothlind, J. (1991). Assessment and classification of attention deficit hyperactive disorders. *School Psychology Review*, 20, 187–202.

Schopler, E., Van Bourgondien, M. E., Wellman, G. J., & Love, S. R. (2010). *Childhood autism rating scale* (2nd ed.). Los Angeles, CA: Western Psychological Services.

Schrank, F. A., Mather, N., & Woodcock, R. W. (2004). *Woodcock–Johnson III diagnostic reading battery*. Rolling Meadows, IL: Riverside Publishing.

Scruggs, T. E., & Mastropieri, M. A. (1998). Summarizing single-subject research: Issues and application. *Behavior Modification*, 22, 221–242.

Shaklee, B. D., Barbour, N. E., Ambrose, R., & Hansford, S. J. (1997). *Designing and using portfolios*. Boston: Allyn & Bacon.

Shapiro, E. S. (1989). *Academic skills problems: Direct assessment and intervention*. New York: Guilford.

Shapiro, E. S. (1996). *Academic skills problems: Direct assessment and intervention* (2nd ed.). New York: Guilford.

Shepherd, K., & Salembier, G. (2011). Improving schools through a response to intervention approach: A cross-case analysis of three rural schools. *Rural Special Education Quarterly*, 30(3), 3–15.

Sheridan, S. M., Cowan, P. J., & Eagle, J. W. (2000). Partnering with parents in educational programming for students with special needs. In C. F. Telzrow & M. Tankersley (Eds.), *IDEA Amendments of 1997: Practice guidelines for school-based teams*. Bethesda, MD: National Association of School Psychologists.

Shinn, M. R. (1989). *Curriculum-based measurement: Assessing special children*. New York: Guilford.

Shinn, M. R. (2002). Best practices in using curriculum-based measurement in a problem-solving model. In A. Thomas & J. Grimes (Eds.), *Best practices in school psychology* (Vol. 4, pp. 671–697). Silver Springs, MD: National Association of School Psychologists.

Shinn, M. R., Habedank, L., Rodden-Nord, K., & Knutson, N. (1993). Using curriculum-based measurement to identify potential candidates for reintegration into general education. *Journal of Special Education*, 27, 202–221.

Shinn, M. R., Nolet, V., & Knutson, N. (1990). Best practices in curriculum-based measurement. In A. Thomas & J. Grimes (Eds.), *Best practices in school psychology*. Washington, DC: National Association of School Psychologists.

Shrank, F. A., Mather, N., & McGrew, K. S. (2014). *Woodcock–Johnson IV*. Rolling Meadows, IL: Riverside Publishing.

Silberglitt, B., & Hintze, J. M. (2007). How much growth can we expect? A conditional analysis of R–CBM growth rates by level of performance. *Exceptional Children*, 74(1), 71–99.

Sinclair, E., Del'Homme, & M. Gonzalez. (1993). Systematic screening for preschool assessment of behavioral disorders. *Behavioral Disorders*, 18, 177–188.

Skiba, R. J., Simmons, A. B., Ritter, S., Gibb, A. C., Rausch, M. K., Cuardrado, J., Chung, C. (2008). Achieving equity in special education: History, status, and current challenges. *Exceptional Children*, 3, 264–288.

Smith, K. G., & Corkum, P. (2007). Systematic review of measures used to diagnose attention-deficit/hyperactivity disorder in research on preschool children. *Topics in Early Childhood Special Education*, 27(3), 164–173.

Snider, V. E. (1995). A primer on phonemic awareness: What it is, why it is important, and how to teach it. *School Psychology Review*, 24(3), 443–455.

Snider, V. E. (1997). The relationship between phonemic awareness and later reading achievement. *Journal of Educational Research*, 90(4), 203–212.

Soodak, L. C., & Podell, D. M. (1993). Teacher efficacy and student problem as factors in special education referral. *Journal of Special Education*, 27(1), 66–81.

Sparrow, S. S., Balla, D. A., & Cicchetti, D. V. (1984). *Vineland adaptive behavior scales*. Circle Pines, MN: American Guidance Service.

Sparrow, S. S., Cicchetti, D. V., & Balla, D. A. (2005). *Vineland–II: Vineland adaptive behavior scales* (2nd ed.). Circle Pines, MN: AGS Publishing Company.

Stecker, P. M. (2007). Tertiary intervention: Using progress monitoring with intensive services. *Teaching Exceptional Children*, May/June 2007, 50–57.

Stoner, G., Carey, S. P., Ikeda, M. J., & Shinn, M. R. (1994). The utility of curriculum-based measurement for evaluating the effects of methylphenidate on academic performance. *Journal of Applied Behavior Analysis*, 27, 101–113.

Sullivan, A. L., & Bal, A. (2013). Disproportionality in special education: Effects of individual and school variables on disability risk. *Exceptional Children*, 79(4), 475–494.

Swanson, H. L., & Watson, B. L. (1989). *Educational and psychological assessment of exceptional children* (2nd ed.). Upper Saddle River, NJ: Merrill/Prentice Hall.

Symons, F. J., & Warren, S. F. (1998). Straw men and strange logic issues and pseudo-issues in special education. *American Psychologist*, 53(10), 1160–1161.

Taylor, R. L. (1993). *Assessment of exceptional students: Educational and psychological procedures* (3rd ed.). Boston: Allyn & Bacon.

Test, D. W., Fowler, C. H., White, J., Richter, S., & Walker, A. (2009). Evidence-based secondary transition practices for enhancing school completion. Exceptionality, 17(1), 16–29.

Tharinger, D. J., & Lambert, N. M. (1990). The contributions of developmental psychology to school psychology. In T. Gutkin & C. R. Reynolds (Eds.), *The handbook of school psychology* (2nd ed.), pp. 74–103. New York: Wiley.

Thoma, C. A., Rogan, P., & Baker, S. R. (2001). Student involvement in transition planning: Unheard voices. *Education and Training in Mental Retardation and Developmental Disabilities*, 36(1), 16–29.

Thompson, S. J., Morse, A. B., Sharpe, M., & Hall, S. (2005). *Accommodations manual: How to select, administer, and evaluate use of accommodations for instruction and assessment of students with disabilities* (2nd ed.). Washington, DC: Council of Chief State School Officers.

Thurlow, M. L., Quenemoen, R. F., Lazarus, S. S., Moen, R. E., Johnstone, C. J., Liu, K. K., Altman, J. (2008). *A principled approach to accountability assessments for students with disabilities* (Synthesis Report 70). Minneapolis, MN: University of Minnesota, National Center on Educational Outcomes.

Thurlow, M. L., Ysseldyke, J. E., & Anderson, C. L. (1995). *High school graduation requirements: What's happening for students with disabilities?* Minneapolis: National Center on Educational Outcomes.

Thurlow, M., & Ysseldyke, J. (1979). Current assessment and decision-making practices in model programs. *Learning Disabilities Quarterly*, 2, 14–24.

Thurlow, M., Christenson, S., & Ysseldyke, J. (1983). *Referral research: An integrative summary of findings* (Research Report No. 141). Minneapolis: University of Minnesota, Institute for Research on Learning Disabilities.

Tucker, J. (1980). Ethnic proportions in classes for the learning disabled: Issues in nonbiased assessment. *Journal of Special Education*, 14, 93–105.

Turnbull, H. R. (1986). *Free and appropriate public education: The law and children with disabilities*. Denver: Love Publishing.

Turnbull, H. R. (1990). *Free and appropriate public education: The law and children with disabilities* (3rd ed.). Denver: Love Publishing.

Turnbull, H. R., Turnbull, A. P., & Strickland, B. (1979). Procedural due process: The two-edged sword that the untrained should not unsheath. *Journal of Education, 161*, 40–59.

Turnbull, R., Turnbull, A., Shank, A., Smith, S., & Leal, D. (2002). *Exceptional lives: Special education in today's schools* (3rd ed.). Upper Saddle River, NJ: Merrill/Prentice Hall.

U.S. Department of Education, Office of Planning, Evaluation, and Policy Development, Policy and Program Studies Service. (2009). *State and local implementation of the No Child Left Behind Act, Volume V-Implementation of the 1 percent rule and 2 percent interim policy option*. Washington, DC: Author.

U.S. Department of Education, Office of Special Education and Rehabilitative Services, Office of Special Education Programs. (2009). *Twenty-eighth annual report to congress on the implementation of the Individuals with Disabilities Education Act, 2006, Vol. 1*. Washington, DC: Author. Retrieved from http://www.ed.gov/about/reports/annual/osep/2006/parts-b-c/index.html

U.S. Department of Education, Office of Special Education and Rehabilitative Services, Office of Special Education Programs. (2009). *Twenty-eighth annual report to congress on the implementation of the Individuals with Disabilities Education Act, 2006, Vol. 2*. Washington, DC: Author. Retrieved from http://www.ed.gov/about/reports/annual/osep/2006/parts-b-c/index.html

U.S. Department of Education. (1991). *Memorandum to chief state school officers*. Washington, DC: Author.

U.S. Department of Education. (1999). *Assistance to states for the education of childern with disabilities and the early intervention Program for infants and toddlers with disabilities: final regulation*. Washington, DC: Author.

U.S. Department of Education. (2000). *The use of tests when making high-stakes decisions for students: A resource guide for educators and policymakers*. Washington, DC: Author.

U.S. Department of Education. (2002). *Twenty-fourth annual report to Congress on the implementation of the Individuals with Disabilities Education Act*. Washington, DC: Author.

U.S. Department of Education. (2004). *Twenty-sixth annual report to Congress on the implementation of the Individuals with Disabilities Education Act*. Washington, DC: Author.

U.S. Office of Technology Assessment. (1992, February). *Testing in American schools: Asking the right questions* (OTA–SET–519). Washington, DC: U.S. Government Printing Office.

Uzgiris, I. C., & Hunt, J. McV. (1975). *Assessment in infancy: Ordinal scales of psychological development*. Urbana: University of Illinois Press.

Vanderheyden, A. M. (2011). Technical adequacy of response to intervention decisions. *Exceptional Children*, 77(3), 335–350.

Vaughn, S., Bos, C., Harrell, J., & Lasky, B. (1988). Parent participation in the initial placement/IEP conference ten years after mandated involvement. *Journal of Learning Disabilities*, 21, 82–89.

Vladescu, J. C. (2007). Test review: *Kaufman Test of Educational Achievement –Second Edition (KTEA–II). Journal of Psychoeducational Assessment*, 25(), 92–100.

Vogel, S. A., Leonard, F., Scales, W., Hayeslip, P., Hermansen, J., & Donnells, L. (1998). The national learning disabilities postsecondary data bank: An overview. *Journal of Learning Disabilities, 31*(3), 234–247.

Vygotsky, L. S. (1993). *The collected works of L. S. Vygotsky: Vol. 2, The fundamentals of defectology (abnormal psychology and learning disabilities)* (J. E. Knox & C. B. Stevens, Trans.). New York: Plenum.

Wallace, T., & Tichá, R. (2006). General outcome measures for students with significant cognitive disabilities: Pilot study. *Technical Report 12: Research Institute on Progress Monitoring*.

Walsh, B., & Betz, N. (1985). *Tests and assessment*. Upper Saddle River, NJ: Prentice Hall.

Wasserman, J. D., & Tulsky, D. S. (2005). A history of intelligence assessment. In D. P. Flanagan & P. L. Harrison (Eds.), *Contemporary intellectual assessment: Theories, tests, and issues* (pp. 3–22). New York: The Guilford Press.

Weber, J., & Stoneman, Z. (1986). Parental nonparticipation as a means of reducing bias in the education of handicapped children. *Special Services in the Schools, 1,* 71–84.

Wechsler, D. (1974). *Manual for the Wechsler intelligence scale for children–revised.* San Antonio: The Psychological Corporation.

Wechsler, D. (2014). Wechsler intelligence scale for children®-fifth edition. Bloomington, MN: Pearson.

Wechsler, D., & Nagliari, J. A. (2006). *Wechsler nonverbal scale of ability.* San Antonio, TX: The Psychological Corporation.

Weller, C., Strawser, S., & Buchanan, M. (1985). Adaptive behavior: Designator of a continuum of severity of learning disabled individuals. *Journal of Learning Disabilities, 18,* 200–203.

Werts, M., Lambert, M., & Carpenter, E. (2009). What special education directors say about RTI. *Learning Disabilities Quarterly, 32*(4), 245–254.

Werts, M. G., & Carpenter, E. S. (2013). Implementation of tasks in RTI: Perceptions of special education teachers. *Teacher Education and Special Education, 36*(3), 247–257.

What Works Clearinghouse (n.d.). *Intervention: Kaplan spell read.* Retrieved from http://ies.ed.gov/ncee/wwc/reports/beginning%5Freading/spellread/

What Works Clearinghouse (n.d.). *Intervention: Saxon middle school math.* Retrieved from http://ies.ed.gov/ncee/wwc/reports/middle_math/smsm/

What Works Clearinghouse (n.d.). *WWC procedures and standards handbook.* Retrieved from http://ies.ed.gov/ncee/wwc/references/idocviewer/Doc.aspx?docId519&tocId54#design

Wiederholt, J. L, & Bryant, B. R. (2012). *Gray Oral Reading Tests,* 5th ed. Austin, TX: Pro-Ed.

Wiener, J. (1986). Alternatives in the assessment of the learning disabled adolescent: A learning strategies approach. *Learning Disabilities Focus, 1,* 97–107.

Wilkinson, G. S. (1993). *The wide range achievement test: Administration manual.* Wilmington, DE: Jastak, Wide Range.

Williams, R., & Zimmerman, D. (1984). On the virtues and vices of standard error of measurement. *Journal of Experimental Education, 52,* 231–233.

Wilson, V. (1987). Percentile scores. In C. R. Reynolds & L. Mann (Eds.), *Encyclopedia of special education: A reference for the education of the handicapped and other exceptional children and adults* (p. 1656). New York: Wiley.

Witt, J. C., Daly, E., & Noell, G. H. (2000). *Functional assessments: A step-by-step guide to solving academic and behavior problems.* Longmont, CO: Sopris West.

Witt, J., & Martens, B. (1984). Adaptive behavior: Tests and assessment issues. *School Psychology Review, 13,* 478–484.

Woodcock, R. W. (2011). *Woodcock reading mastery tests,* 3rd ed. Bloomington, MN: Pearson.

Woodcock, R. W., Schrank, F. A., McGrew, K. S., & Mather, N. (2014). *Woodcock-Johnson IV Tests of Achievement.* Rolling Meadow, IL: Houghton Mifflin Harcourt.

Yeh, S. S. (2006). High stakes testing: Can rapid assessment reduce the pressure? *Teachers College Record, 108*(4), 621–661.

Yell, M. L. (1995). Least restrictive environment, inclusion, and students with disabilities: A legal analysis. *Journal of Special Education, 28,* 389–404.

Yell, M. L. (1997). *The law and special education.* Upper Saddle River, NJ: Merrill/ Prentice Hall.

Yell, M. L., Drasgow, E., & Ford, L. (2000). The Individuals with Disabilities Education Act amendments of 1997: Implications for school-based teams. In C. F. Telzrow & M. Tankersley (Eds.), *IDEA: Amendments of 1997: Practice guidelines for school-based teams* (pp. 1–28). Bethesda, MD: National Association of School Psychologists.

Yovanoff, P., & Tindal, G. (2007). Scaling early reading alternate assessments with statewide measures. *Exceptional Children, 73*(2), 184–201.

Yssel, N., Adams, C., Clarke, L. S., & Jones, R. (2014). Applying an RTI model for students with learning disabilities who are gifted. *Teaching Exceptional Children, 46*(3), 42–52.

Ysseldyke, J. E., Nelson, J. R., & House, A. L. (2000). Statewide and district-wide assessments: Current status and guidelines for student accommodations and alternate assessments. In C. F. Telzrow and M. Tankersley (Eds.), *IDEA Amendments of 1997: Practice guidelines for school-based teams.* Bethesda, MD: National Association of School Psychologists.

Ysseldyke, J. E., Thurlow, M. L., Kozleski, E., & Reschly, D. (1998). *Accountability for the results of educating students with disabilities: Assessment conference report on the new assessment provisions of the 1997 Amendments to the Individuals with Disabilities Education Act.* (EC 306929). National Center on Educational Outcomes. (ERIC Document Reproduction Service No. ED 425 588).

Ysseldyke, J., & Thurlow, M. (1983). *Identification/classification research: An integrative summary of findings* (Research Report No. 142). Minneapolis: University of Minnesota, Institute for Research on Learning Disabilities.

Ysseldyke, J., Algozzine, B., Regan, R., & Potter, M. (1980). Technical adequacy of tests used by professionals in simulated decision making. *Psychology in the Schools, 17,* 202–209.

Ysseldyke, J., Algozzine, B., Richey, L., & Graden, J. (1982). Declaring students eligible for learning disability services: Why bother with the data? *Learning Disabilities Quarterly, 5,* 37–44.

Ysseldyke, J., Christenson, S., Pianta, B., & Algozzine, B. (1983). An analysis of teachers' reasons and desired outcomes for students referred for psychoeducational assessment. *Journal of Psychoeducational Assessment, 1,* 73–83.

Zhang, D., Katsiyannis, A., Ju, S., & Roberts, E. (2014). Minority representation in special education: 5-year trends. *Journal of Child & Family Studies, 23:* 118–127. DOI:10.1007/s10826-012-9698-6

Zirkel, P., & Thomas, L. B. (2010). State laws for RTI: An updated snapshot. *Teaching Exceptional Children, 42*(3), 56–63.

Zirkel, P. A. (2011). State special education laws for functional behavioral assessment and behavior intervention plans. *Behavioral Disorders, 36*(4), 262–278.

Zirkel, P. A. (2012). The legal dimension of RTI-Confusion confirmed: A response to Walker and Daves. *Learning Disabilities Quarterly, 35*(2), 72–75.

Name Index

Note: Illustrations are noted with an *f*; tables are noted with a *t*.

Note: Illustrations are noted with an *f*; tables are noted with a *t*.